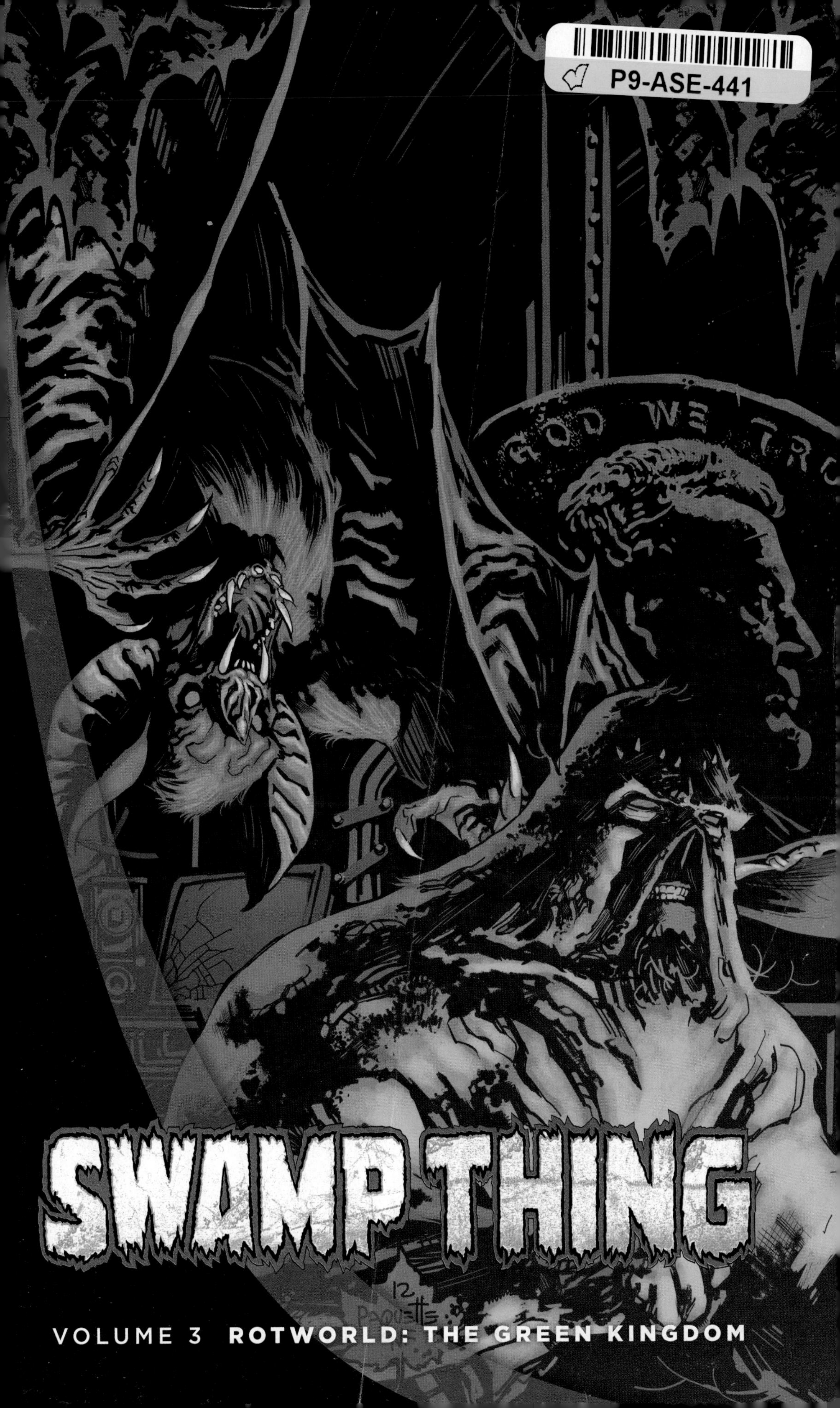

SWAMP THING

VOLUME 3 **ROTWORLD: THE GREEN KINGDOM**

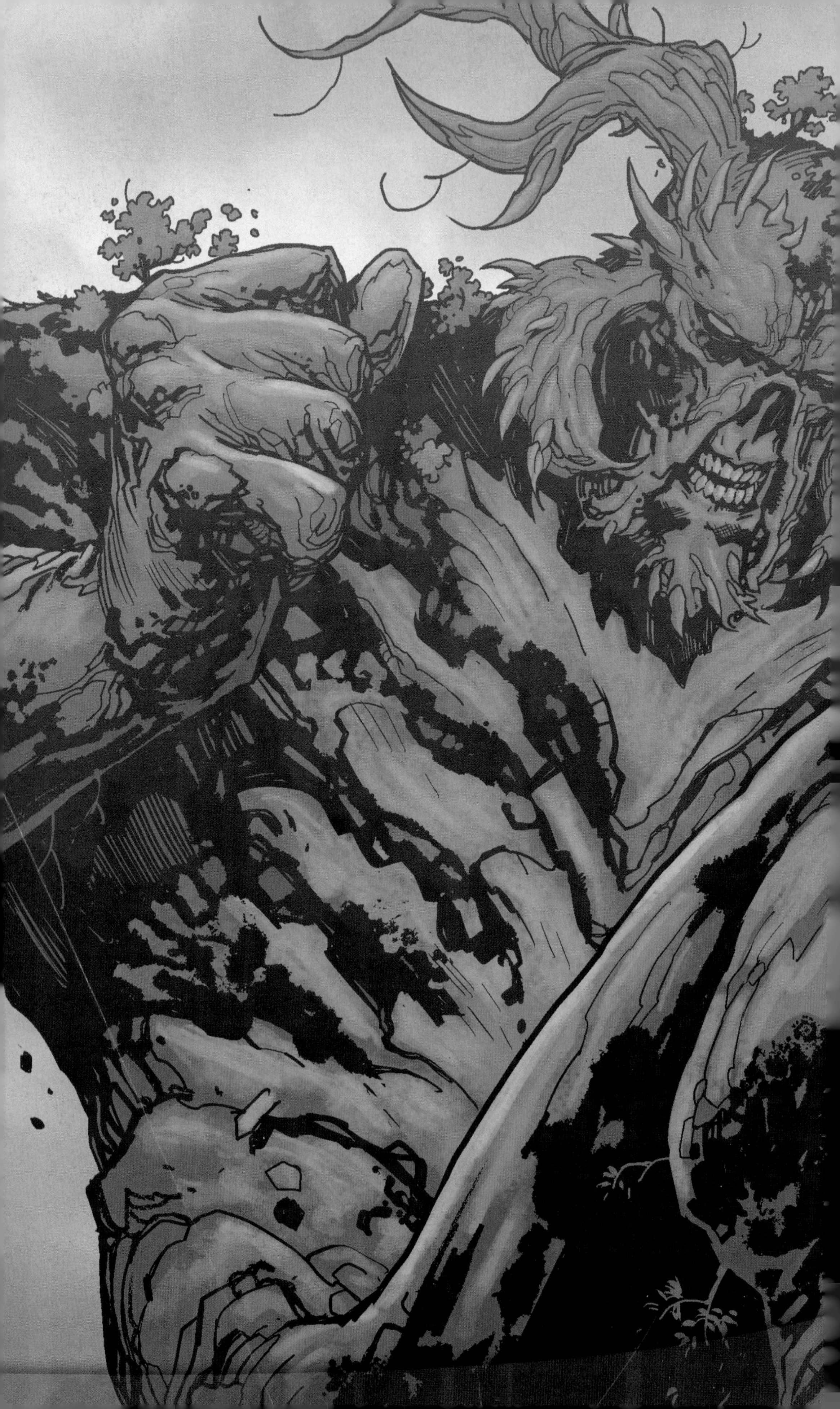

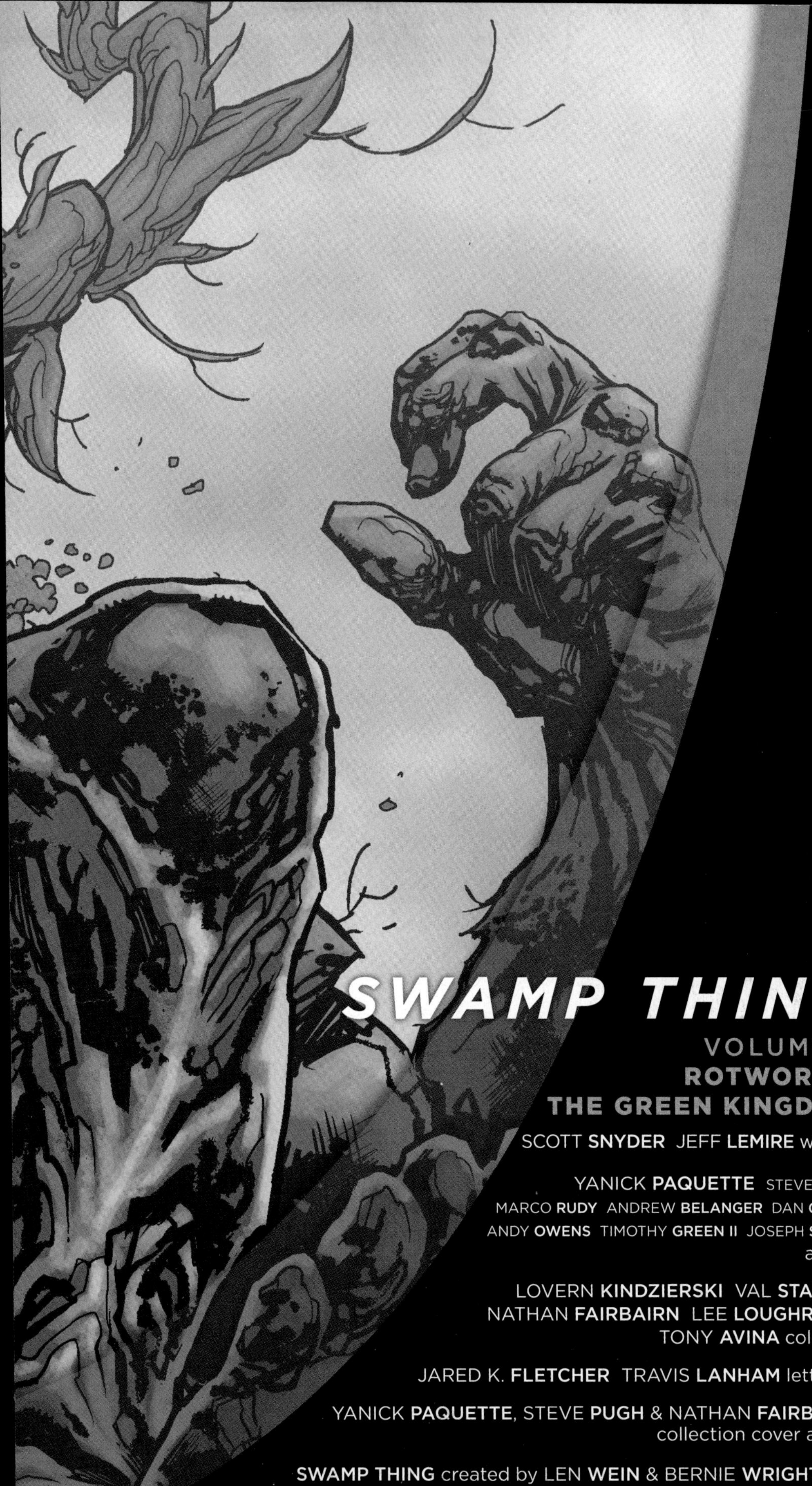

SWAMP THING

VOLUME 3
ROTWORLD: THE GREEN KINGDOM

SCOTT **SNYDER** JEFF **LEMIRE** writers

YANICK **PAQUETTE** STEVE **PUGH**
MARCO **RUDY** ANDREW **BELANGER** DAN **GREEN**
ANDY **OWENS** TIMOTHY **GREEN II** JOSEPH **SILVER**
artists

LOVERN **KINDZIERSKI** VAL **STAPLES**
NATHAN **FAIRBAIRN** LEE **LOUGHRIDGE**
TONY **AVINA** colorists

JARED K. **FLETCHER** TRAVIS **LANHAM** letterers

YANICK **PAQUETTE**, STEVE **PUGH** & NATHAN **FAIRBAIRN**
collection cover artists

SWAMP THING created by LEN **WEIN** & BERNIE **WRIGHTSON**

MATT IDELSON JOEY CAVALIERI Editors – Original Series CHRIS CONROY Associate Editor – Original Series
KATE STEWART Assistant Editor – Original Series ROWENA YOW Editor
ROBBIN BROSTERMAN Design Director – Books ROBBIE BIEDERMAN Publication Design

BOB HARRAS Senior VP – Editor-in-Chief, DC Comics

DIANE NELSON President DAN DIDIO and JIM LEE Co-Publishers GEOFF JOHNS Chief Creative Officer
JOHN ROOD Executive VP – Sales, Marketing and Business Development AMY GENKINS Senior VP – Business and Legal Affairs
NAIRI GARDINER Senior VP – Finance JEFF BOISON VP – Publishing Planning
MARK CHIARELLO VP – Art Direction and Design JOHN CUNNINGHAM VP – Marketing
TERRI CUNNINGHAM VP – Editorial Administration ALISON GILL Senior VP – Manufacturing and Operations
HANK KANALZ Senior VP – Vertigo & Integrated Publishing JAY KOGAN VP – Business and Legal Affairs, Publishing
JACK MAHAN VP – Business Affairs, Talent NICK NAPOLITANO VP – Manufacturing Administration
SUE POHJA VP – Book Sales COURTNEY SIMMONS Senior VP – Publicity BOB WAYNE Senior VP – Sales

SWAMP THING VOLUME 3: ROTWORLD: THE GREEN KINGDOM

DC Comics, 1700 Broadway, New York, NY 10019
A Warner Bros. Entertainment Company.
Printed by RR Donnelley, Salem, VA, USA. 10/11/13. First Printing.

ISBN: 978-1-4012-4264-0

Library of Congress Cataloging-in-Publication Data

Snyder, Scott.
Swamp Thing. Volume 3, Rotworld / The Green Kingdom /Scott Snyder, Yanick Paquette, Jeff Lemire.
pages cm
"Originally published in single magazine form as SWAMP THING 12-18, ANIMAL MAN 12, 17."
ISBN 978-1-4012-4264-0
1. Graphic novels. I. Paquette, Yanick, illustrator. II. Lemire, Jeff, illustrator III. Title. IV. Title: Rotworld.
PN6728.S93S74 2013
741.5'973—dc23
2013026267

SUSTAINABLE Certified Chain of Custody
FORESTRY At Least 20% Certified Forest Content
INITIATIVE
www.sfiprogram.org
SFI-01042
APPLIES TO TEXT STOCK ONLY

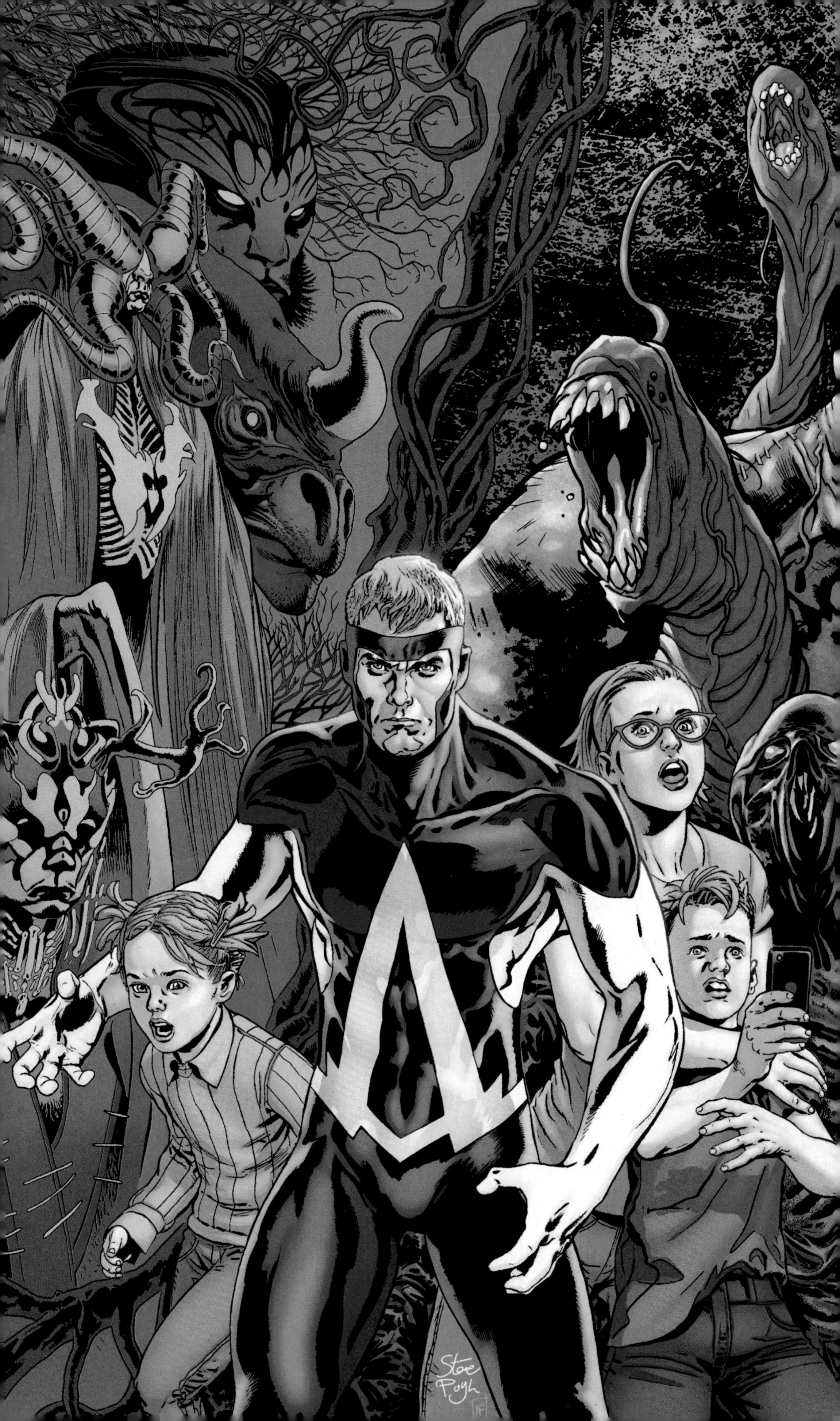
Steve
Pugh

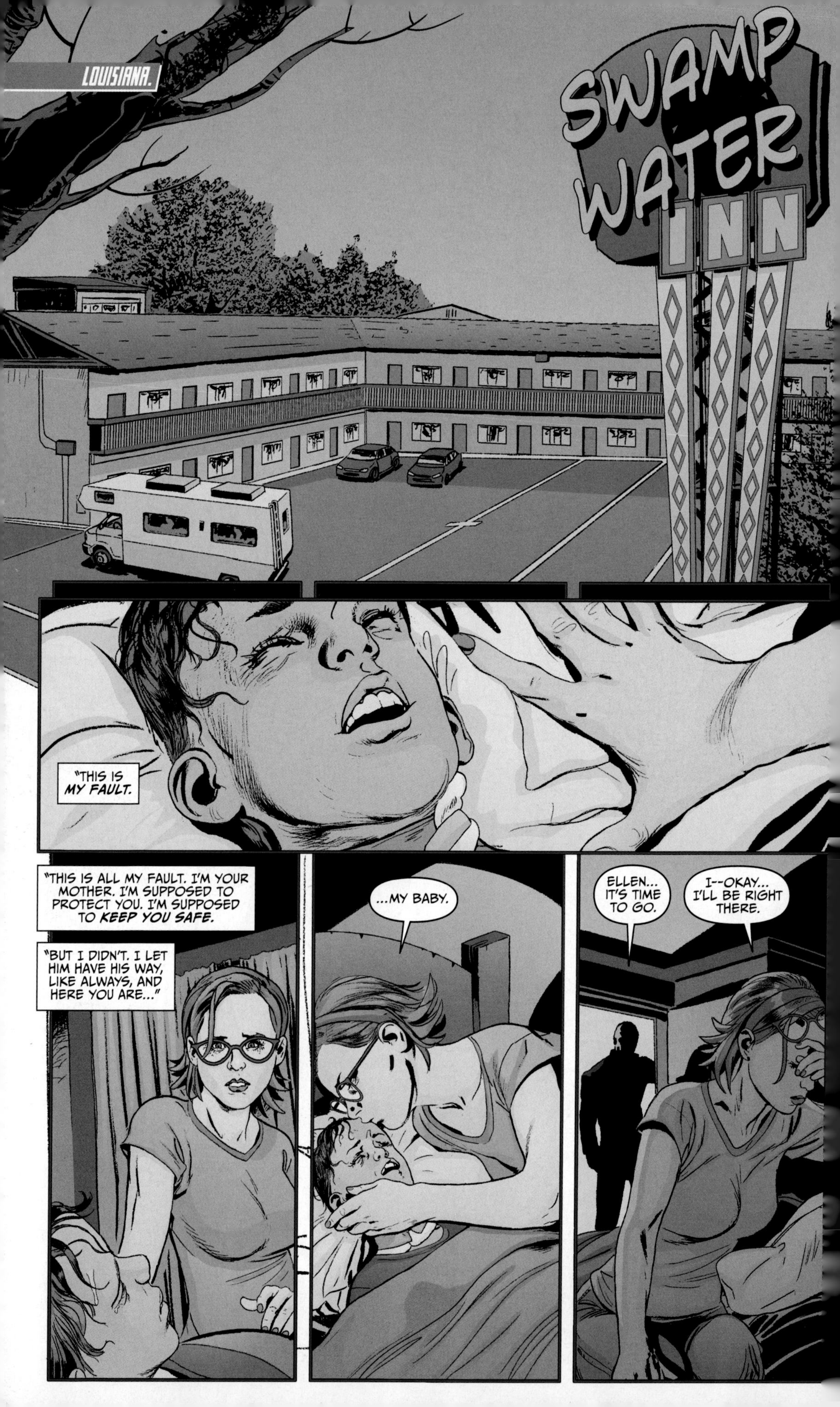

LOUISIANA.
SWAMP WATER INN
"THIS IS MY FAULT.
"THIS IS ALL MY FAULT. I'M YOUR MOTHER. I'M SUPPOSED TO PROTECT YOU. I'M SUPPOSED TO KEEP YOU SAFE.
"BUT I DIDN'T. I LET HIM HAVE HIS WAY, LIKE ALWAYS, AND HERE YOU ARE..."
...MY BABY.
ELLEN... IT'S TIME TO GO.
I--OKAY... I'LL BE RIGHT THERE.

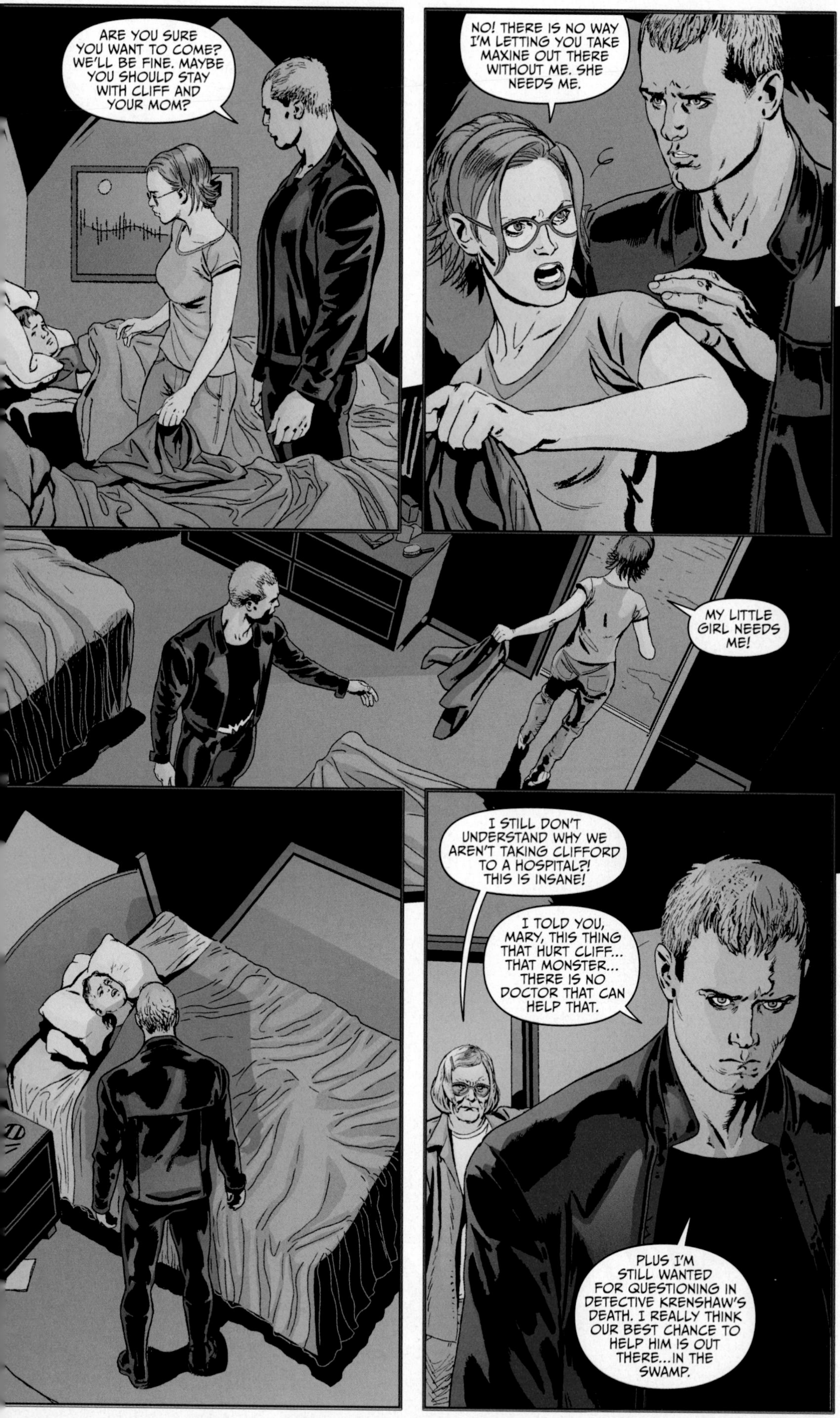
ARE YOU SURE YOU WANT TO COME? WE'LL BE FINE. MAYBE YOU SHOULD STAY WITH CLIFF AND YOUR MOM?
NO! THERE IS NO WAY I'M LETTING YOU TAKE MAXINE OUT THERE WITHOUT ME. SHE NEEDS ME.
MY LITTLE GIRL NEEDS ME!
I STILL DON'T UNDERSTAND WHY WE AREN'T TAKING CLIFFORD TO A HOSPITAL?! THIS IS INSANE!
I TOLD YOU, MARY, THIS THING THAT HURT CLIFF... THAT MONSTER... THERE IS NO DOCTOR THAT CAN HELP THAT.
PLUS I'M STILL WANTED FOR QUESTIONING IN DETECTIVE KRENSHAW'S DEATH. I REALLY THINK OUR BEST CHANCE TO HELP HIM IS OUT THERE...IN THE SWAMP.

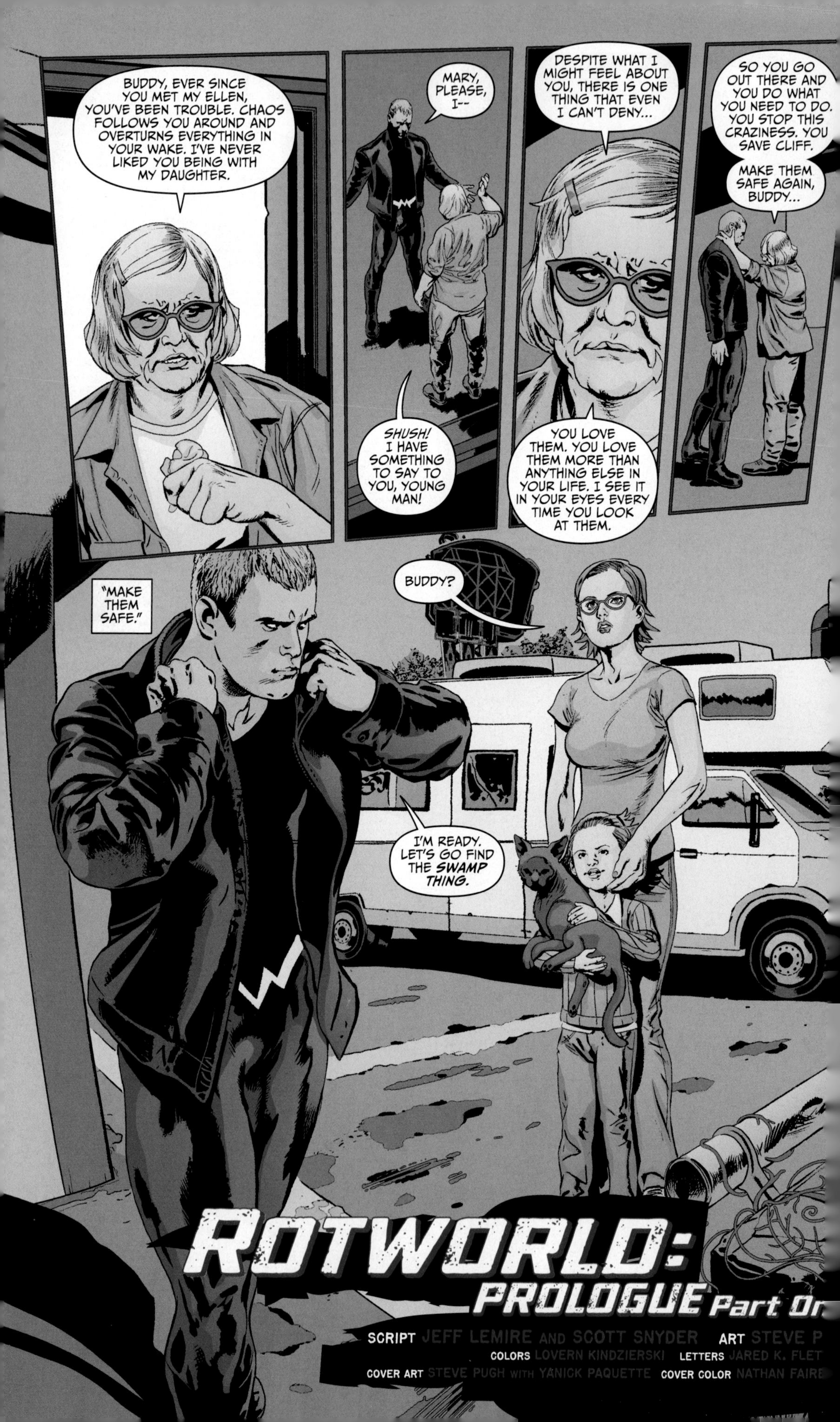
BUDDY, EVER SINCE YOU MET MY ELLEN, YOU'VE BEEN TROUBLE. CHAOS FOLLOWS YOU AROUND AND OVERTURNS EVERYTHING IN YOUR WAKE. I'VE NEVER LIKED YOU BEING WITH MY DAUGHTER.
MARY, PLEASE, I--
SHUSH! I HAVE SOMETHING TO SAY TO YOU, YOUNG MAN!
DESPITE WHAT I MIGHT FEEL ABOUT YOU, THERE IS ONE THING THAT EVEN I CAN'T DENY...
YOU LOVE THEM. YOU LOVE THEM MORE THAN ANYTHING ELSE IN YOUR LIFE. I SEE IT IN YOUR EYES EVERY TIME YOU LOOK AT THEM.
SO YOU GO OUT THERE AND YOU DO WHAT YOU NEED TO DO. YOU STOP THIS CRAZINESS. YOU SAVE CLIFF.
MAKE THEM SAFE AGAIN, BUDDY...
"MAKE THEM SAFE."
BUDDY?
I'M READY. LET'S GO FIND THE *SWAMP THING.*
ROTWORLD:
PROLOGUE Part On
SCRIPT JEFF LEMIRE AND SCOTT SNYDER ART STEVE P
COLORS LOVERN KINDZIERSKI LETTERS JARED K. FLET
COVER ART STEVE PUGH WITH YANICK PAQUETTE COVER COLOR NATHAN FAIRB

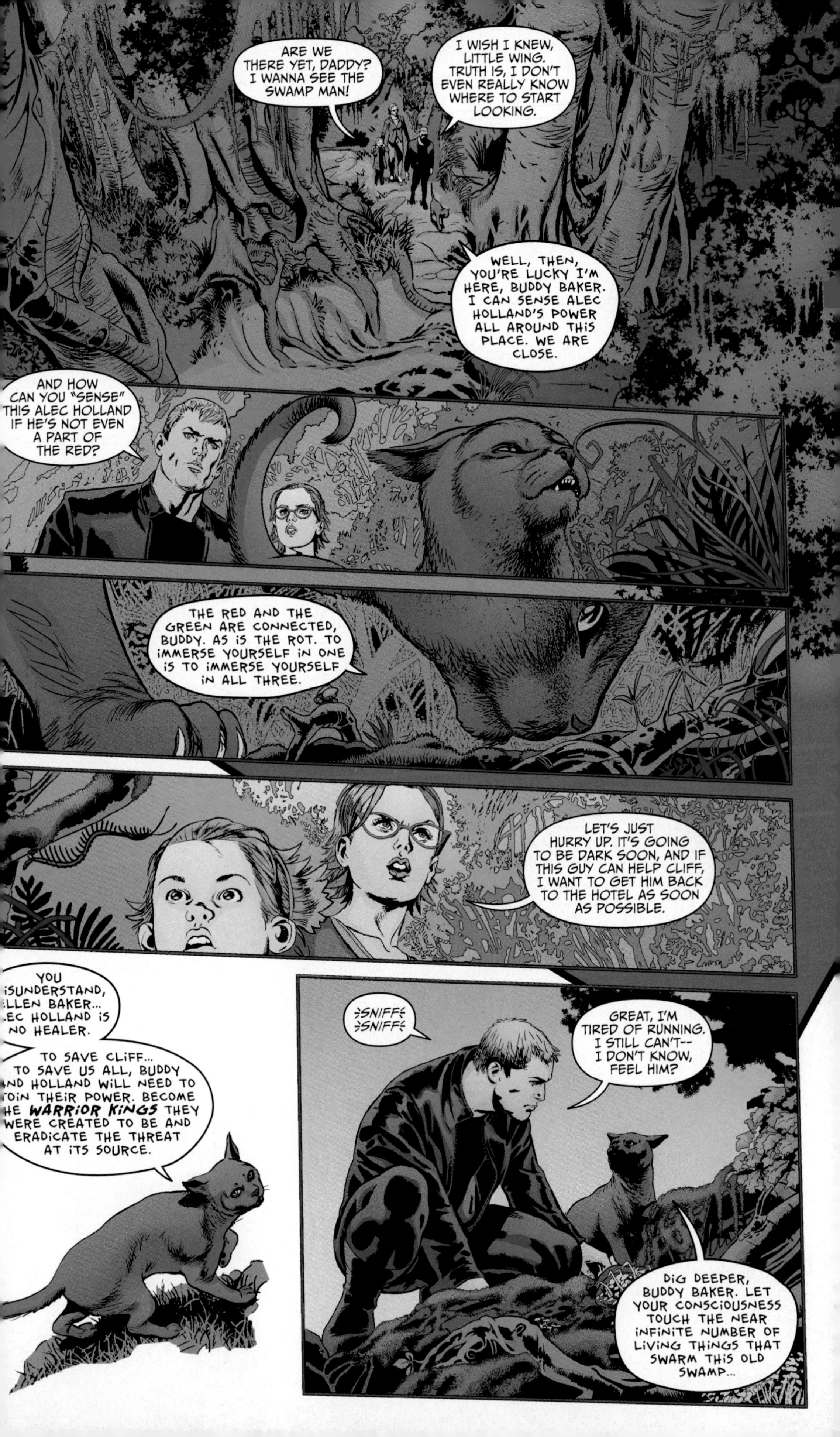
ARE WE THERE YET, DADDY? I WANNA SEE THE SWAMP MAN!
I WISH I KNEW, LITTLE WING. TRUTH IS, I DON'T EVEN REALLY KNOW WHERE TO START LOOKING.
WELL, THEN, YOU'RE LUCKY I'M HERE, BUDDY BAKER. I CAN SENSE ALEC HOLLAND'S POWER ALL AROUND THIS PLACE. WE ARE CLOSE.
AND HOW CAN YOU "SENSE" THIS ALEC HOLLAND IF HE'S NOT EVEN A PART OF THE RED?
THE RED AND THE GREEN ARE CONNECTED, BUDDY. AS IS THE ROT. TO IMMERSE YOURSELF IN ONE IS TO IMMERSE YOURSELF IN ALL THREE.
LET'S JUST HURRY UP. IT'S GOING TO BE DARK SOON, AND IF THIS GUY CAN HELP CLIFF, I WANT TO GET HIM BACK TO THE HOTEL AS SOON AS POSSIBLE.
YOU ISUNDERSTAND, ELLEN BAKER... LEC HOLLAND IS NO HEALER.
TO SAVE CLIFF... TO SAVE US ALL, BUDDY ND HOLLAND WILL NEED TO OIN THEIR POWER. BECOME HE WARRIOR KINGS THEY WERE CREATED TO BE AND ERADICATE THE THREAT AT ITS SOURCE.
SNIFF SNIFF
GREAT, I'M TIRED OF RUNNING. I STILL CAN'T-- I DON'T KNOW, FEEL HIM?
DIG DEEPER, BUDDY BAKER. LET YOUR CONSCIOUSNESS TOUCH THE NEAR INFINITE NUMBER OF LIVING THINGS THAT SWARM THIS OLD SWAMP...

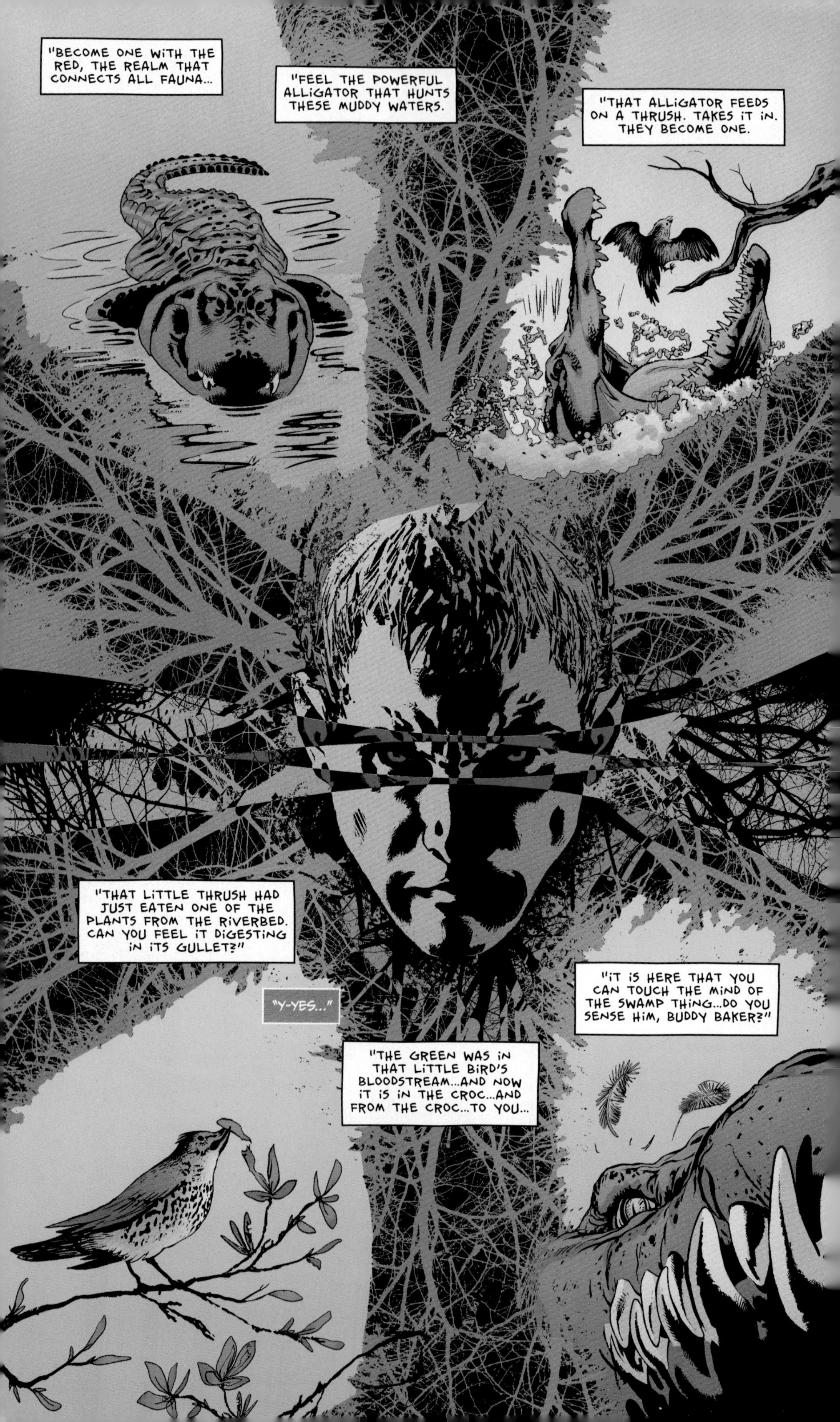
"BECOME ONE WITH THE RED, THE REALM THAT CONNECTS ALL FAUNA...
"FEEL THE POWERFUL ALLIGATOR THAT HUNTS THESE MUDDY WATERS.
"THAT ALLIGATOR FEEDS ON A THRUSH. TAKES IT IN. THEY BECOME ONE.
"THAT LITTLE THRUSH HAD JUST EATEN ONE OF THE PLANTS FROM THE RIVERBED. CAN YOU FEEL IT DIGESTING IN ITS GULLET?"
"Y-YES..."
"IT IS HERE THAT YOU CAN TOUCH THE MIND OF THE SWAMP THING...DO YOU SENSE HIM, BUDDY BAKER?"
"THE GREEN WAS IN THAT LITTLE BIRD'S BLOODSTREAM...AND NOW IT IS IN THE CROC...AND FROM THE CROC...TO YOU...

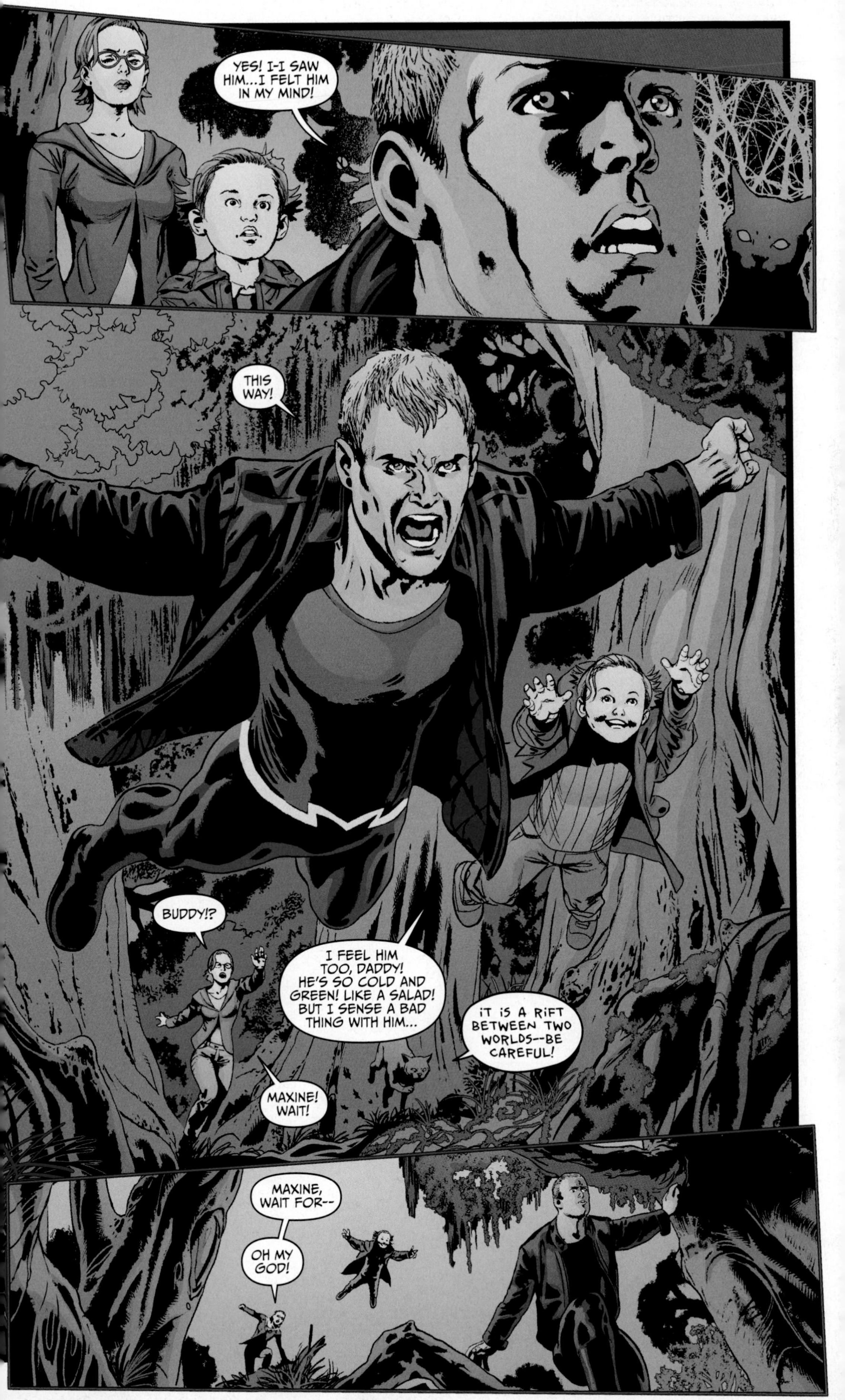
YES! I-I SAW HIM...I FELT HIM IN MY MIND!
THIS WAY!
BUDDY!?
I FEEL HIM TOO, DADDY! HE'S SO COLD AND GREEN! LIKE A SALAD! BUT I SENSE A BAD THING WITH HIM...
IT IS A RIFT BETWEEN TWO WORLDS--BE CAREFUL!
MAXINE! WAIT!
MAXINE, WAIT FOR--
OH MY GOD!

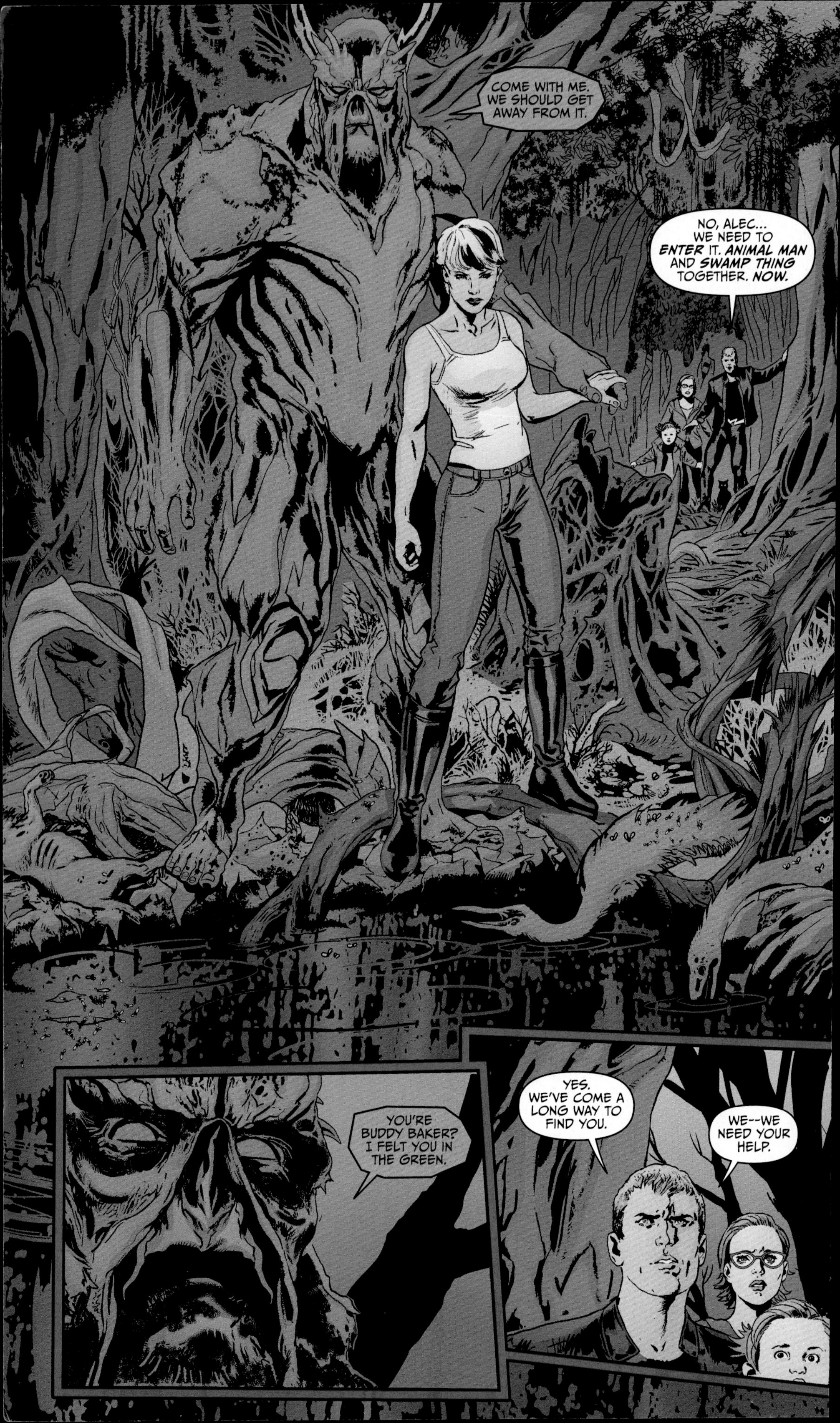
COME WITH ME. WE SHOULD GET AWAY FROM IT.
NO, ALEC... WE NEED TO ENTER IT. ANIMAL MAN AND SWAMP THING TOGETHER. NOW.
YOU'RE BUDDY BAKER? I FELT YOU IN THE GREEN.
YES. WE'VE COME A LONG WAY TO FIND YOU.
WE--WE NEED YOUR HELP.

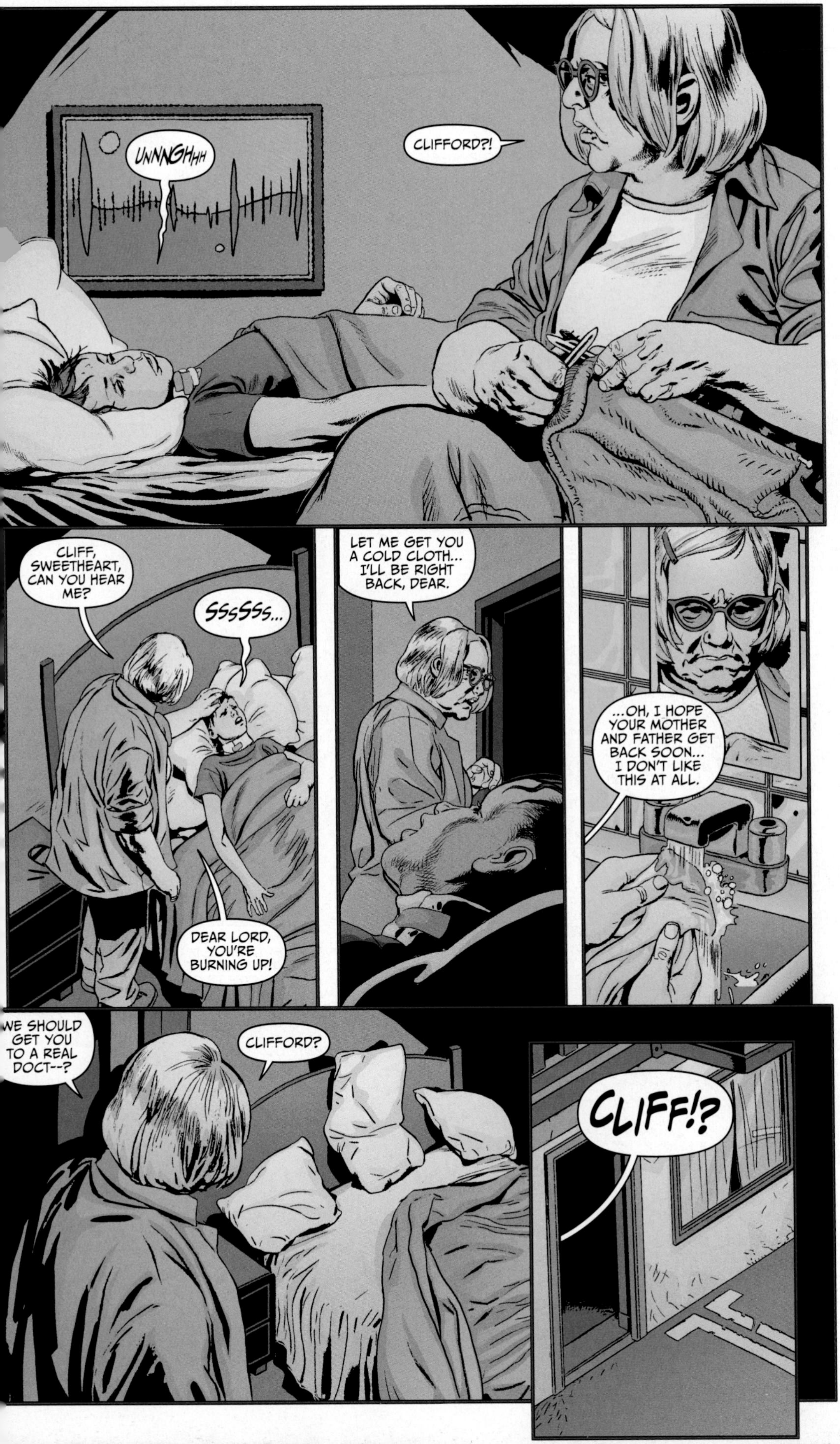
UNNNGHHH
CLIFFORD?!
CLIFF, SWEETHEART, CAN YOU HEAR ME?
SSSSSS...
DEAR LORD, YOU'RE BURNING UP!
LET ME GET YOU A COLD CLOTH... I'LL BE RIGHT BACK, DEAR.
...OH, I HOPE YOUR MOTHER AND FATHER GET BACK SOON... I DON'T LIKE THIS AT ALL.
WE SHOULD GET YOU TO A REAL DOCT--?
CLIFFORD?
CLIFF!?

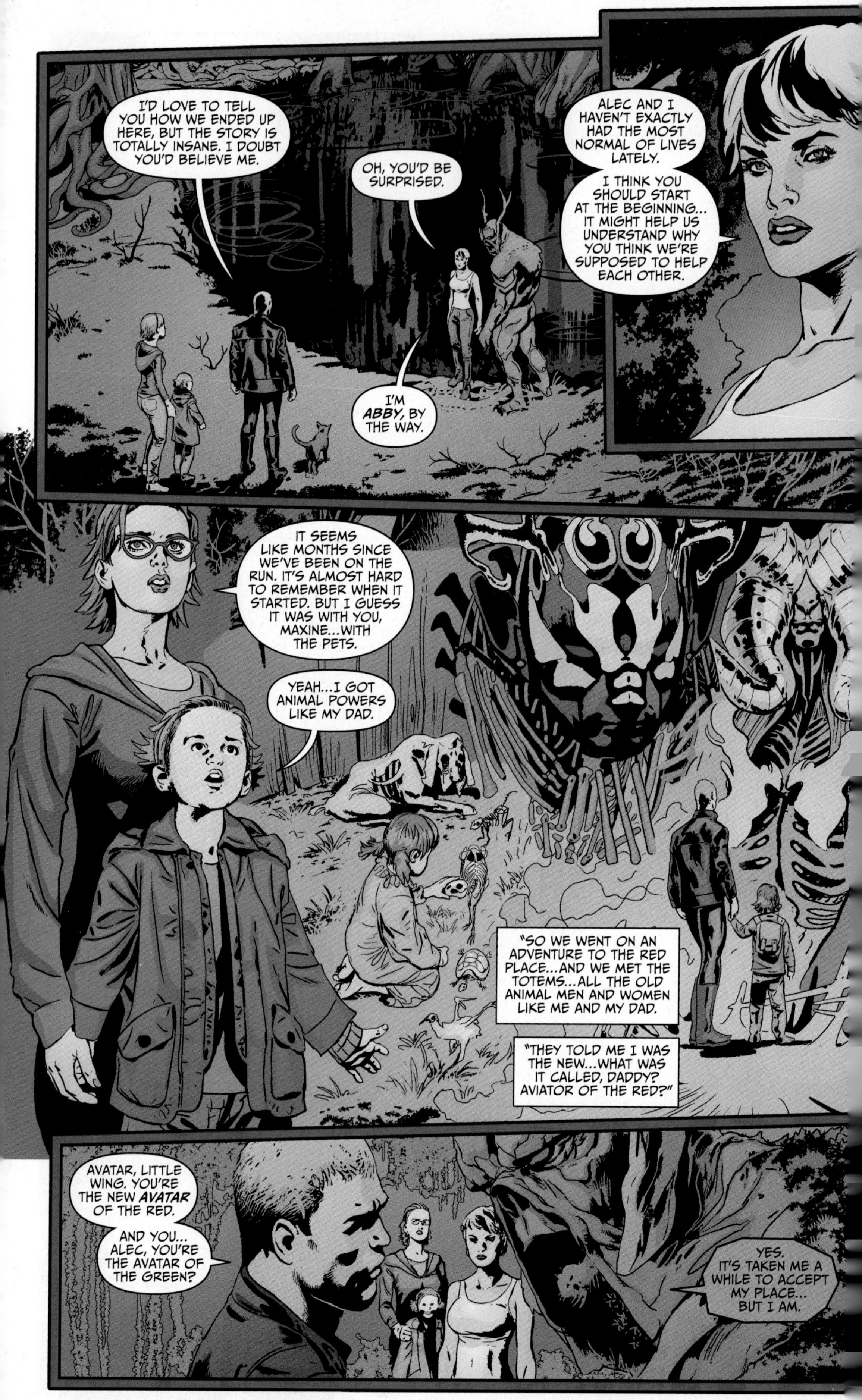
I'D LOVE TO TELL YOU HOW WE ENDED UP HERE, BUT THE STORY IS TOTALLY INSANE. I DOUBT YOU'D BELIEVE ME.
OH, YOU'D BE SURPRISED.
I'M *ABBY,* BY THE WAY.
ALEC AND I HAVEN'T EXACTLY HAD THE MOST NORMAL OF LIVES LATELY.
I THINK YOU SHOULD START AT THE BEGINNING... IT MIGHT HELP US UNDERSTAND WHY YOU THINK WE'RE SUPPOSED TO HELP EACH OTHER.
IT SEEMS LIKE MONTHS SINCE WE'VE BEEN ON THE RUN. IT'S ALMOST HARD TO REMEMBER WHEN IT STARTED. BUT I GUESS IT WAS WITH YOU, MAXINE...WITH THE PETS.
YEAH...I GOT ANIMAL POWERS LIKE MY DAD.
"SO WE WENT ON AN ADVENTURE TO THE RED PLACE...AND WE MET THE TOTEMS...ALL THE OLD ANIMAL MEN AND WOMEN LIKE ME AND MY DAD.
"THEY TOLD ME I WAS THE NEW...WHAT WAS IT CALLED, DADDY? AVIATOR OF THE RED?"
AVATAR, LITTLE WING. YOU'RE THE NEW *AVATAR* OF THE RED.
AND YOU... ALEC, YOU'RE THE AVATAR OF THE GREEN?
YES. IT'S TAKEN ME A WHILE TO ACCEPT MY PLACE... BUT I AM.

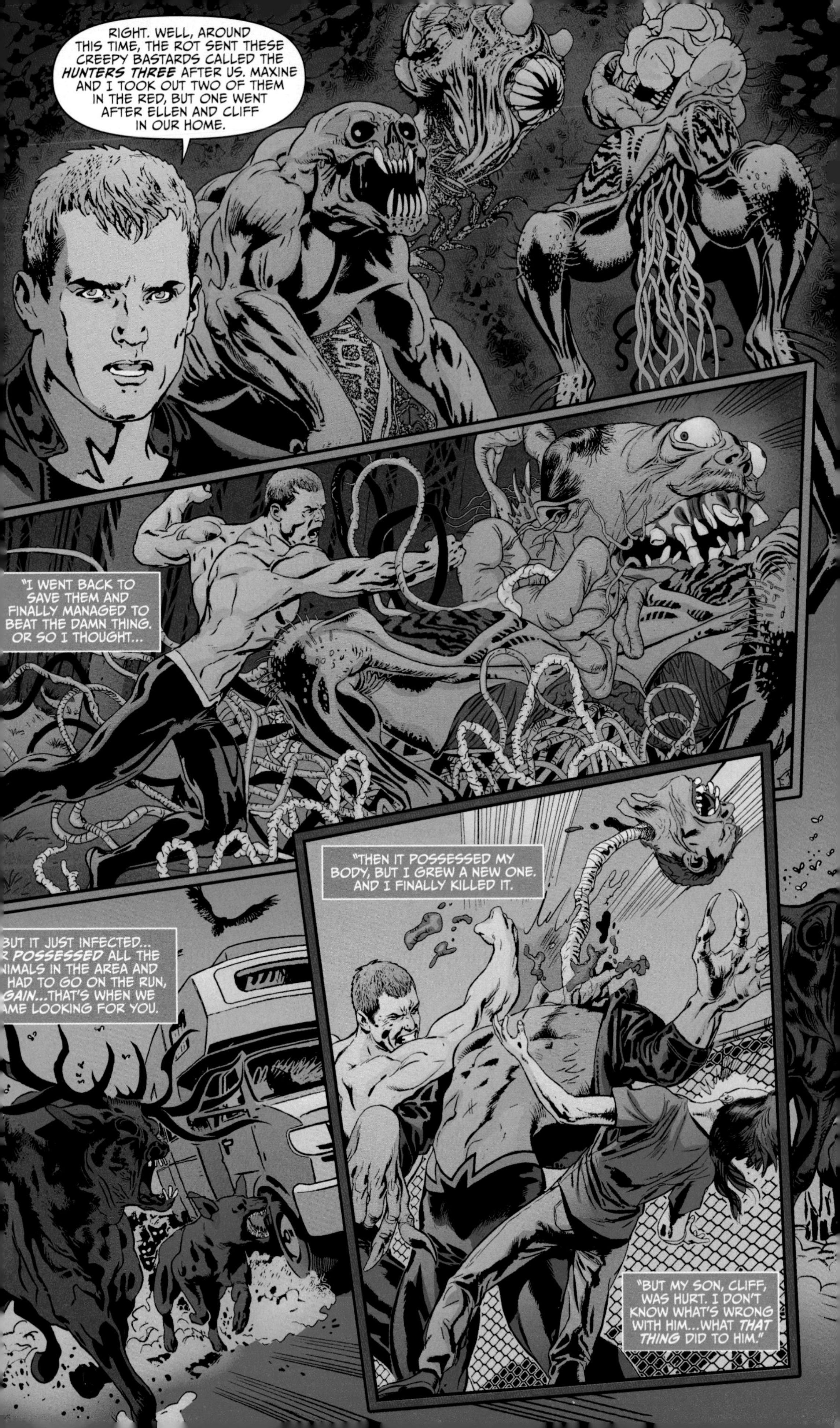
RIGHT. WELL, AROUND THIS TIME, THE ROT SENT THESE CREEPY BASTARDS CALLED THE *HUNTERS THREE* AFTER US. MAXINE AND I TOOK OUT TWO OF THEM IN THE RED, BUT ONE WENT AFTER ELLEN AND CLIFF IN OUR HOME.
"I WENT BACK TO SAVE THEM AND FINALLY MANAGED TO BEAT THE DAMN THING. OR SO I THOUGHT...
"THEN IT POSSESSED MY BODY, BUT I GREW A NEW ONE. AND I FINALLY KILLED IT.
BUT IT JUST INFECTED... *POSSESSED* ALL THE NIMALS IN THE AREA AND HAD TO GO ON THE RUN, *GAIN*...THAT'S WHEN WE AME LOOKING FOR YOU.
"BUT MY SON, CLIFF, WAS HURT. I DON'T KNOW WHAT'S WRONG WITH HIM...WHAT *THAT THING* DID TO HIM."

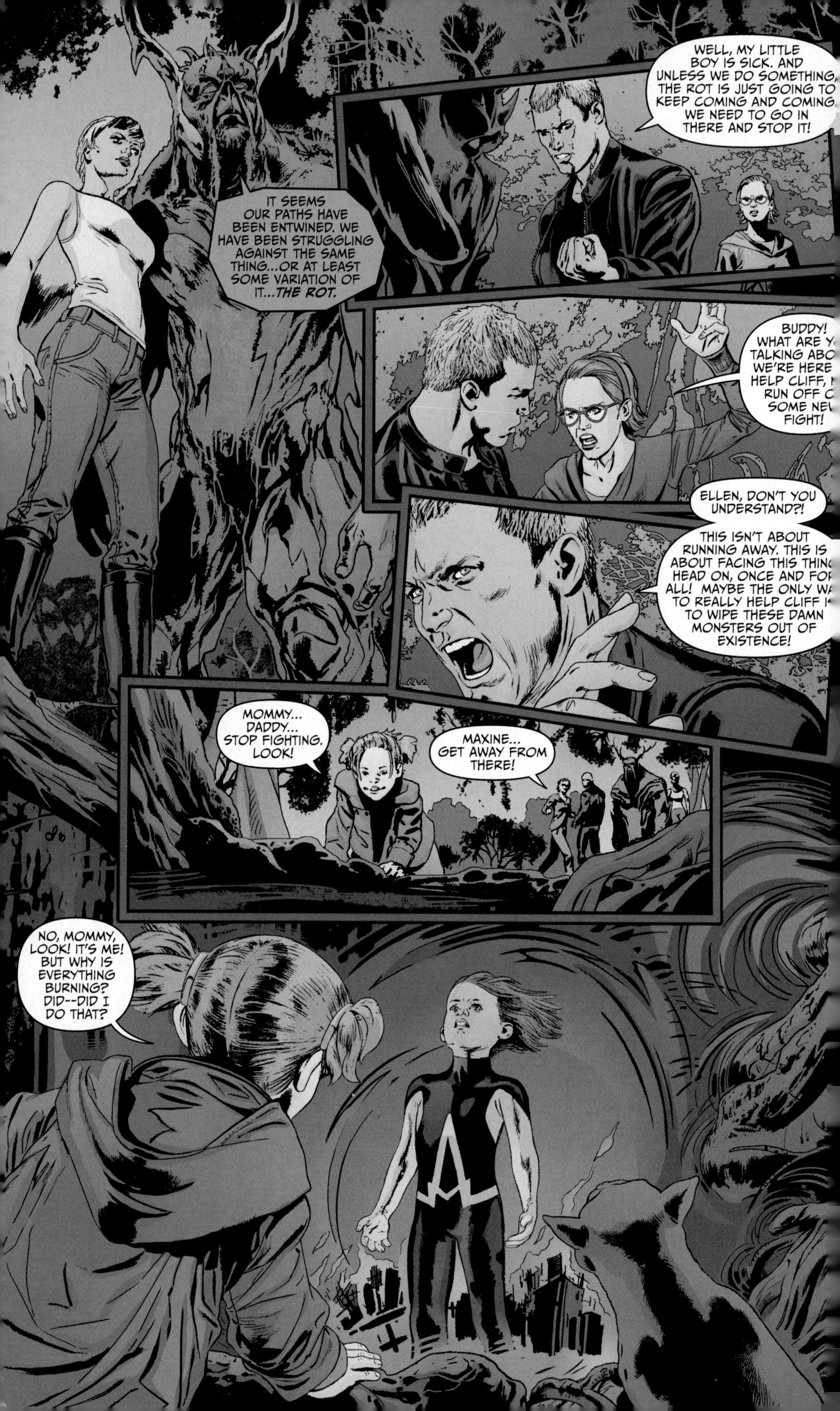
IT SEEMS OUR PATHS HAVE BEEN ENTWINED. WE HAVE BEEN STRUGGLING AGAINST THE SAME THING...OR AT LEAST SOME VARIATION OF IT...*THE ROT.*
WELL, MY LITTLE BOY IS SICK. AND UNLESS WE DO SOMETHING, THE ROT IS JUST GOING TO KEEP COMING AND COMING. WE NEED TO GO IN THERE AND STOP IT!
BUDDY! WHAT ARE Y TALKING ABO WE'RE HERE HELP CLIFF, RUN OFF SOME NEW FIGHT!
ELLEN, DON'T YOU UNDERSTAND?!
THIS ISN'T ABOUT RUNNING AWAY. THIS IS ABOUT FACING THIS THIN HEAD ON, ONCE AND FO ALL! MAYBE THE ONLY WA TO REALLY HELP CLIFF I TO WIPE THESE DAMN MONSTERS OUT OF EXISTENCE!
MOMMY... DADDY... STOP FIGHTING. LOOK!
MAXINE... GET AWAY FROM THERE!
NO, MOMMY, LOOK! IT'S ME! BUT WHY IS EVERYTHING BURNING? DID--DID I DO THAT?

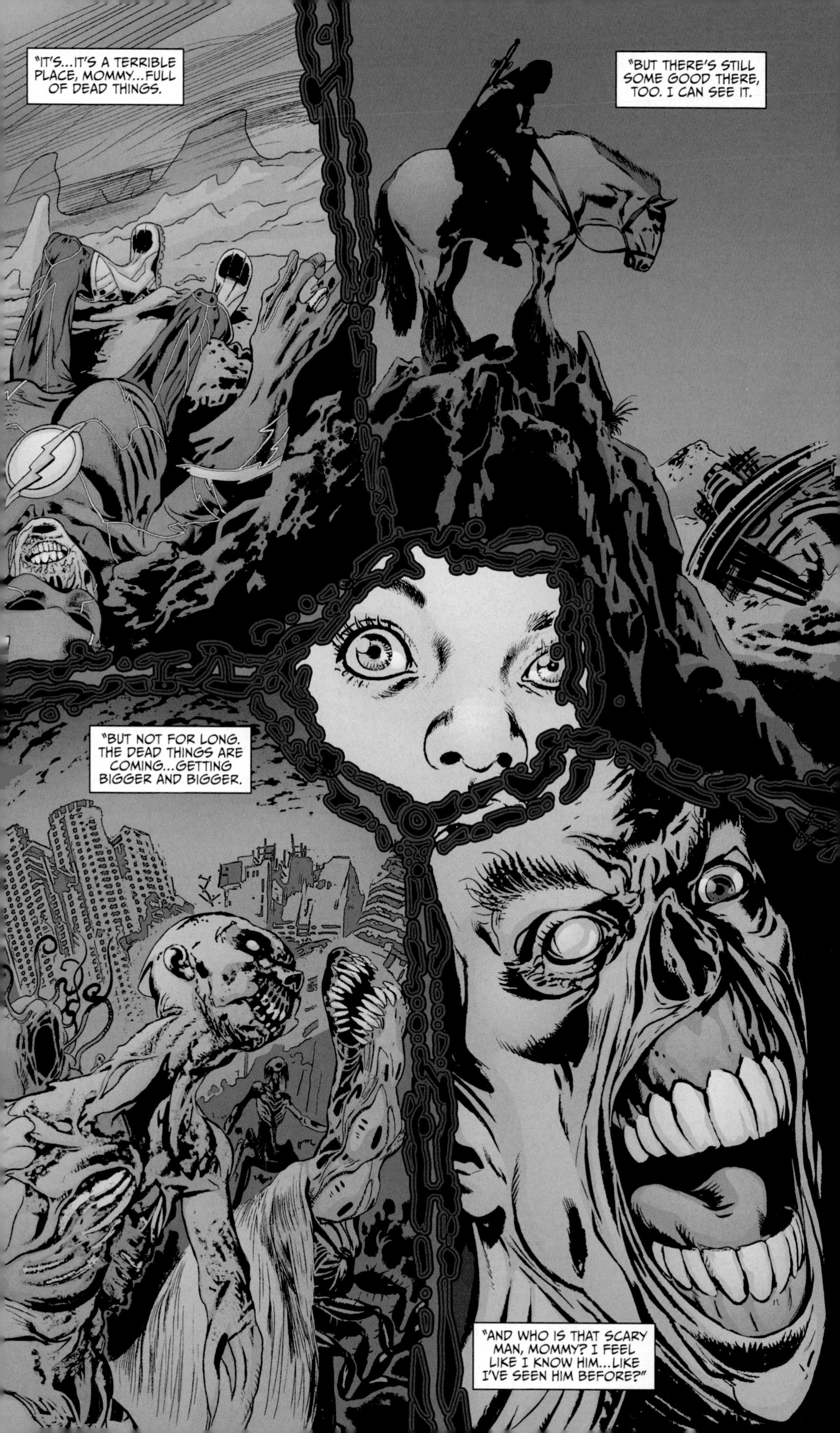
"IT'S...IT'S A TERRIBLE PLACE, MOMMY...FULL OF DEAD THINGS.
"BUT THERE'S STILL SOME GOOD THERE, TOO. I CAN SEE IT.
"BUT NOT FOR LONG. THE DEAD THINGS ARE COMING...GETTING BIGGER AND BIGGER.
"AND WHO IS THAT SCARY MAN, MOMMY? I FEEL LIKE I KNOW HIM...LIKE I'VE SEEN HIM BEFORE?"

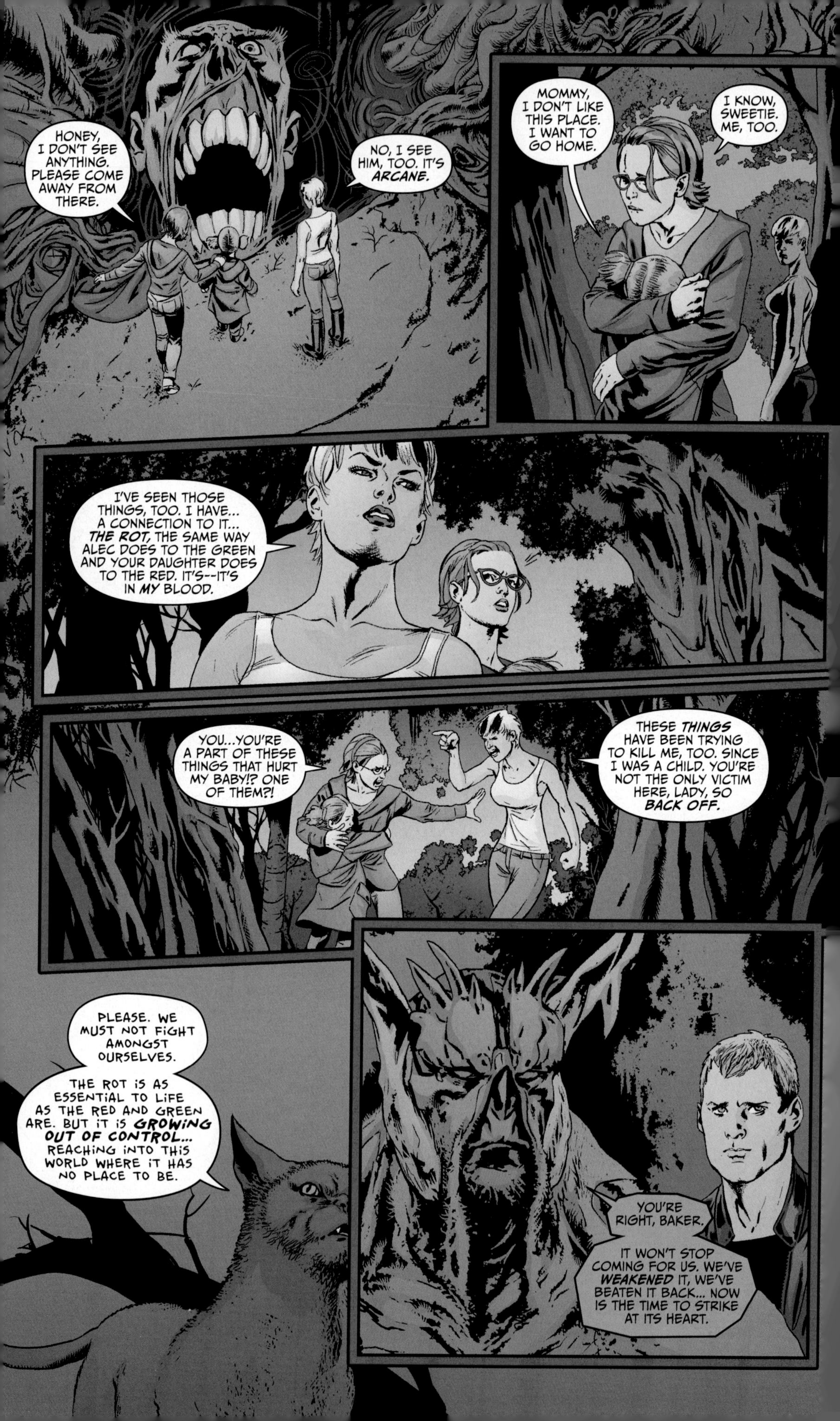
HONEY, I DON'T SEE ANYTHING. PLEASE COME AWAY FROM THERE.
NO, I SEE HIM, TOO. IT'S ARCANE.
MOMMY, I DON'T LIKE THIS PLACE. I WANT TO GO HOME.
I KNOW, SWEETIE. ME, TOO.
I'VE SEEN THOSE THINGS, TOO. I HAVE... A CONNECTION TO IT... THE ROT, THE SAME WAY ALEC DOES TO THE GREEN AND YOUR DAUGHTER DOES TO THE RED. IT'S--IT'S IN MY BLOOD.
YOU...YOU'RE A PART OF THESE THINGS THAT HURT MY BABY!? ONE OF THEM?!
THESE THINGS HAVE BEEN TRYING TO KILL ME, TOO. SINCE I WAS A CHILD. YOU'RE NOT THE ONLY VICTIM HERE, LADY, SO BACK OFF.
PLEASE. WE MUST NOT FIGHT AMONGST OURSELVES.
THE ROT IS AS ESSENTIAL TO LIFE AS THE RED AND GREEN ARE. BUT IT IS GROWING OUT OF CONTROL... REACHING INTO THIS WORLD WHERE IT HAS NO PLACE TO BE.
YOU'RE RIGHT, BAKER.
IT WON'T STOP COMING FOR US. WE'VE WEAKENED IT, WE'VE BEATEN IT BACK... NOW IS THE TIME TO STRIKE AT ITS HEART.

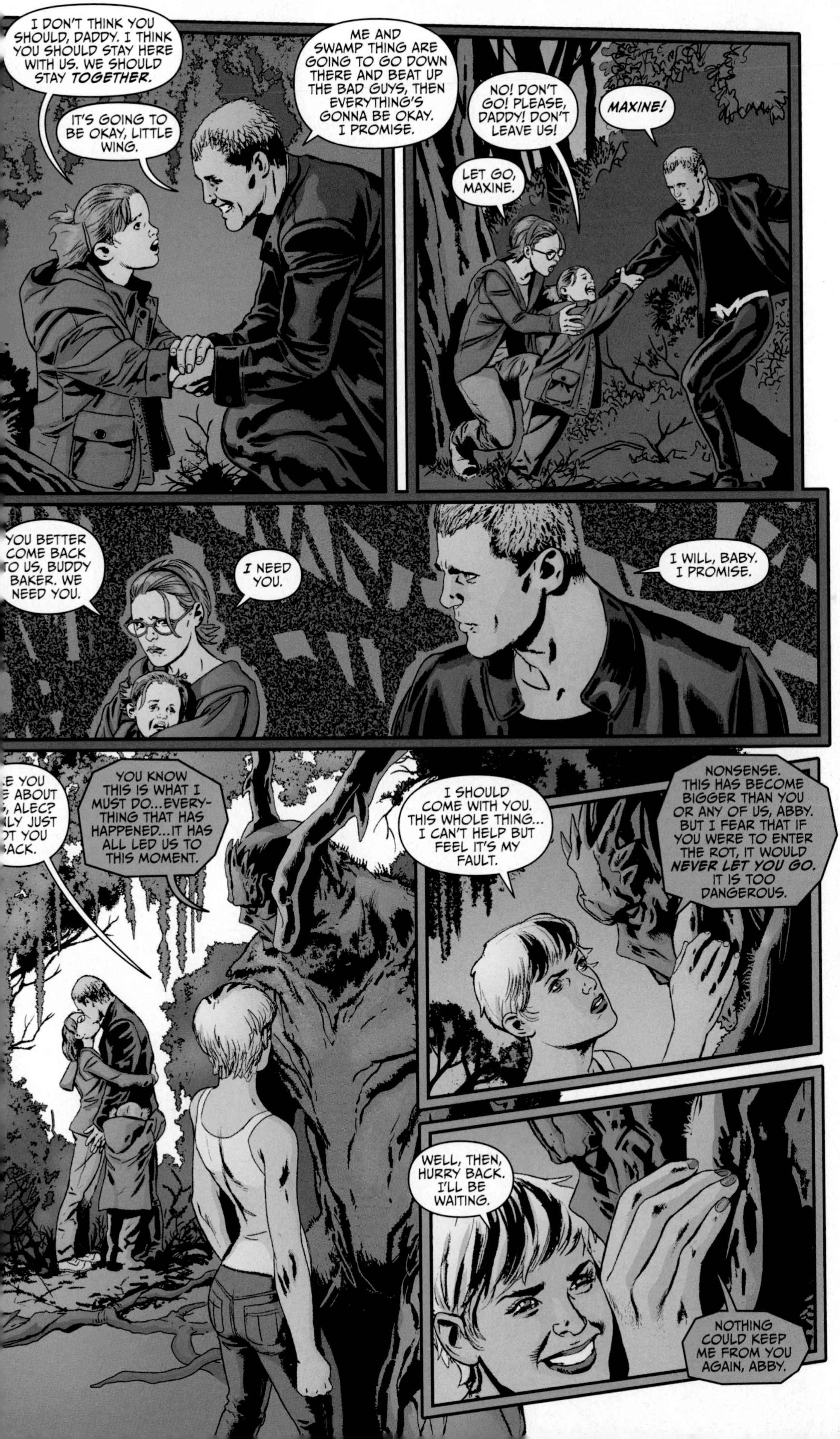
I DON'T THINK YOU SHOULD, DADDY. I THINK YOU SHOULD STAY HERE WITH US. WE SHOULD STAY TOGETHER.
IT'S GOING TO BE OKAY, LITTLE WING.
ME AND SWAMP THING ARE GOING TO GO DOWN THERE AND BEAT UP THE BAD GUYS, THEN EVERYTHING'S GONNA BE OKAY. I PROMISE.
NO! DON'T GO! PLEASE, DADDY! DON'T LEAVE US!
MAXINE!
LET GO, MAXINE.
YOU BETTER COME BACK TO US, BUDDY BAKER. WE NEED YOU.
I NEED YOU.
I WILL, BABY. I PROMISE.
YOU KNOW THIS IS WHAT I MUST DO...EVERYTHING THAT HAS HAPPENED...IT HAS ALL LED US TO THIS MOMENT.
I SHOULD COME WITH YOU. THIS WHOLE THING... I CAN'T HELP BUT FEEL IT'S MY FAULT.
NONSENSE. THIS HAS BECOME BIGGER THAN YOU OR ANY OF US, ABBY. BUT I FEAR THAT IF YOU WERE TO ENTER THE ROT, IT WOULD NEVER LET YOU GO. IT IS TOO DANGEROUS.
WELL, THEN, HURRY BACK. I'LL BE WAITING.
NOTHING COULD KEEP ME FROM YOU AGAIN, ABBY.

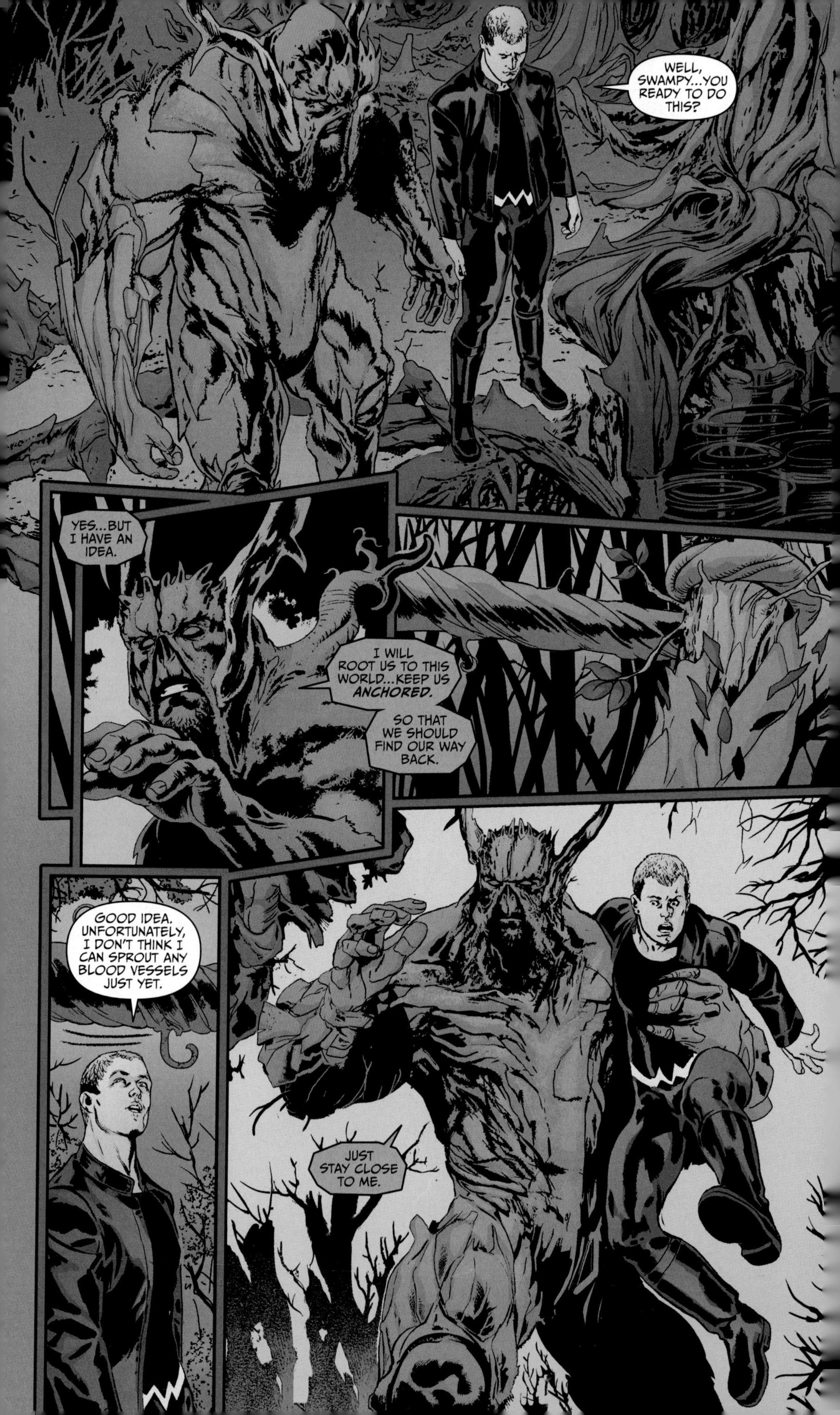
WELL, SWAMPY...YOU READY TO DO THIS?
YES...BUT I HAVE AN IDEA.
I WILL ROOT US TO THIS WORLD...KEEP US ANCHORED.
SO THAT WE SHOULD FIND OUR WAY BACK.
GOOD IDEA. UNFORTUNATELY, I DON'T THINK I CAN SPROUT ANY BLOOD VESSELS JUST YET.
JUST STAY CLOSE TO ME.

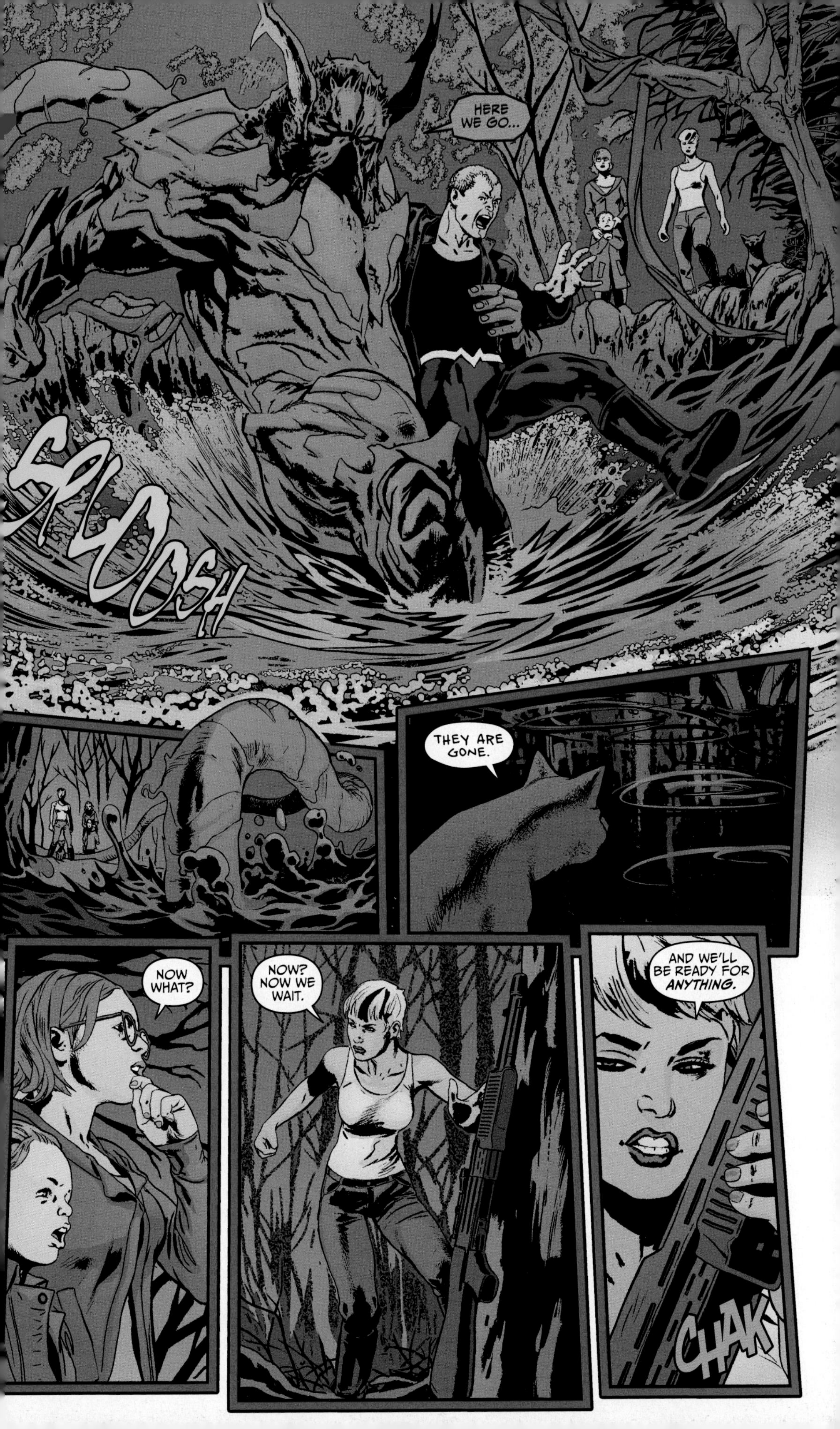
HERE WE GO...
SPLOOSH
THEY ARE GONE.
NOW WHAT?
NOW? NOW WE WAIT.
AND WE'LL BE READY FOR *ANYTHING.*
CHAK

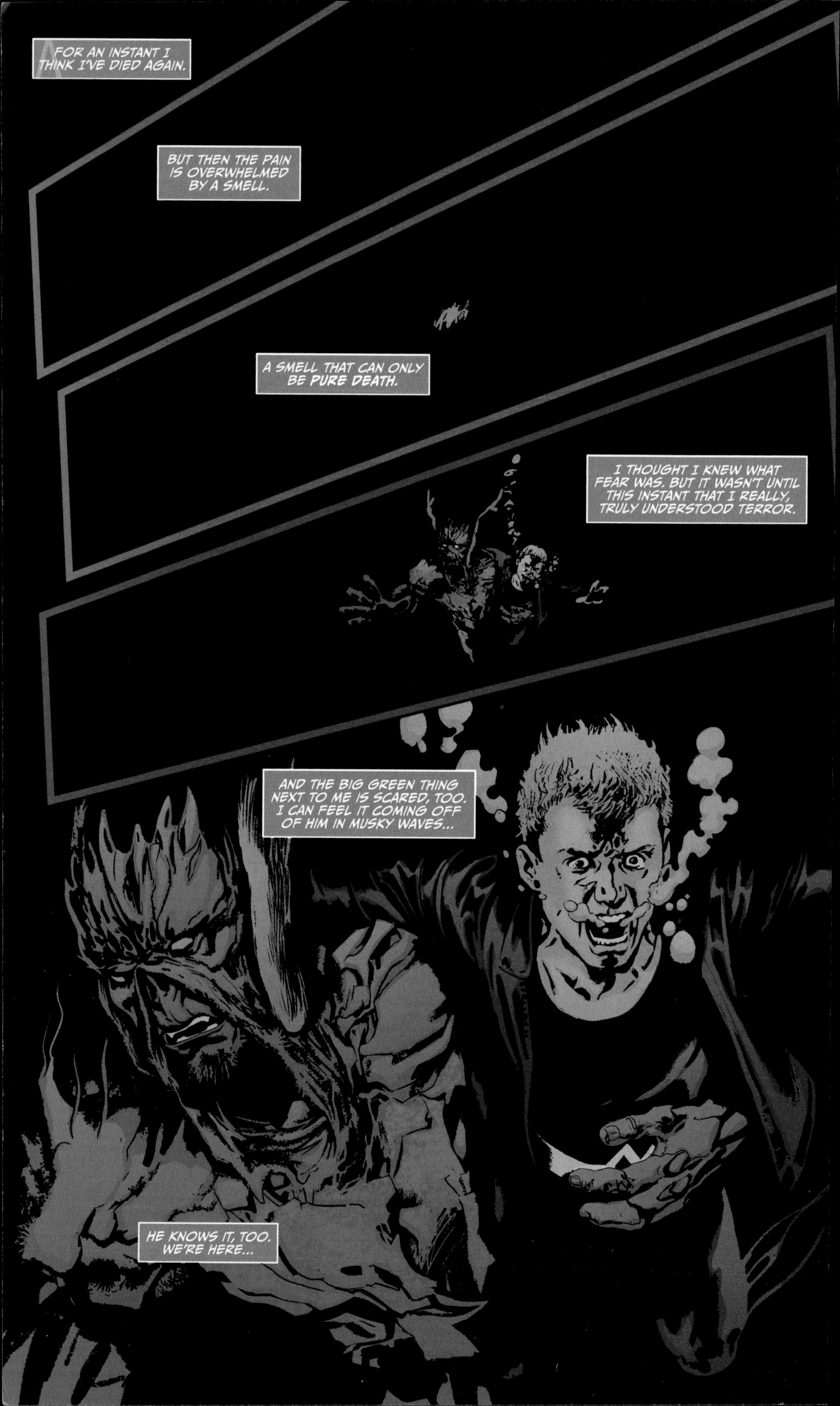

FOR AN INSTANT I THINK I'VE DIED AGAIN.
BUT THEN THE PAIN IS OVERWHELMED BY A SMELL.
A SMELL THAT CAN ONLY BE PURE DEATH.
I THOUGHT I KNEW WHAT FEAR WAS. BUT IT WASN'T UNTIL THIS INSTANT THAT I REALLY, TRULY UNDERSTOOD TERROR.
AND THE BIG GREEN THING NEXT TO ME IS SCARED, TOO. I CAN FEEL IT COMING OFF OF HIM IN MUSKY WAVES...
HE KNOWS IT, TOO. WE'RE HERE...

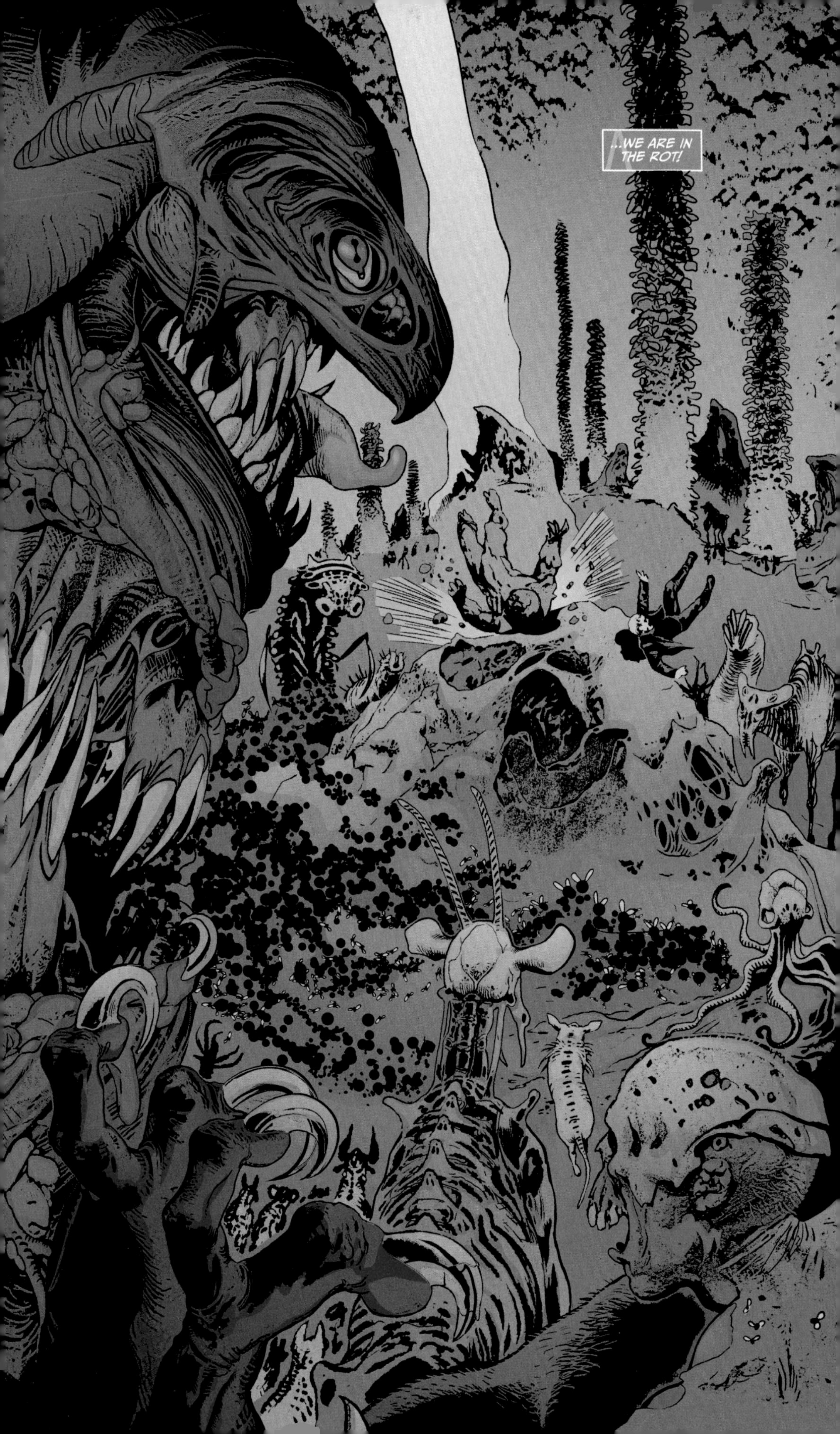
...WE ARE IN THE ROT!

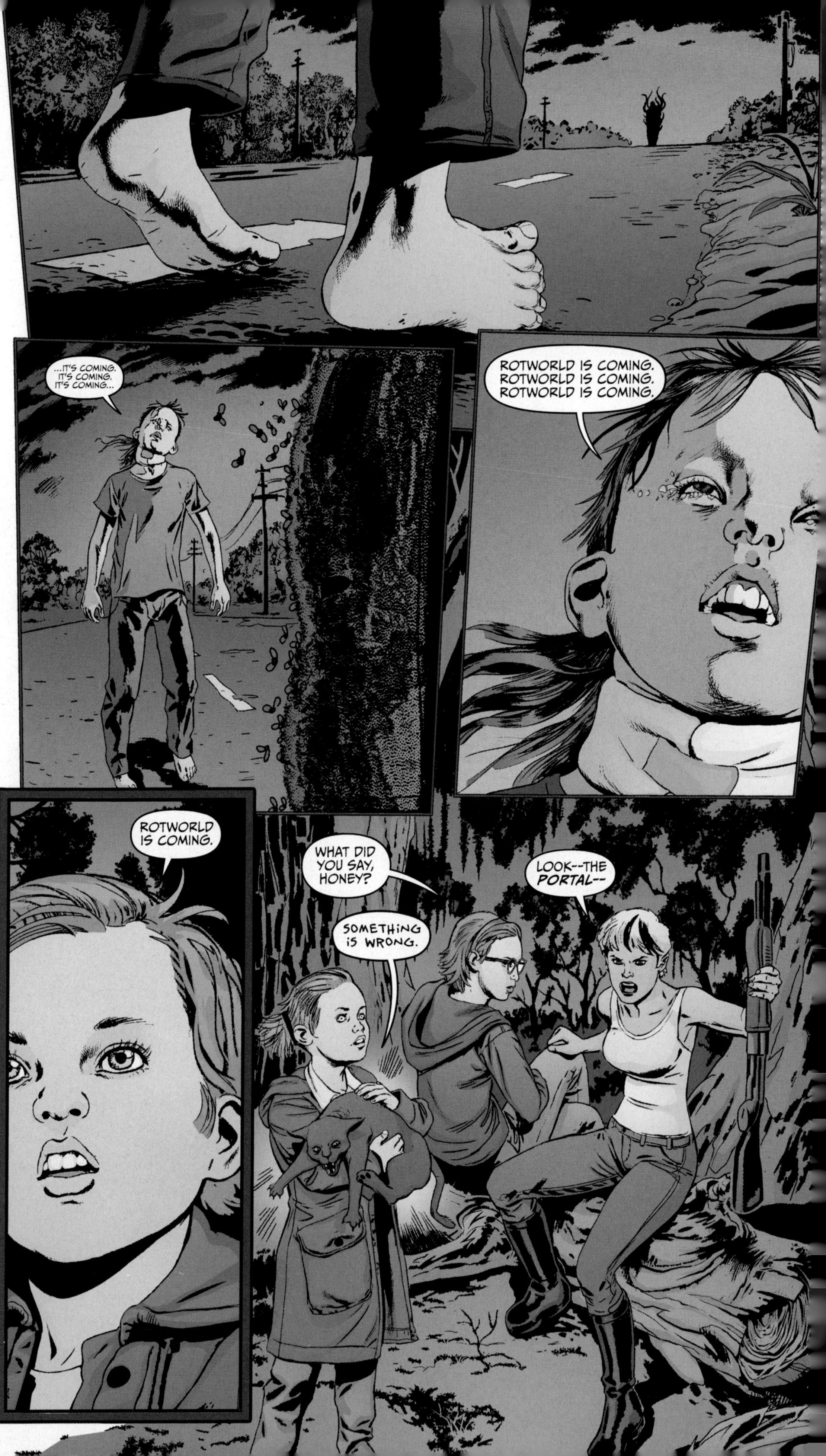
...IT'S COMING. IT'S COMING. IT'S COMING...
ROTWORLD IS COMING. ROTWORLD IS COMING. ROTWORLD IS COMING.
ROTWORLD IS COMING.
WHAT DID YOU SAY, HONEY?
SOMETHING IS WRONG.
LOOK--THE PORTAL--

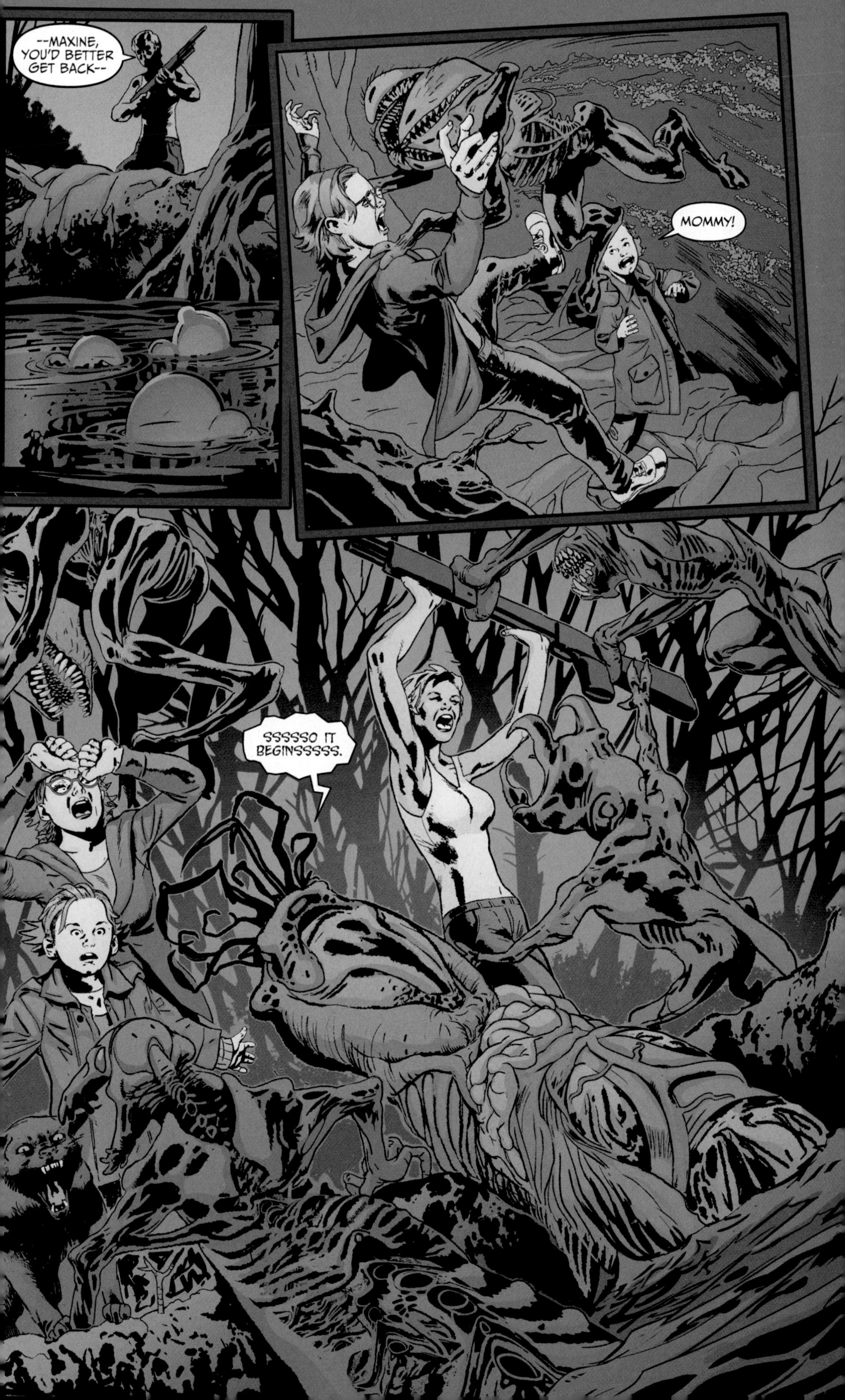
--MAXINE, YOU'D BETTER GET BACK--
MOMMY!
SSSSSO IT BEGINSSSSS.

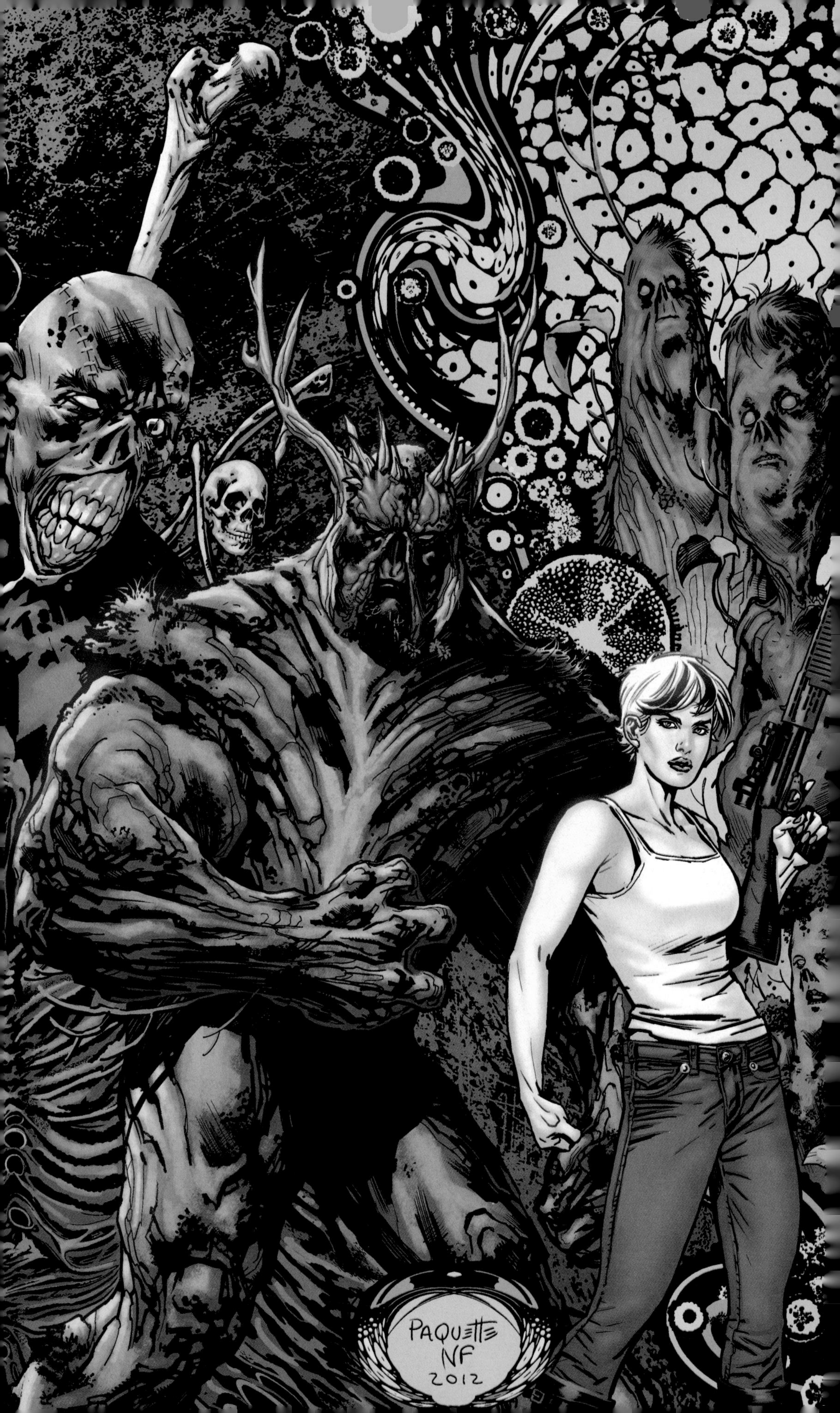
PAQUETTE
NF
2012

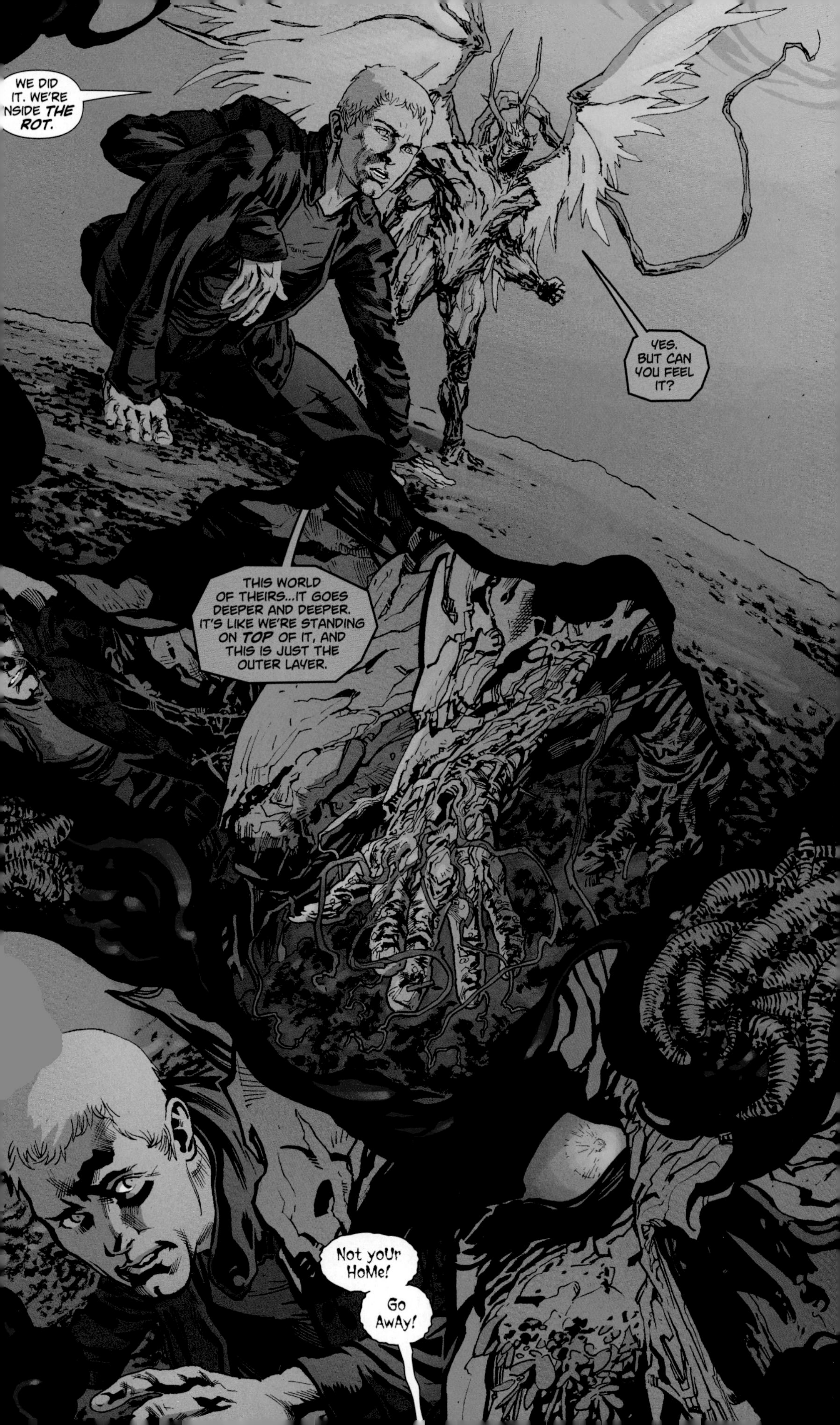
WE DID IT. WE'RE NSIDE THE ROT.
YES. BUT CAN YOU FEEL IT?
THIS WORLD OF THEIRS...IT GOES DEEPER AND DEEPER. IT'S LIKE WE'RE STANDING ON TOP OF IT, AND THIS IS JUST THE OUTER LAYER.
Not yoUr HoMe!
Go AwAy!

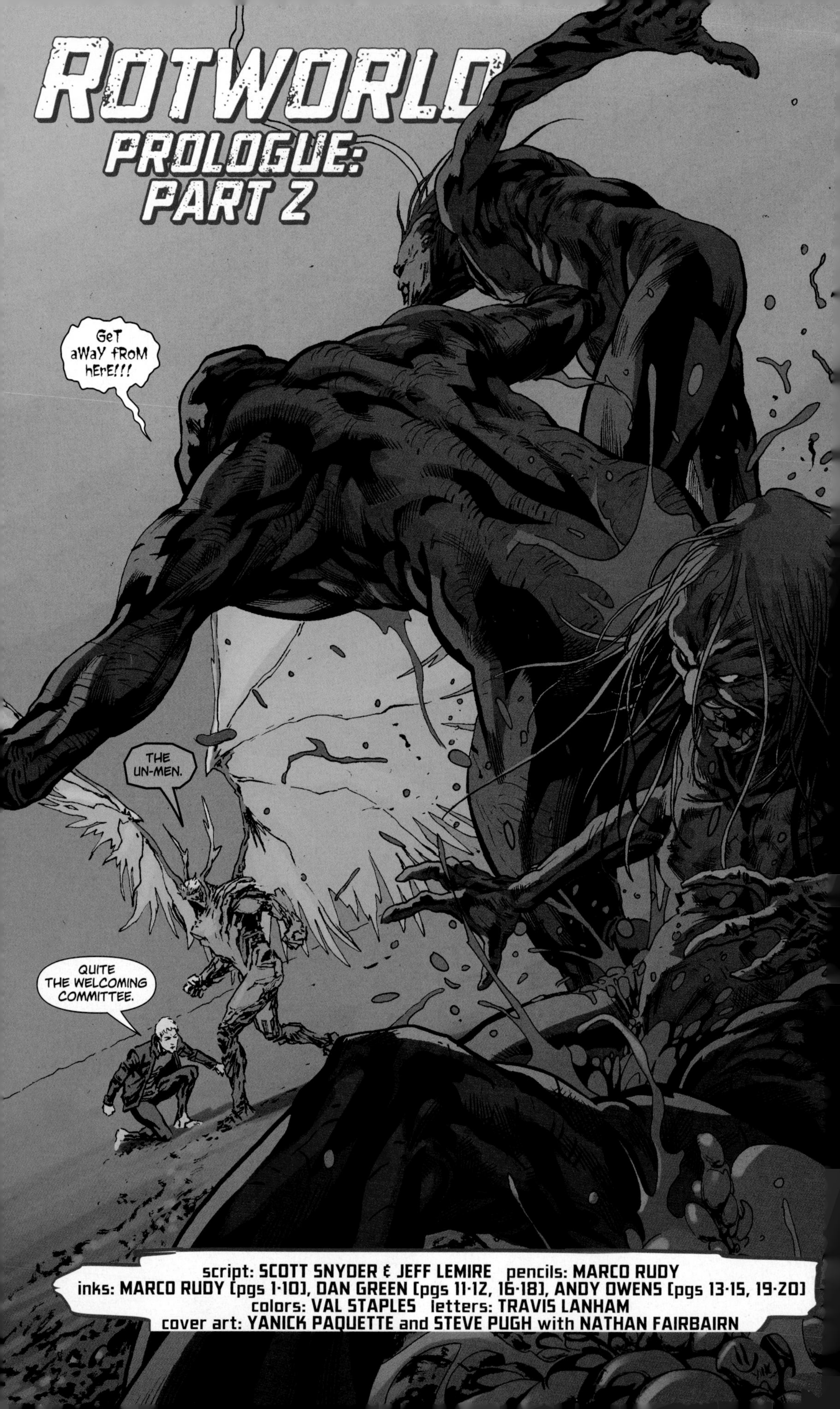
ROTWORLD
PROLOGUE: PART 2
GeT aWaY fROM hErE!!!
THE UN-MEN.
QUITE THE WELCOMING COMMITTEE.
script: SCOTT SNYDER & JEFF LEMIRE pencils: MARCO RUDY
inks: MARCO RUDY [pgs 1-10], DAN GREEN [pgs 11-12, 16-18], ANDY OWENS [pgs 13-15, 19-20]
colors: VAL STAPLES letters: TRAVIS LANHAM
cover art: YANICK PAQUETTE and STEVE PUGH with NATHAN FAIRBAIRN

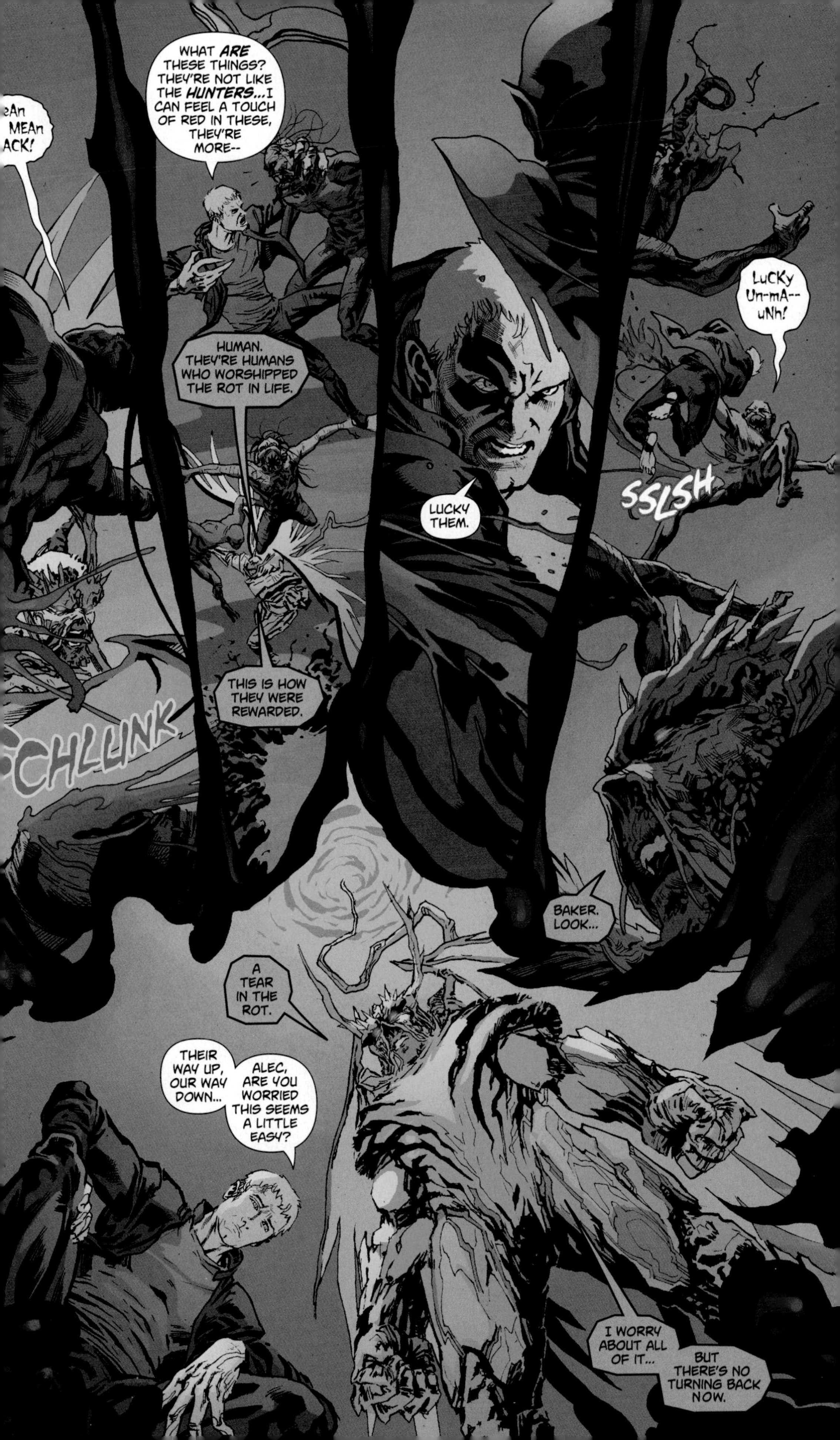
eAn MEAn ACK!
WHAT ARE THESE THINGS? THEY'RE NOT LIKE THE HUNTERS...I CAN FEEL A TOUCH OF RED IN THESE, THEY'RE MORE--
HUMAN. THEY'RE HUMANS WHO WORSHIPPED THE ROT IN LIFE.
THIS IS HOW THEY WERE REWARDED.
CHLUNK
LUCKY THEM.
LuCKy Un-mA--uNh!
SSLSH
BAKER. LOOK...
A TEAR IN THE ROT.
THEIR WAY UP, OUR WAY DOWN...
ALEC, ARE YOU WORRIED THIS SEEMS A LITTLE EASY?
I WORRY ABOUT ALL OF IT...
BUT THERE'S NO TURNING BACK NOW.

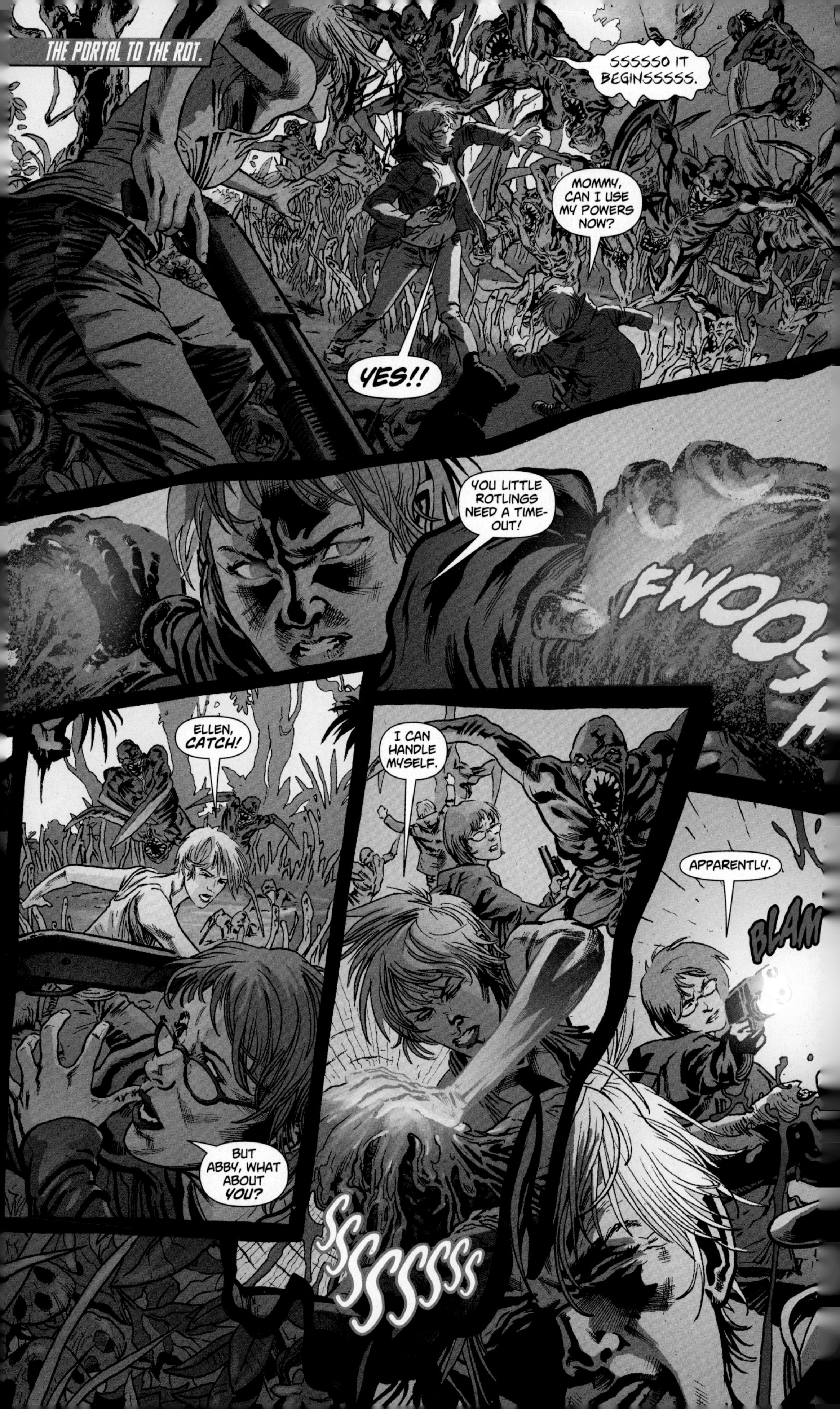
THE PORTAL TO THE ROT.
SSSSSO IT BEGINSSSSS.
MOMMY, CAN I USE MY POWERS NOW?
YES!!
YOU LITTLE ROTLINGS NEED A TIME-OUT!
FWOOSH
ELLEN, CATCH!
BUT ABBY, WHAT ABOUT YOU?
I CAN HANDLE MYSELF.
APPARENTLY.
BLAM
SSSSSSS

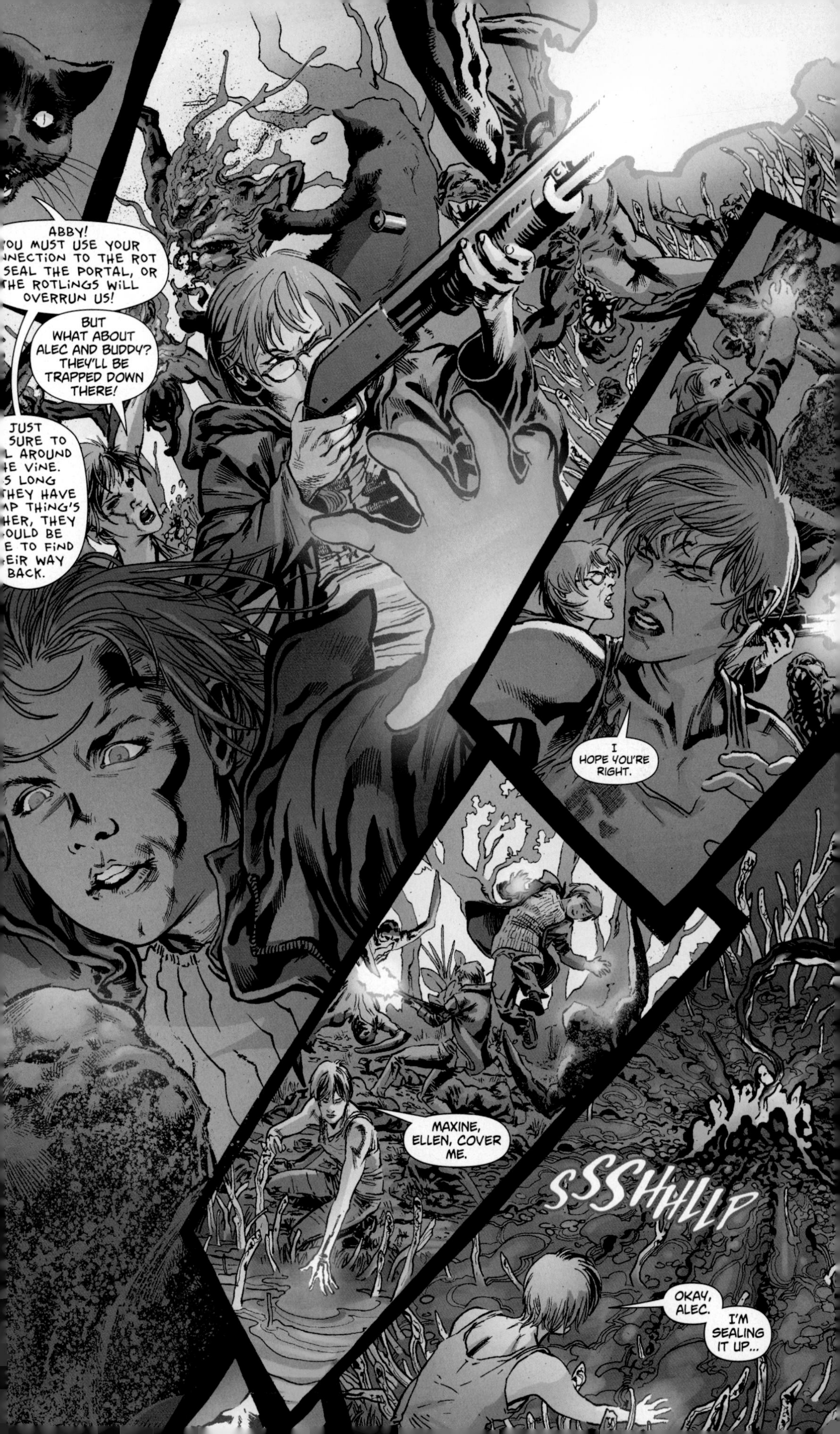
ABBY! YOU MUST USE YOUR NNECTION TO THE ROT SEAL THE PORTAL, OR THE ROTLINGS WILL OVERRUN US!
BUT WHAT ABOUT ALEC AND BUDDY? THEY'LL BE TRAPPED DOWN THERE!
JUST SURE TO L AROUND E VINE. S LONG THEY HAVE MP THING'S HER, THEY OULD BE E TO FIND EIR WAY BACK.
I HOPE YOU'RE RIGHT.
MAXINE, ELLEN, COVER ME.
SSSHHLLP
OKAY, ALEC.
I'M SEALING IT UP...

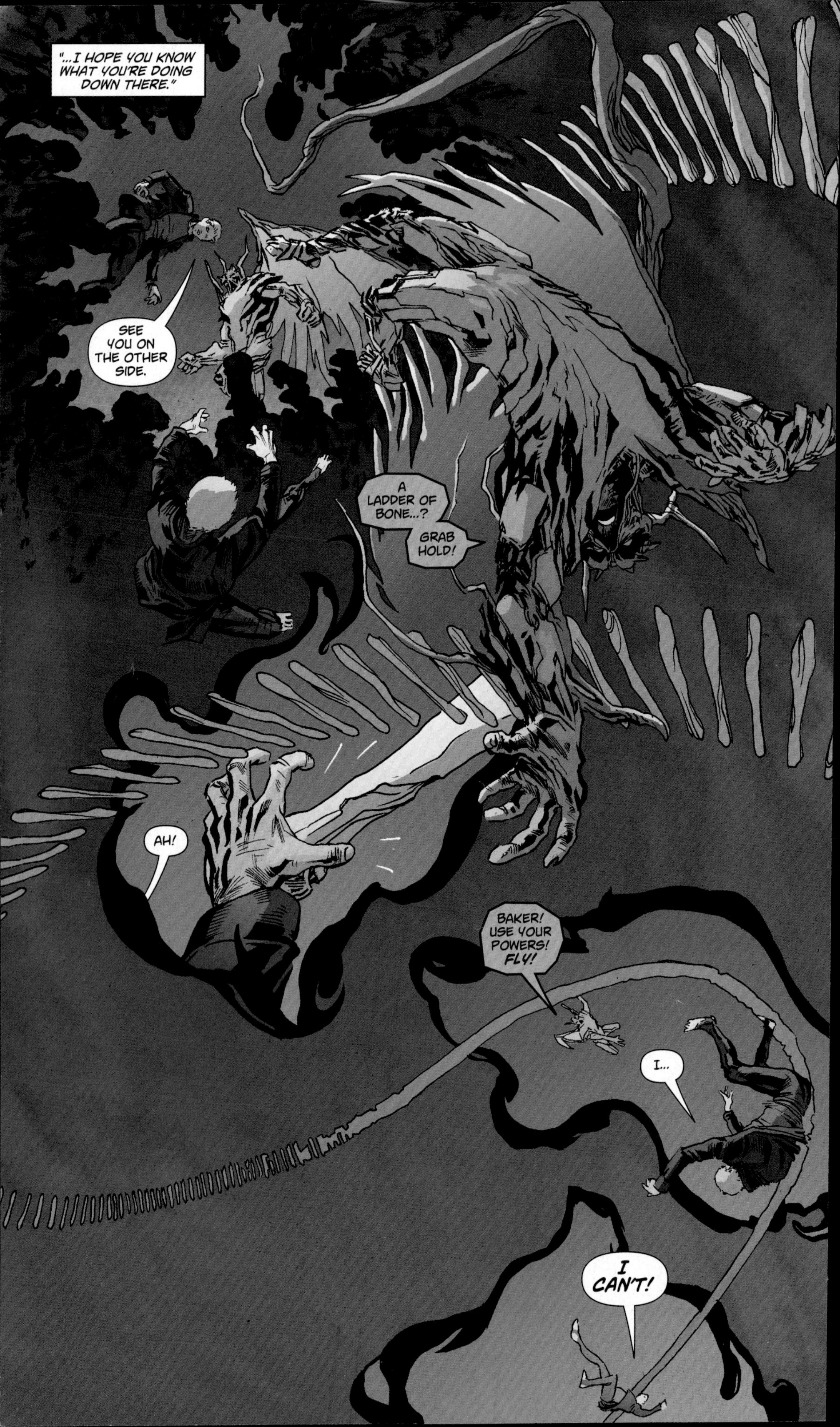
"...I HOPE YOU KNOW WHAT YOU'RE DOING DOWN THERE."
SEE YOU ON THE OTHER SIDE.
A LADDER OF BONE...?
GRAB HOLD!
AH!
BAKER! USE YOUR POWERS! FLY!
I...
I CAN'T!

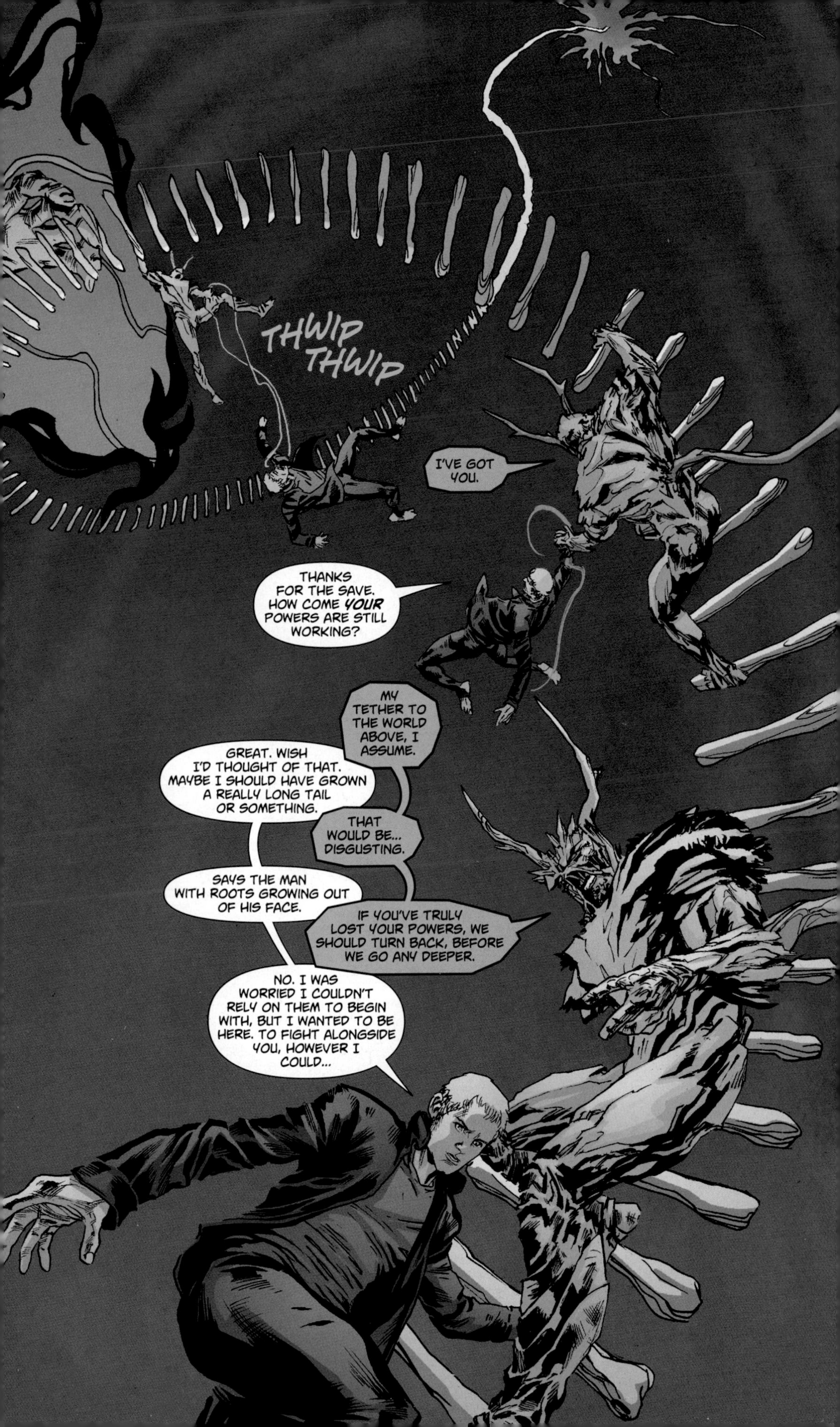
THWIP THWIP
I'VE GOT YOU.
THANKS FOR THE SAVE. HOW COME YOUR POWERS ARE STILL WORKING?
MY TETHER TO THE WORLD ABOVE, I ASSUME.
GREAT. WISH I'D THOUGHT OF THAT. MAYBE I SHOULD HAVE GROWN A REALLY LONG TAIL OR SOMETHING.
THAT WOULD BE... DISGUSTING.
SAYS THE MAN WITH ROOTS GROWING OUT OF HIS FACE.
IF YOU'VE TRULY LOST YOUR POWERS, WE SHOULD TURN BACK, BEFORE WE GO ANY DEEPER.
NO. I WAS WORRIED I COULDN'T RELY ON THEM TO BEGIN WITH, BUT I WANTED TO BE HERE. TO FIGHT ALONGSIDE YOU, HOWEVER I COULD...

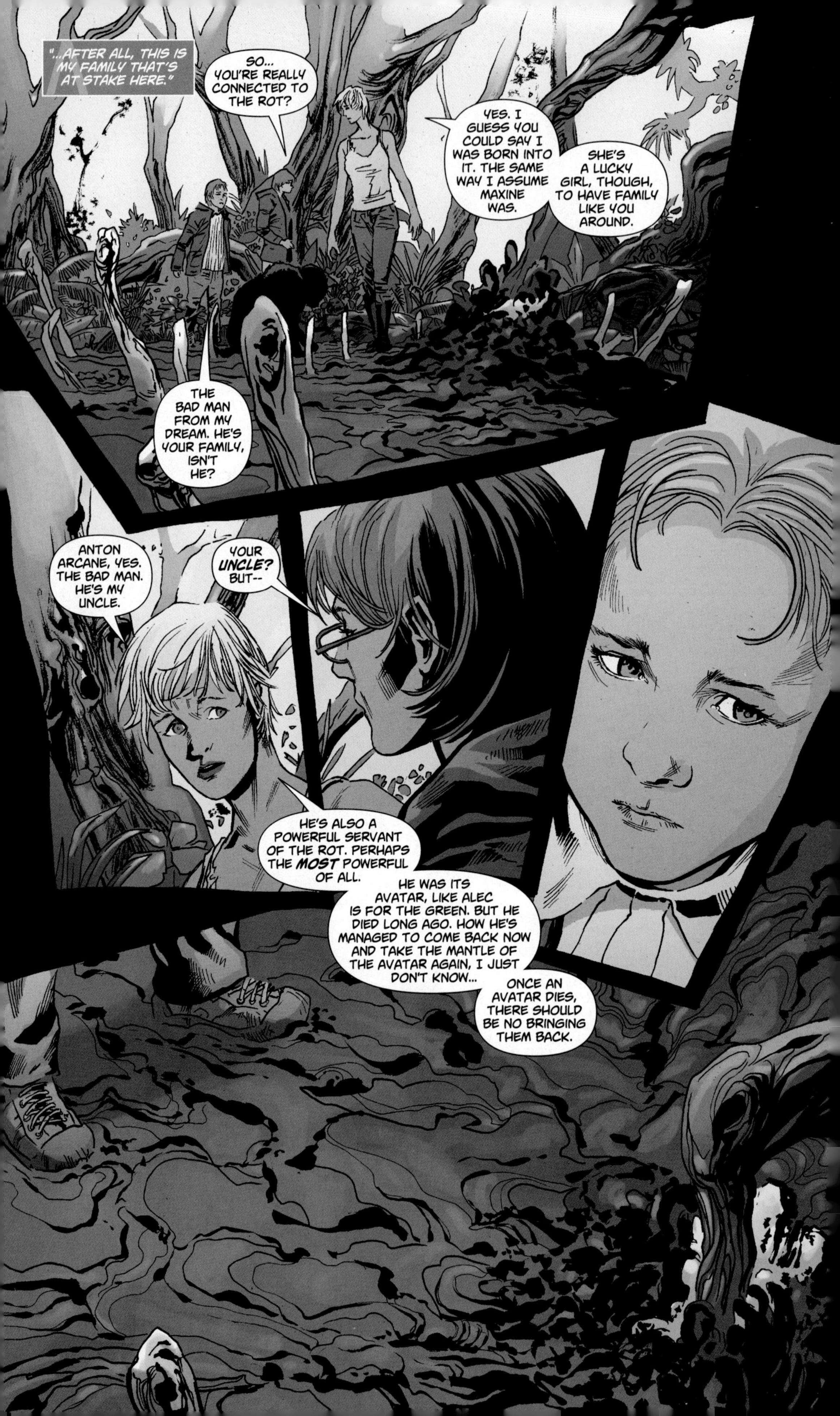
"...AFTER ALL, THIS IS MY FAMILY THAT'S AT STAKE HERE."
SO... YOU'RE REALLY CONNECTED TO THE ROT?
YES. I GUESS YOU COULD SAY I WAS BORN INTO IT. THE SAME WAY I ASSUME MAXINE WAS.
SHE'S A LUCKY GIRL, THOUGH, TO HAVE FAMILY LIKE YOU AROUND.
THE BAD MAN FROM MY DREAM. HE'S YOUR FAMILY, ISN'T HE?
ANTON ARCANE, YES. THE BAD MAN. HE'S MY UNCLE.
YOUR *UNCLE?* BUT--
HE'S ALSO A POWERFUL SERVANT OF THE ROT. PERHAPS THE *MOST* POWERFUL OF ALL.
HE WAS ITS AVATAR, LIKE ALEC IS FOR THE GREEN. BUT HE DIED LONG AGO. HOW HE'S MANAGED TO COME BACK NOW AND TAKE THE MANTLE OF THE AVATAR AGAIN, I JUST DON'T KNOW...
ONCE AN AVATAR DIES, THERE SHOULD BE NO BRINGING THEM BACK.

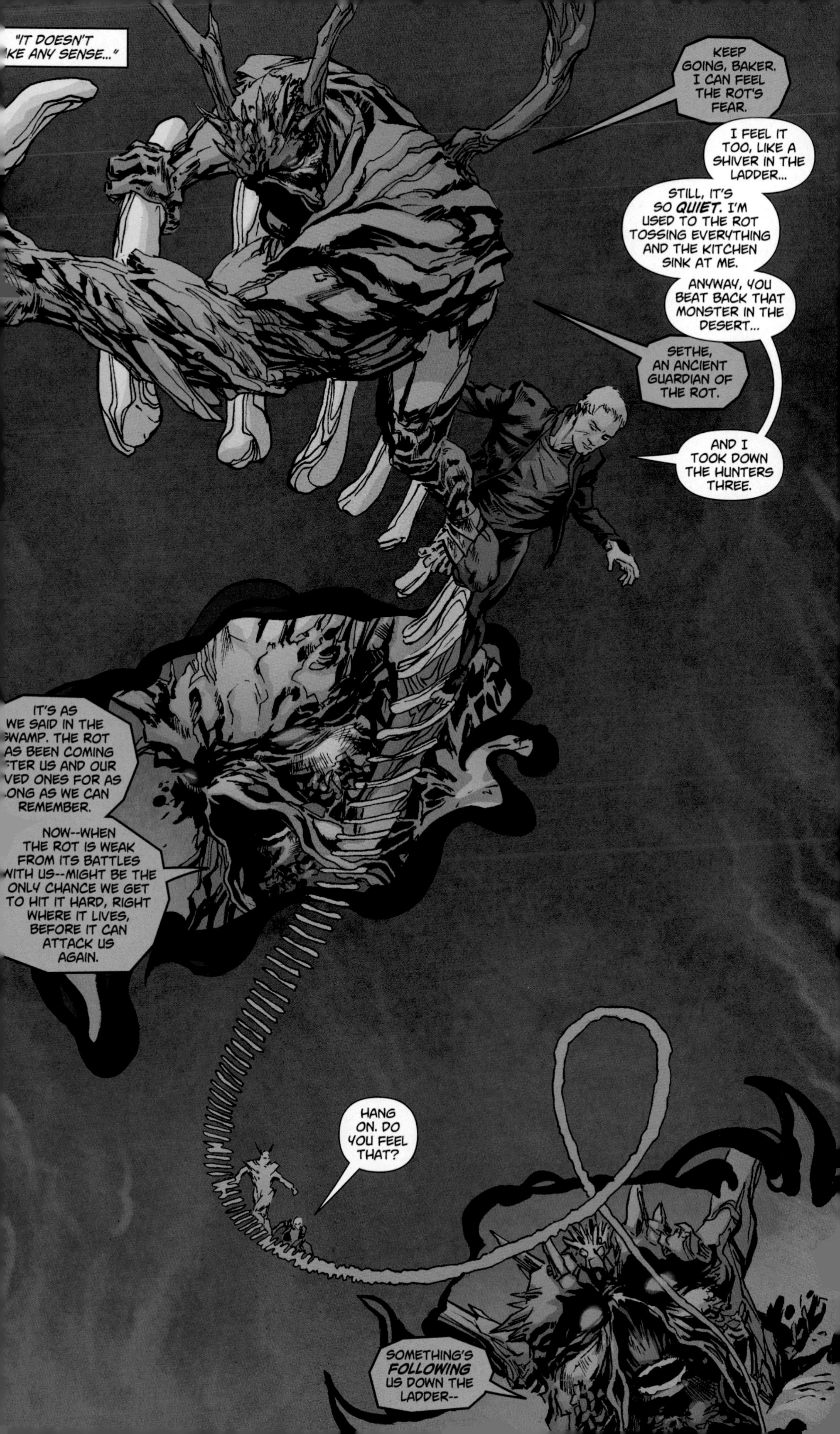
"IT DOESN'T
KE ANY SENSE..."
KEEP GOING, BAKER. I CAN FEEL THE ROT'S FEAR.
I FEEL IT TOO, LIKE A SHIVER IN THE LADDER...
STILL, IT'S SO QUIET. I'M USED TO THE ROT TOSSING EVERYTHING AND THE KITCHEN SINK AT ME.
ANYWAY, YOU BEAT BACK THAT MONSTER IN THE DESERT...
SETHE, AN ANCIENT GUARDIAN OF THE ROT.
AND I TOOK DOWN THE HUNTERS THREE.
IT'S AS WE SAID IN THE SWAMP. THE ROT AS BEEN COMING TER US AND OUR VED ONES FOR AS ONG AS WE CAN REMEMBER.
NOW--WHEN THE ROT IS WEAK FROM ITS BATTLES WITH US--MIGHT BE THE ONLY CHANCE WE GET TO HIT IT HARD, RIGHT WHERE IT LIVES, BEFORE IT CAN ATTACK US AGAIN.
HANG ON. DO YOU FEEL THAT?
SOMETHING'S FOLLOWING US DOWN THE LADDER--

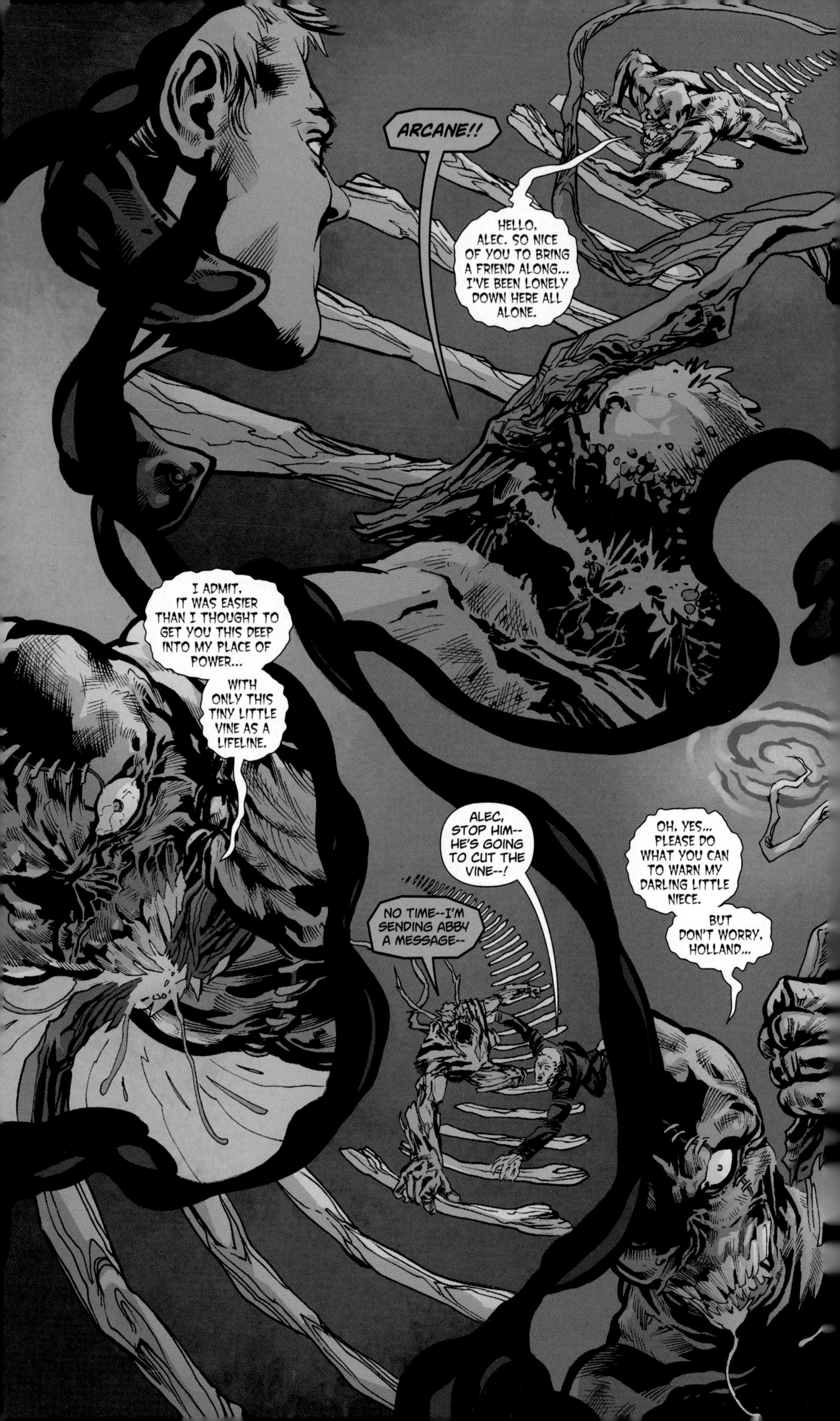
ARCANE!!
HELLO, ALEC. SO NICE OF YOU TO BRING A FRIEND ALONG... I'VE BEEN LONELY DOWN HERE ALL ALONE.
I ADMIT, IT WAS EASIER THAN I THOUGHT TO GET YOU THIS DEEP INTO MY PLACE OF POWER...
WITH ONLY THIS TINY LITTLE VINE AS A LIFELINE.
ALEC, STOP HIM-- HE'S GOING TO CUT THE VINE--!
NO TIME--I'M SENDING ABBY A MESSAGE--
OH, YES... PLEASE DO WHAT YOU CAN TO WARN MY DARLING LITTLE NIECE.
BUT DON'T WORRY, HOLLAND...

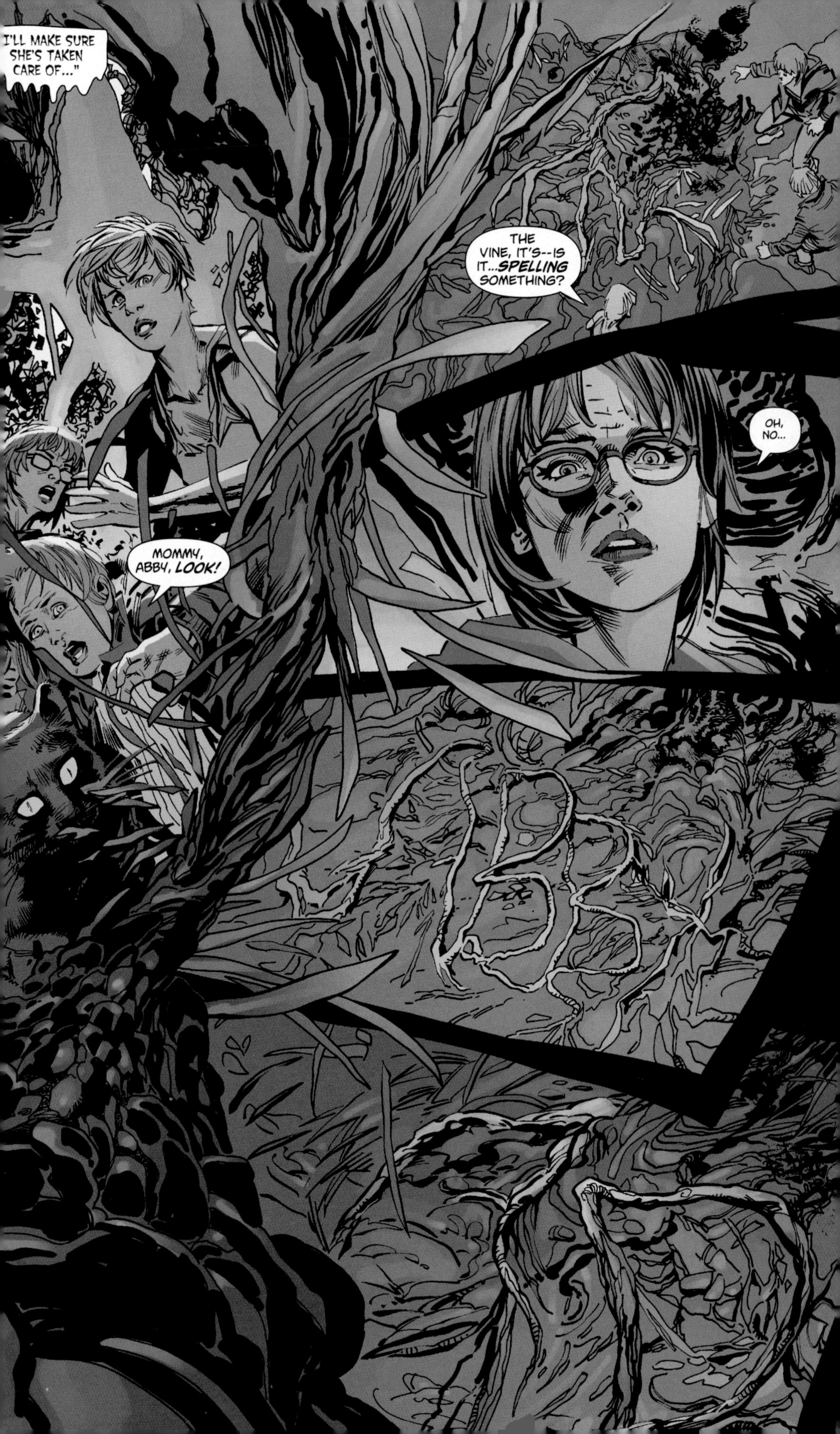
I'LL MAKE SURE SHE'S TAKEN CARE OF..."
THE VINE, IT'S--IS IT...SPELLING SOMETHING?
MOMMY, ABBY, LOOK!
OH, NO...

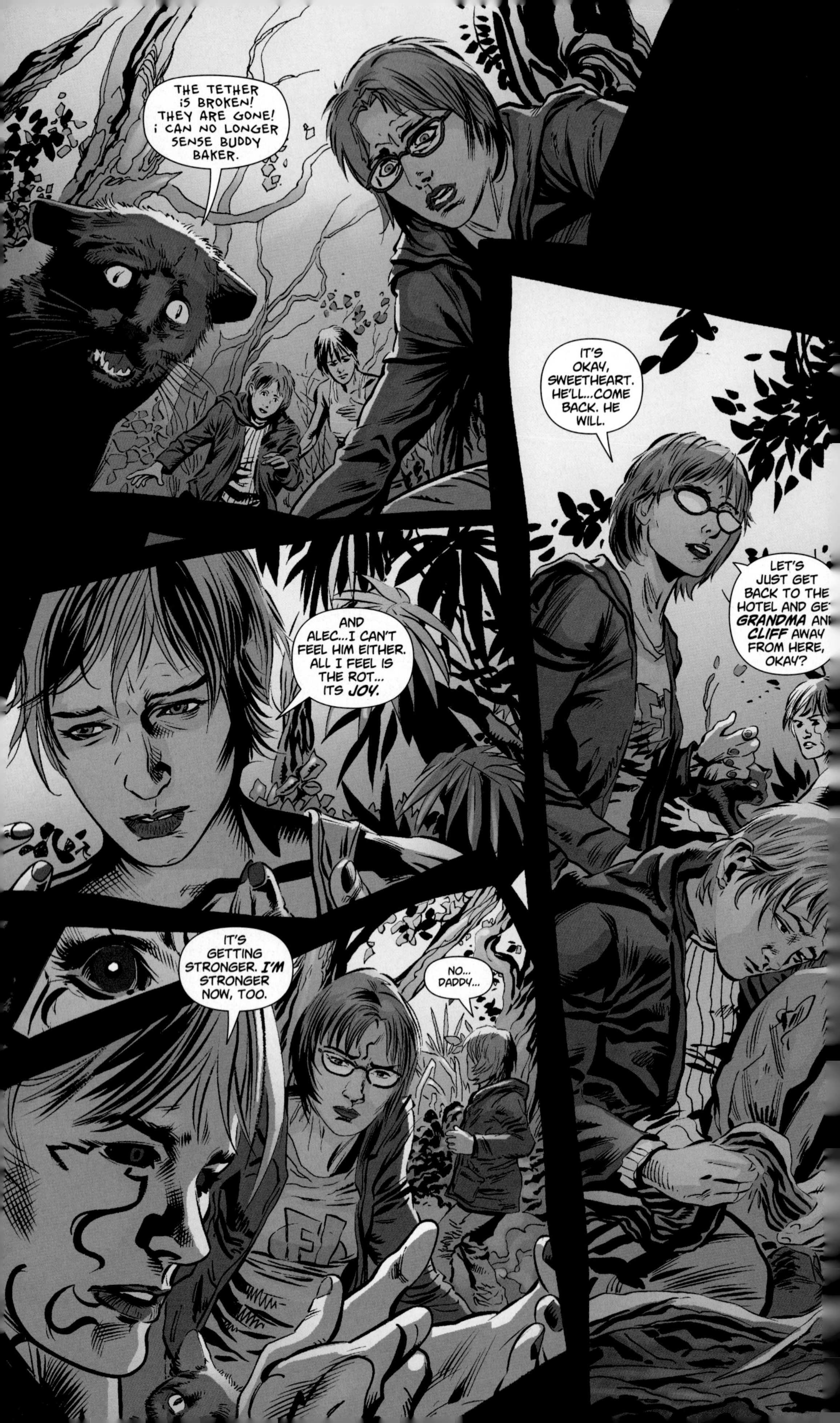
THE TETHER IS BROKEN! THEY ARE GONE! I CAN NO LONGER SENSE BUDDY BAKER.
IT'S OKAY, SWEETHEART. HE'LL...COME BACK. HE WILL.
AND ALEC...I CAN'T FEEL HIM EITHER. ALL I FEEL IS THE ROT... ITS JOY.
LET'S JUST GET BACK TO THE HOTEL AND GET GRANDMA AND CLIFF AWAY FROM HERE, OKAY?
IT'S GETTING STRONGER. I'M STRONGER NOW, TOO.
NO... DADDY...

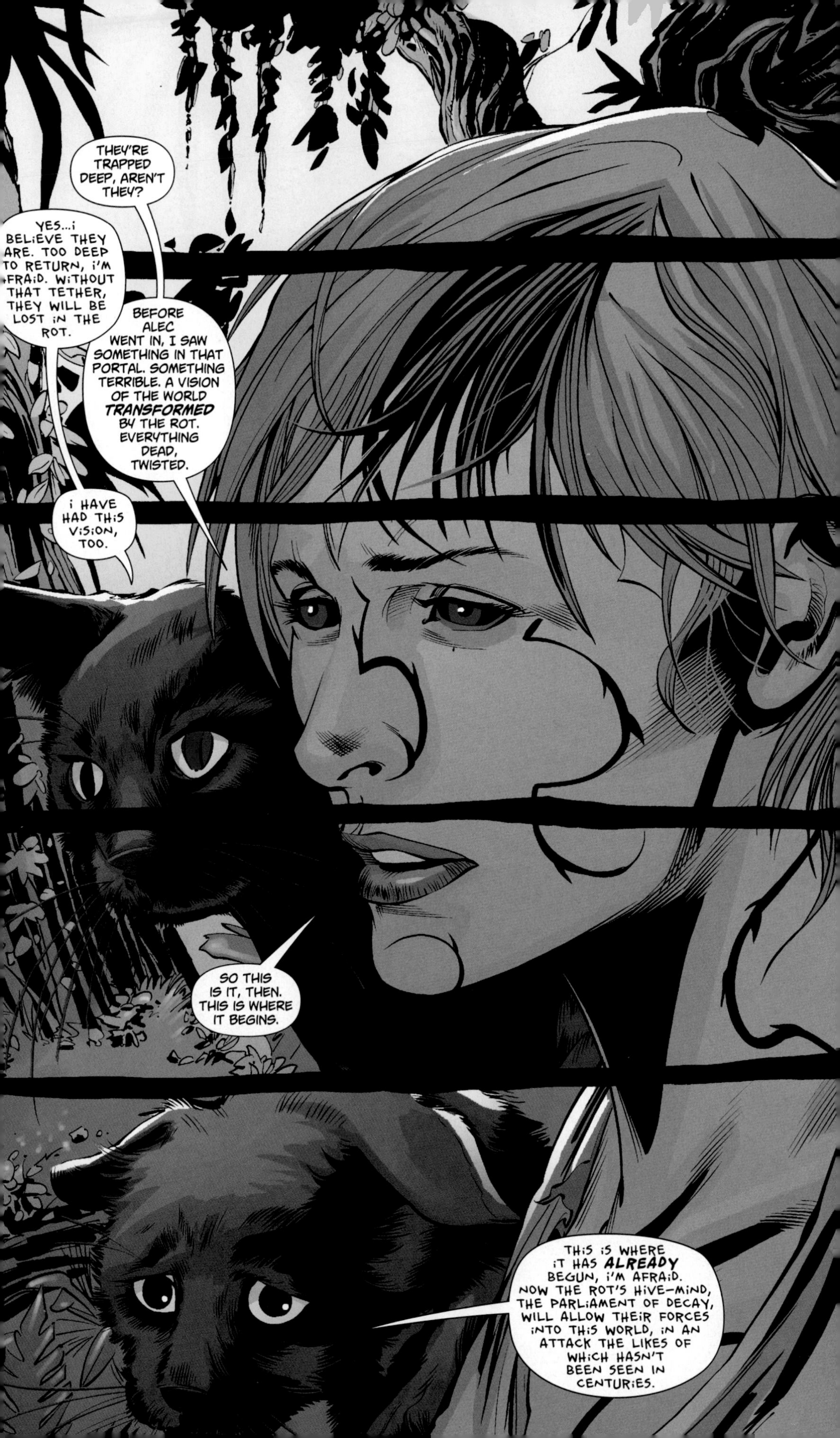
THEY'RE TRAPPED DEEP, AREN'T THEY?
YES...i BELiEVE THEY ARE. TOO DEEP TO RETURN, i'M AFRAiD. WiTHOUT THAT TETHER, THEY WiLL BE LOST iN THE ROT.
BEFORE ALEC WENT IN, I SAW SOMETHING IN THAT PORTAL. SOMETHING TERRIBLE. A VISION OF THE WORLD TRANSFORMED BY THE ROT. EVERYTHING DEAD, TWISTED.
i HAVE HAD THiS ViSiON, TOO.
SO THIS IS IT, THEN. THIS IS WHERE IT BEGINS.
THiS iS WHERE iT HAS ALREADY BEGUN, i'M AFRAiD. NOW THE ROT'S HiVE-MiND, THE PARLiAMENT OF DECAY, WiLL ALLOW THEiR FORCES iNTO THiS WORLD, iN AN ATTACK THE LiKES OF WHiCH HASN'T BEEN SEEN iN CENTURiES.

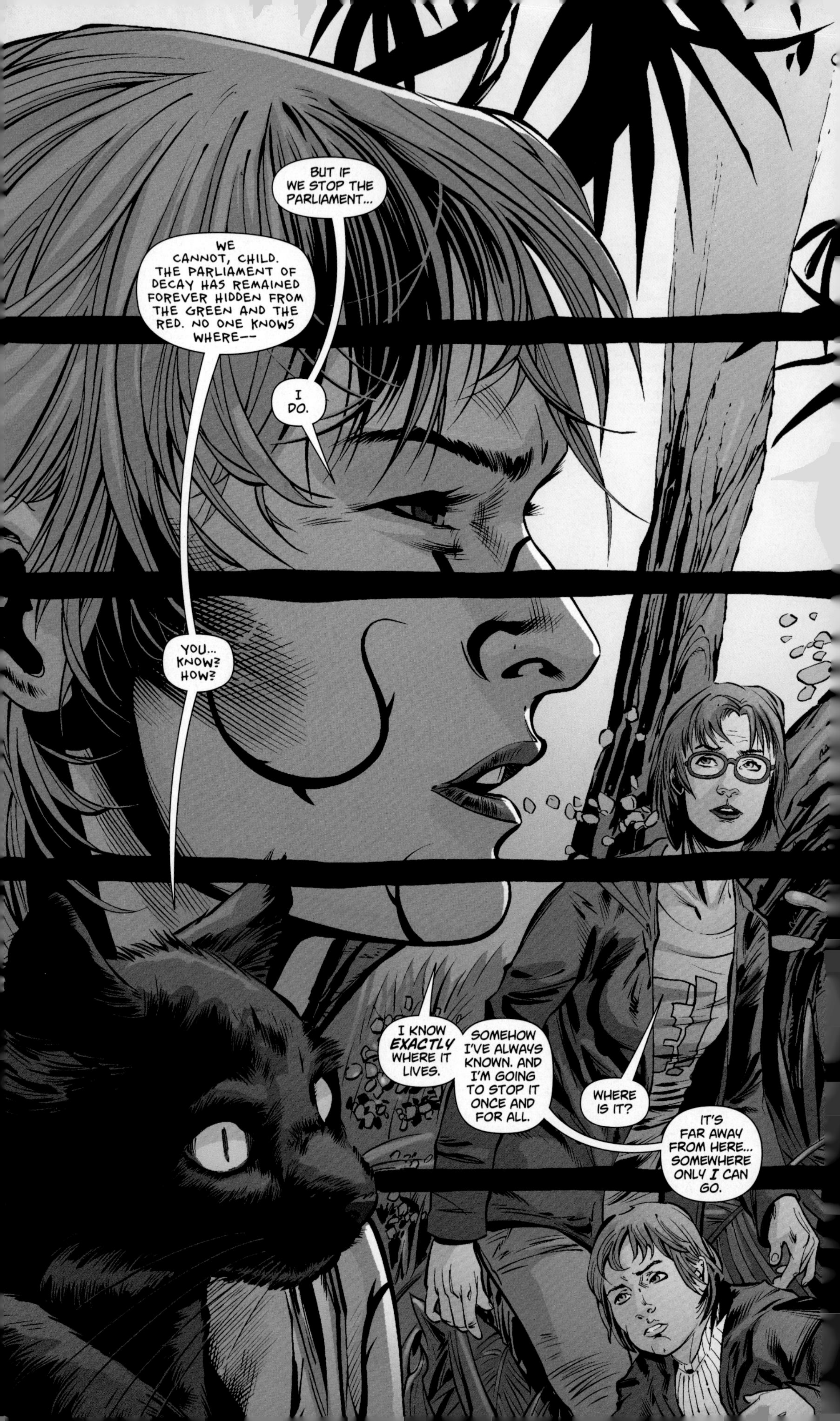
BUT IF WE STOP THE PARLIAMENT...
WE CANNOT, CHILD. THE PARLIAMENT OF DECAY HAS REMAINED FOREVER HIDDEN FROM THE GREEN AND THE RED. NO ONE KNOWS WHERE--
I DO.
YOU... KNOW? HOW?
I KNOW EXACTLY WHERE IT LIVES.
SOMEHOW I'VE ALWAYS KNOWN. AND I'M GOING TO STOP IT ONCE AND FOR ALL.
WHERE IS IT?
IT'S FAR AWAY FROM HERE... SOMEWHERE ONLY I CAN GO.

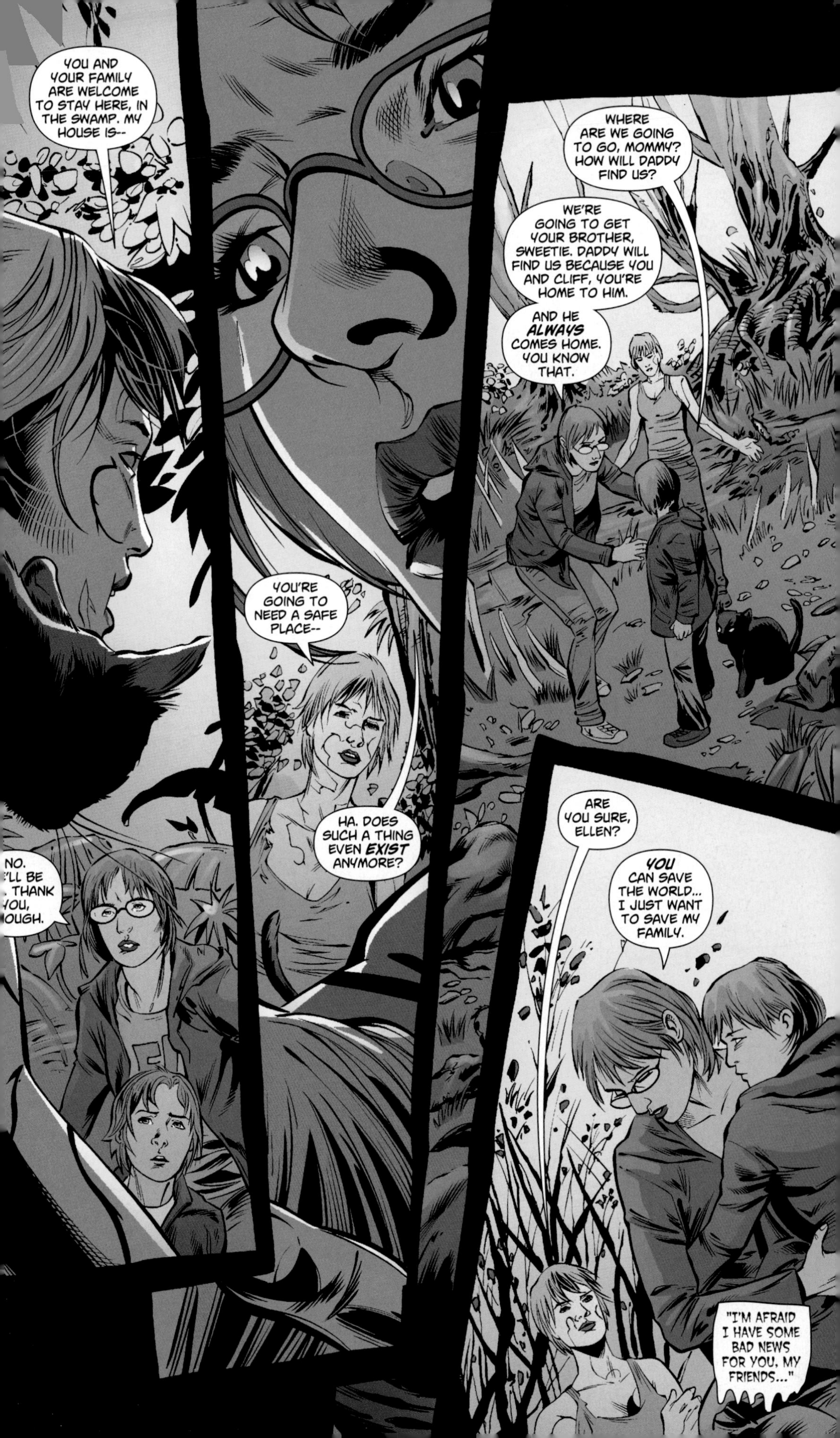

YOU AND YOUR FAMILY ARE WELCOME TO STAY HERE, IN THE SWAMP. MY HOUSE IS--
NO. 'LL BE . THANK YOU, OUGH.
YOU'RE GOING TO NEED A SAFE PLACE--
HA. DOES SUCH A THING EVEN EXIST ANYMORE?
WHERE ARE WE GOING TO GO, MOMMY? HOW WILL DADDY FIND US?
WE'RE GOING TO GET YOUR BROTHER, SWEETIE. DADDY WILL FIND US BECAUSE YOU AND CLIFF, YOU'RE HOME TO HIM.
AND HE ALWAYS COMES HOME. YOU KNOW THAT.
ARE YOU SURE, ELLEN?
YOU CAN SAVE THE WORLD... I JUST WANT TO SAVE MY FAMILY.
"I'M AFRAID I HAVE SOME BAD NEWS FOR YOU, MY FRIENDS..."

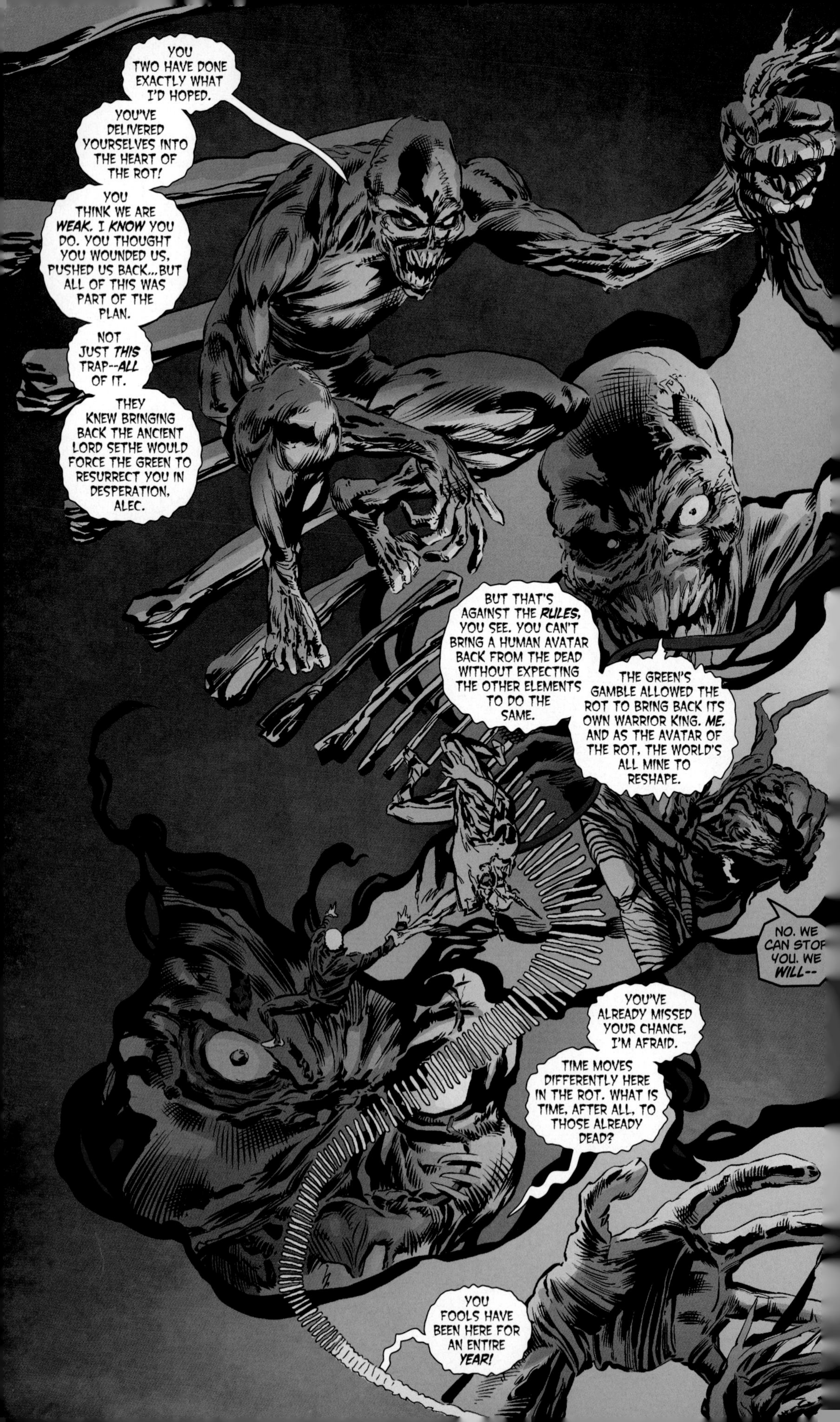
YOU TWO HAVE DONE EXACTLY WHAT I'D HOPED.
YOU'VE DELIVERED YOURSELVES INTO THE HEART OF THE ROT!
YOU THINK WE ARE *WEAK*. I *KNOW* YOU DO. YOU THOUGHT YOU WOUNDED US, PUSHED US BACK...BUT ALL OF THIS WAS PART OF THE PLAN.
NOT JUST *THIS* TRAP--*ALL* OF IT.
THEY KNEW BRINGING BACK THE ANCIENT LORD SETHE WOULD FORCE THE GREEN TO RESURRECT YOU IN DESPERATION, ALEC.
BUT THAT'S AGAINST THE *RULES*, YOU SEE. YOU CAN'T BRING A HUMAN AVATAR BACK FROM THE DEAD WITHOUT EXPECTING THE OTHER ELEMENTS TO DO THE SAME.
THE GREEN'S GAMBLE ALLOWED THE ROT TO BRING BACK ITS OWN WARRIOR KING. *ME*. AND AS THE AVATAR OF THE ROT, THE WORLD'S ALL MINE TO RESHAPE.
NO. WE CAN STOP YOU. WE *WILL*--
YOU'VE ALREADY MISSED YOUR CHANCE, I'M AFRAID.
TIME MOVES DIFFERENTLY HERE IN THE ROT. WHAT IS TIME, AFTER ALL, TO THOSE ALREADY DEAD?
YOU FOOLS HAVE BEEN HERE FOR AN ENTIRE *YEAR*!

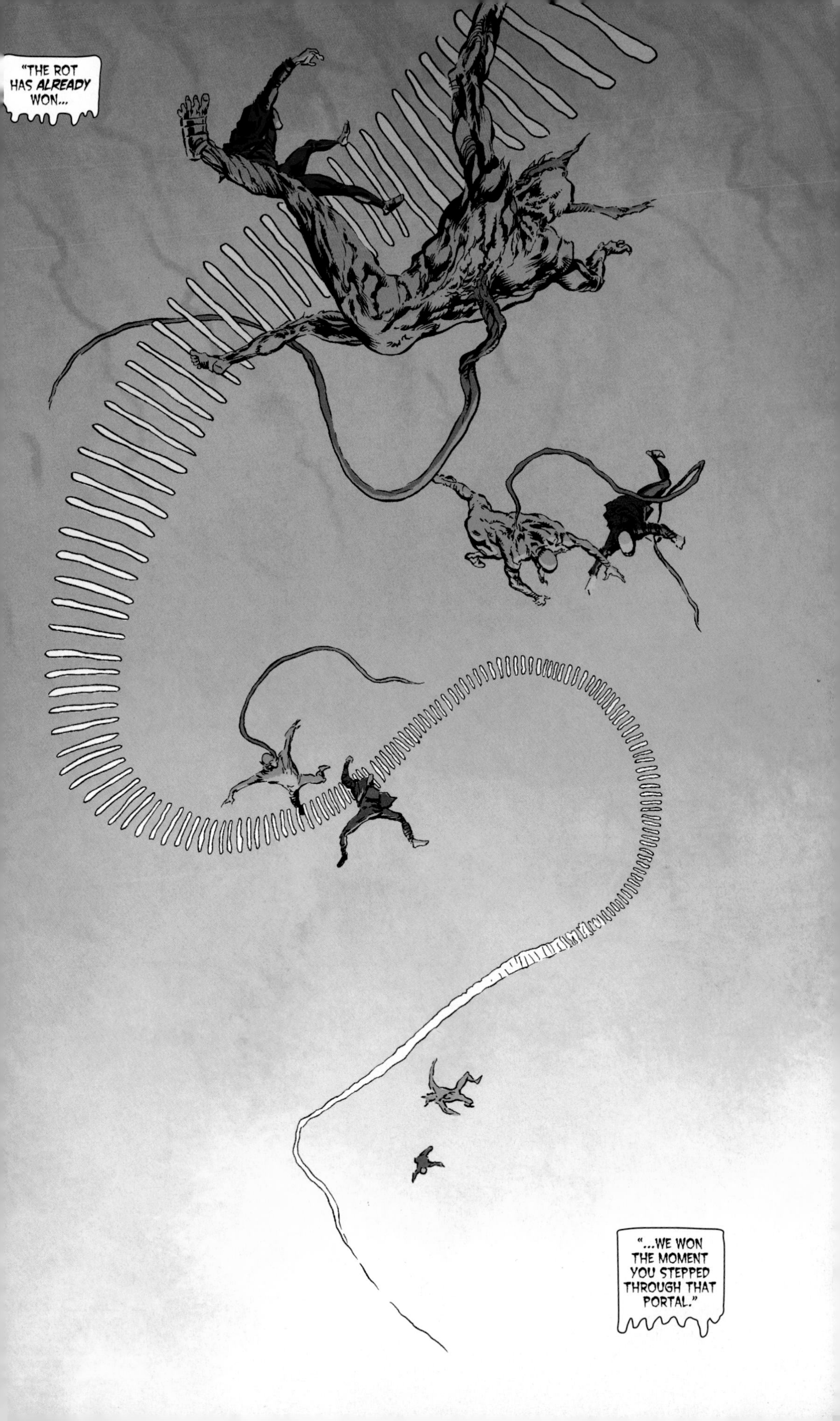
"THE ROT HAS *ALREADY* WON...
"...WE WON THE MOMENT YOU STEPPED THROUGH THAT PORTAL."

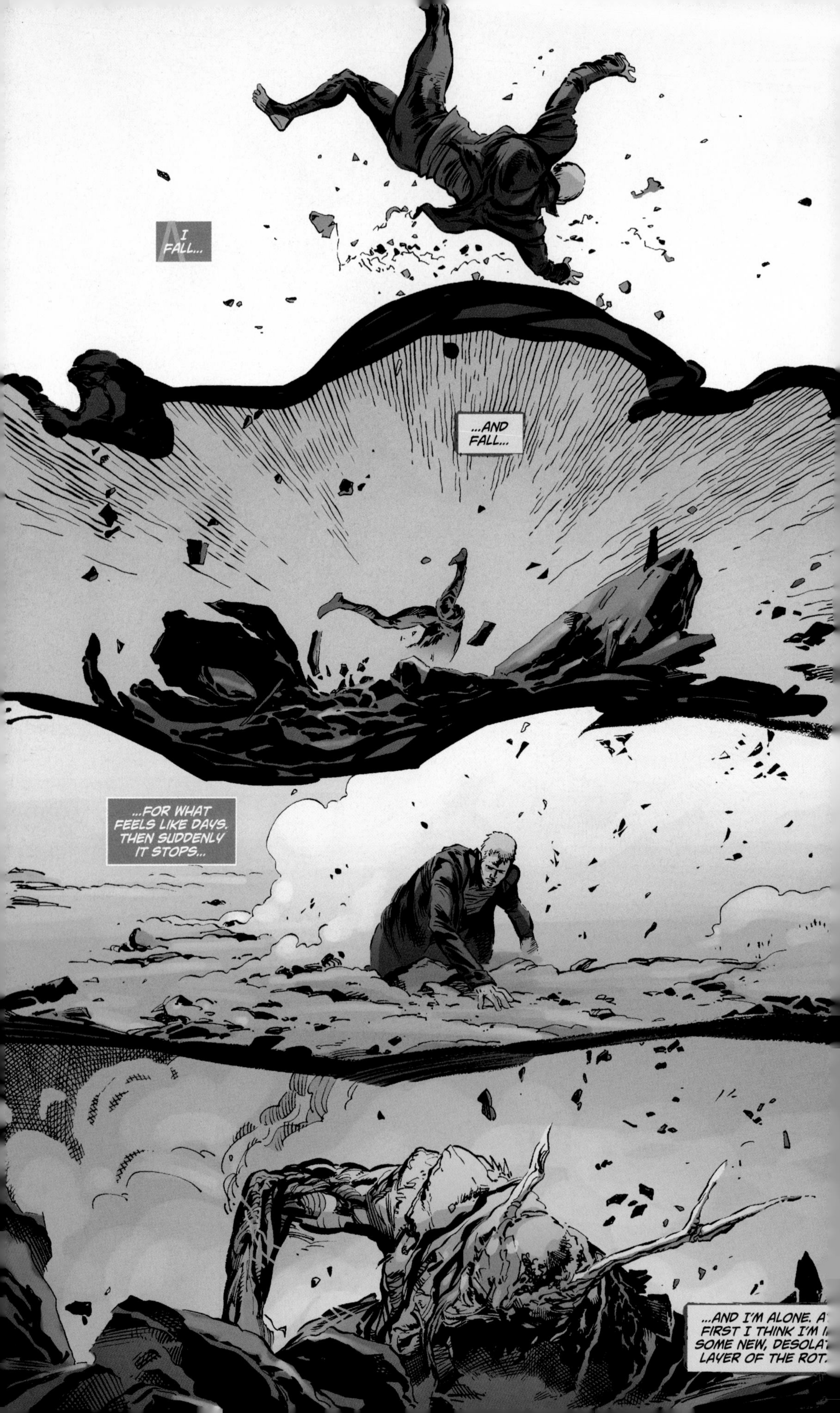
I FALL...
...AND FALL...
...FOR WHAT FEELS LIKE DAYS. THEN SUDDENLY IT STOPS...
...AND I'M ALONE. A FIRST I THINK I'M I SOME NEW, DESOLA LAYER OF THE ROT.

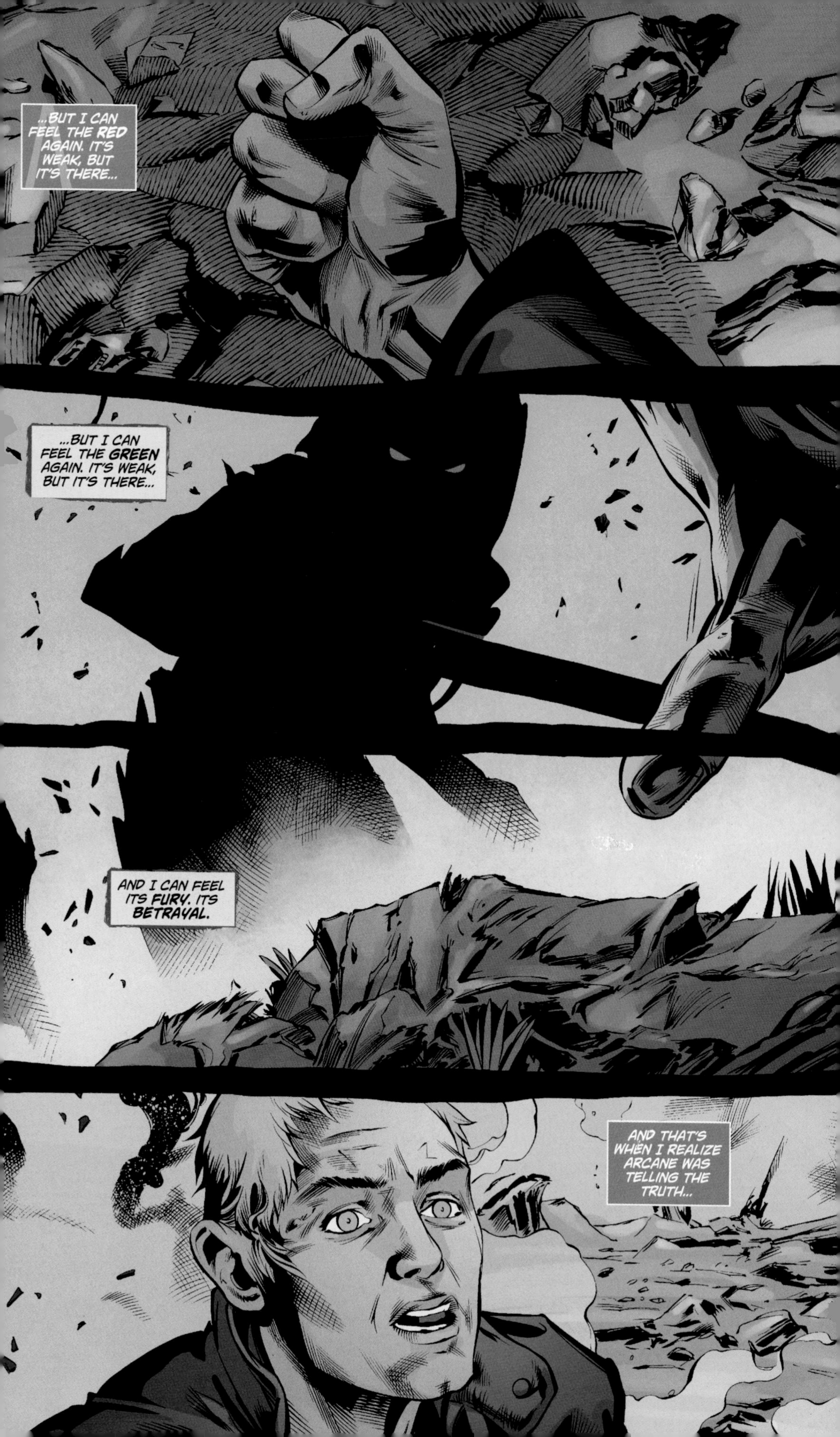
...BUT I CAN FEEL THE RED AGAIN. IT'S WEAK, BUT IT'S THERE...
...BUT I CAN FEEL THE GREEN AGAIN. IT'S WEAK, BUT IT'S THERE...
AND I CAN FEEL ITS FURY. ITS BETRAYAL.
AND THAT'S WHEN I REALIZE ARCANE WAS TELLING THE TRUTH...

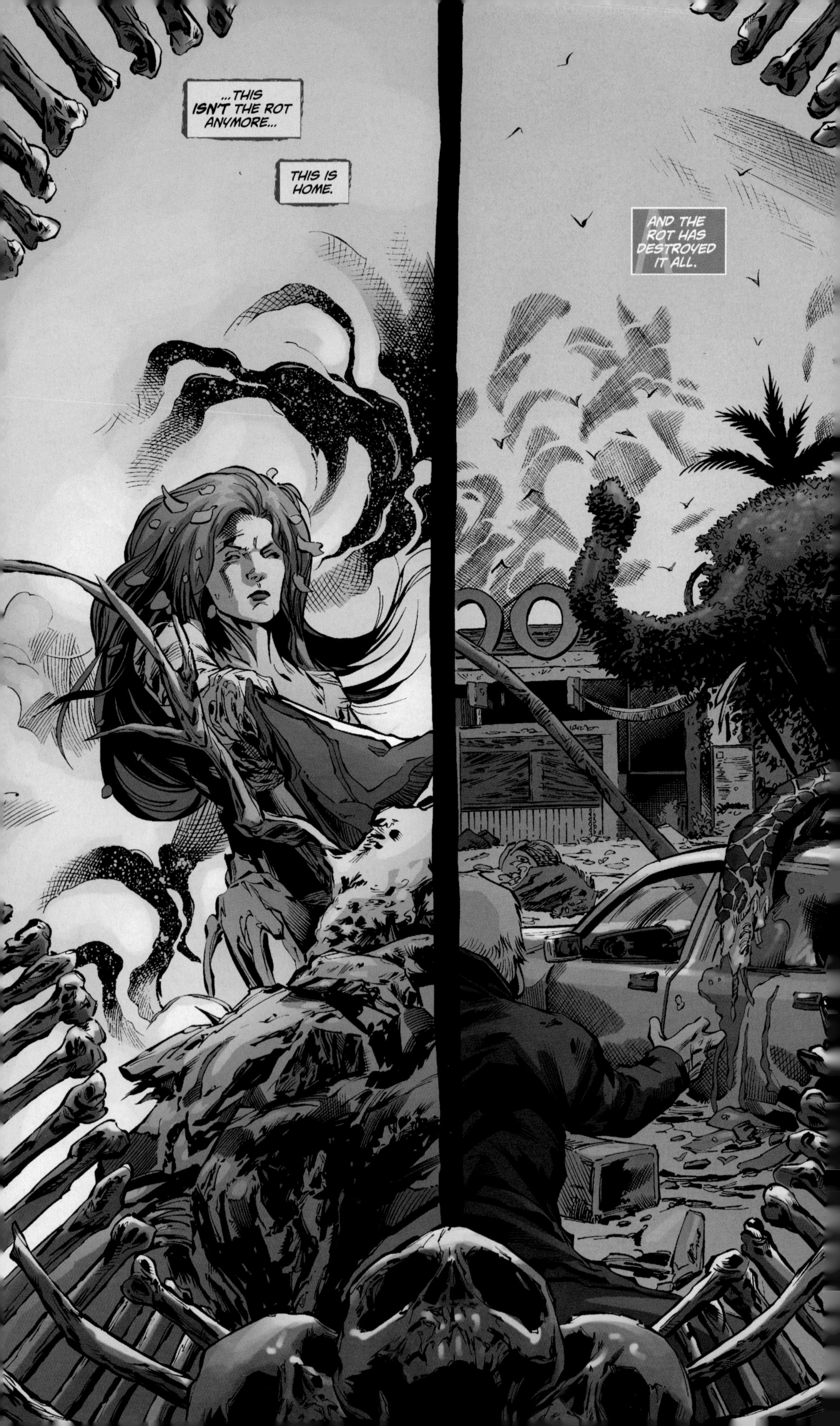
...THIS ISN'T THE ROT ANYMORE...
THIS IS HOME.
AND THE ROT HAS DESTROYED IT ALL.

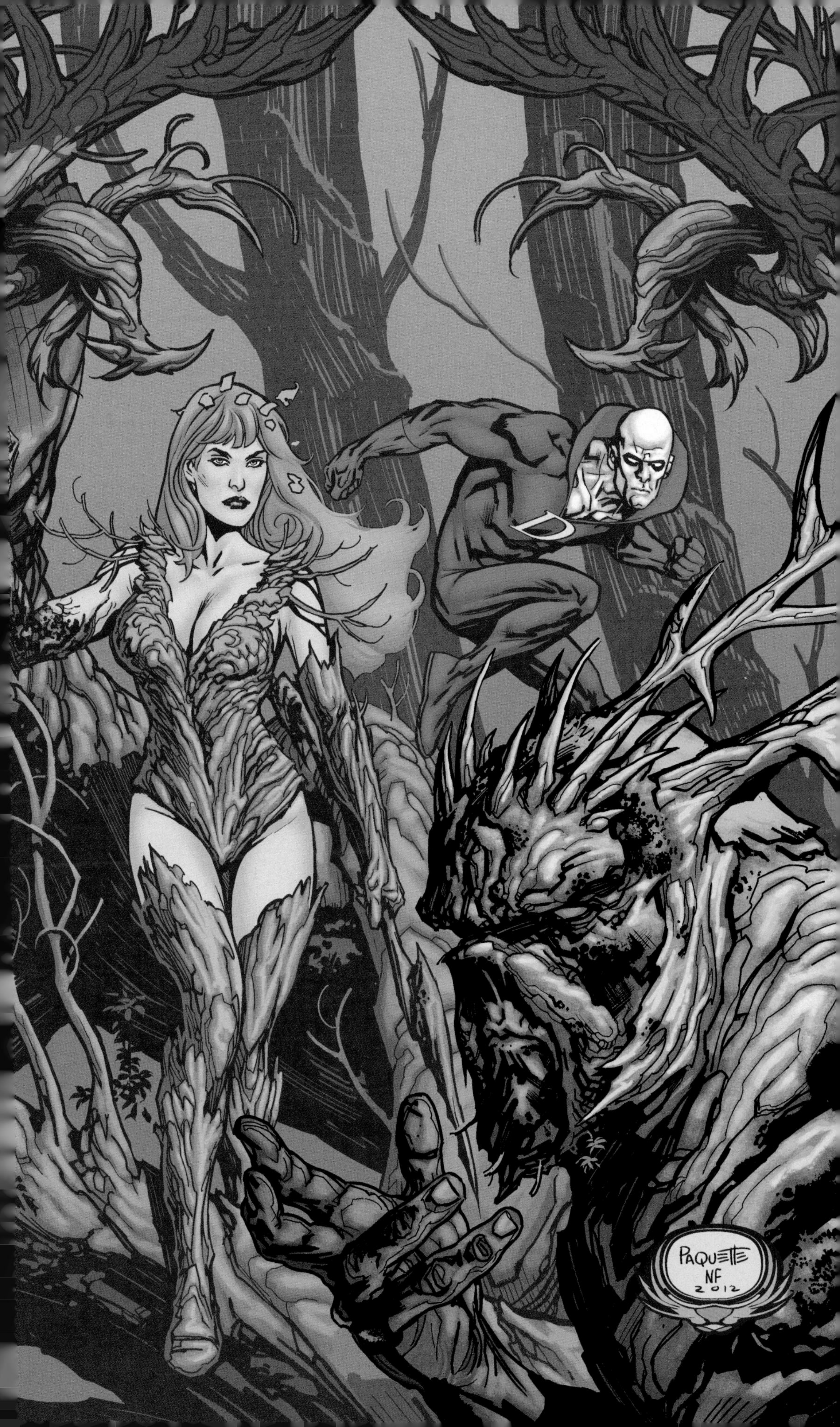
PAQUETTE
NF
2012

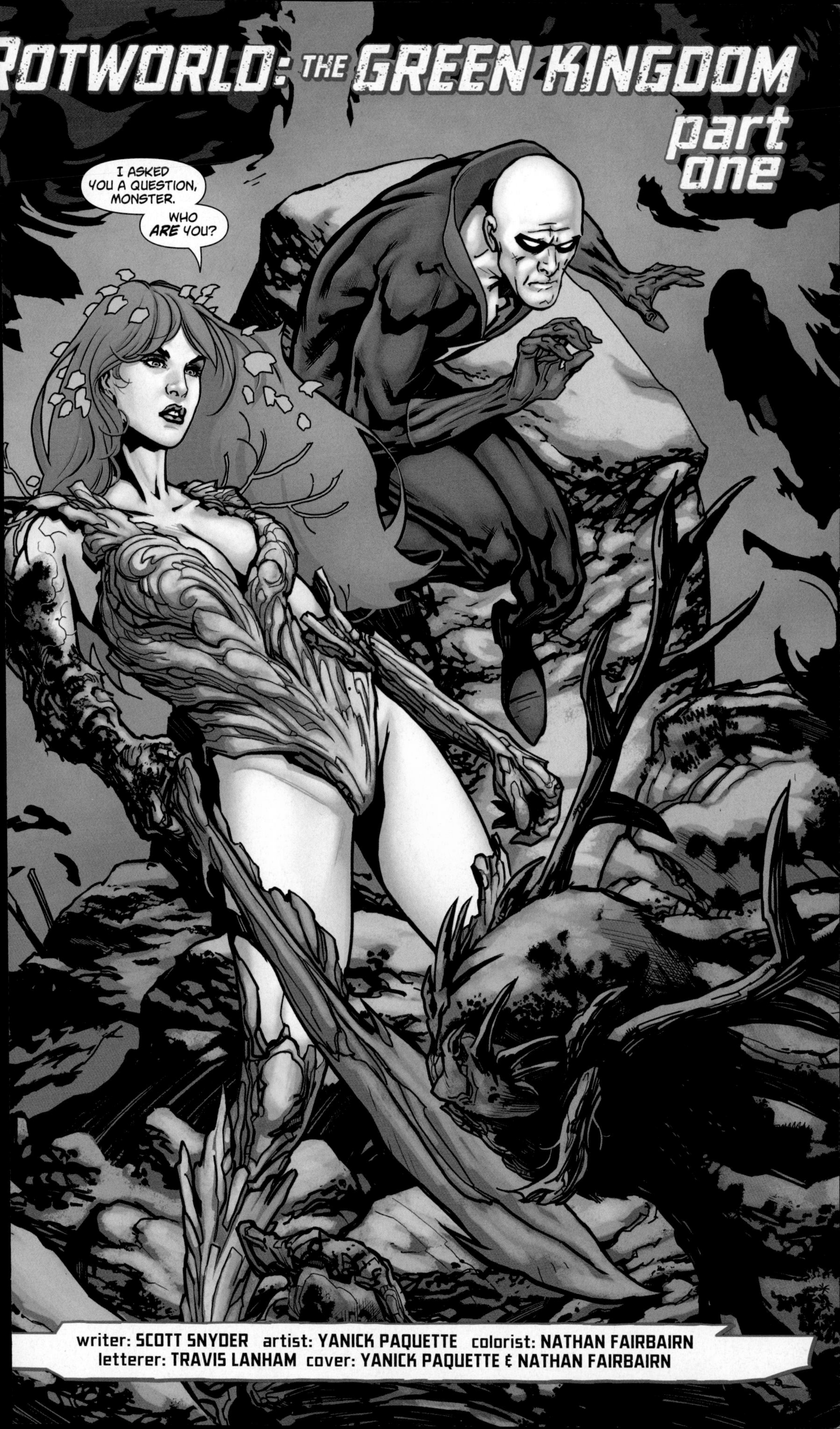
ROTWORLD: THE GREEN KINGDOM
part one
I ASKED YOU A QUESTION, MONSTER.
WHO ARE YOU?
writer: SCOTT SNYDER artist: YANICK PAQUETTE colorist: NATHAN FAIRBAIRN
letterer: TRAVIS LANHAM cover: YANICK PAQUETTE & NATHAN FAIRBAIRN

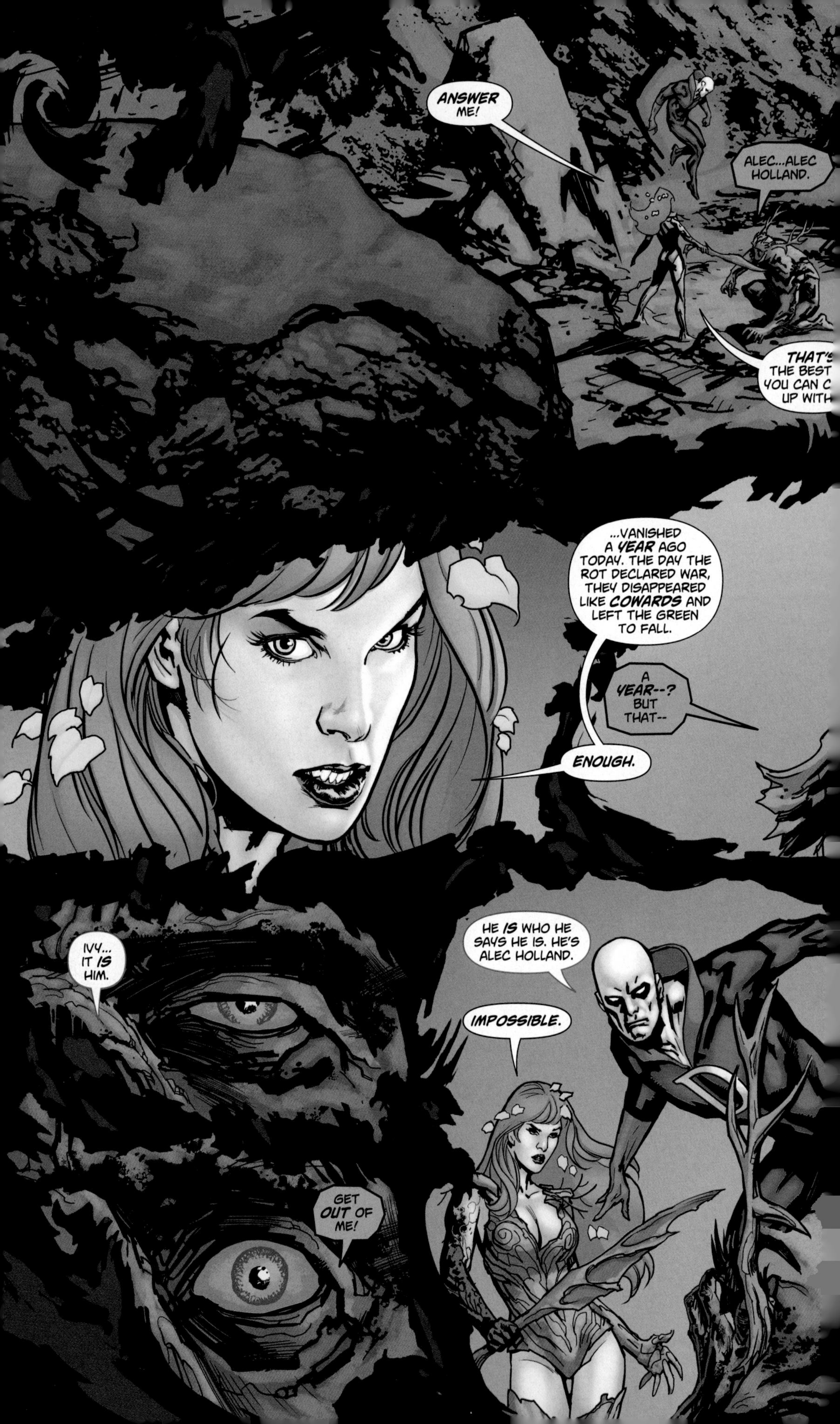
ANSWER ME!
ALEC...ALEC HOLLAND.
THAT'S THE BEST YOU CAN C UP WITH
...VANISHED A YEAR AGO TODAY. THE DAY THE ROT DECLARED WAR, THEY DISAPPEARED LIKE COWARDS AND LEFT THE GREEN TO FALL.
A YEAR--? BUT THAT--
ENOUGH.
IVY... IT IS HIM.
HE IS WHO HE SAYS HE IS. HE'S ALEC HOLLAND.
IMPOSSIBLE.
GET OUT OF ME!

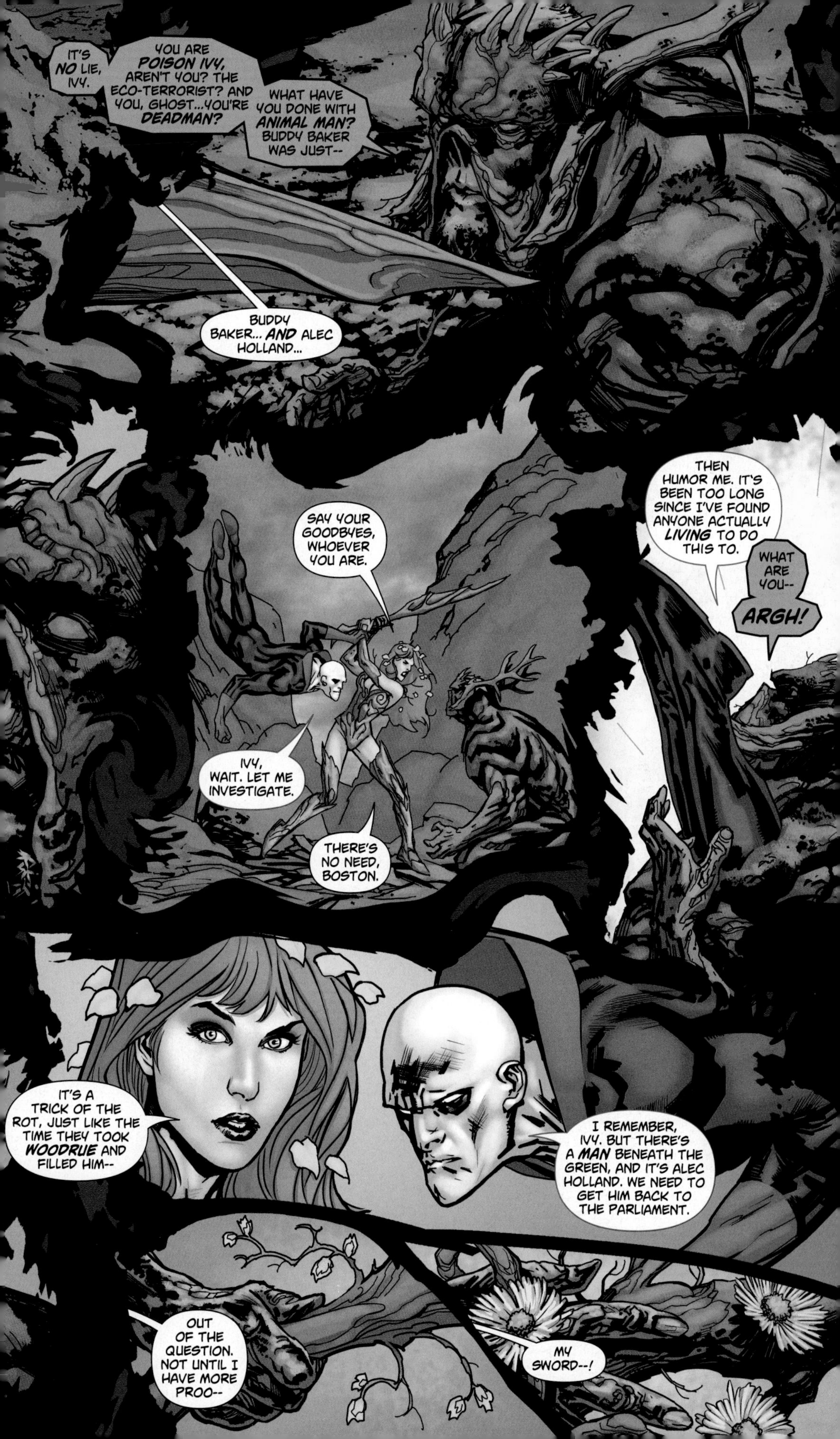
IT'S NO LIE, IVY.
YOU ARE POISON IVY, AREN'T YOU? THE ECO-TERRORIST? AND YOU, GHOST...YOU'RE DEADMAN?
WHAT HAVE YOU DONE WITH ANIMAL MAN? BUDDY BAKER WAS JUST--
BUDDY BAKER... AND ALEC HOLLAND...
SAY YOUR GOODBYES, WHOEVER YOU ARE.
THEN HUMOR ME. IT'S BEEN TOO LONG SINCE I'VE FOUND ANYONE ACTUALLY LIVING TO DO THIS TO.
WHAT ARE YOU--
ARGH!
IVY, WAIT. LET ME INVESTIGATE.
THERE'S NO NEED, BOSTON.
IT'S A TRICK OF THE ROT, JUST LIKE THE TIME THEY TOOK WOODRUE AND FILLED HIM--
I REMEMBER, IVY. BUT THERE'S A MAN BENEATH THE GREEN, AND IT'S ALEC HOLLAND. WE NEED TO GET HIM BACK TO THE PARLIAMENT.
OUT OF THE QUESTION. NOT UNTIL I HAVE MORE PROO--
MY SWORD--!

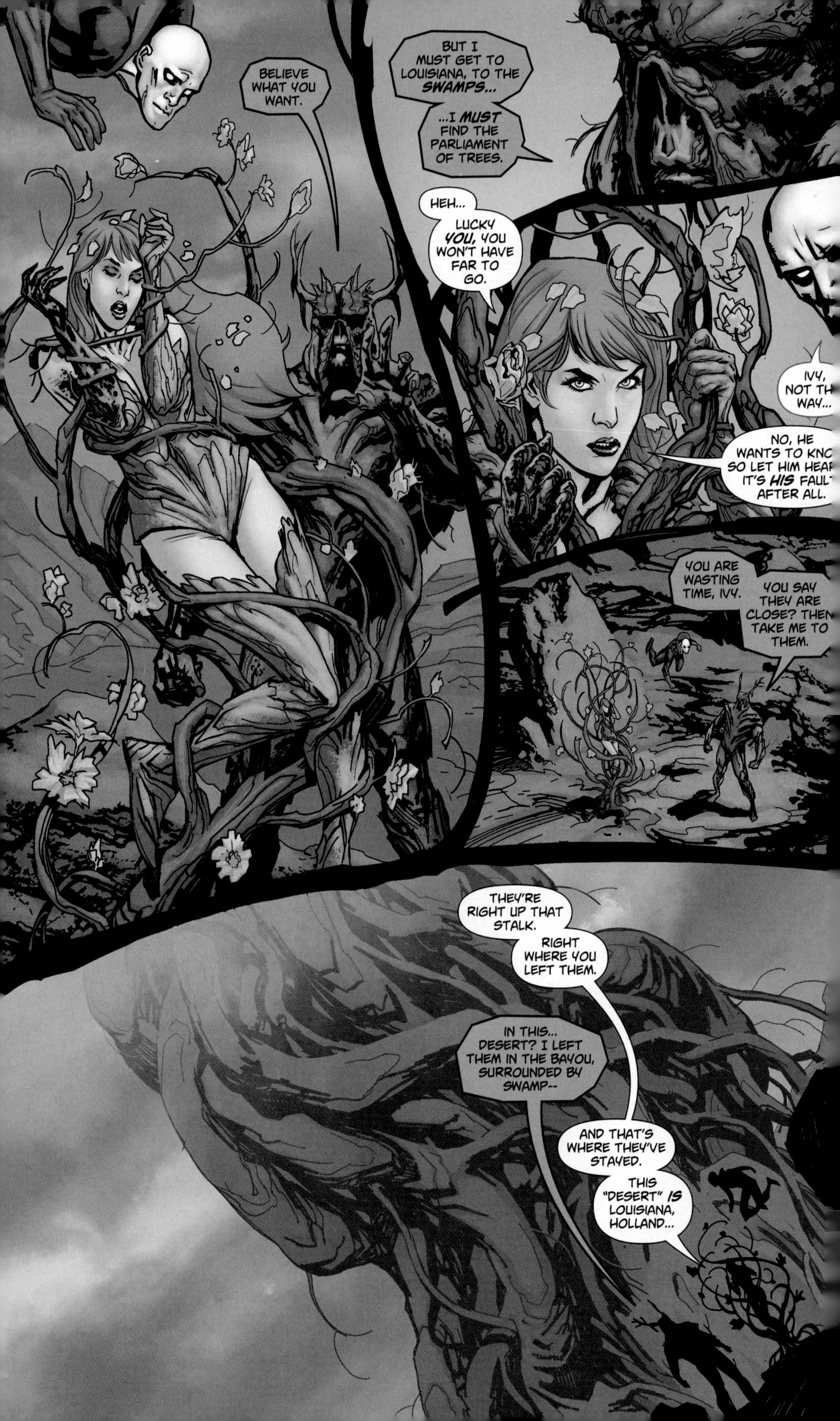
BELIEVE WHAT YOU WANT.
BUT I MUST GET TO LOUISIANA, TO THE SWAMPS...
...I MUST FIND THE PARLIAMENT OF TREES.
HEH...
LUCKY YOU, YOU WON'T HAVE FAR TO GO.
IVY, NOT TH WAY...
NO, HE WANTS TO KNO SO LET HIM HEAR IT'S HIS FAUL AFTER ALL.
YOU ARE WASTING TIME, IVY.
YOU SAY THEY ARE CLOSE? THEN TAKE ME TO THEM.
THEY'RE RIGHT UP THAT STALK.
RIGHT WHERE YOU LEFT THEM.
IN THIS... DESERT? I LEFT THEM IN THE BAYOU, SURROUNDED BY SWAMP--
AND THAT'S WHERE THEY'VE STAYED.
THIS "DESERT" IS LOUISIANA, HOLLAND...

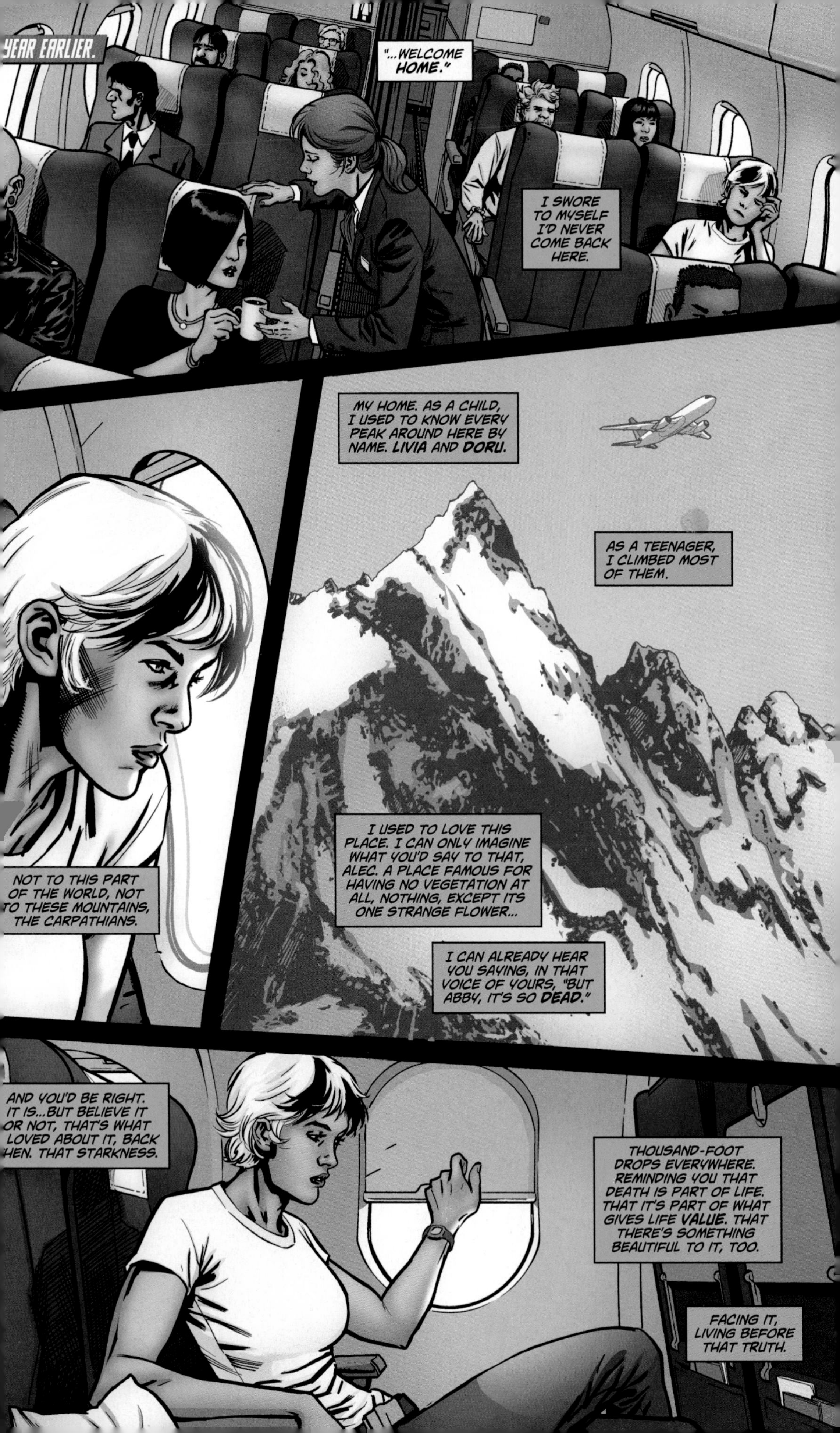
YEAR EARLIER.
"...WELCOME HOME."
I SWORE TO MYSELF I'D NEVER COME BACK HERE.
NOT TO THIS PART OF THE WORLD, NOT TO THESE MOUNTAINS, THE CARPATHIANS.
MY HOME. AS A CHILD, I USED TO KNOW EVERY PEAK AROUND HERE BY NAME. LIVIA AND DORU.
AS A TEENAGER, I CLIMBED MOST OF THEM.
I USED TO LOVE THIS PLACE. I CAN ONLY IMAGINE WHAT YOU'D SAY TO THAT, ALEC. A PLACE FAMOUS FOR HAVING NO VEGETATION AT ALL, NOTHING, EXCEPT ITS ONE STRANGE FLOWER...
I CAN ALREADY HEAR YOU SAYING, IN THAT VOICE OF YOURS, "BUT ABBY, IT'S SO DEAD."
AND YOU'D BE RIGHT. IT IS...BUT BELIEVE IT OR NOT, THAT'S WHAT LOVED ABOUT IT, BACK HEN. THAT STARKNESS.
THOUSAND-FOOT DROPS EVERYWHERE. REMINDING YOU THAT DEATH IS PART OF LIFE. THAT IT'S PART OF WHAT GIVES LIFE VALUE. THAT THERE'S SOMETHING BEAUTIFUL TO IT, TOO.
FACING IT, LIVING BEFORE THAT TRUTH.

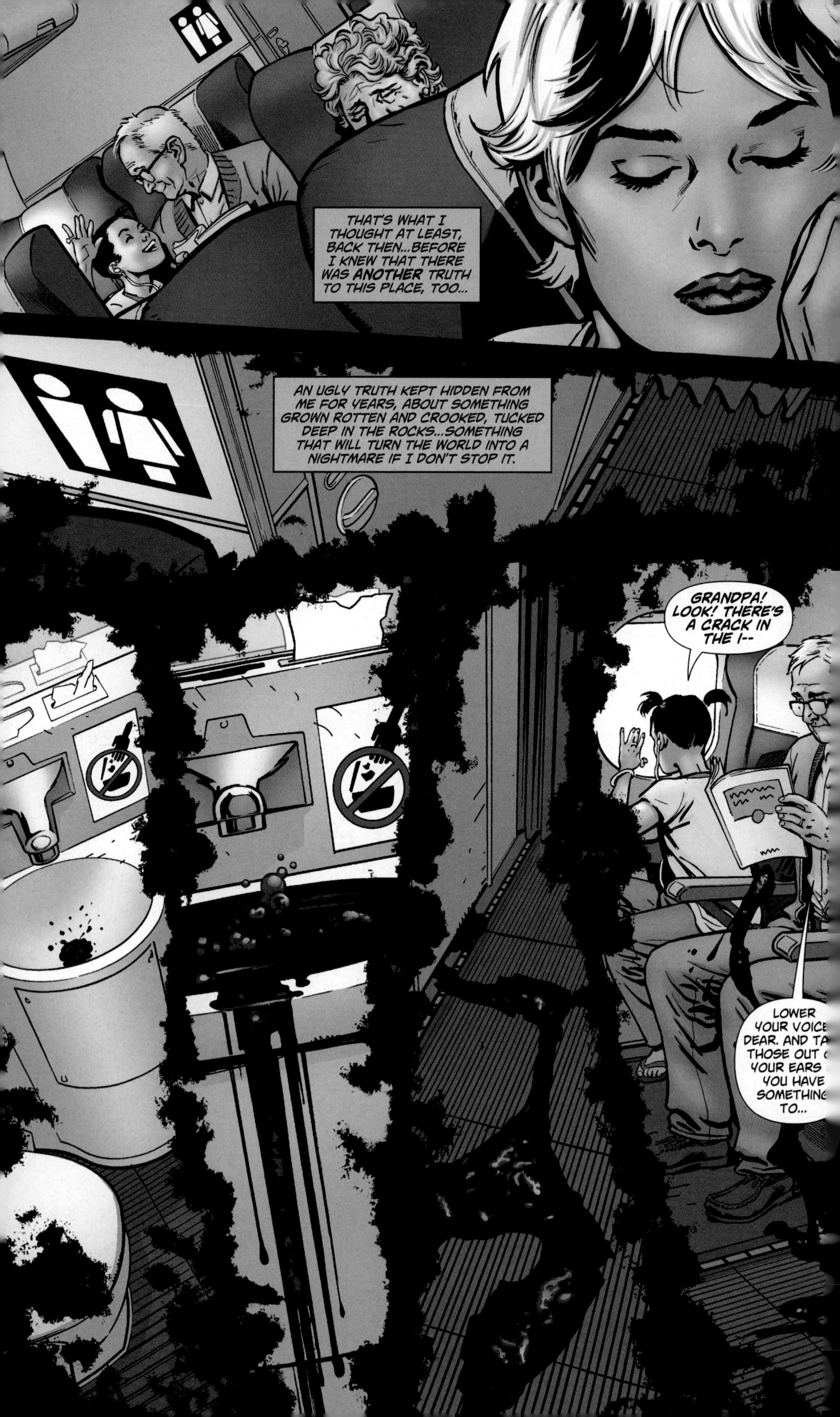
THAT'S WHAT I THOUGHT AT LEAST, BACK THEN...BEFORE I KNEW THAT THERE WAS ANOTHER TRUTH TO THIS PLACE, TOO...
AN UGLY TRUTH KEPT HIDDEN FROM ME FOR YEARS, ABOUT SOMETHING GROWN ROTTEN AND CROOKED, TUCKED DEEP IN THE ROCKS...SOMETHING THAT WILL TURN THE WORLD INTO A NIGHTMARE IF I DON'T STOP IT.
GRANDPA! LOOK! THERE'S A CRACK IN THE I--
LOWER YOUR VOICE DEAR. AND TA THOSE OUT YOUR EARS YOU HAVE SOMETHING TO...

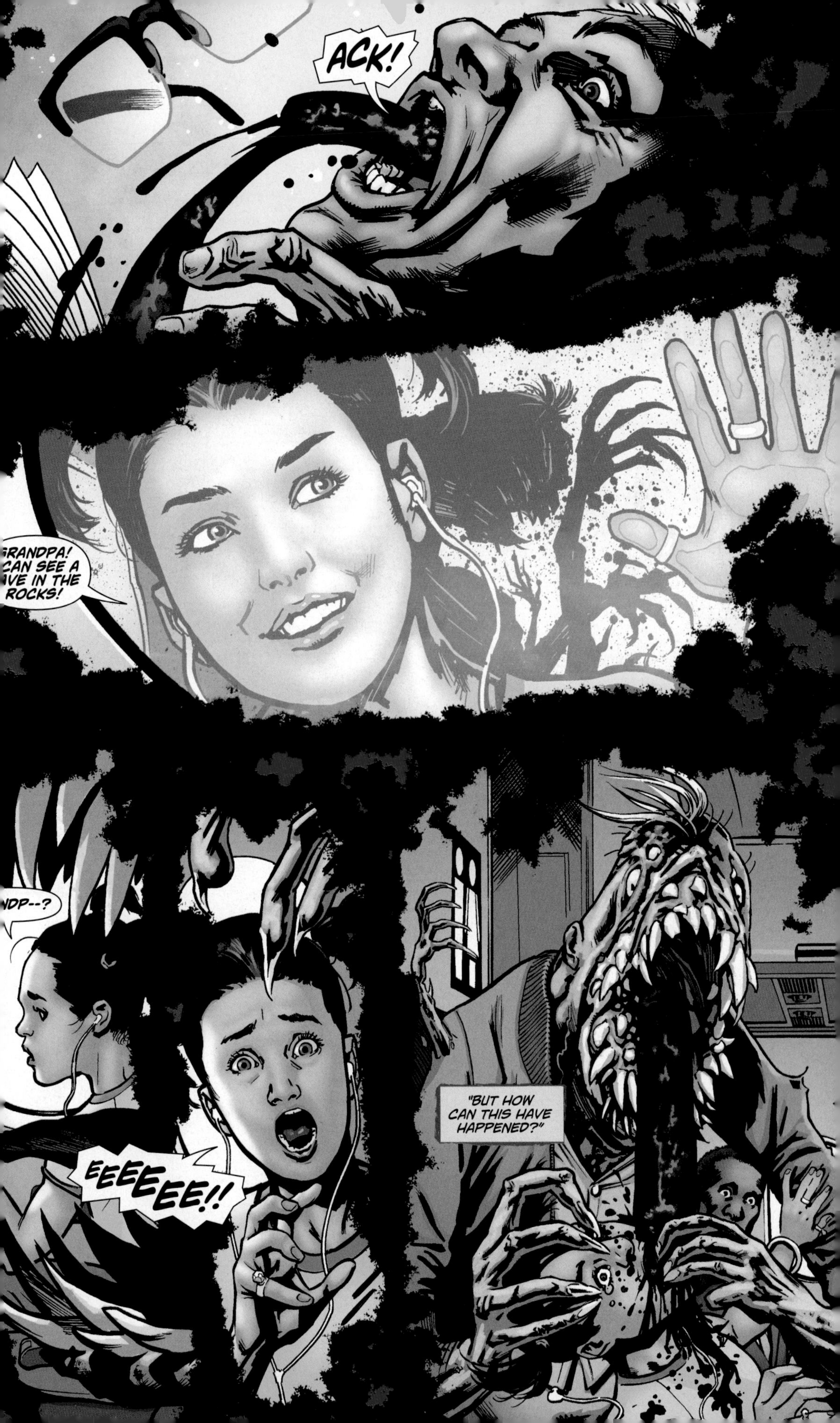
ACK!
GRANDPA! CAN SEE A VE IN THE ROCKS!
NDP--?
EEEEEE!!
"BUT HOW CAN THIS HAVE HAPPENED?"

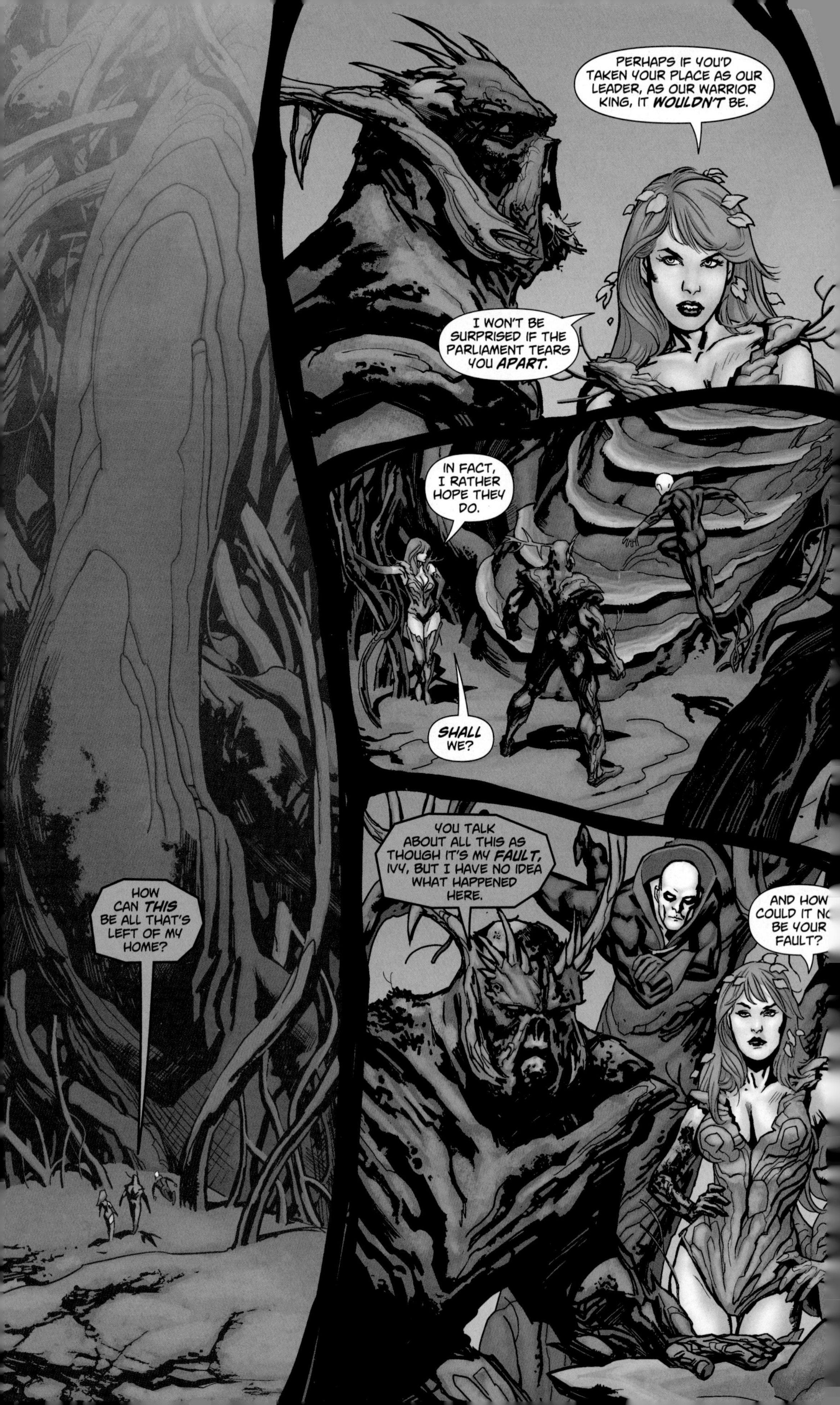

PERHAPS IF YOU'D TAKEN YOUR PLACE AS OUR LEADER, AS OUR WARRIOR KING, IT *WOULDN'T* BE.
I WON'T BE SURPRISED IF THE PARLIAMENT TEARS YOU *APART*.
IN FACT, I RATHER HOPE THEY DO.
SHALL WE?
HOW CAN *THIS* BE ALL THAT'S LEFT OF MY HOME?
YOU TALK ABOUT ALL THIS AS THOUGH IT'S MY *FAULT*, IVY, BUT I HAVE NO IDEA WHAT HAPPENED HERE.
AND HOW COULD IT NO BE YOUR FAULT?

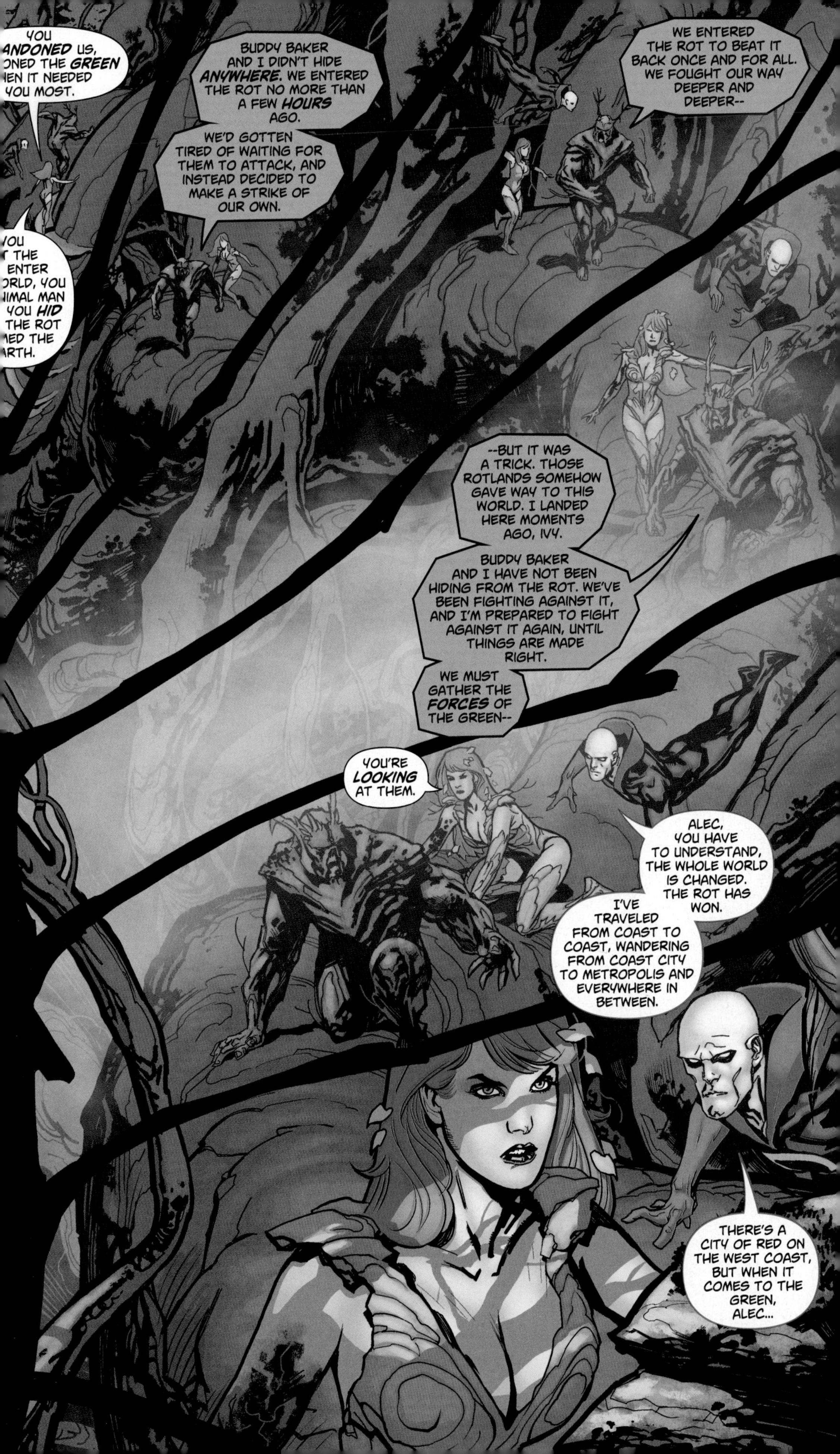
YOU ...ANDONED US, ...ONED THE GREEN ...HEN IT NEEDED YOU MOST.
BUDDY BAKER AND I DIDN'T HIDE ANYWHERE. WE ENTERED THE ROT NO MORE THAN A FEW HOURS AGO.
WE'D GOTTEN TIRED OF WAITING FOR THEM TO ATTACK, AND INSTEAD DECIDED TO MAKE A STRIKE OF OUR OWN.
WE ENTERED THE ROT TO BEAT IT BACK ONCE AND FOR ALL. WE FOUGHT OUR WAY DEEPER AND DEEPER--
...OU ...T THE ENTER ...ORLD, YOU ...NIMAL MAN YOU HID THE ROT ...MED THE ...ARTH.
--BUT IT WAS A TRICK. THOSE ROTLANDS SOMEHOW GAVE WAY TO THIS WORLD. I LANDED HERE MOMENTS AGO, IVY.
BUDDY BAKER AND I HAVE NOT BEEN HIDING FROM THE ROT. WE'VE BEEN FIGHTING AGAINST IT, AND I'M PREPARED TO FIGHT AGAINST IT AGAIN, UNTIL THINGS ARE MADE RIGHT.
WE MUST GATHER THE FORCES OF THE GREEN--
YOU'RE LOOKING AT THEM.
ALEC, YOU HAVE TO UNDERSTAND, THE WHOLE WORLD IS CHANGED. THE ROT HAS WON.
I'VE TRAVELED FROM COAST TO COAST, WANDERING FROM COAST CITY TO METROPOLIS AND EVERYWHERE IN BETWEEN.
THERE'S A CITY OF RED ON THE WEST COAST, BUT WHEN IT COMES TO THE GREEN, ALEC...

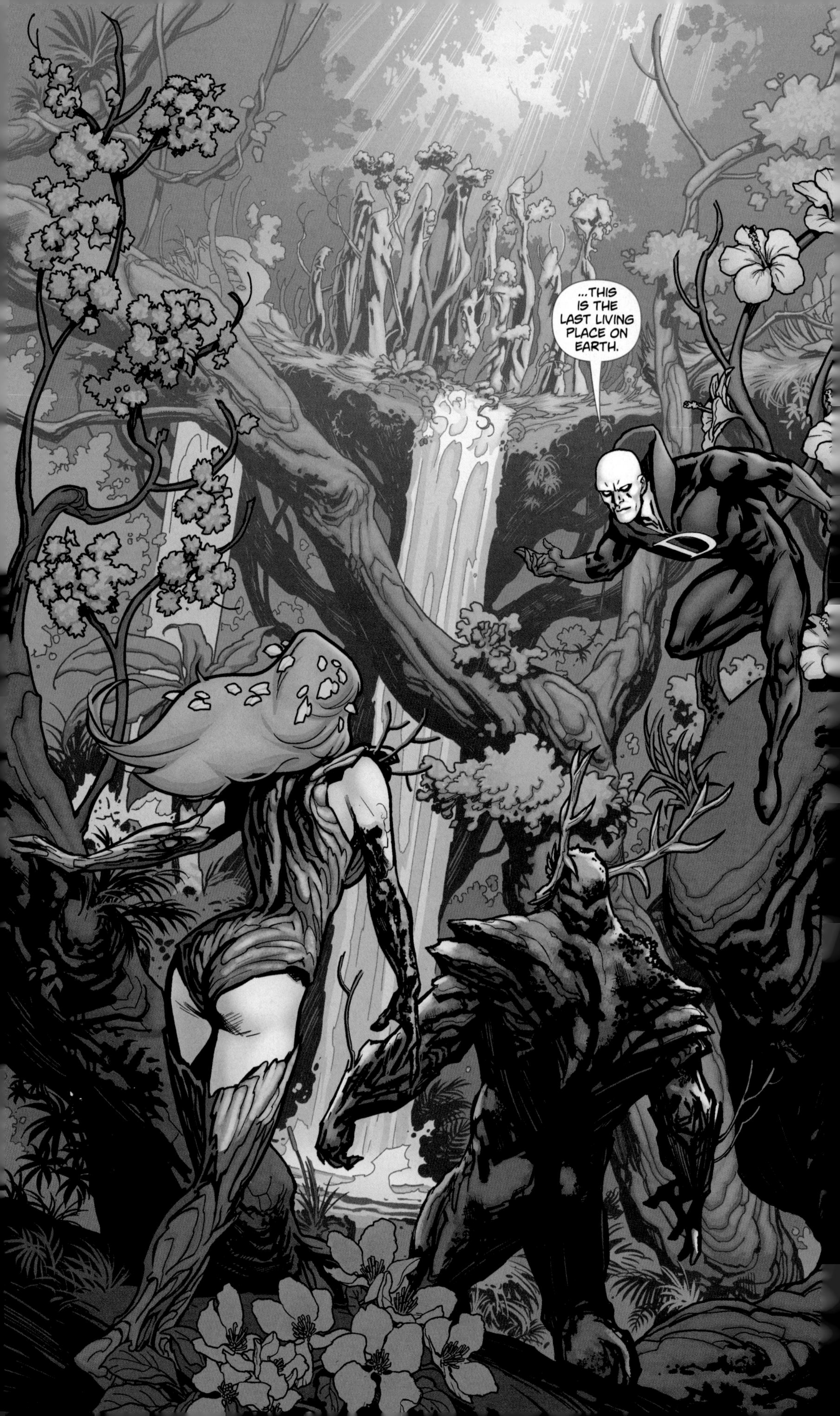
...THIS IS THE LAST LIVING PLACE ON EARTH.

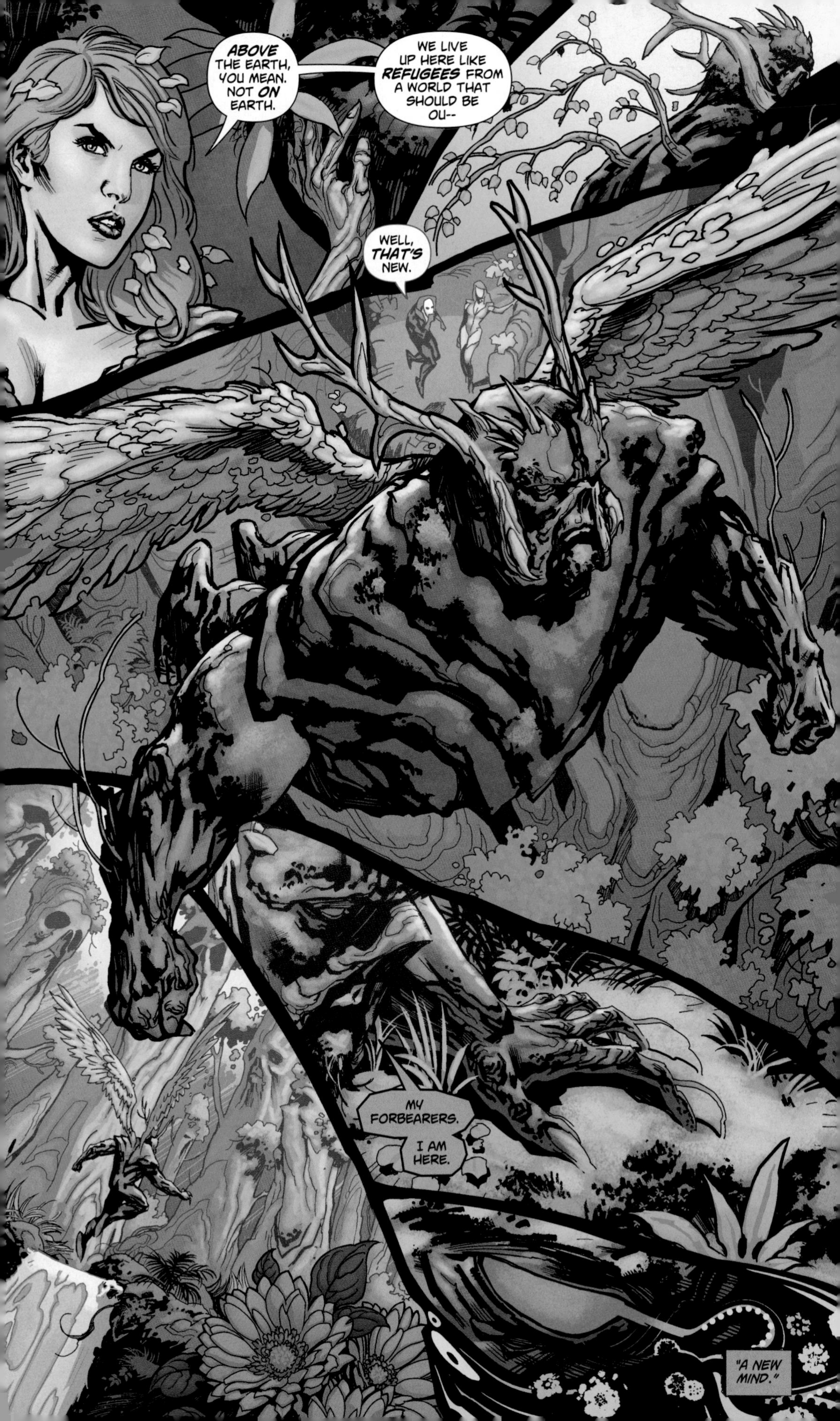
ABOVE THE EARTH, YOU MEAN. NOT ON EARTH.
WE LIVE UP HERE LIKE REFUGEES FROM A WORLD THAT SHOULD BE OU--
WELL, THAT'S NEW.
MY FORBEARERS.
I AM HERE.
"A NEW MIND."

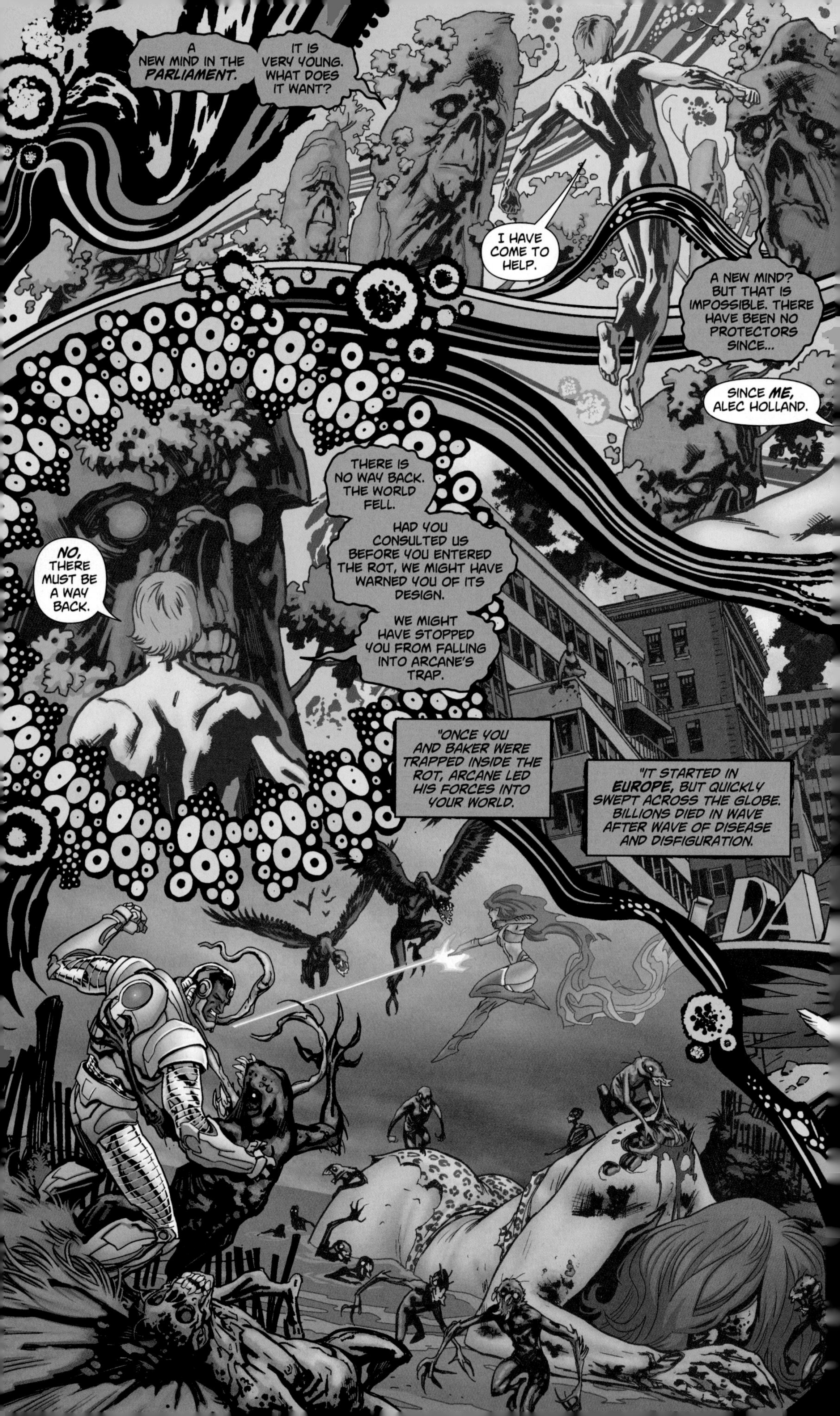
A NEW MIND IN THE PARLIAMENT.
IT IS VERY YOUNG. WHAT DOES IT WANT?
I HAVE COME TO HELP.
A NEW MIND? BUT THAT IS IMPOSSIBLE. THERE HAVE BEEN NO PROTECTORS SINCE...
SINCE ME, ALEC HOLLAND.
THERE IS NO WAY BACK. THE WORLD FELL.
HAD YOU CONSULTED US BEFORE YOU ENTERED THE ROT, WE MIGHT HAVE WARNED YOU OF ITS DESIGN.
WE MIGHT HAVE STOPPED YOU FROM FALLING INTO ARCANE'S TRAP.
NO, THERE MUST BE A WAY BACK.
"ONCE YOU AND BAKER WERE TRAPPED INSIDE THE ROT, ARCANE LED HIS FORCES INTO YOUR WORLD.
"IT STARTED IN EUROPE, BUT QUICKLY SWEPT ACROSS THE GLOBE. BILLIONS DIED IN WAVE AFTER WAVE OF DISEASE AND DISFIGURATION.

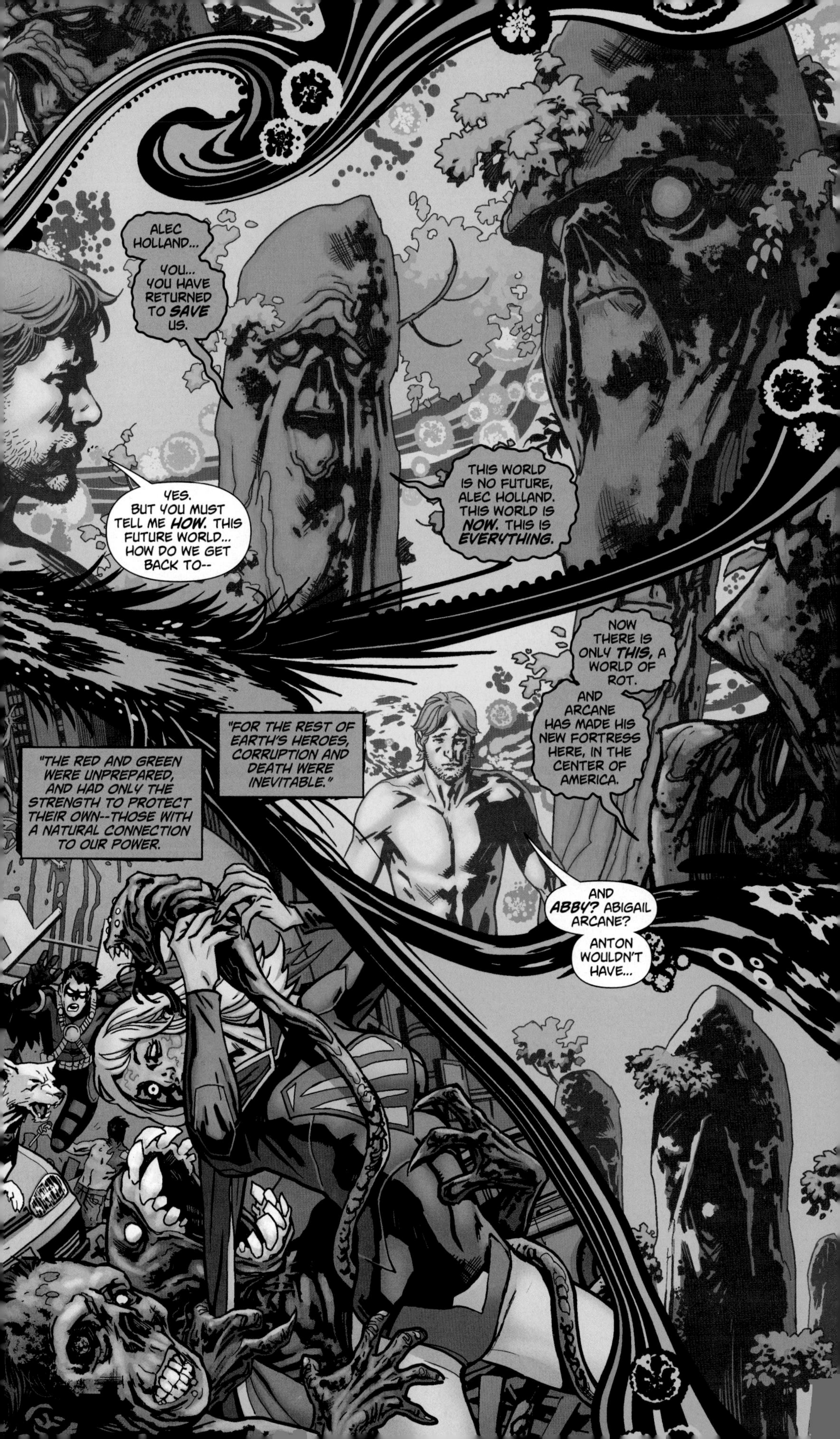
ALEC HOLLAND... YOU... YOU HAVE RETURNED TO SAVE US.
YES. BUT YOU MUST TELL ME HOW. THIS FUTURE WORLD... HOW DO WE GET BACK TO--
THIS WORLD IS NO FUTURE, ALEC HOLLAND. THIS WORLD IS NOW. THIS IS EVERYTHING.
NOW THERE IS ONLY THIS, A WORLD OF ROT.
AND ARCANE HAS MADE HIS NEW FORTRESS HERE, IN THE CENTER OF AMERICA.
"FOR THE REST OF EARTH'S HEROES, CORRUPTION AND DEATH WERE INEVITABLE."
"THE RED AND GREEN WERE UNPREPARED, AND HAD ONLY THE STRENGTH TO PROTECT THEIR OWN--THOSE WITH A NATURAL CONNECTION TO OUR POWER.
AND ABBY? ABIGAIL ARCANE?
ANTON WOULDN'T HAVE...

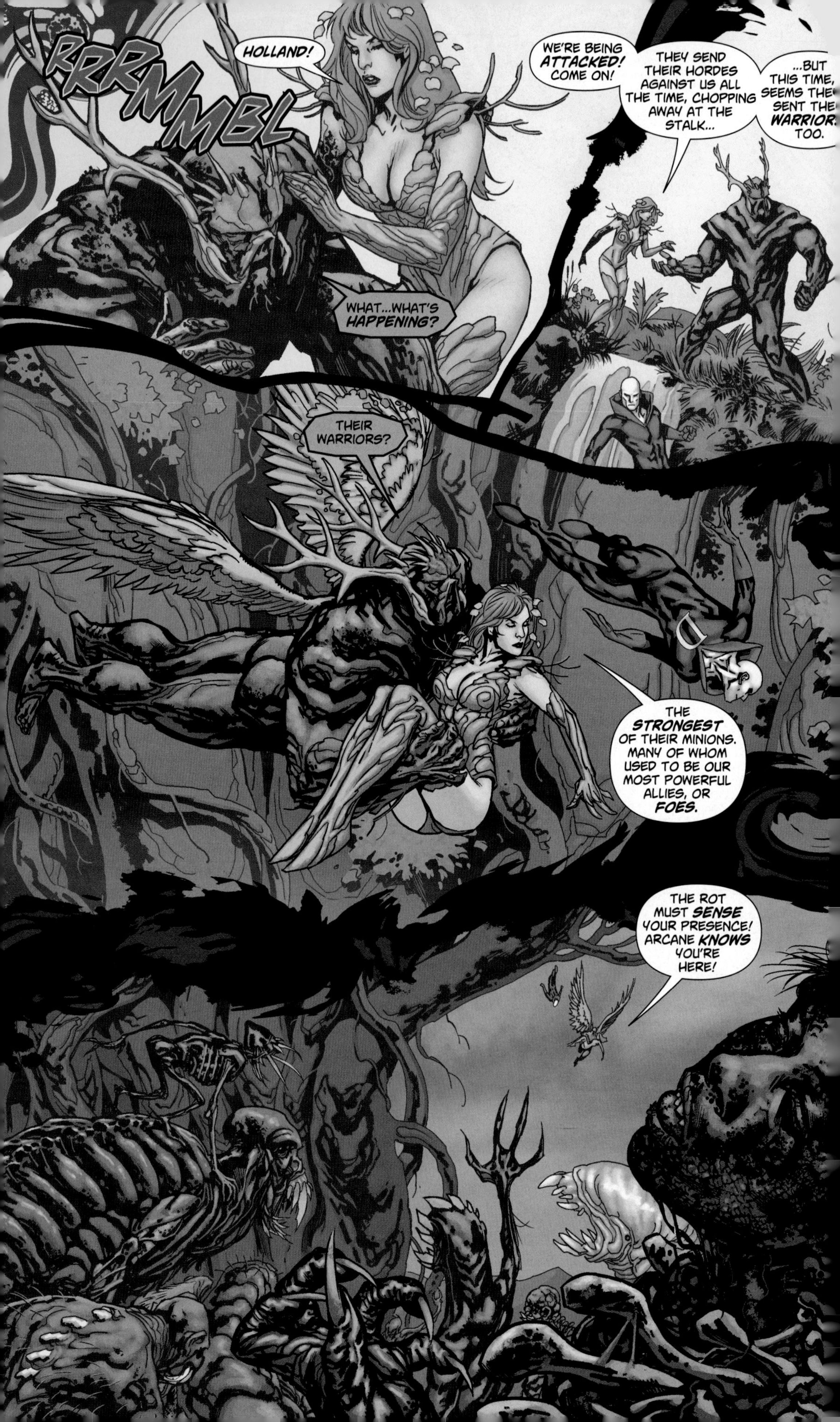

RRRMMMBL
HOLLAND!
WE'RE BEING ATTACKED! COME ON!
THEY SEND THEIR HORDES AGAINST US ALL THE TIME, CHOPPING AWAY AT THE STALK...
...BUT THIS TIME, SEEMS THE SENT THE WARRIOR TOO.
WHAT...WHAT'S HAPPENING?
THEIR WARRIORS?
THE STRONGEST OF THEIR MINIONS. MANY OF WHOM USED TO BE OUR MOST POWERFUL ALLIES, OR FOES.
THE ROT MUST SENSE YOUR PRESENCE! ARCANE KNOWS YOU'RE HERE!

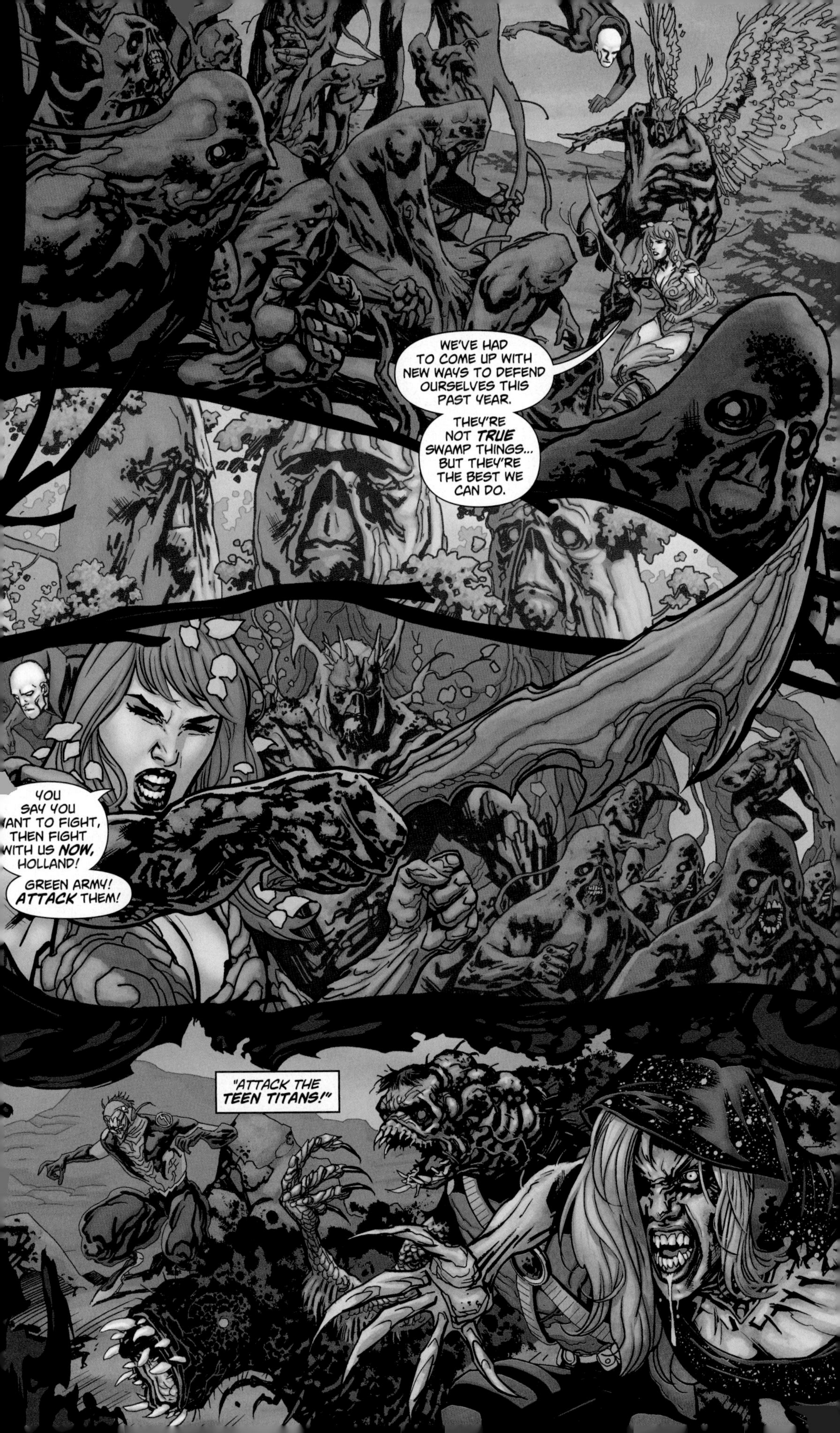

WE'VE HAD TO COME UP WITH NEW WAYS TO DEFEND OURSELVES THIS PAST YEAR.
THEY'RE NOT TRUE SWAMP THINGS... BUT THEY'RE THE BEST WE CAN DO.
YOU SAY YOU WANT TO FIGHT, THEN FIGHT WITH US NOW, HOLLAND!
GREEN ARMY! ATTACK THEM!
"ATTACK THE TEEN TITANS!"

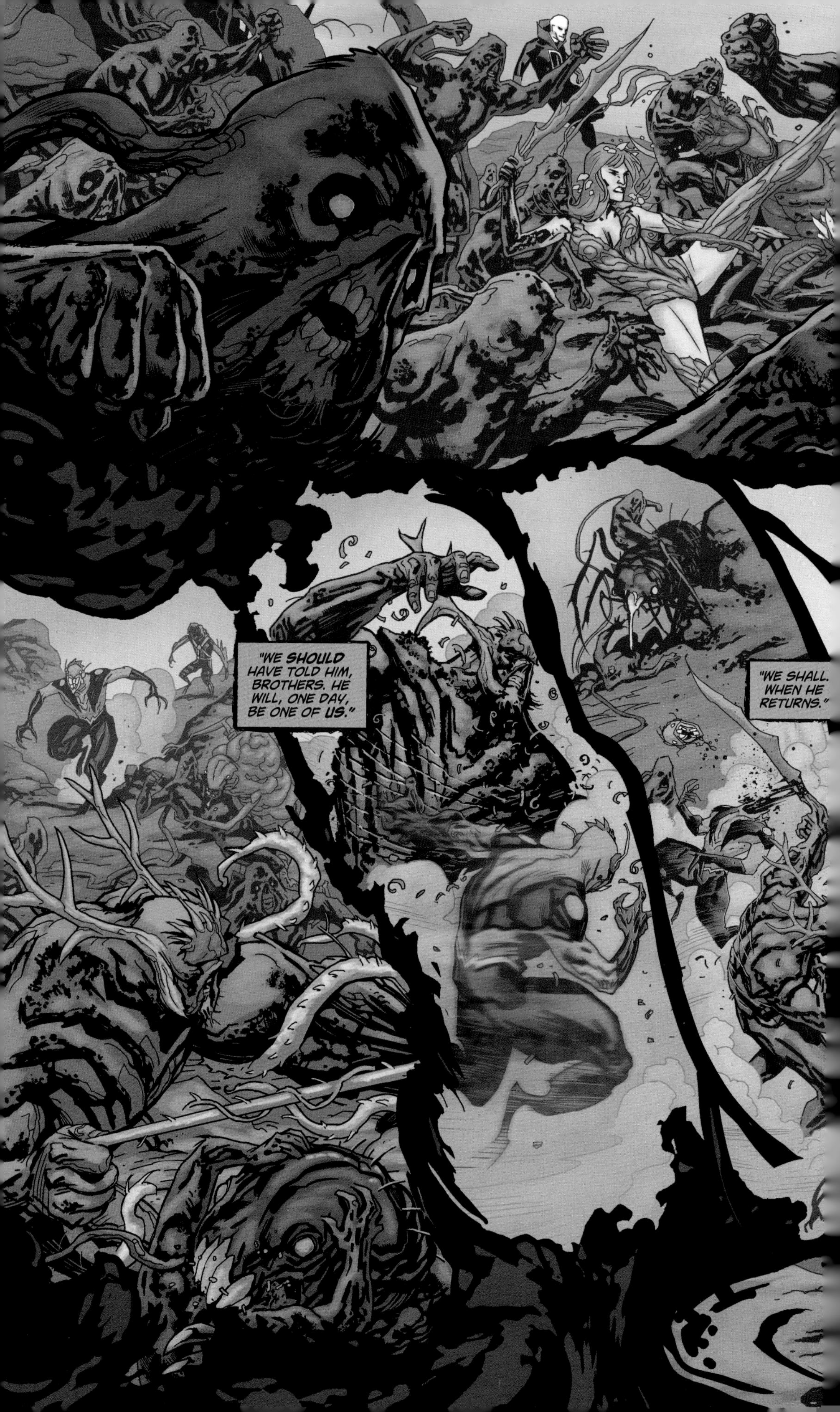
"WE SHOULD HAVE TOLD HIM, BROTHERS. HE WILL, ONE DAY, BE ONE OF US."
"WE SHALL. WHEN HE RETURNS."

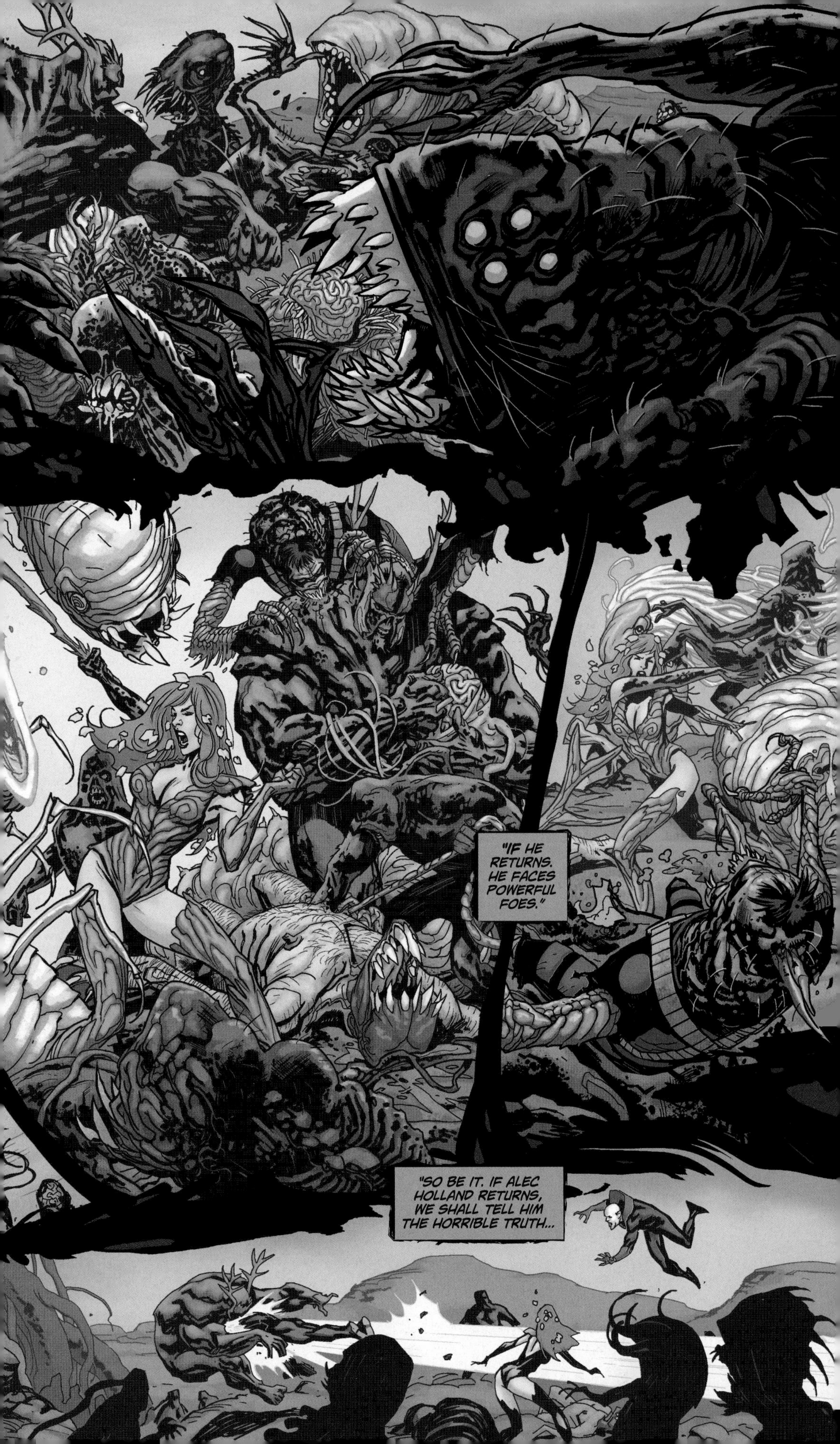
"IF HE RETURNS, HE FACES POWERFUL FOES."
"SO BE IT. IF ALEC HOLLAND RETURNS, WE SHALL TELL HIM THE HORRIBLE TRUTH...

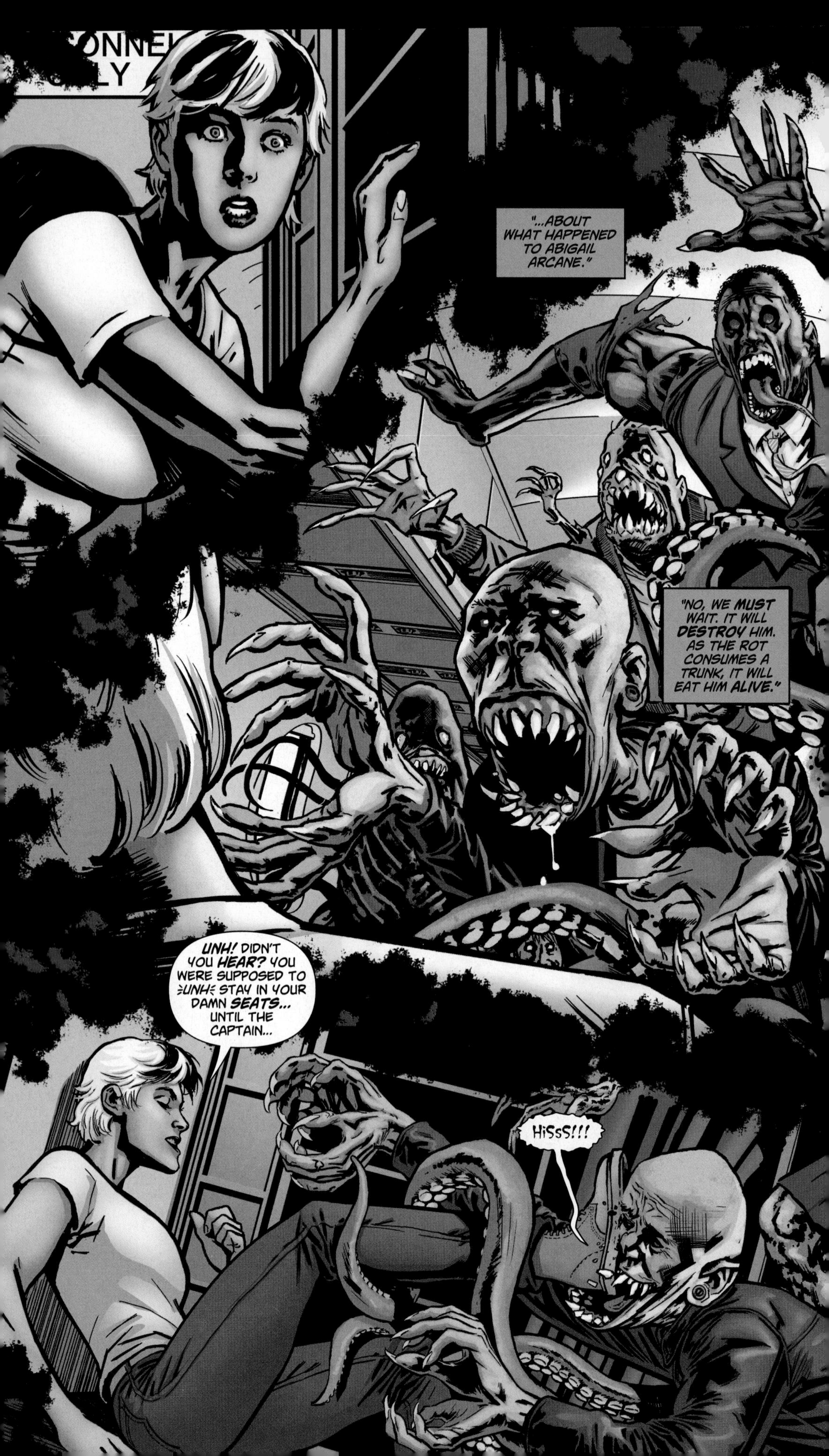
"...ABOUT WHAT HAPPENED TO ABIGAIL ARCANE."
"NO, WE MUST WAIT. IT WILL DESTROY HIM. AS THE ROT CONSUMES A TRUNK, IT WILL EAT HIM ALIVE."
UNH! DIDN'T YOU HEAR? YOU WERE SUPPOSED TO UNH STAY IN YOUR DAMN SEATS... UNTIL THE CAPTAIN...
HISSS!!!

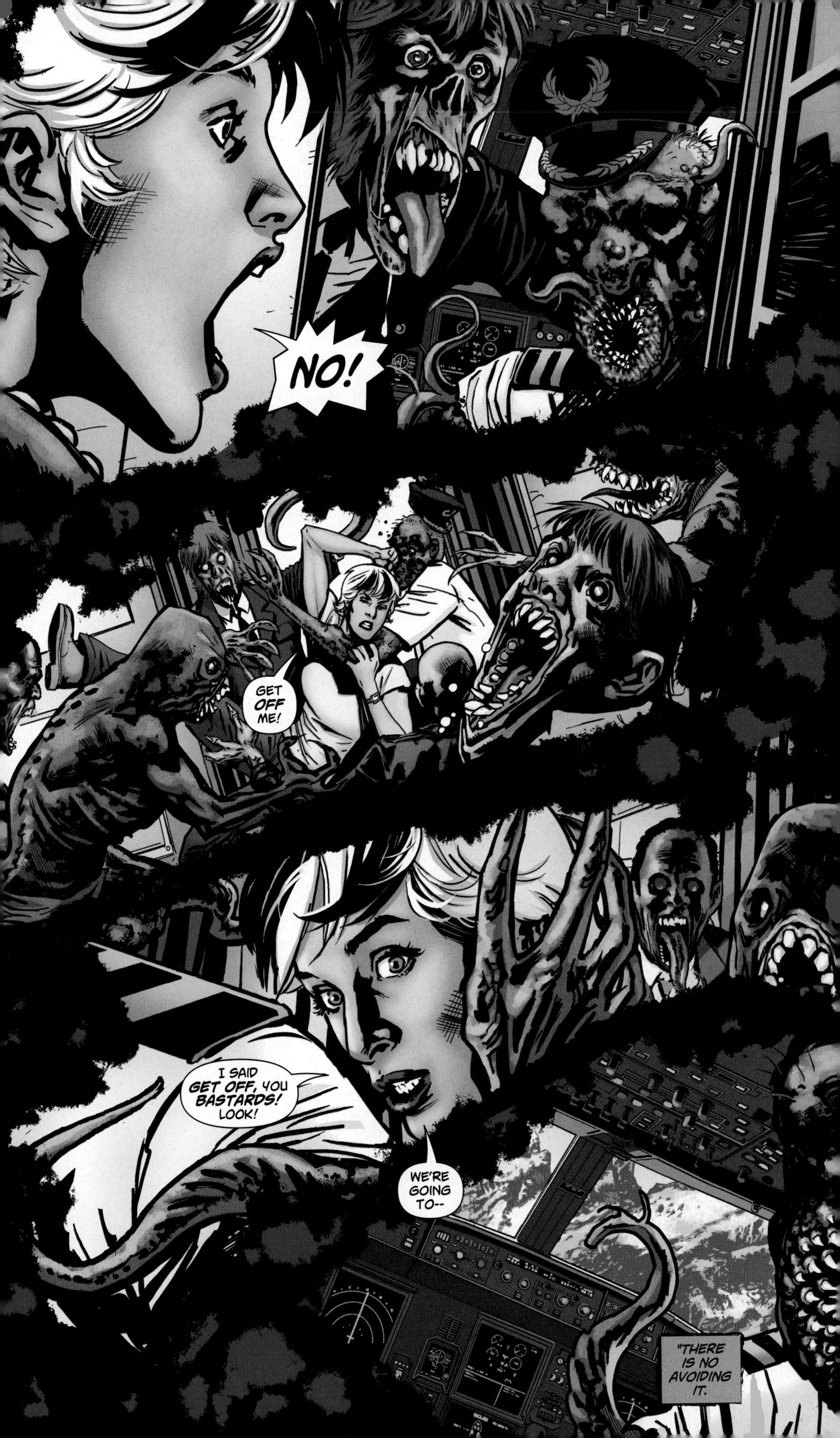
NO!
GET OFF ME!
I SAID GET OFF, YOU BASTARDS! LOOK!
WE'RE GOING TO--
"THERE IS NO AVOIDING IT.

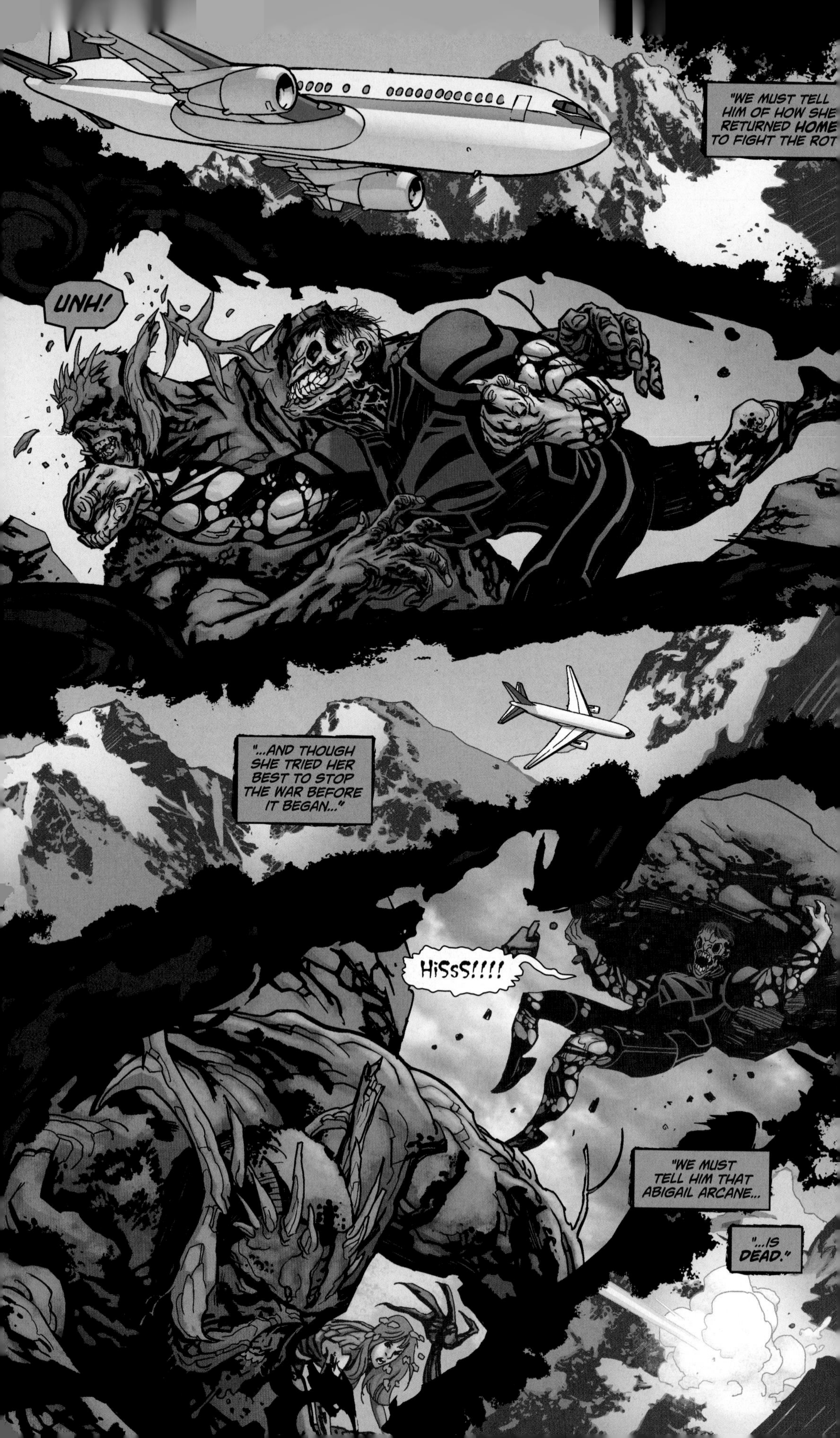
"WE MUST TELL HIM OF HOW SHE RETURNED HOME TO FIGHT THE ROT
UNH!
"...AND THOUGH SHE TRIED HER BEST TO STOP THE WAR BEFORE IT BEGAN..."
HiSsS!!!!
"WE MUST TELL HIM THAT ABIGAIL ARCANE...
"...IS DEAD."

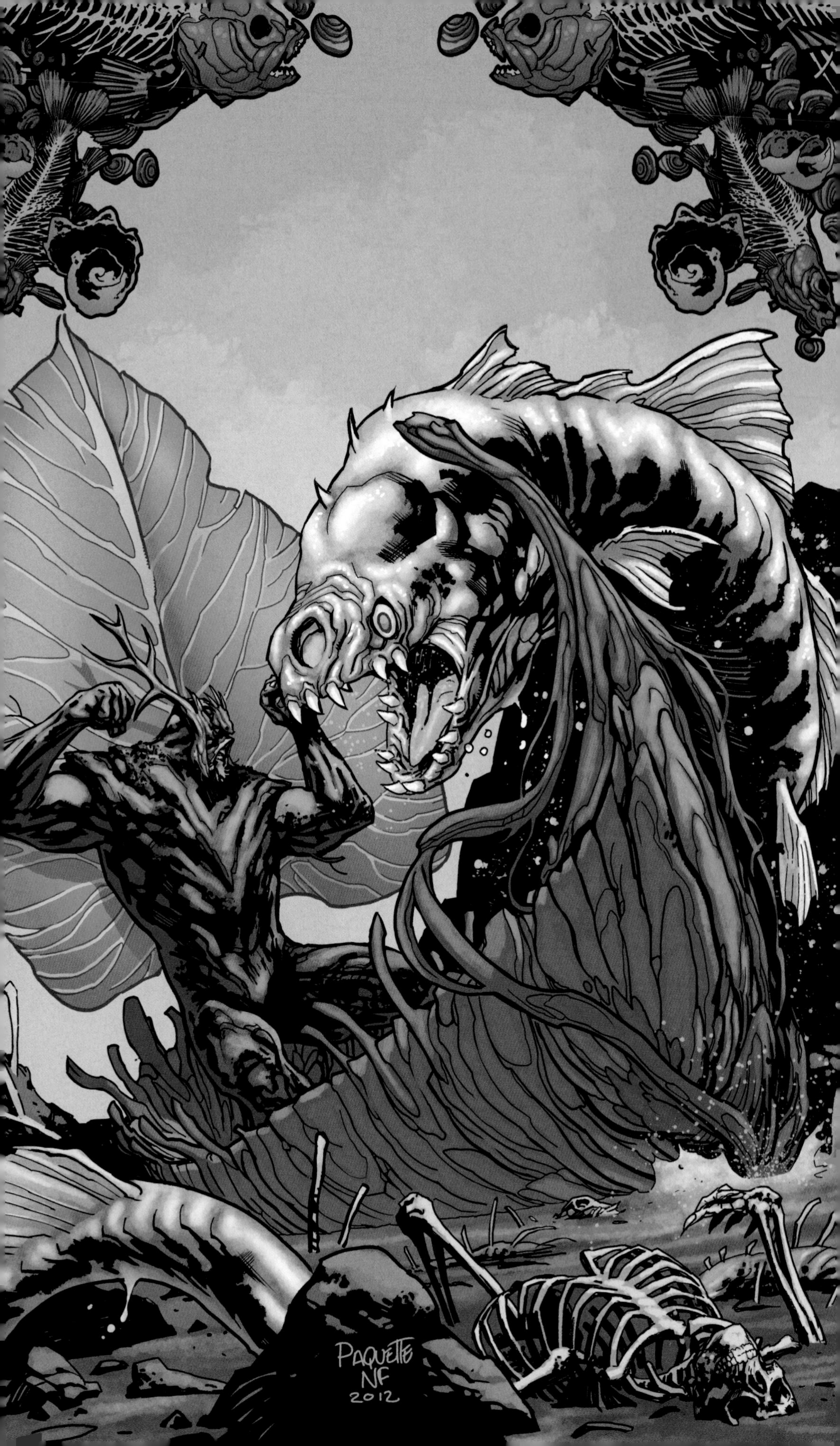
PAQUETTE
NF
2012

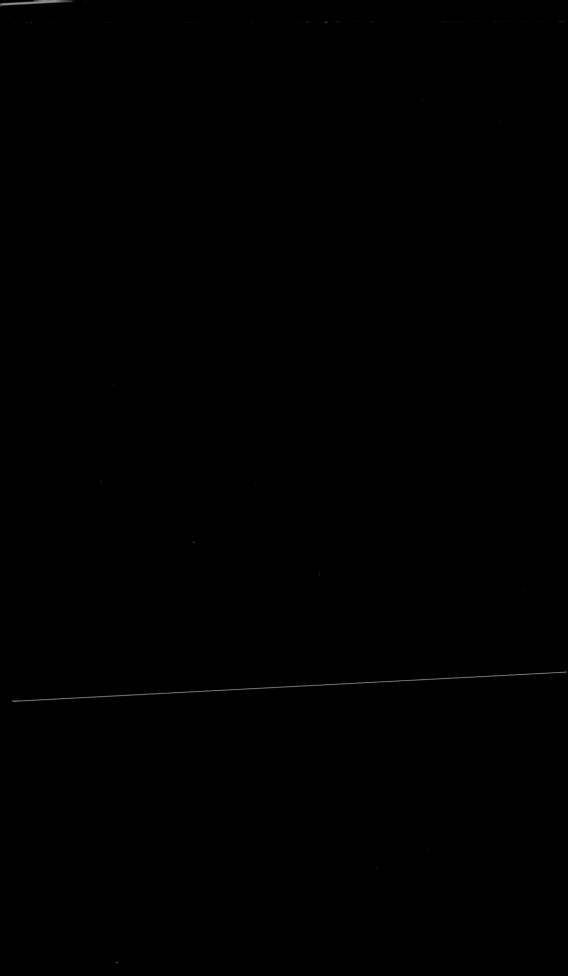

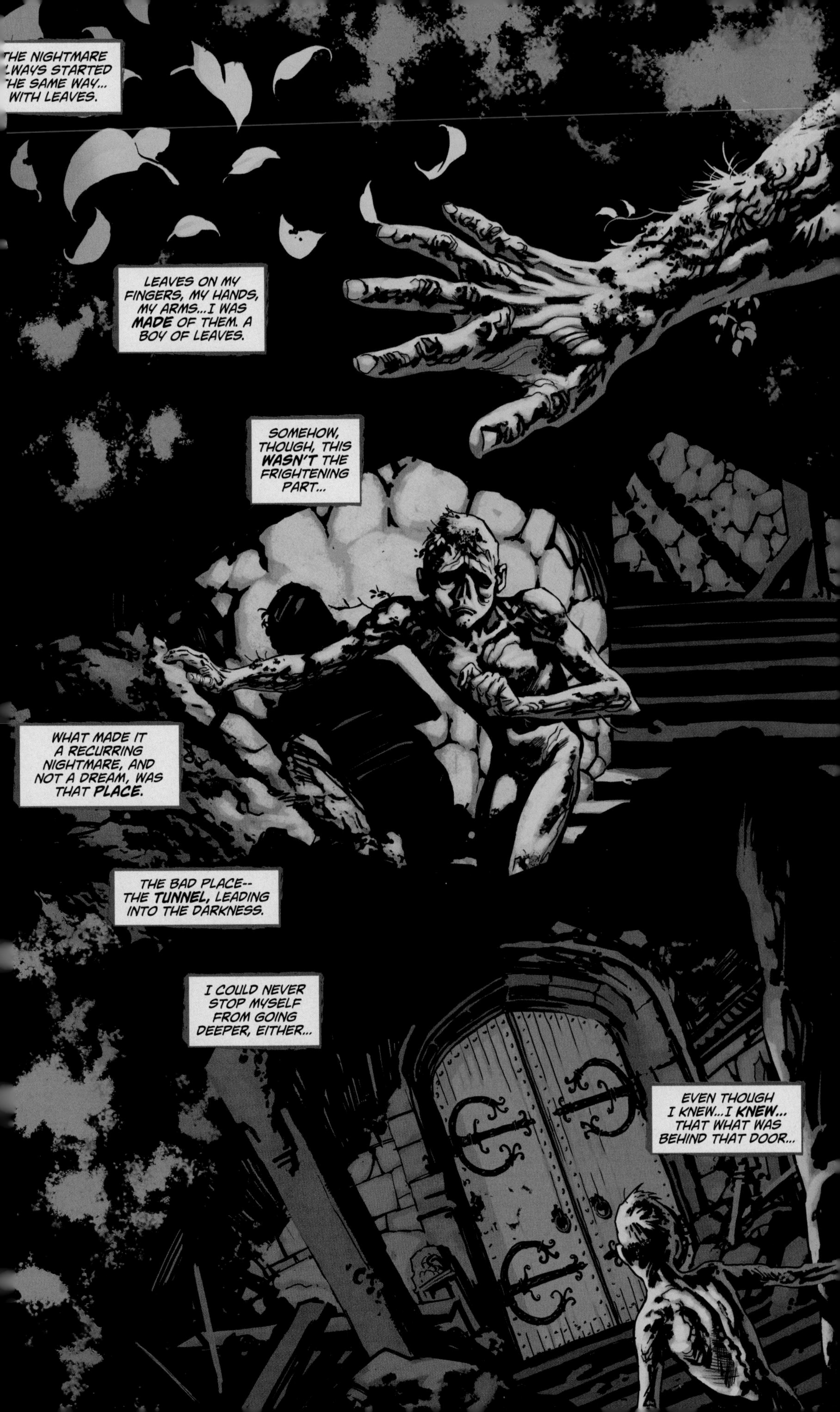
THE NIGHTMARE ALWAYS STARTED THE SAME WAY... WITH LEAVES.
LEAVES ON MY FINGERS, MY HANDS, MY ARMS...I WAS MADE OF THEM. A BOY OF LEAVES.
SOMEHOW, THOUGH, THIS WASN'T THE FRIGHTENING PART...
WHAT MADE IT A RECURRING NIGHTMARE, AND NOT A DREAM, WAS THAT PLACE.
THE BAD PLACE-- THE TUNNEL, LEADING INTO THE DARKNESS.
I COULD NEVER STOP MYSELF FROM GOING DEEPER, EITHER...
EVEN THOUGH I KNEW...I KNEW... THAT WHAT WAS BEHIND THAT DOOR...

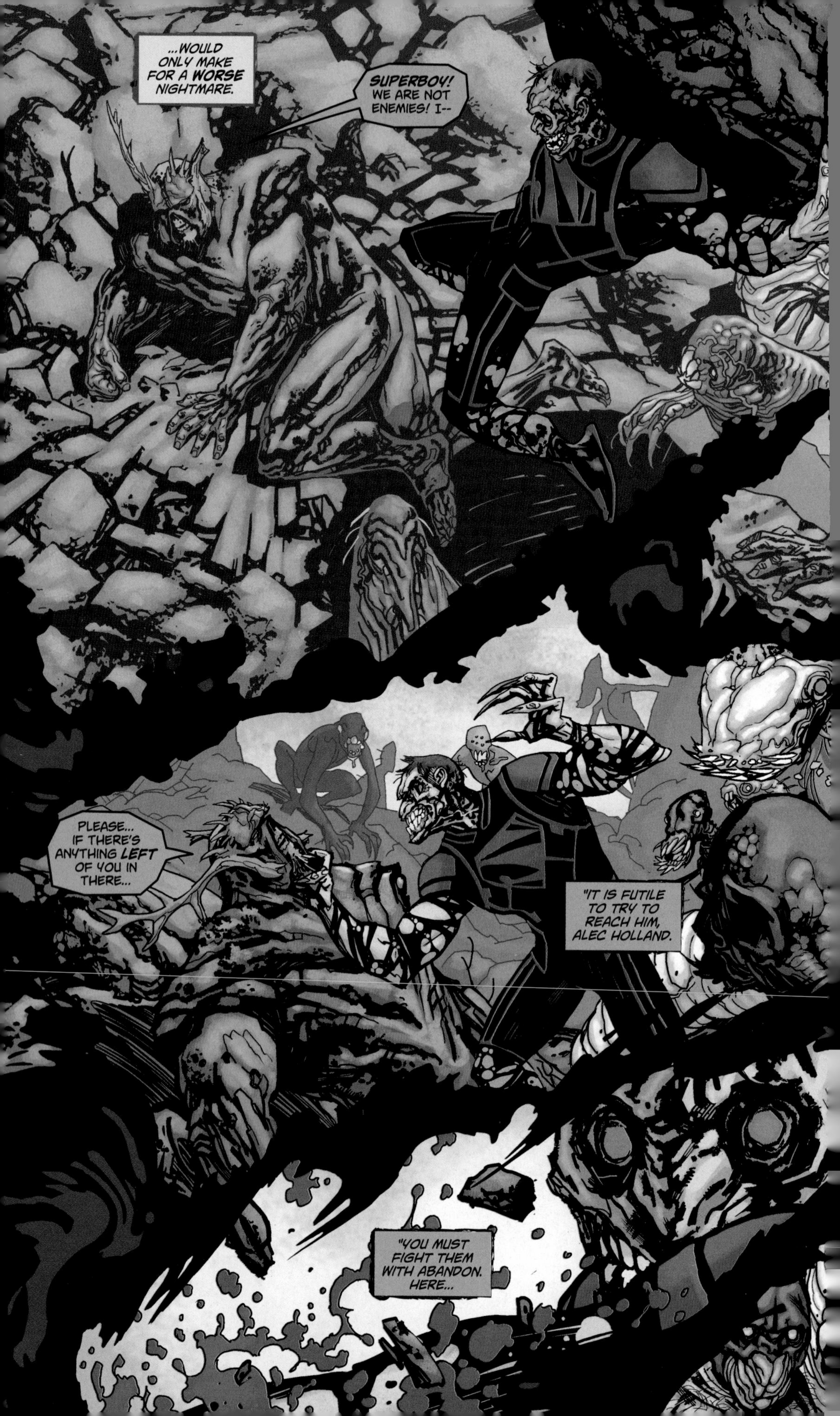
...WOULD ONLY MAKE FOR A WORSE NIGHTMARE.
SUPERBOY! WE ARE NOT ENEMIES! I--
PLEASE... IF THERE'S ANYTHING LEFT OF YOU IN THERE...
"IT IS FUTILE TO TRY TO REACH HIM, ALEC HOLLAND.
"YOU MUST FIGHT THEM WITH ABANDON. HERE...

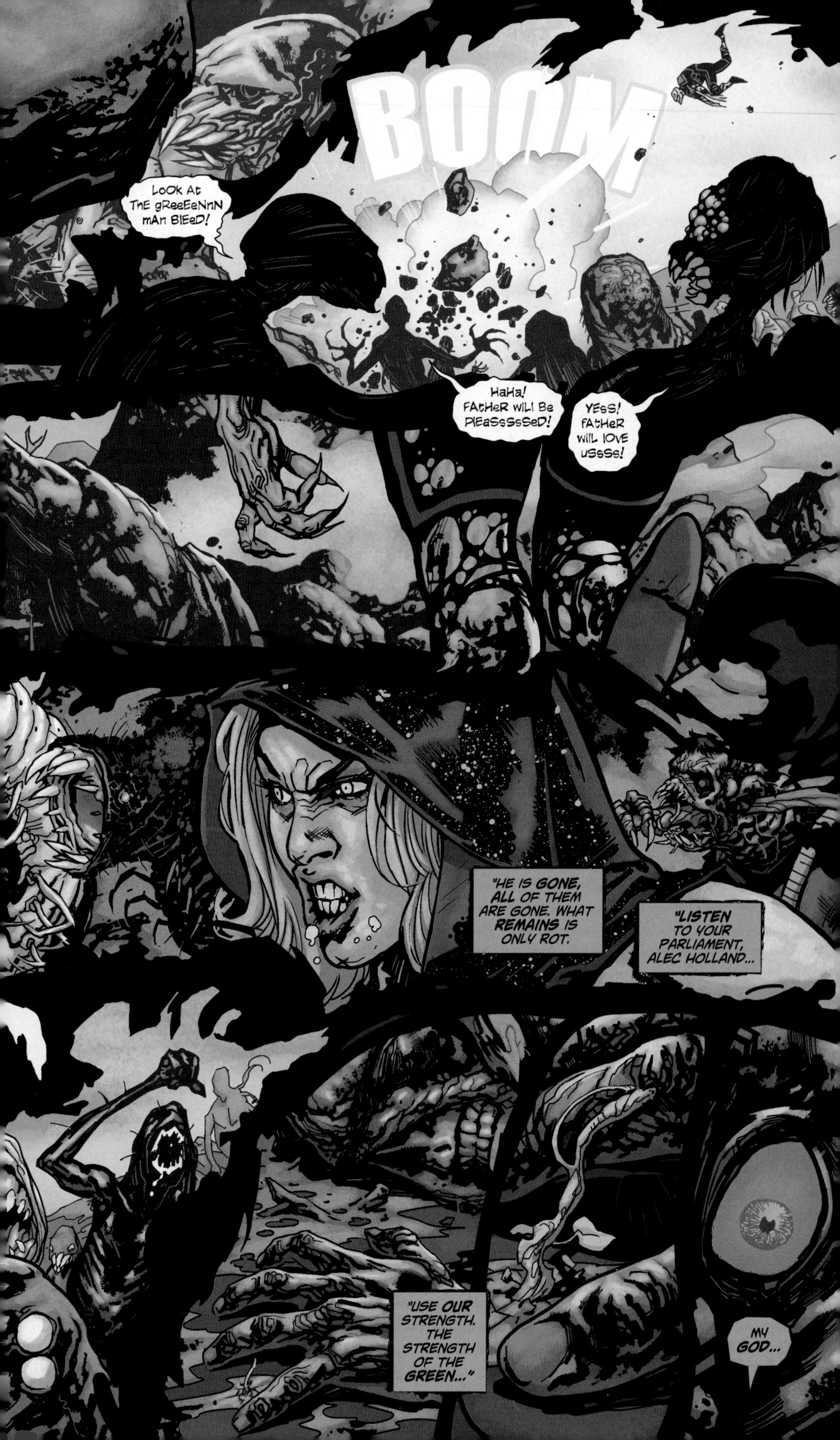
BOOM
LOOK AT THE gREEEENNN mAN BlEED!
HAHA! FATHER WILL BE PLEASSSSSED!
YESS! FATHER WILL LOVE USSSS!
"HE IS GONE, ALL OF THEM ARE GONE. WHAT REMAINS IS ONLY ROT.
"LISTEN TO YOUR PARLIAMENT, ALEC HOLLAND...
"USE OUR STRENGTH. THE STRENGTH OF THE GREEN..."
MY GOD...

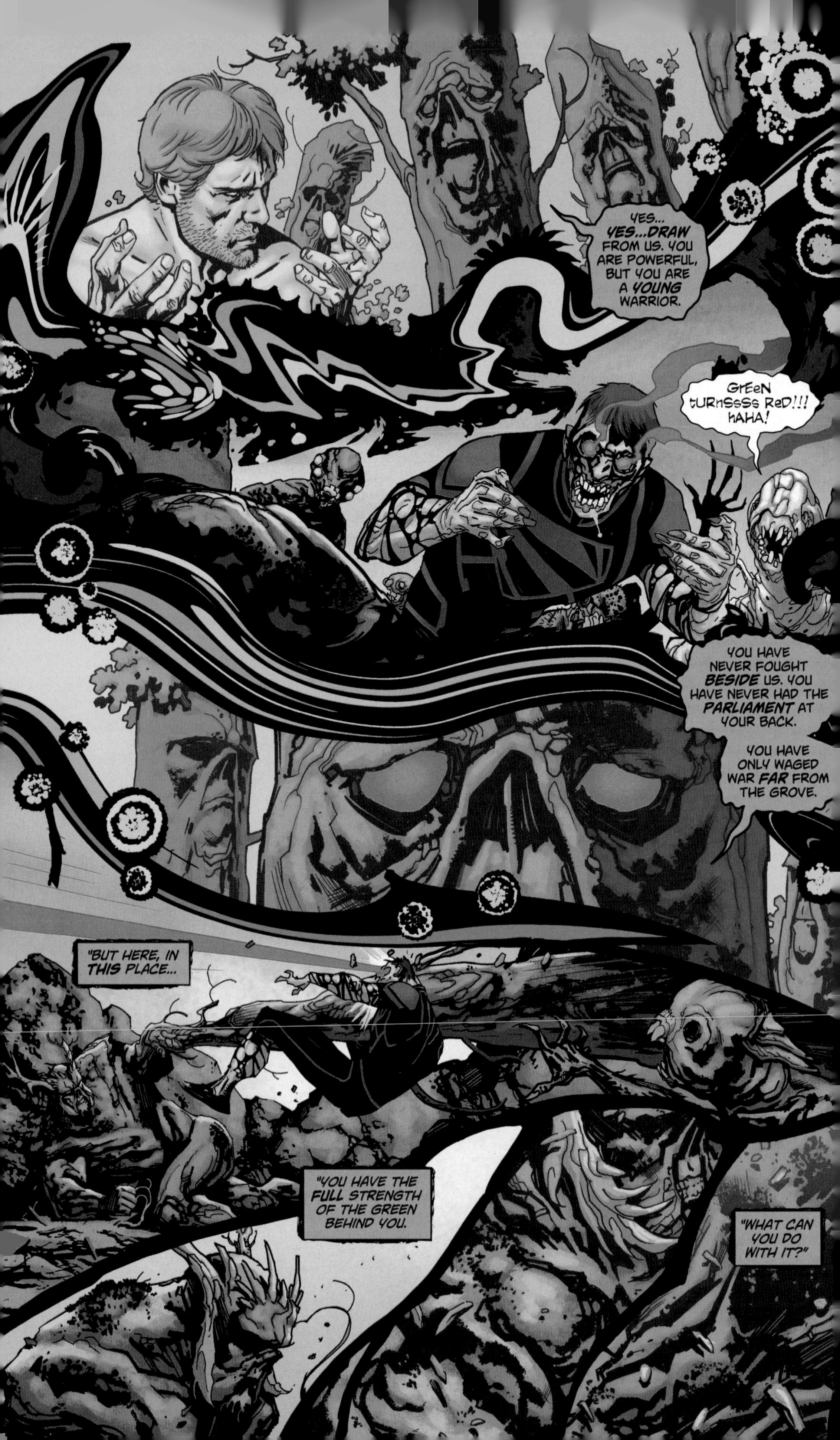
YES... YES...DRAW FROM US. YOU ARE POWERFUL, BUT YOU ARE A YOUNG WARRIOR.
GrEeN tURnSSSS ReD!!! hAHA!
YOU HAVE NEVER FOUGHT BESIDE US. YOU HAVE NEVER HAD THE PARLIAMENT AT YOUR BACK.
YOU HAVE ONLY WAGED WAR FAR FROM THE GROVE.
"BUT HERE, IN THIS PLACE...
"YOU HAVE THE FULL STRENGTH OF THE GREEN BEHIND YOU.
"WHAT CAN YOU DO WITH IT?"

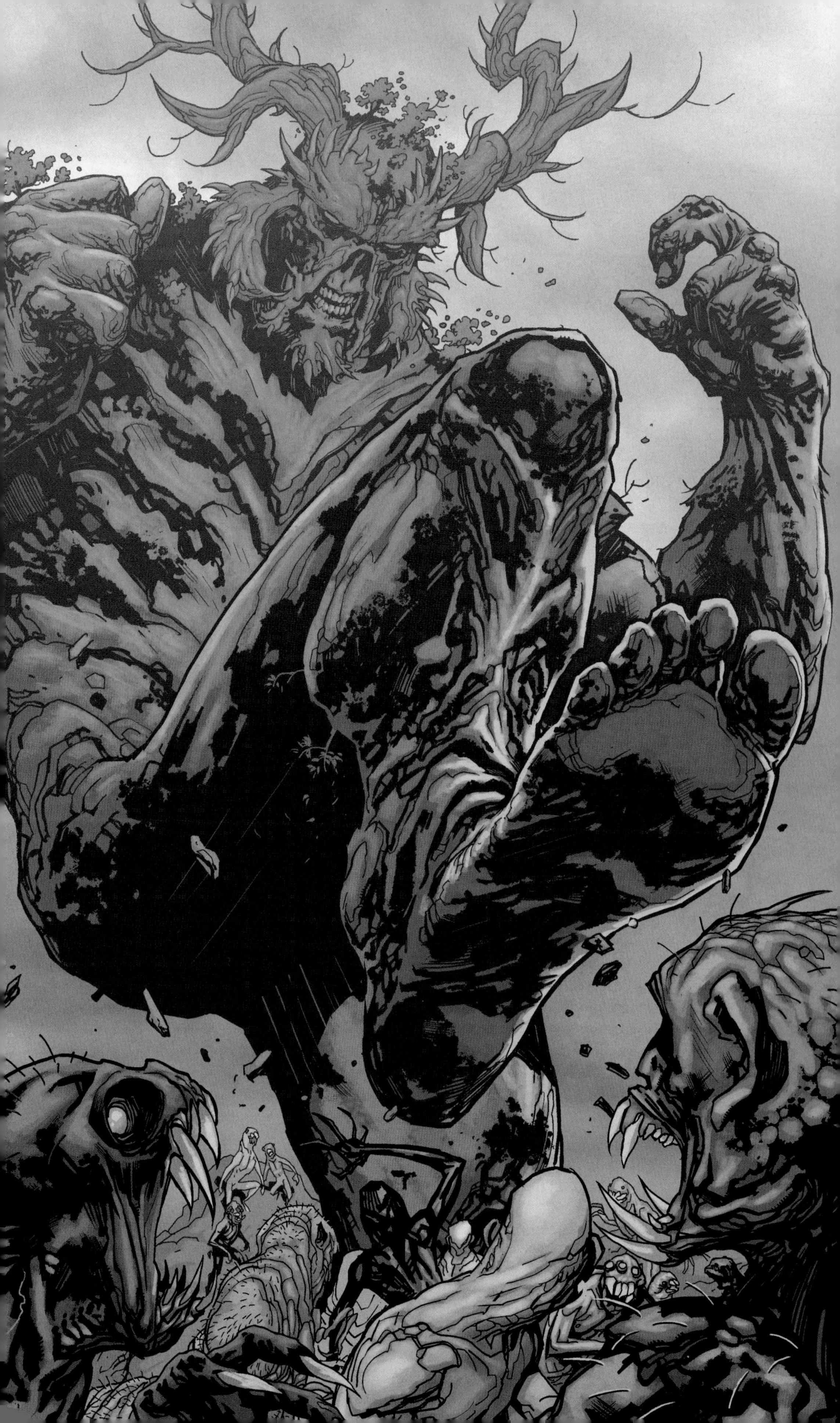

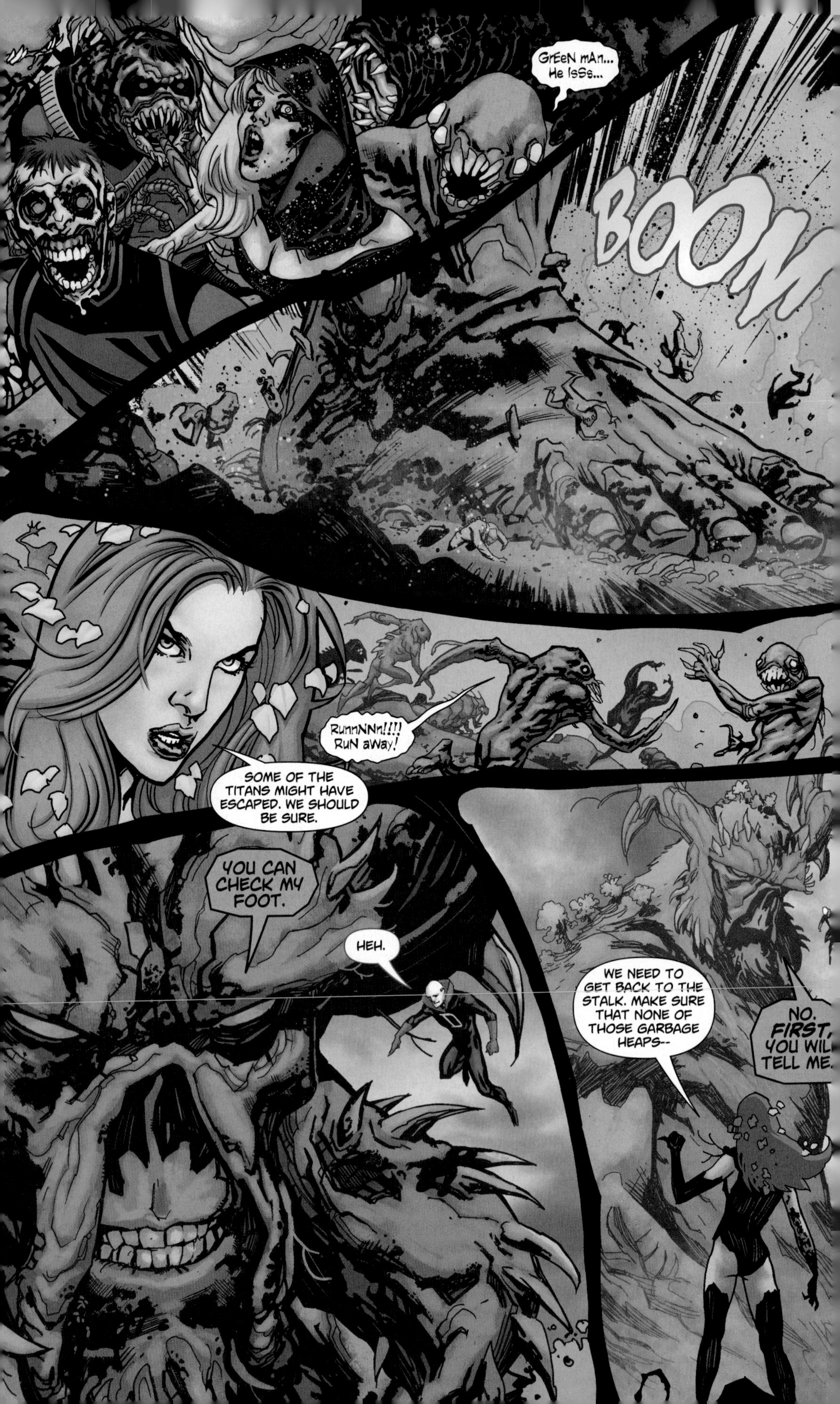
GrEeN mAn... He IsSs...
BOOM
RunnNNn!!!! RuN away!
SOME OF THE TITANS MIGHT HAVE ESCAPED. WE SHOULD BE SURE.
YOU CAN CHECK MY FOOT.
HEH.
WE NEED TO GET BACK TO THE STALK. MAKE SURE THAT NONE OF THOSE GARBAGE HEAPS--
NO. FIRST, YOU WIL TELL ME.

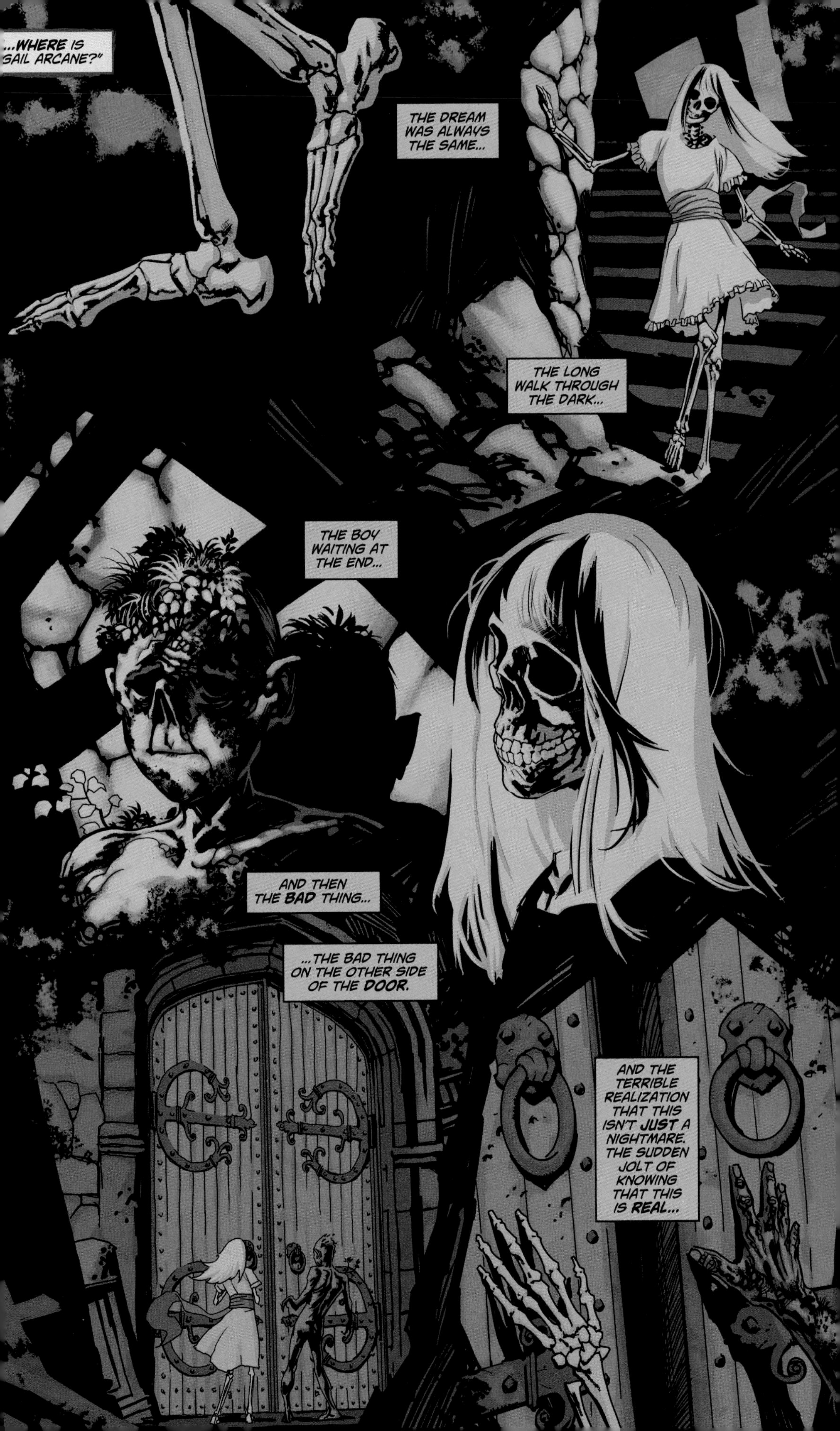
...WHERE IS
SAIL ARCANE?"
THE DREAM WAS ALWAYS THE SAME...
THE LONG WALK THROUGH THE DARK...
THE BOY WAITING AT THE END...
AND THEN THE BAD THING...
...THE BAD THING ON THE OTHER SIDE OF THE DOOR.
AND THE TERRIBLE REALIZATION THAT THIS ISN'T JUST A NIGHTMARE. THE SUDDEN JOLT OF KNOWING THAT THIS IS REAL...

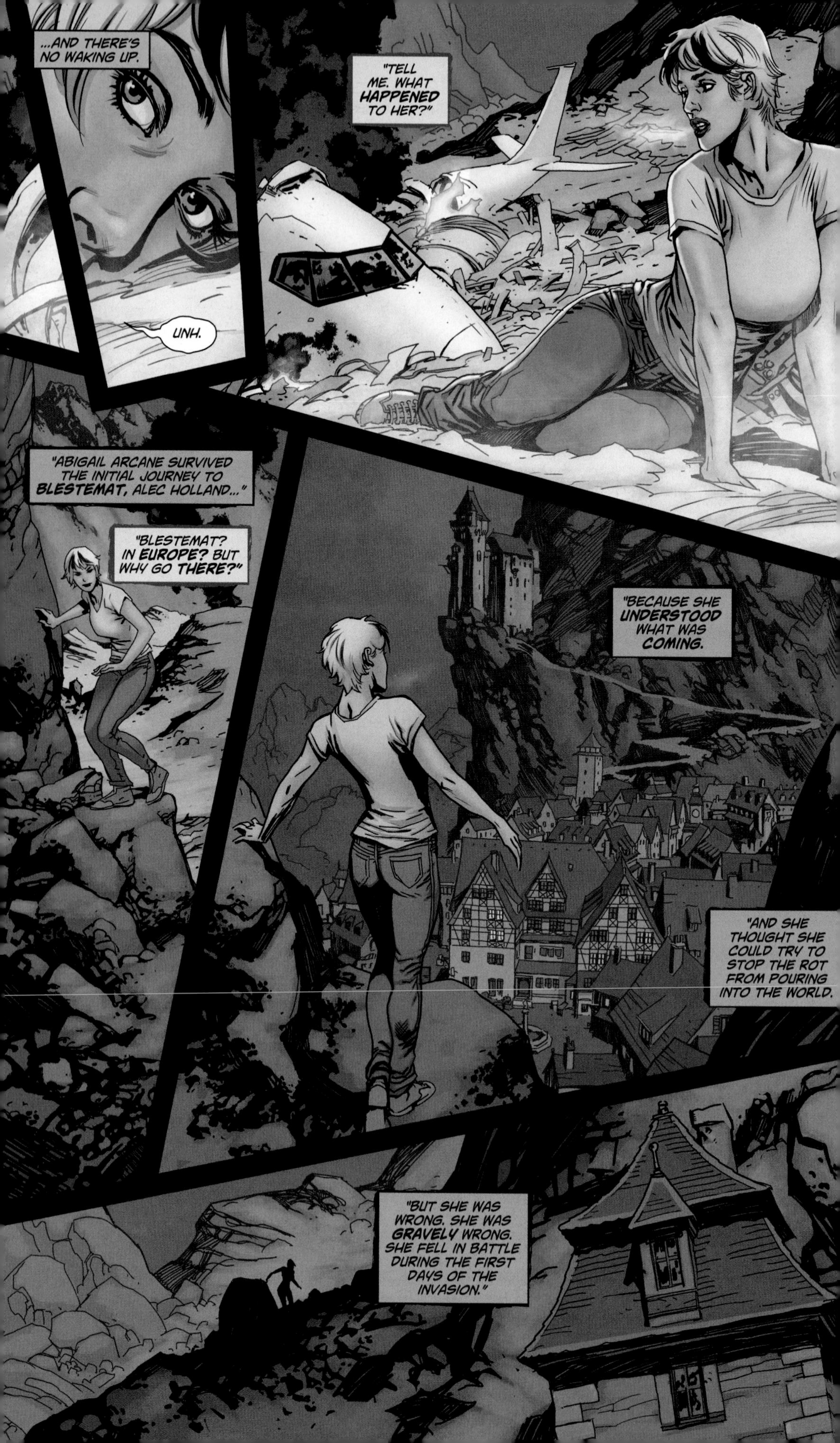
...AND THERE'S NO WAKING UP.
"TELL ME. WHAT HAPPENED TO HER?"
UNH.
"ABIGAIL ARCANE SURVIVED THE INITIAL JOURNEY TO BLESTEMAT, ALEC HOLLAND..."
"BLESTEMAT? IN EUROPE? BUT WHY GO THERE?"
"BECAUSE SHE UNDERSTOOD WHAT WAS COMING.
"AND SHE THOUGHT SHE COULD TRY TO STOP THE ROT FROM POURING INTO THE WORLD.
"BUT SHE WAS WRONG. SHE WAS GRAVELY WRONG. SHE FELL IN BATTLE DURING THE FIRST DAYS OF THE INVASION."

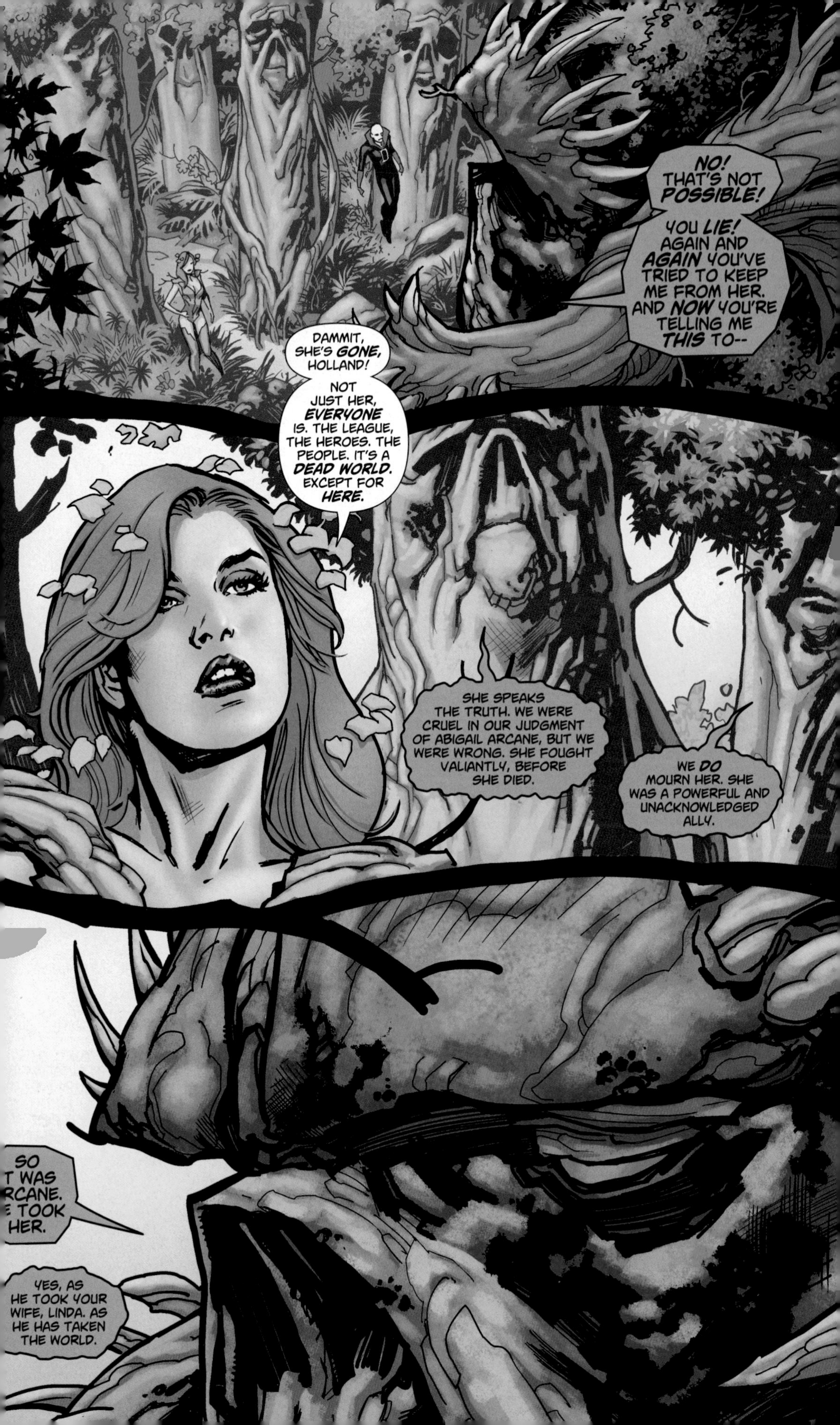
NO! THAT'S NOT POSSIBLE!
YOU LIE! AGAIN AND AGAIN YOU'VE TRIED TO KEEP ME FROM HER. AND NOW YOU'RE TELLING ME THIS TO--
DAMMIT, SHE'S GONE, HOLLAND!
NOT JUST HER, EVERYONE IS. THE LEAGUE, THE HEROES. THE PEOPLE. IT'S A DEAD WORLD. EXCEPT FOR HERE.
SHE SPEAKS THE TRUTH. WE WERE CRUEL IN OUR JUDGMENT OF ABIGAIL ARCANE, BUT WE WERE WRONG. SHE FOUGHT VALIANTLY, BEFORE SHE DIED.
WE DO MOURN HER. SHE WAS A POWERFUL AND UNACKNOWLEDGED ALLY.
YES, AS HE TOOK YOUR WIFE, LINDA. AS HE HAS TAKEN THE WORLD.

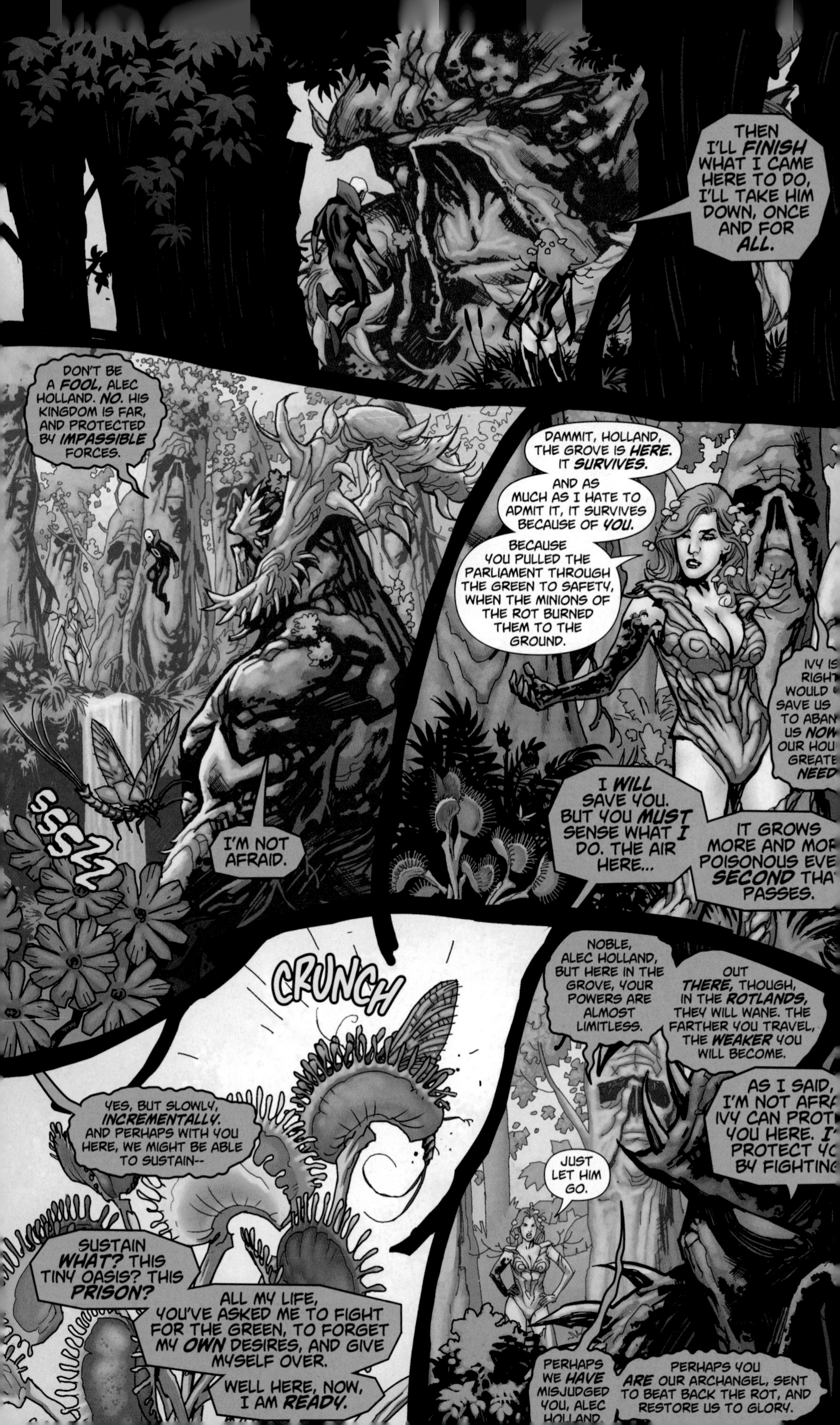

THEN I'LL FINISH WHAT I CAME HERE TO DO, I'LL TAKE HIM DOWN, ONCE AND FOR ALL.
DON'T BE A FOOL, ALEC HOLLAND. NO. HIS KINGDOM IS FAR, AND PROTECTED BY IMPASSIBLE FORCES.
I'M NOT AFRAID.
SSSZZ
DAMMIT, HOLLAND, THE GROVE IS HERE. IT SURVIVES.
AND AS MUCH AS I HATE TO ADMIT IT, IT SURVIVES BECAUSE OF YOU.
BECAUSE YOU PULLED THE PARLIAMENT THROUGH THE GREEN TO SAFETY, WHEN THE MINIONS OF THE ROT BURNED THEM TO THE GROUND.
I WILL SAVE YOU. BUT YOU MUST SENSE WHAT I DO. THE AIR HERE...
CRUNCH
YES, BUT SLOWLY, INCREMENTALLY. AND PERHAPS WITH YOU HERE, WE MIGHT BE ABLE TO SUSTAIN--
SUSTAIN WHAT? THIS TINY OASIS? THIS PRISON?
ALL MY LIFE, YOU'VE ASKED ME TO FIGHT FOR THE GREEN, TO FORGET MY OWN DESIRES, AND GIVE MYSELF OVER.
WELL HERE, NOW, I AM READY.
NOBLE, ALEC HOLLAND, BUT HERE IN THE GROVE, YOUR POWERS ARE ALMOST LIMITLESS.
OUT THERE, THOUGH, IN THE ROTLANDS, THEY WILL WANE. THE FARTHER YOU TRAVEL, THE WEAKER YOU WILL BECOME.
JUST LET HIM GO.
PERHAPS WE HAVE MISJUDGED YOU, ALEC HOLLAND.
PERHAPS YOU ARE OUR ARCHANGEL, SENT TO BEAT BACK THE ROT, AND RESTORE US TO GLORY.

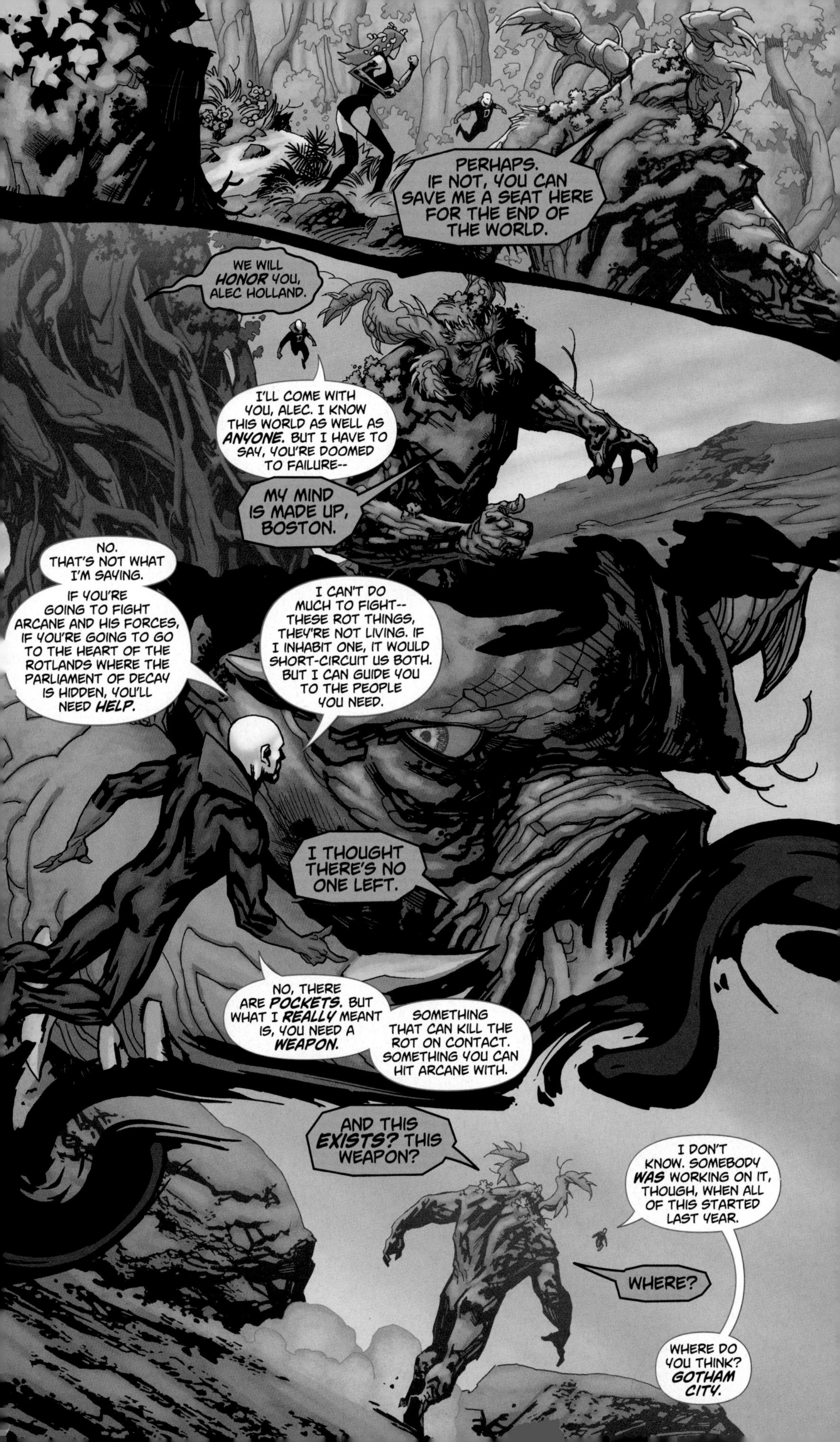
PERHAPS. IF NOT, YOU CAN SAVE ME A SEAT HERE FOR THE END OF THE WORLD.
WE WILL HONOR YOU, ALEC HOLLAND.
I'LL COME WITH YOU, ALEC. I KNOW THIS WORLD AS WELL AS ANYONE. BUT I HAVE TO SAY, YOU'RE DOOMED TO FAILURE--
MY MIND IS MADE UP, BOSTON.
NO. THAT'S NOT WHAT I'M SAYING.
IF YOU'RE GOING TO FIGHT ARCANE AND HIS FORCES, IF YOU'RE GOING TO GO TO THE HEART OF THE ROTLANDS WHERE THE PARLIAMENT OF DECAY IS HIDDEN, YOU'LL NEED HELP.
I CAN'T DO MUCH TO FIGHT-- THESE ROT THINGS, THEY'RE NOT LIVING. IF I INHABIT ONE, IT WOULD SHORT-CIRCUIT US BOTH. BUT I CAN GUIDE YOU TO THE PEOPLE YOU NEED.
I THOUGHT THERE'S NO ONE LEFT.
NO, THERE ARE POCKETS. BUT WHAT I REALLY MEANT IS, YOU NEED A WEAPON.
SOMETHING THAT CAN KILL THE ROT ON CONTACT. SOMETHING YOU CAN HIT ARCANE WITH.
AND THIS EXISTS? THIS WEAPON?
I DON'T KNOW. SOMEBODY WAS WORKING ON IT, THOUGH, WHEN ALL OF THIS STARTED LAST YEAR.
WHERE?
WHERE DO YOU THINK? GOTHAM CITY.

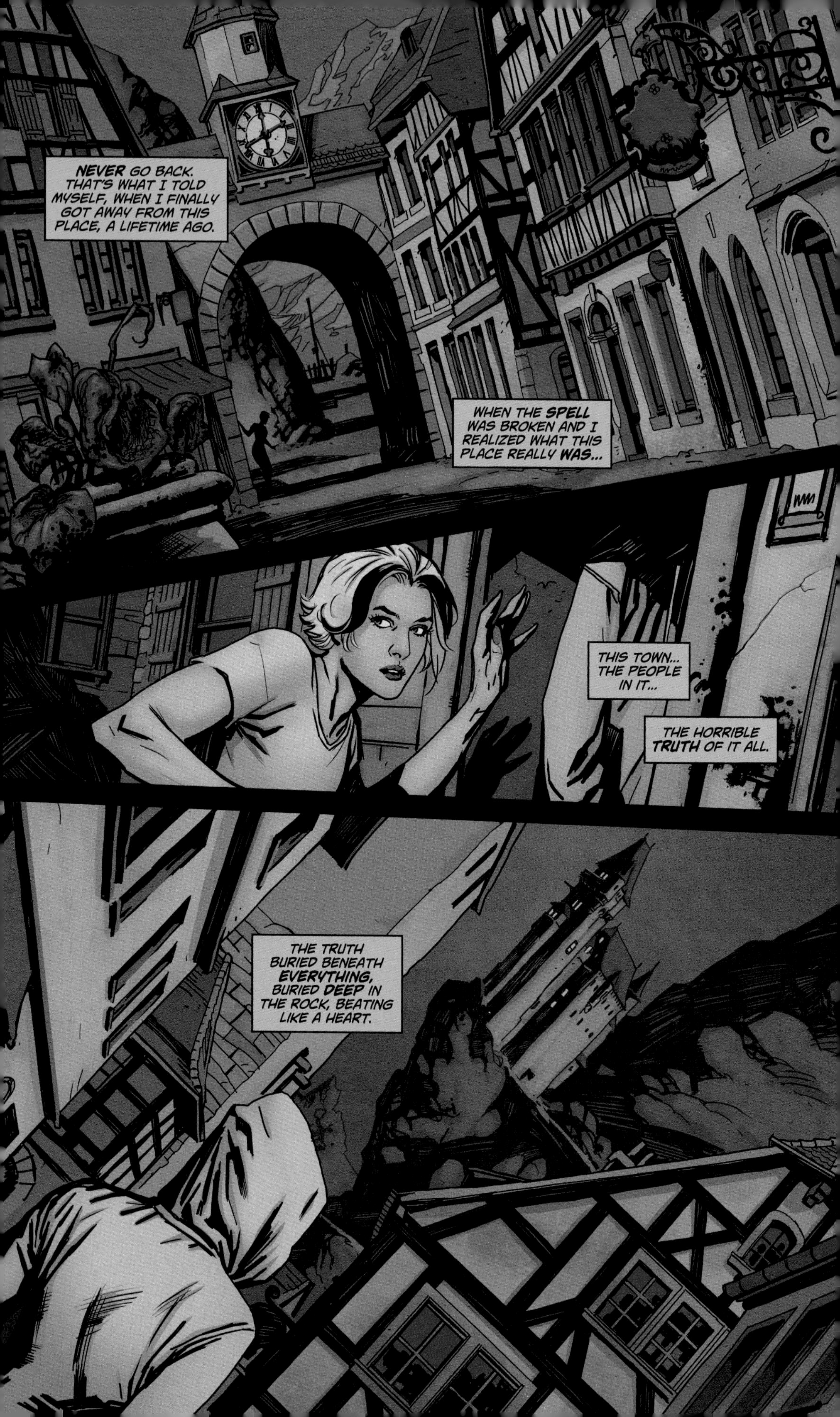
NEVER GO BACK. THAT'S WHAT I TOLD MYSELF, WHEN I FINALLY GOT AWAY FROM THIS PLACE, A LIFETIME AGO.
WHEN THE SPELL WAS BROKEN AND I REALIZED WHAT THIS PLACE REALLY WAS...
THIS TOWN... THE PEOPLE IN IT...
THE HORRIBLE TRUTH OF IT ALL.
THE TRUTH BURIED BENEATH EVERYTHING, BURIED DEEP IN THE ROCK, BEATING LIKE A HEART.

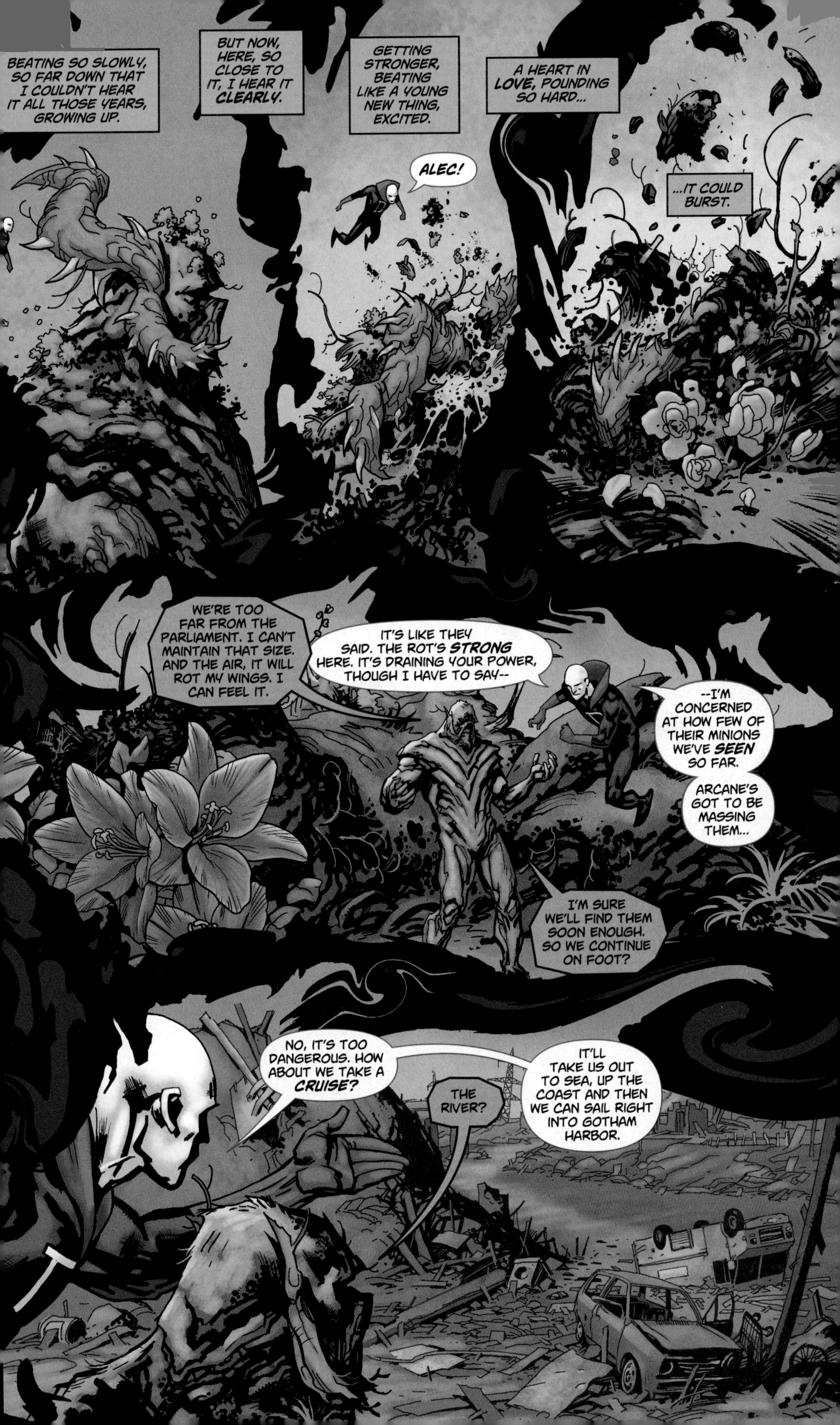
BEATING SO SLOWLY, SO FAR DOWN THAT I COULDN'T HEAR IT ALL THOSE YEARS, GROWING UP.
BUT NOW, HERE, SO CLOSE TO IT, I HEAR IT CLEARLY.
GETTING STRONGER, BEATING LIKE A YOUNG NEW THING, EXCITED.
A HEART IN LOVE, POUNDING SO HARD...
ALEC!
...IT COULD BURST.
WE'RE TOO FAR FROM THE PARLIAMENT. I CAN'T MAINTAIN THAT SIZE. AND THE AIR, IT WILL ROT MY WINGS. I CAN FEEL IT.
IT'S LIKE THEY SAID. THE ROT'S STRONG HERE. IT'S DRAINING YOUR POWER, THOUGH I HAVE TO SAY--
--I'M CONCERNED AT HOW FEW OF THEIR MINIONS WE'VE SEEN SO FAR.
ARCANE'S GOT TO BE MASSING THEM...
I'M SURE WE'LL FIND THEM SOON ENOUGH. SO WE CONTINUE ON FOOT?
NO, IT'S TOO DANGEROUS. HOW ABOUT WE TAKE A CRUISE?
THE RIVER?
IT'LL TAKE US OUT TO SEA, UP THE COAST AND THEN WE CAN SAIL RIGHT INTO GOTHAM HARBOR.

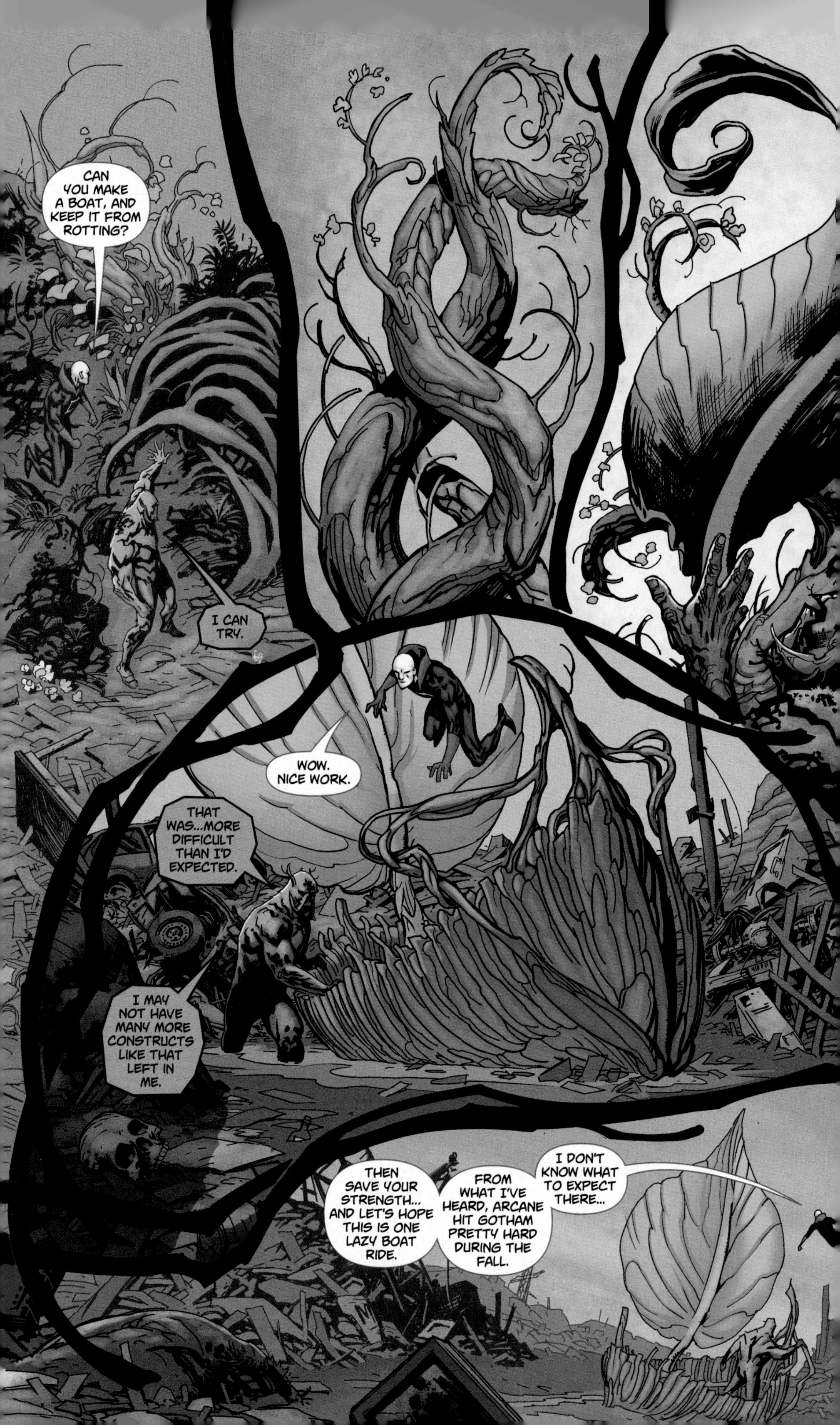
CAN YOU MAKE A BOAT, AND KEEP IT FROM ROTTING?
I CAN TRY.
WOW. NICE WORK.
THAT WAS...MORE DIFFICULT THAN I'D EXPECTED.
I MAY NOT HAVE MANY MORE CONSTRUCTS LIKE THAT LEFT IN ME.
THEN SAVE YOUR STRENGTH... AND LET'S HOPE THIS IS ONE LAZY BOAT RIDE.
FROM WHAT I'VE HEARD, ARCANE HIT GOTHAM PRETTY HARD DURING THE FALL.
I DON'T KNOW WHAT TO EXPECT THERE...

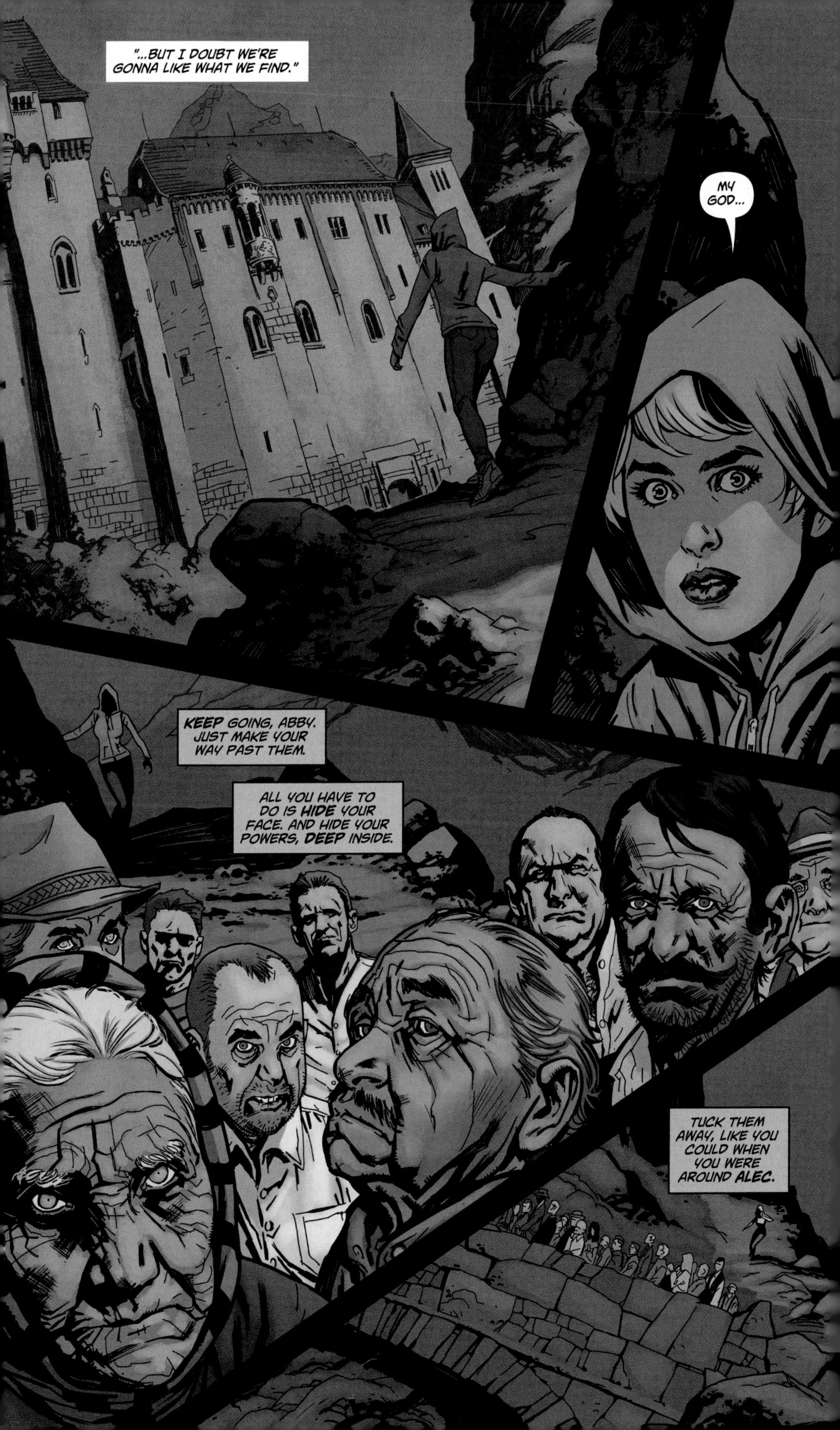
"...BUT I DOUBT WE'RE GONNA LIKE WHAT WE FIND."
MY GOD...
KEEP GOING, ABBY. JUST MAKE YOUR WAY PAST THEM.
ALL YOU HAVE TO DO IS HIDE YOUR FACE. AND HIDE YOUR POWERS, DEEP INSIDE.
TUCK THEM AWAY, LIKE YOU COULD WHEN YOU WERE AROUND ALEC.

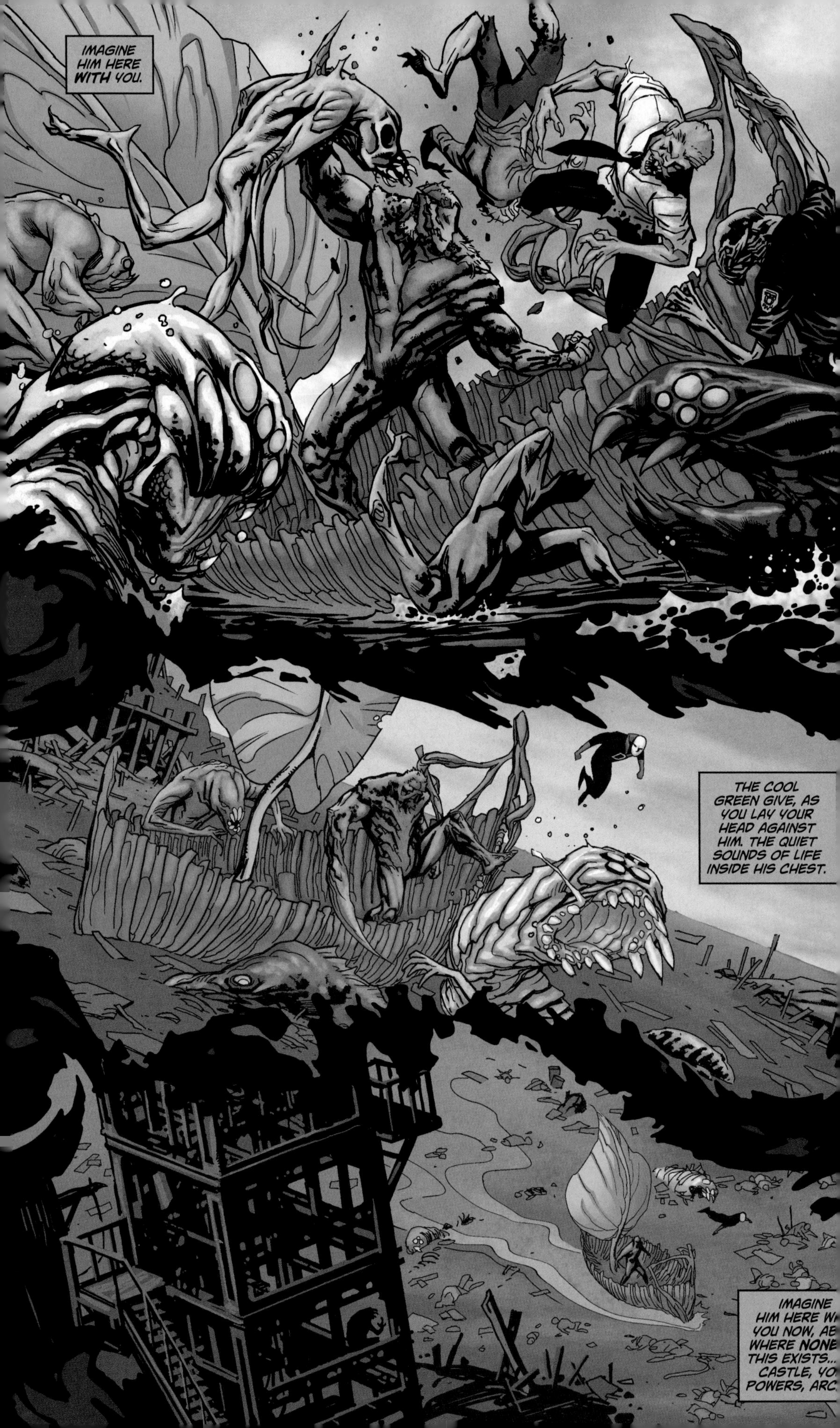
IMAGINE HIM HERE WITH YOU.
THE COOL GREEN GIVE, AS YOU LAY YOUR HEAD AGAINST HIM. THE QUIET SOUNDS OF LIFE INSIDE HIS CHEST.
IMAGINE HIM HERE W YOU NOW, AB WHERE NONE THIS EXISTS... CASTLE, YO POWERS, ARC

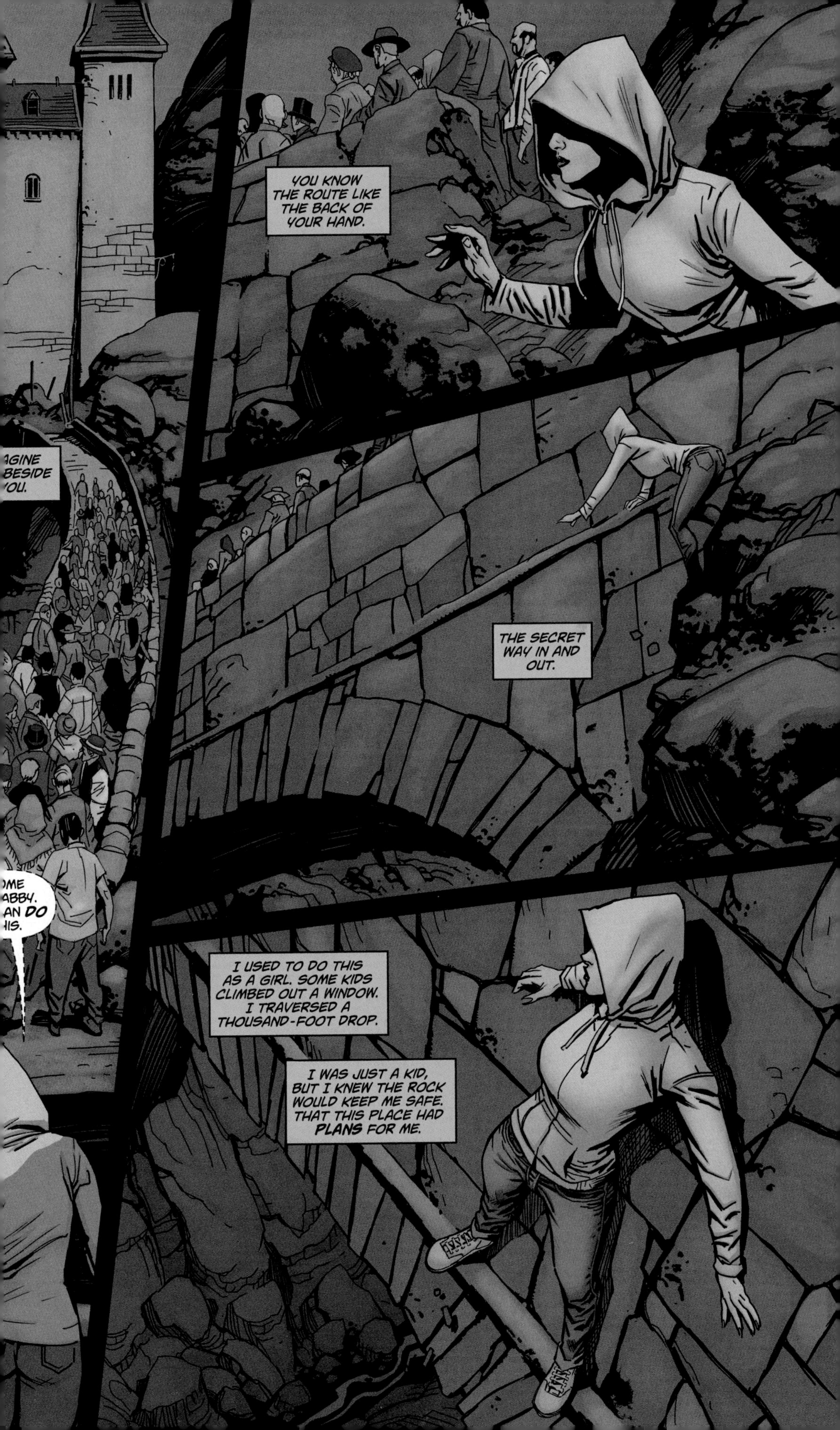
AGINE
BESIDE
YOU.
YOU KNOW THE ROUTE LIKE THE BACK OF YOUR HAND.
THE SECRET WAY IN AND OUT.
OME
ABBY.
AN DO
HIS.
I USED TO DO THIS AS A GIRL. SOME KIDS CLIMBED OUT A WINDOW. I TRAVERSED A THOUSAND-FOOT DROP.
I WAS JUST A KID, BUT I KNEW THE ROCK WOULD KEEP ME SAFE. THAT THIS PLACE HAD PLANS FOR ME.

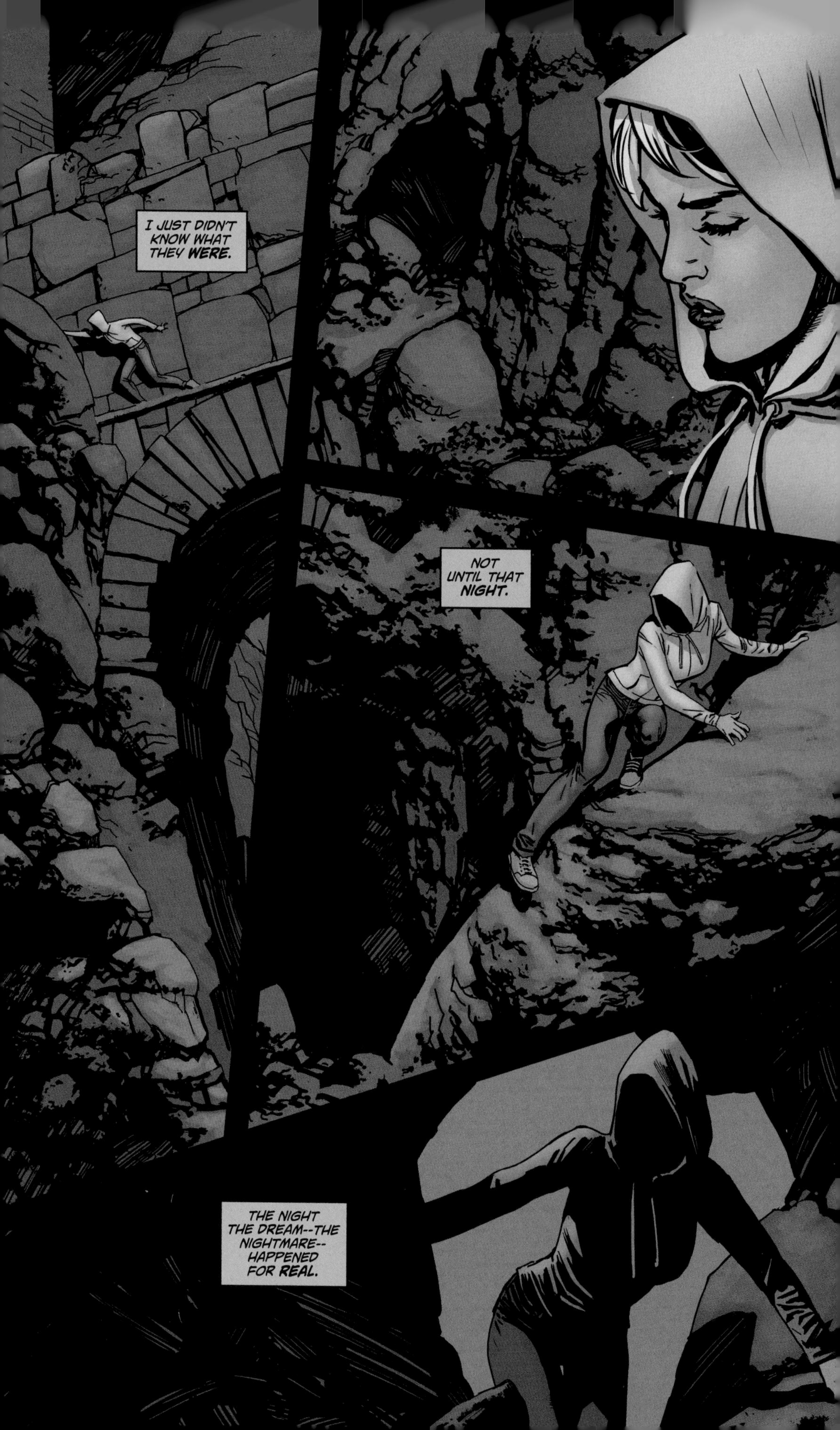
I JUST DIDN'T KNOW WHAT THEY WERE.
NOT UNTIL THAT NIGHT.
THE NIGHT THE DREAM--THE NIGHTMARE--HAPPENED FOR REAL.

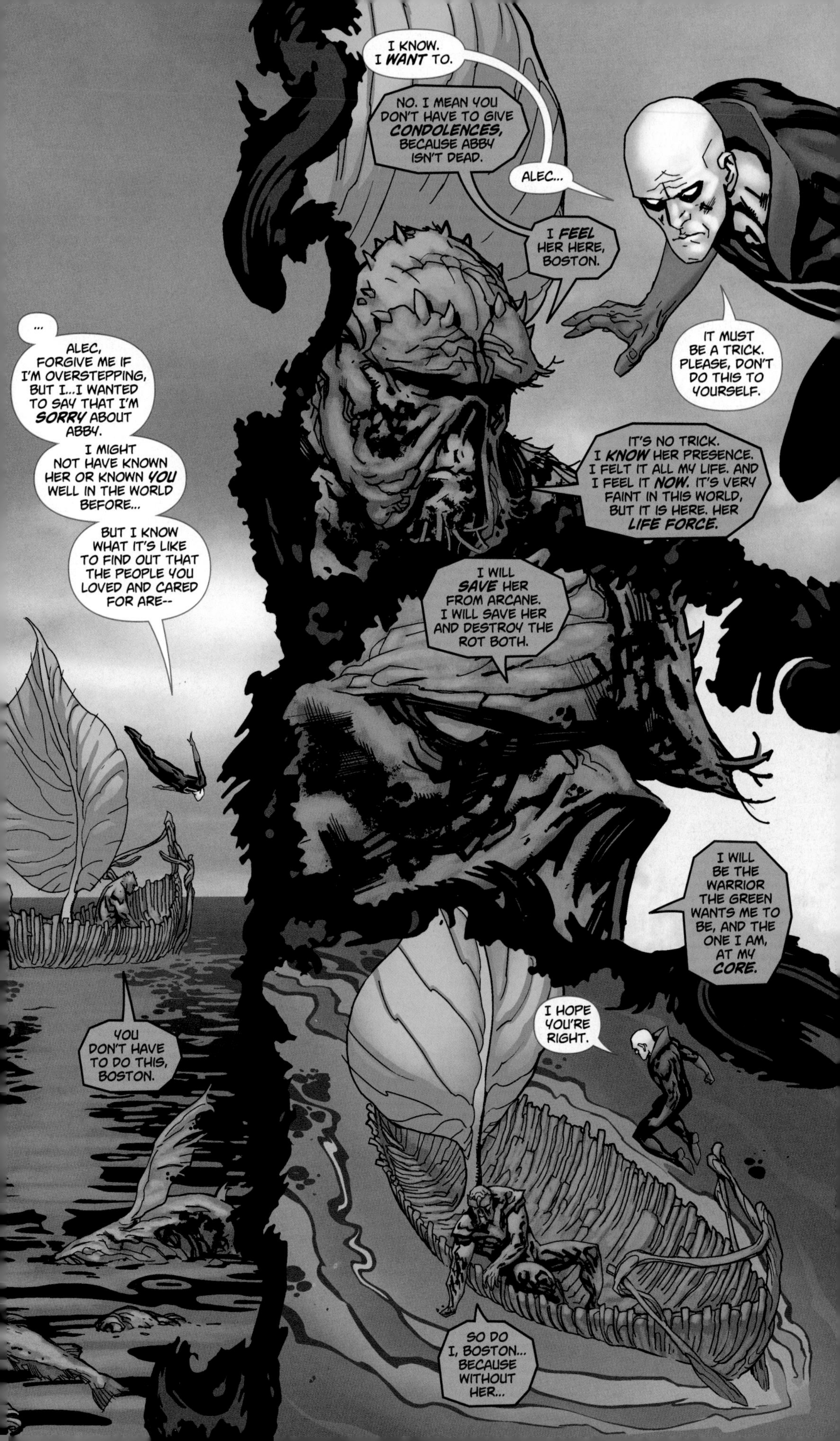
...
ALEC, FORGIVE ME IF I'M OVERSTEPPING, BUT I...I WANTED TO SAY THAT I'M SORRY ABOUT ABBY.
I MIGHT NOT HAVE KNOWN HER OR KNOWN YOU WELL IN THE WORLD BEFORE...
BUT I KNOW WHAT IT'S LIKE TO FIND OUT THAT THE PEOPLE YOU LOVED AND CARED FOR ARE--
I KNOW. I WANT TO.
NO. I MEAN YOU DON'T HAVE TO GIVE CONDOLENCES, BECAUSE ABBY ISN'T DEAD.
ALEC...
I FEEL HER HERE, BOSTON.
IT MUST BE A TRICK. PLEASE, DON'T DO THIS TO YOURSELF.
IT'S NO TRICK. I KNOW HER PRESENCE. I FELT IT ALL MY LIFE. AND I FEEL IT NOW. IT'S VERY FAINT IN THIS WORLD, BUT IT IS HERE. HER LIFE FORCE.
I WILL SAVE HER FROM ARCANE. I WILL SAVE HER AND DESTROY THE ROT BOTH.
I WILL BE THE WARRIOR THE GREEN WANTS ME TO BE, AND THE ONE I AM, AT MY CORE.
YOU DON'T HAVE TO DO THIS, BOSTON.
I HOPE YOU'RE RIGHT.
SO DO I, BOSTON... BECAUSE WITHOUT HER...

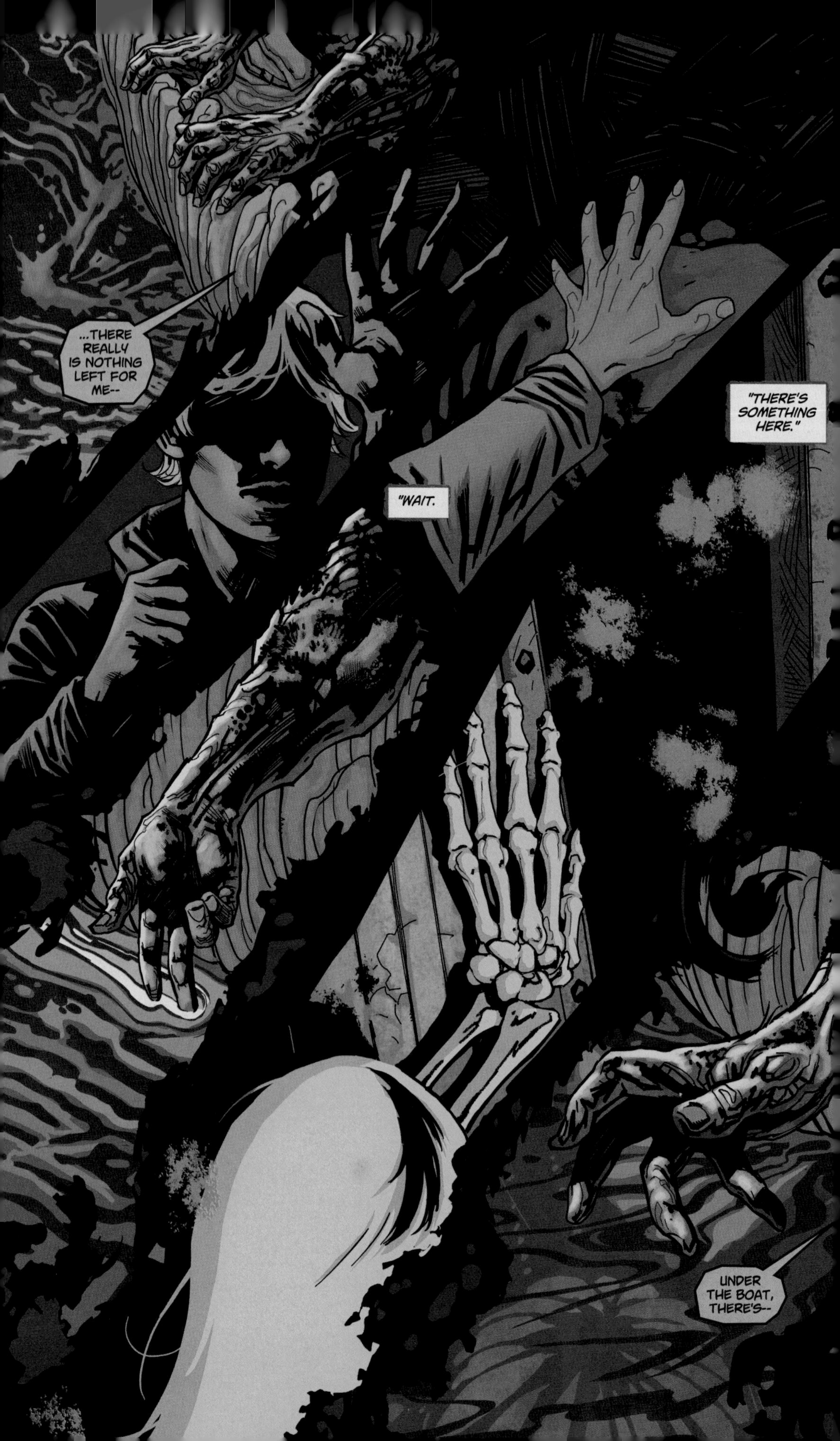
...THERE REALLY IS NOTHING LEFT FOR ME--
"WAIT.
"THERE'S SOMETHING HERE."
UNDER THE BOAT, THERE'S--

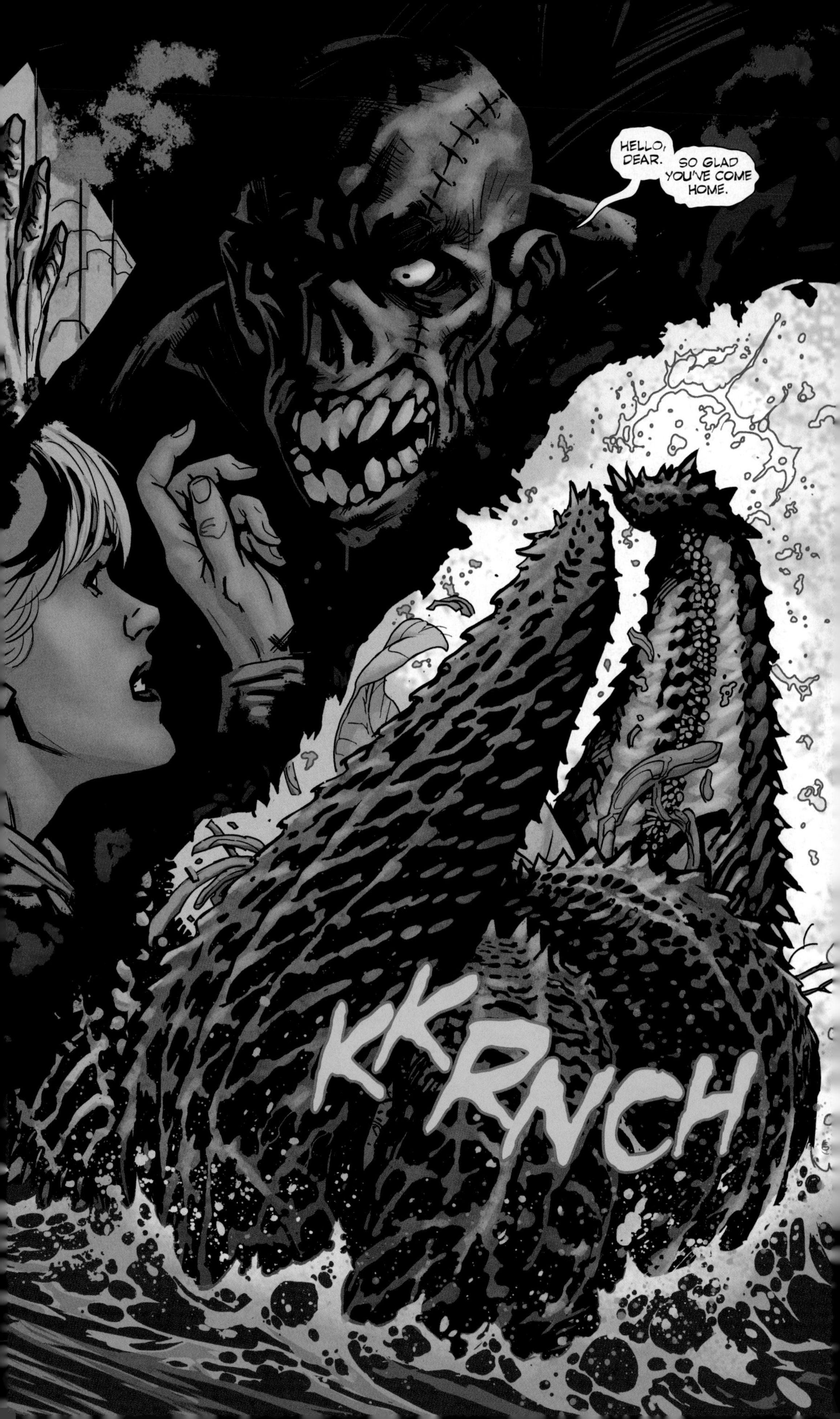
HELLO, DEAR.
SO GLAD YOU'VE COME HOME.
KKRNCH

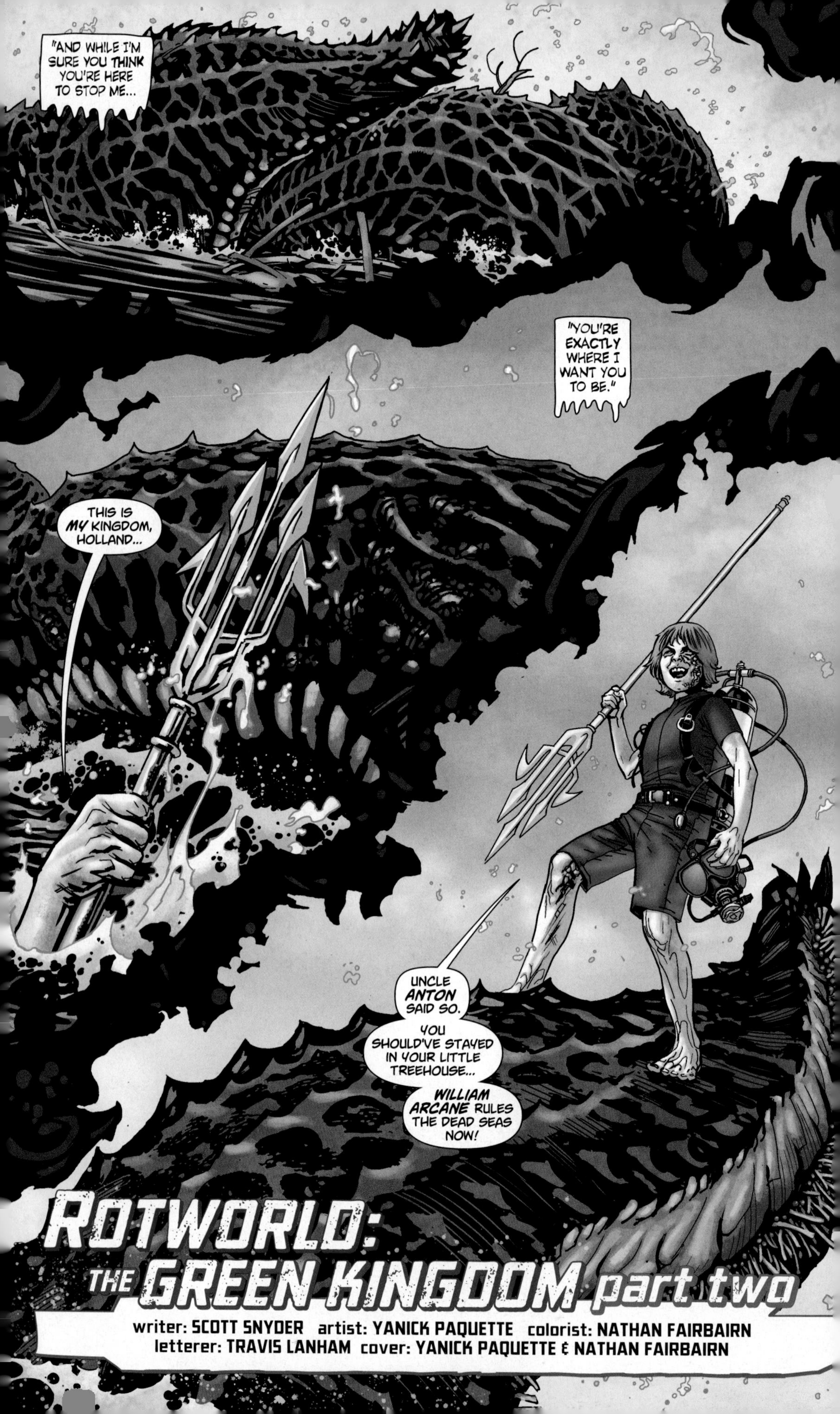
"AND WHILE I'M SURE YOU THINK YOU'RE HERE TO STOP ME...
"YOU'RE EXACTLY WHERE I WANT YOU TO BE."
THIS IS MY KINGDOM, HOLLAND...
UNCLE ANTON SAID SO.
YOU SHOULD'VE STAYED IN YOUR LITTLE TREEHOUSE...
WILLIAM ARCANE RULES THE DEAD SEAS NOW!
ROTWORLD: THE GREEN KINGDOM part two
writer: SCOTT SNYDER artist: YANICK PAQUETTE colorist: NATHAN FAIRBAIRN
letterer: TRAVIS LANHAM cover: YANICK PAQUETTE & NATHAN FAIRBAIRN

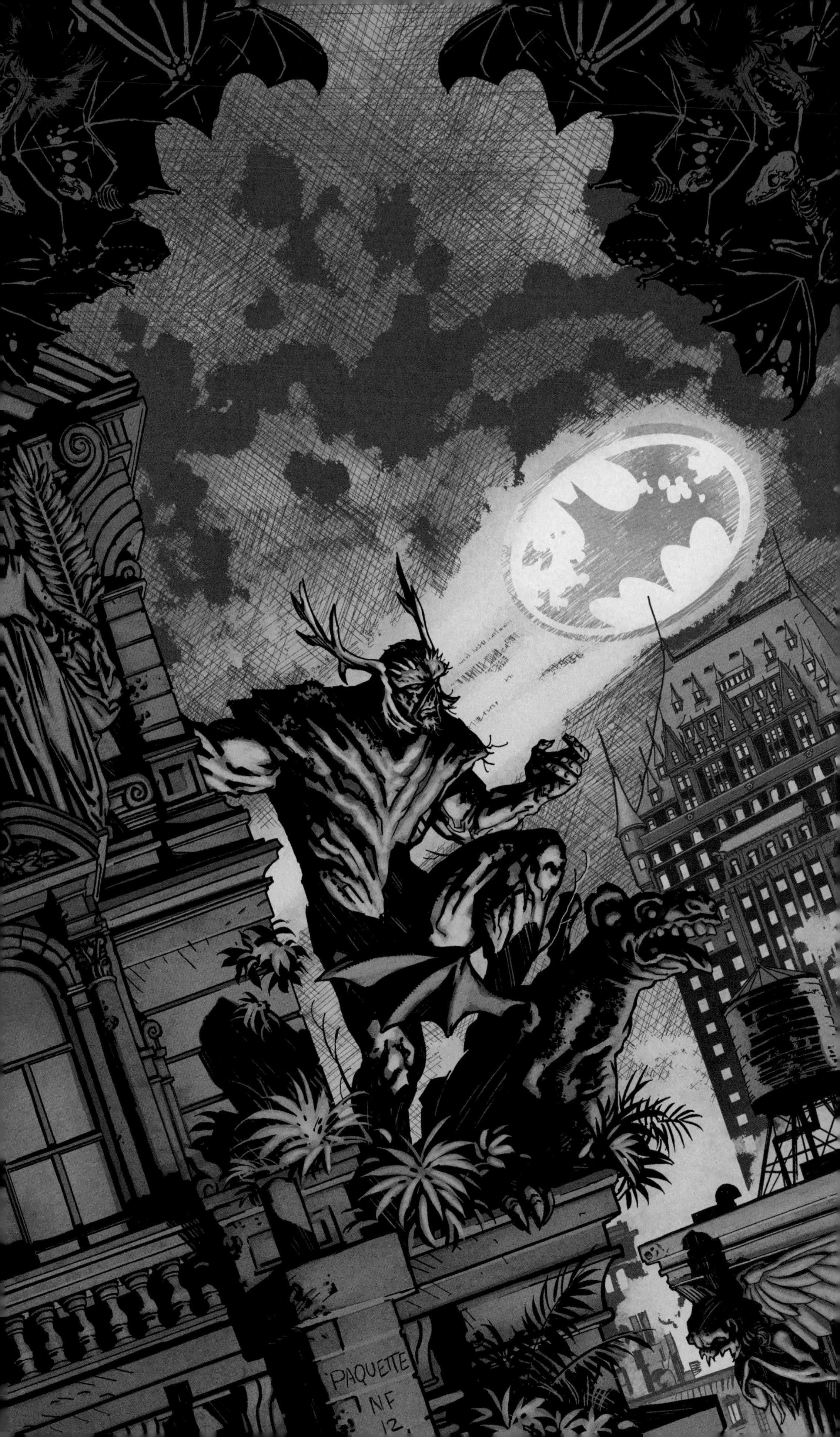
PAQUETTE
NF
12.

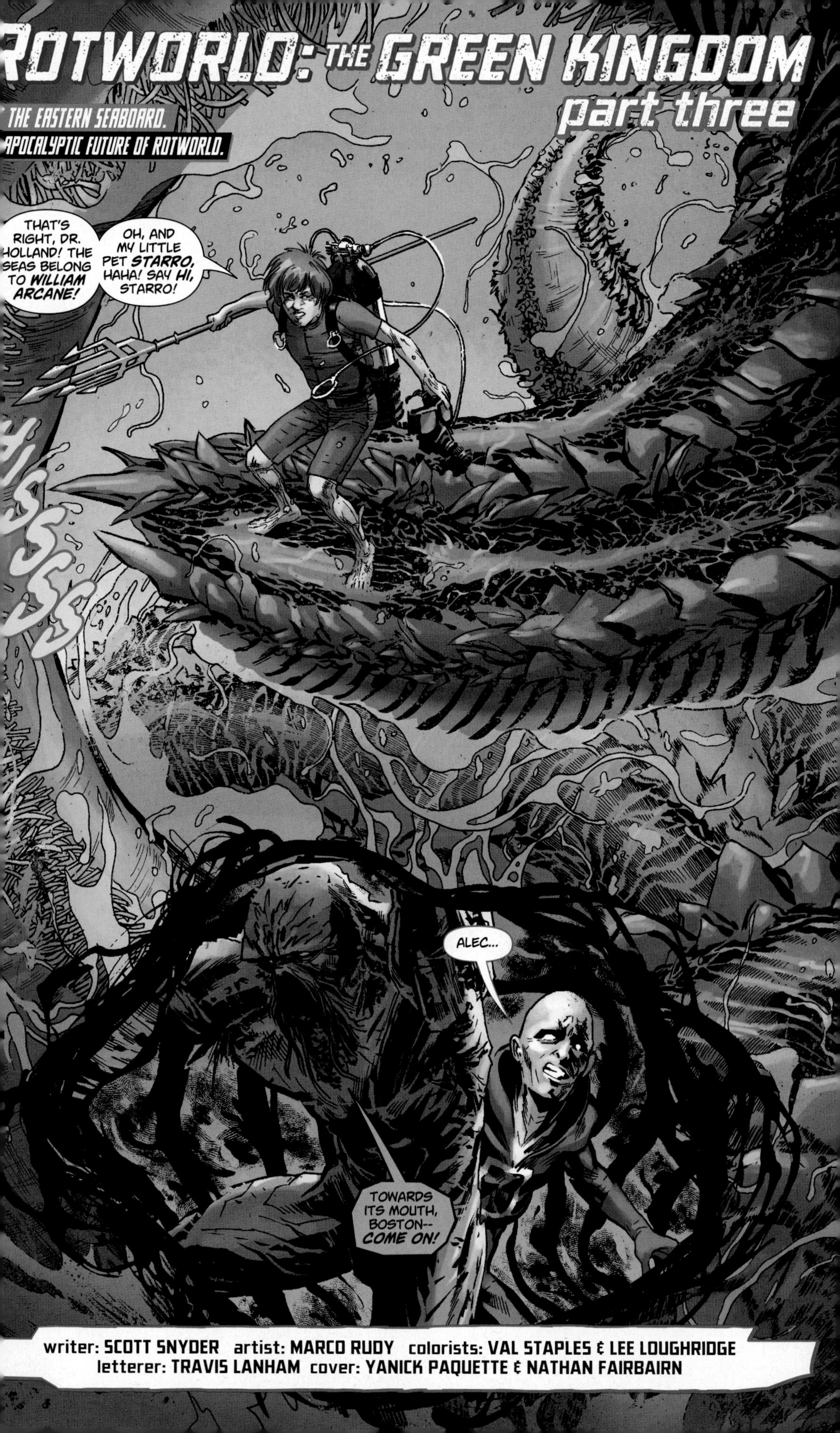
ROTWORLD: THE GREEN KINGDOM
part three
THE EASTERN SEABOARD.
APOCALYPTIC FUTURE OF ROTWORLD.
THAT'S RIGHT, DR. HOLLAND! THE SEAS BELONG TO WILLIAM ARCANE!
OH, AND MY LITTLE PET STARRO, HAHA! SAY HI, STARRO!
HISSSSS
ALEC...
TOWARDS ITS MOUTH, BOSTON-- COME ON!
writer: SCOTT SNYDER artist: MARCO RUDY colorists: VAL STAPLES & LEE LOUGHRIDGE
letterer: TRAVIS LANHAM cover: YANICK PAQUETTE & NATHAN FAIRBAIRN

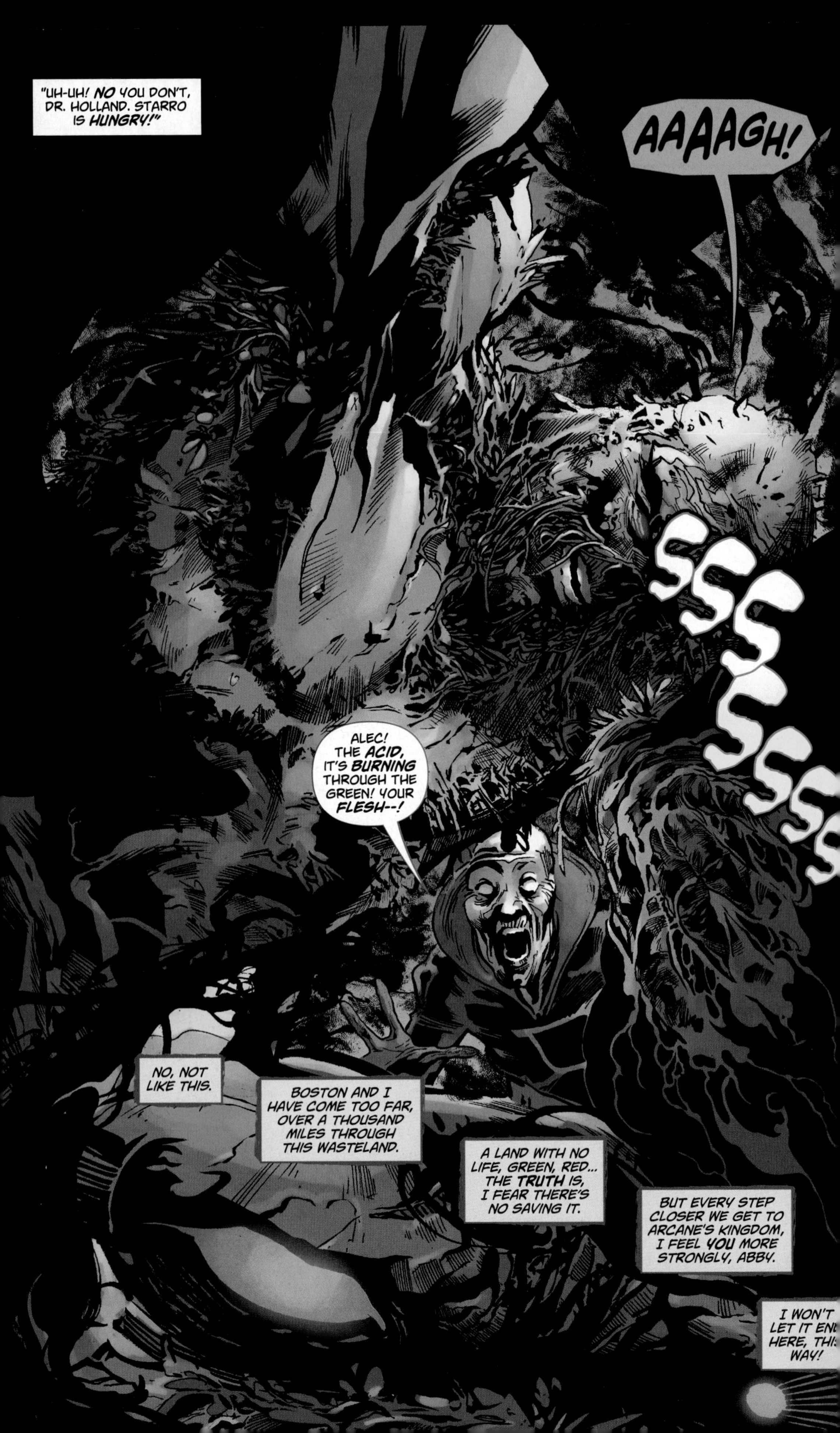
"UH-UH! NO YOU DON'T, DR. HOLLAND. STARRO IS HUNGRY!"
AAAAGH!
SSSSSSSS
ALEC! THE ACID, IT'S BURNING THROUGH THE GREEN! YOUR FLESH--!
NO, NOT LIKE THIS.
BOSTON AND I HAVE COME TOO FAR, OVER A THOUSAND MILES THROUGH THIS WASTELAND.
A LAND WITH NO LIFE, GREEN, RED... THE TRUTH IS, I FEAR THERE'S NO SAVING IT.
BUT EVERY STEP CLOSER WE GET TO ARCANE'S KINGDOM, I FEEL YOU MORE STRONGLY, ABBY.
I WON'T LET IT END HERE, THIS WAY!

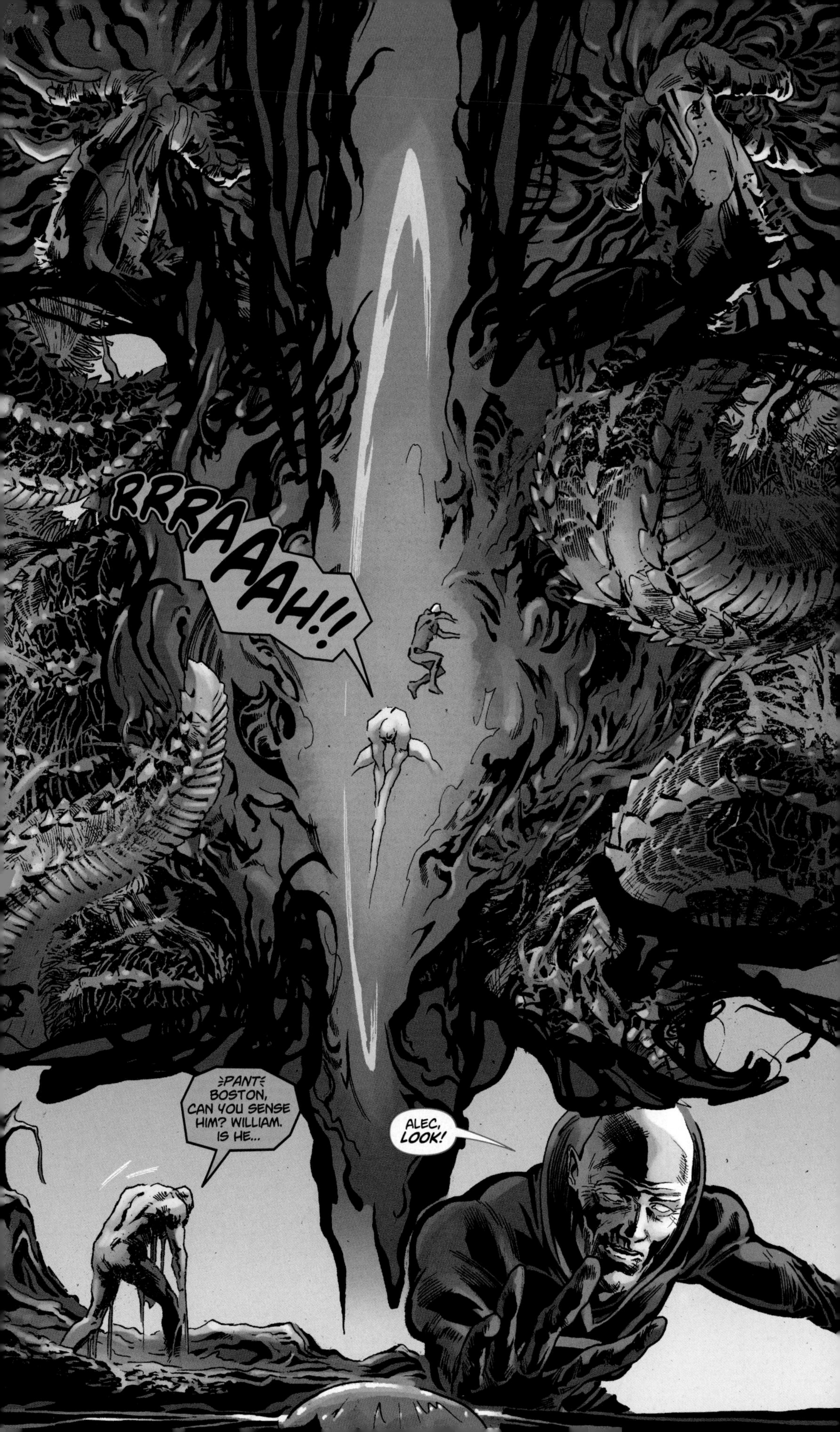
RRRAAAAH!!
≈PANT≈ BOSTON, CAN YOU SENSE HIM? WILLIAM. IS HE...
ALEC, LOOK!

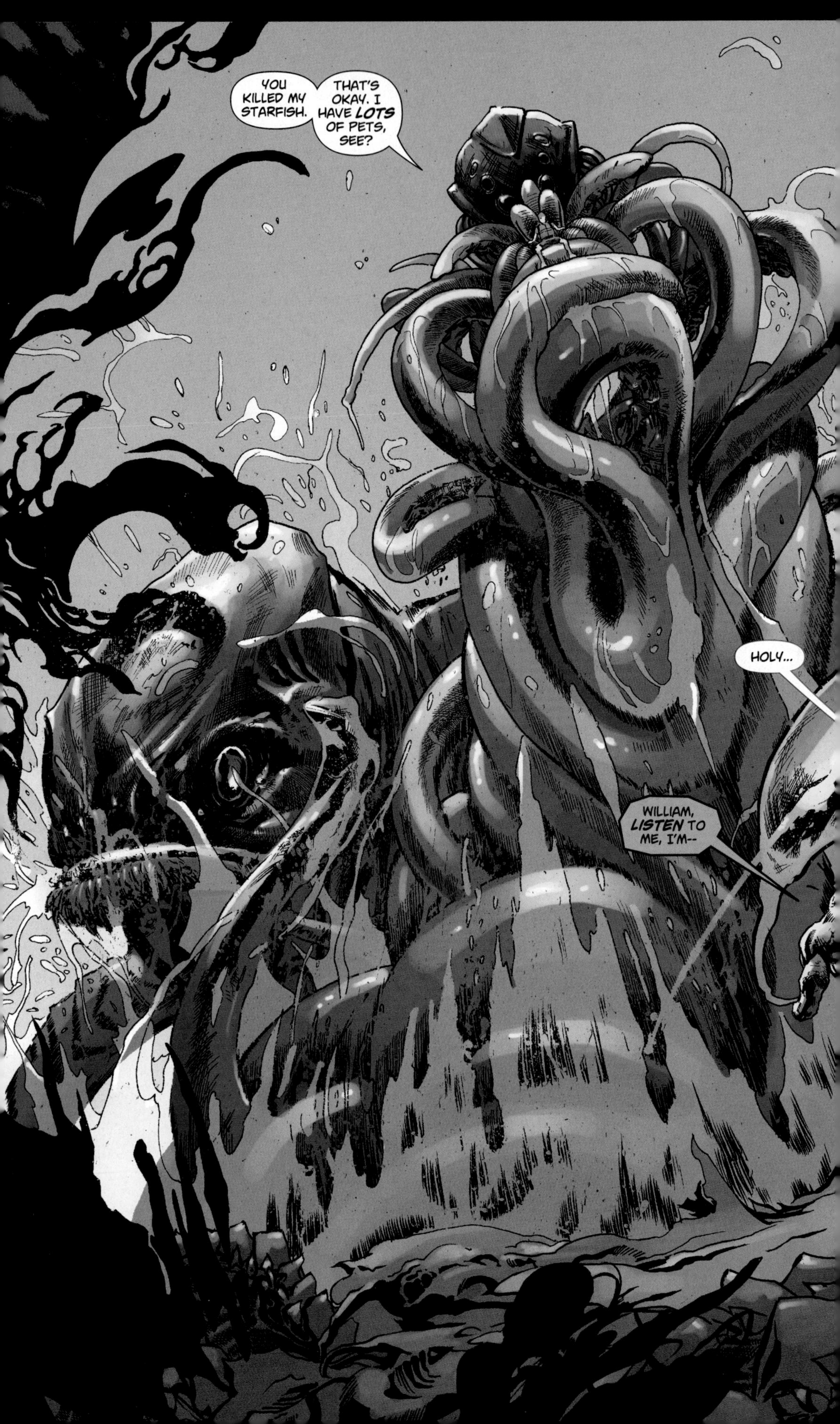
YOU KILLED MY STARFISH.
THAT'S OKAY. I HAVE LOTS OF PETS, SEE?
HOLY...
WILLIAM, LISTEN TO ME, I'M--

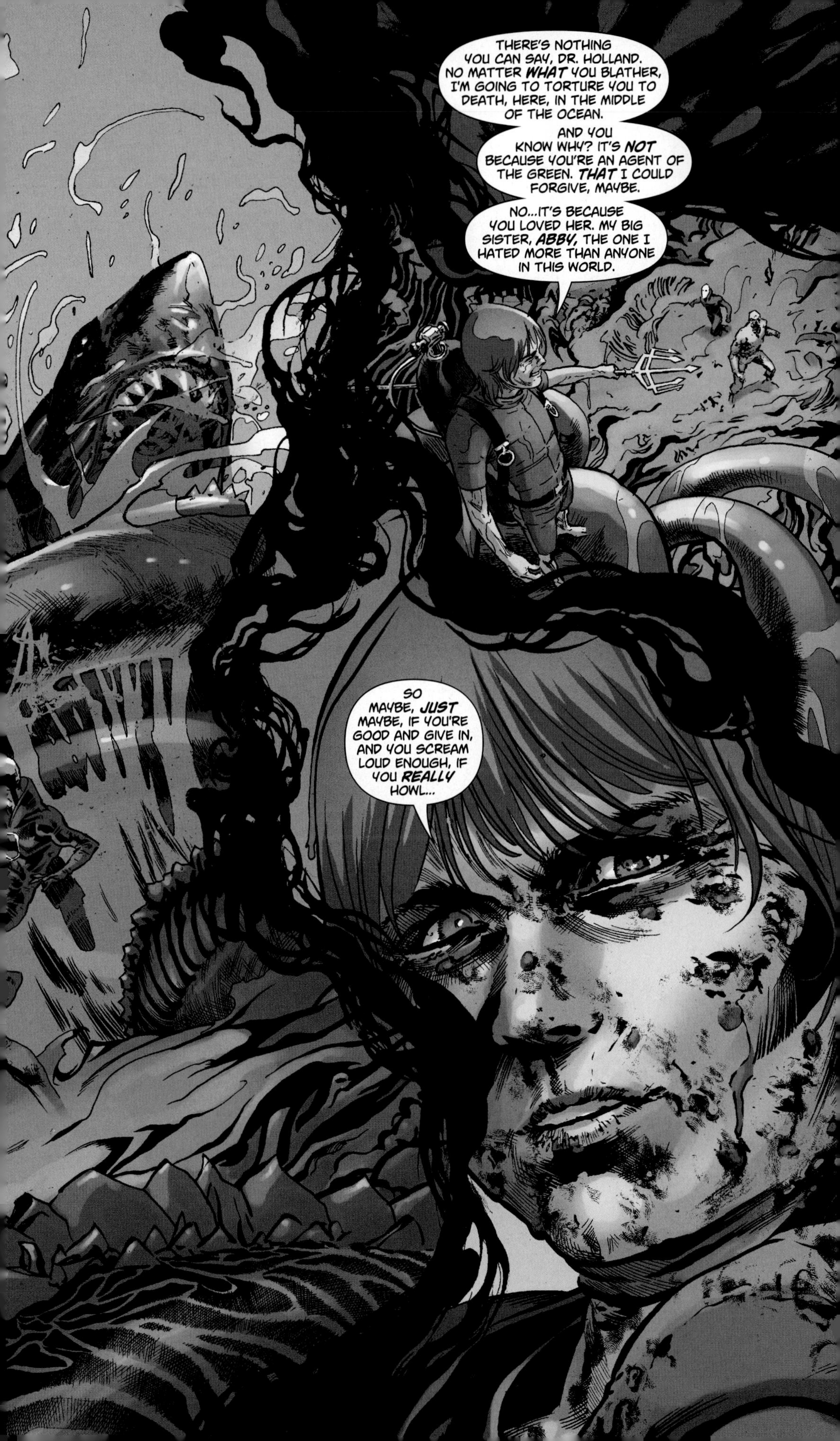
THERE'S NOTHING YOU CAN SAY, DR. HOLLAND. NO MATTER WHAT YOU BLATHER, I'M GOING TO TORTURE YOU TO DEATH, HERE, IN THE MIDDLE OF THE OCEAN.
AND YOU KNOW WHY? IT'S NOT BECAUSE YOU'RE AN AGENT OF THE GREEN. THAT I COULD FORGIVE, MAYBE.
NO...IT'S BECAUSE YOU LOVED HER. MY BIG SISTER, ABBY, THE ONE I HATED MORE THAN ANYONE IN THIS WORLD.
SO MAYBE, JUST MAYBE, IF YOU'RE GOOD AND GIVE IN, AND YOU SCREAM LOUD ENOUGH, IF YOU REALLY HOWL...

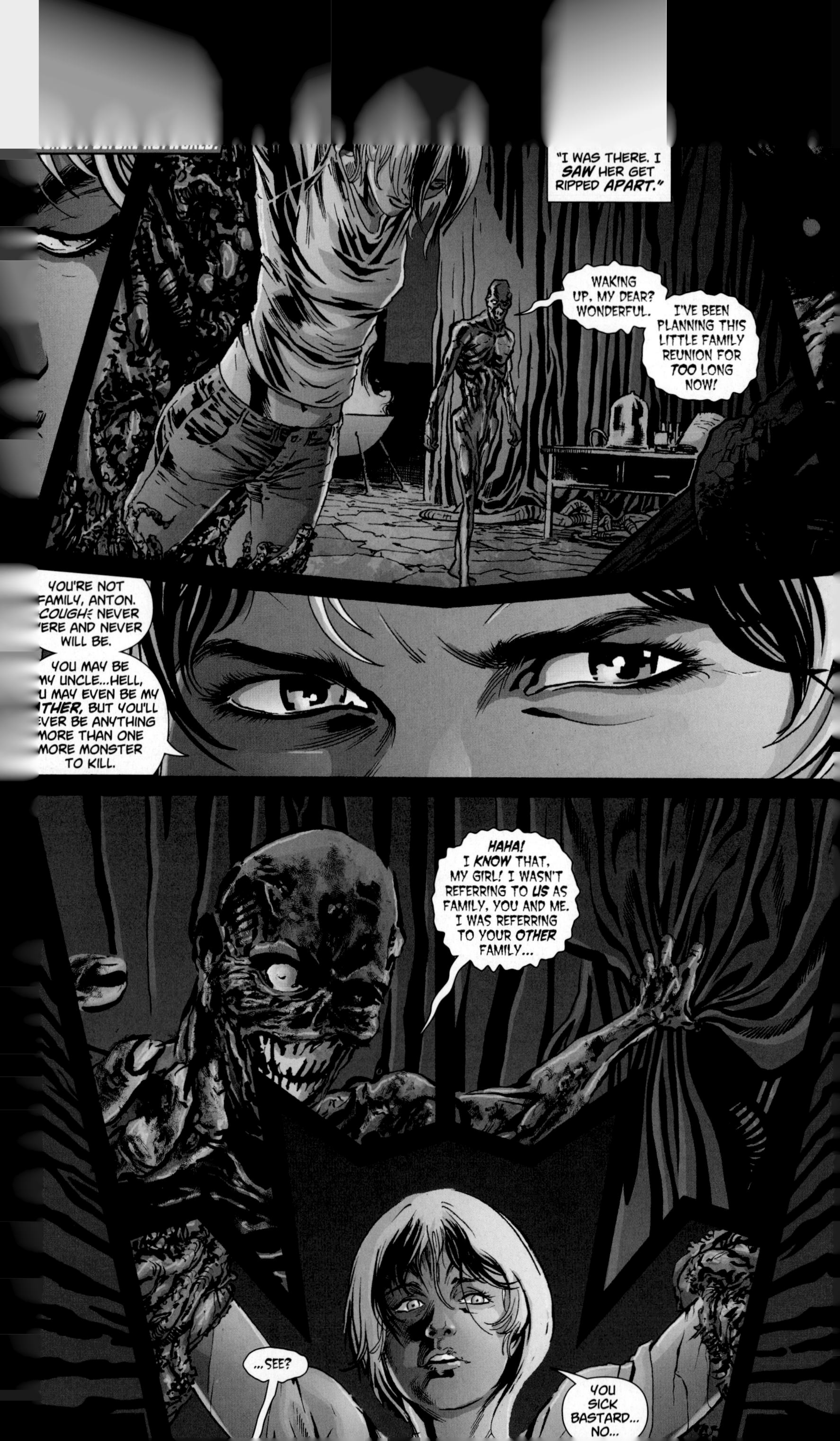
"I WAS THERE. I SAW HER GET RIPPED APART."
WAKING UP, MY DEAR? WONDERFUL.
I'VE BEEN PLANNING THIS LITTLE FAMILY REUNION FOR TOO LONG NOW!
YOU'RE NOT FAMILY, ANTON. COUGH NEVER WERE AND NEVER WILL BE.
YOU MAY BE MY UNCLE...HELL, YOU MAY EVEN BE MY FATHER, BUT YOU'LL NEVER BE ANYTHING MORE THAN ONE MORE MONSTER TO KILL.
HAHA! I KNOW THAT, MY GIRL! I WASN'T REFERRING TO US AS FAMILY, YOU AND ME. I WAS REFERRING TO YOUR OTHER FAMILY...
...SEE?
YOU SICK BASTARD... NO...

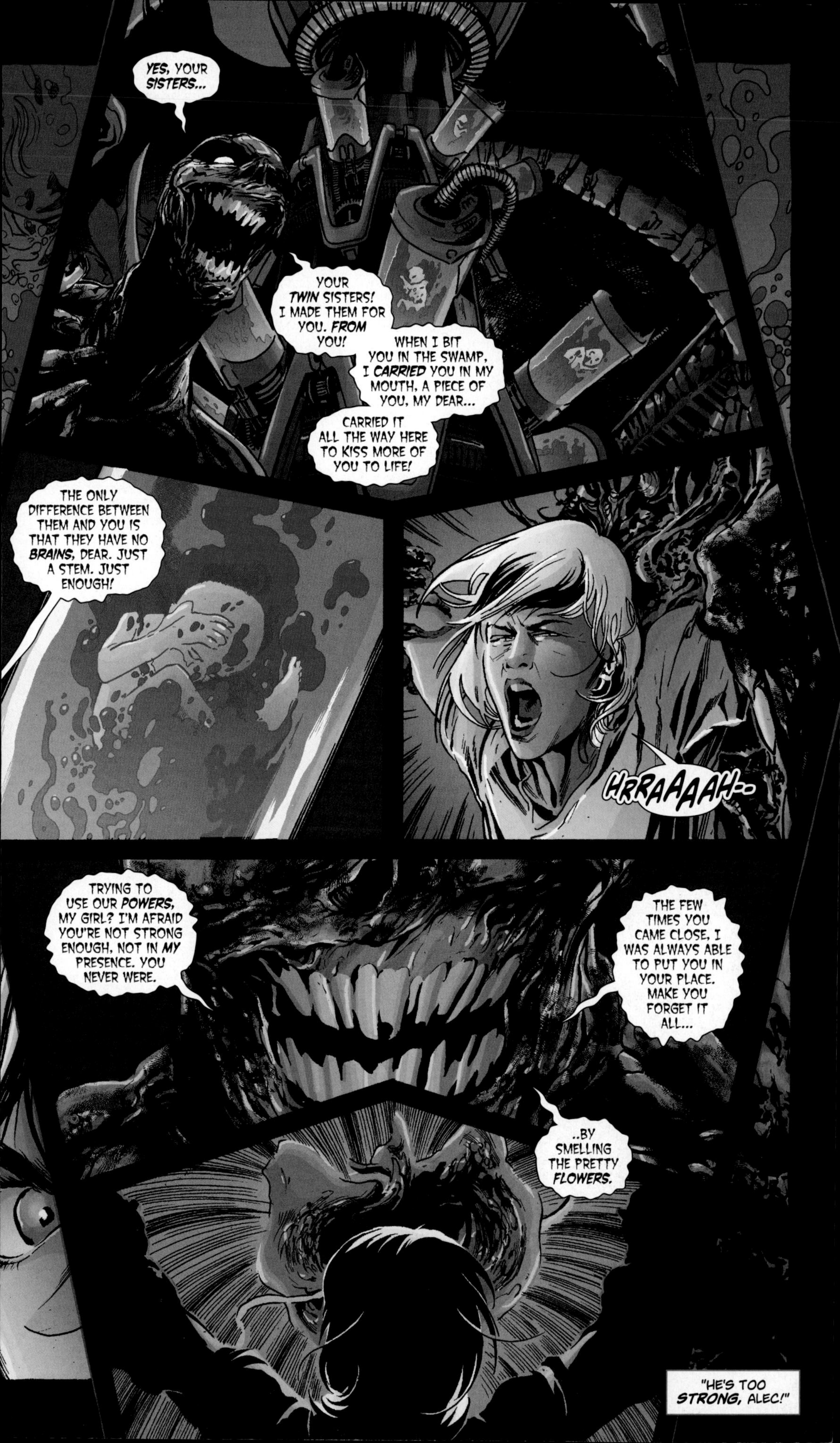
YES, YOUR SISTERS...
YOUR TWIN SISTERS! I MADE THEM FOR YOU. FROM YOU!
WHEN I BIT YOU IN THE SWAMP, I CARRIED YOU IN MY MOUTH, A PIECE OF YOU, MY DEAR...
CARRIED IT ALL THE WAY HERE TO KISS MORE OF YOU TO LIFE!
THE ONLY DIFFERENCE BETWEEN THEM AND YOU IS THAT THEY HAVE NO BRAINS, DEAR. JUST A STEM. JUST ENOUGH!
HRRAAAAH--
TRYING TO USE OUR POWERS, MY GIRL? I'M AFRAID YOU'RE NOT STRONG ENOUGH, NOT IN MY PRESENCE. YOU NEVER WERE.
THE FEW TIMES YOU CAME CLOSE, I WAS ALWAYS ABLE TO PUT YOU IN YOUR PLACE. MAKE YOU FORGET IT ALL...
..BY SMELLING THE PRETTY FLOWERS.
"HE'S TOO STRONG, ALEC!"

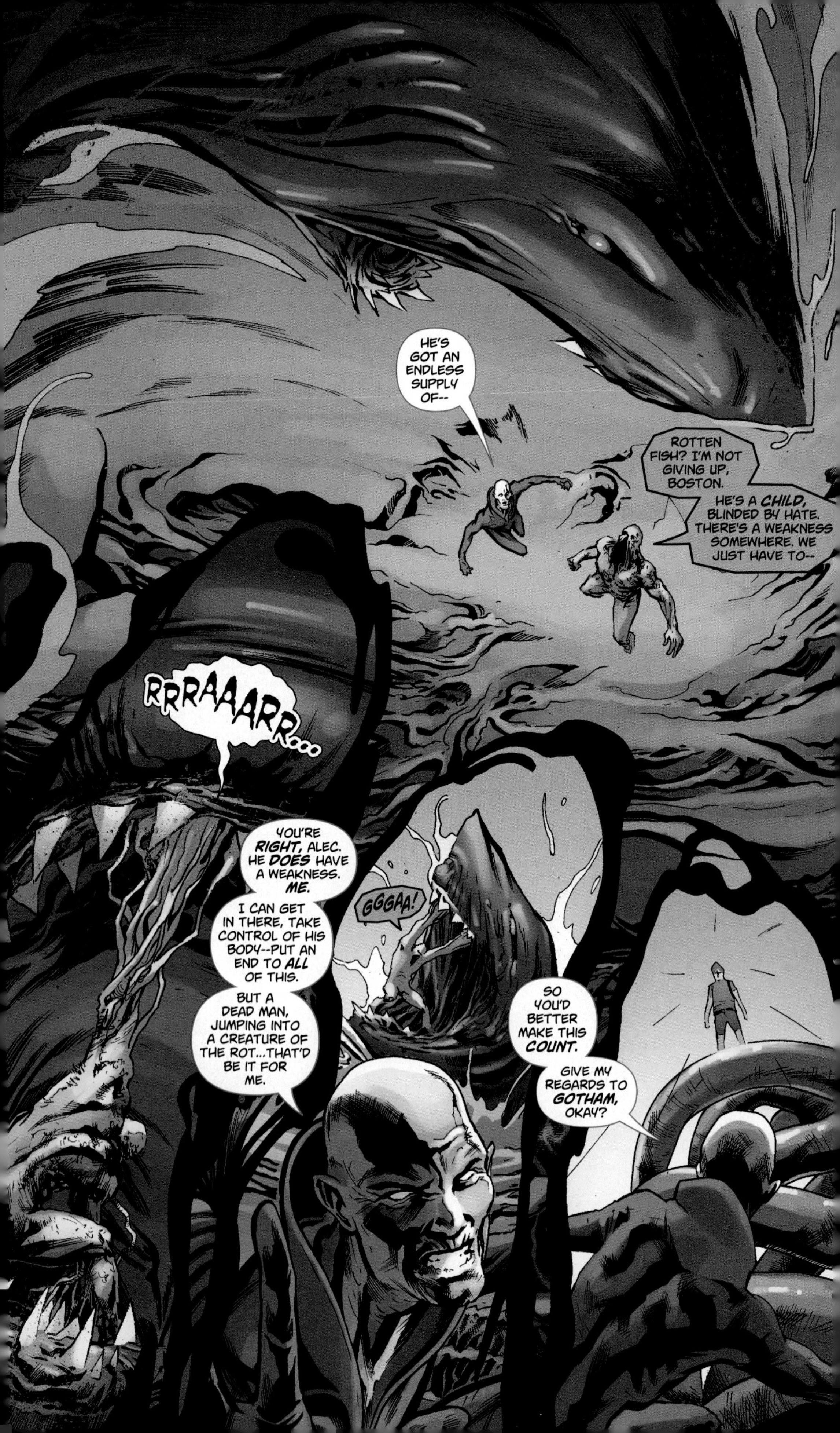
HE'S GOT AN ENDLESS SUPPLY OF--
ROTTEN FISH? I'M NOT GIVING UP, BOSTON.
HE'S A CHILD, BLINDED BY HATE. THERE'S A WEAKNESS SOMEWHERE. WE JUST HAVE TO--
RRRAAAARR...
GGGAA!
YOU'RE RIGHT, ALEC. HE DOES HAVE A WEAKNESS. ME.
I CAN GET IN THERE, TAKE CONTROL OF HIS BODY--PUT AN END TO ALL OF THIS.
BUT A DEAD MAN, JUMPING INTO A CREATURE OF THE ROT...THAT'D BE IT FOR ME.
SO YOU'D BETTER MAKE THIS COUNT.
GIVE MY REGARDS TO GOTHAM, OKAY?

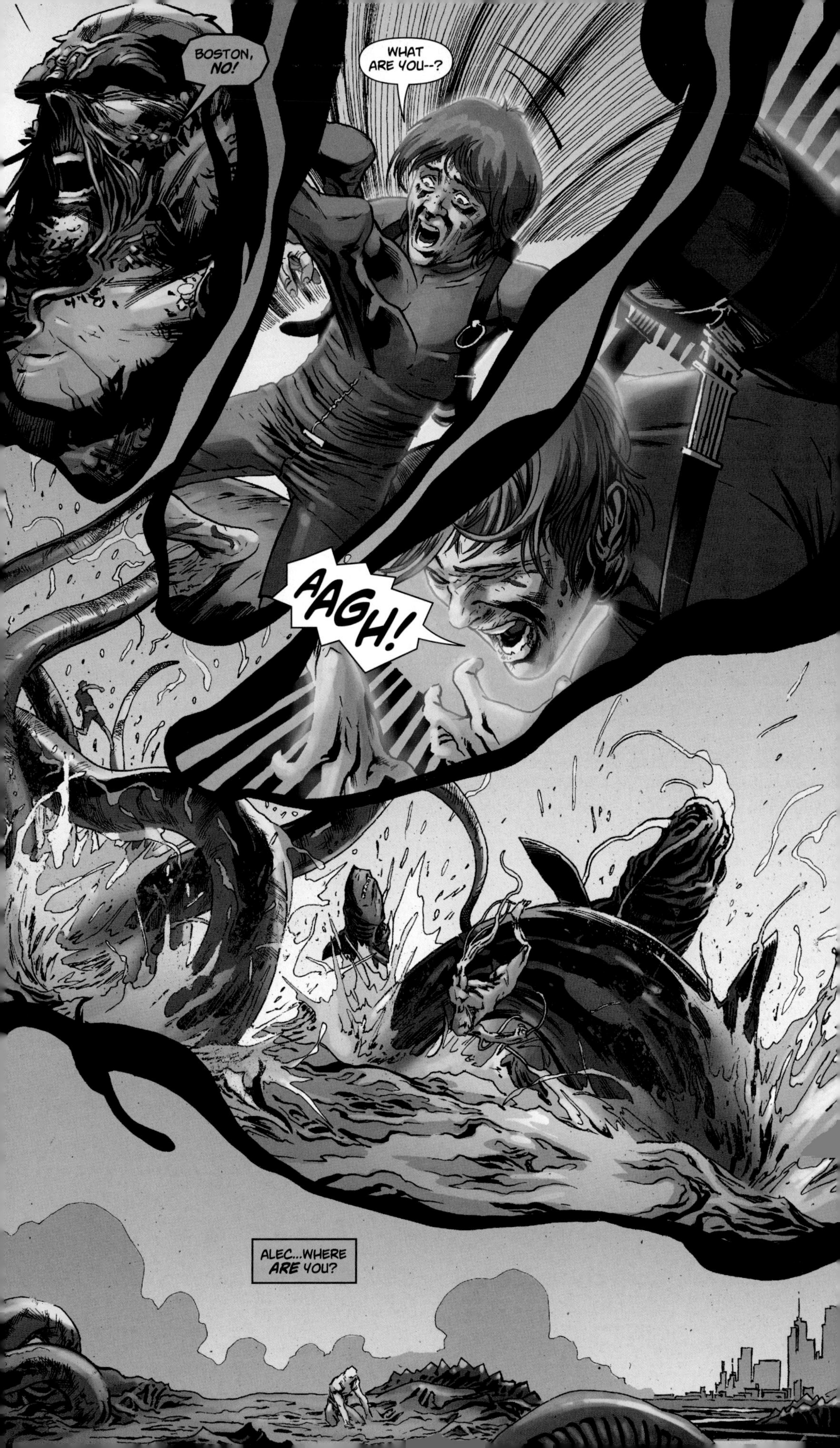
BOSTON, NO!
WHAT ARE YOU--?
AAGH!
ALEC...WHERE ARE YOU?

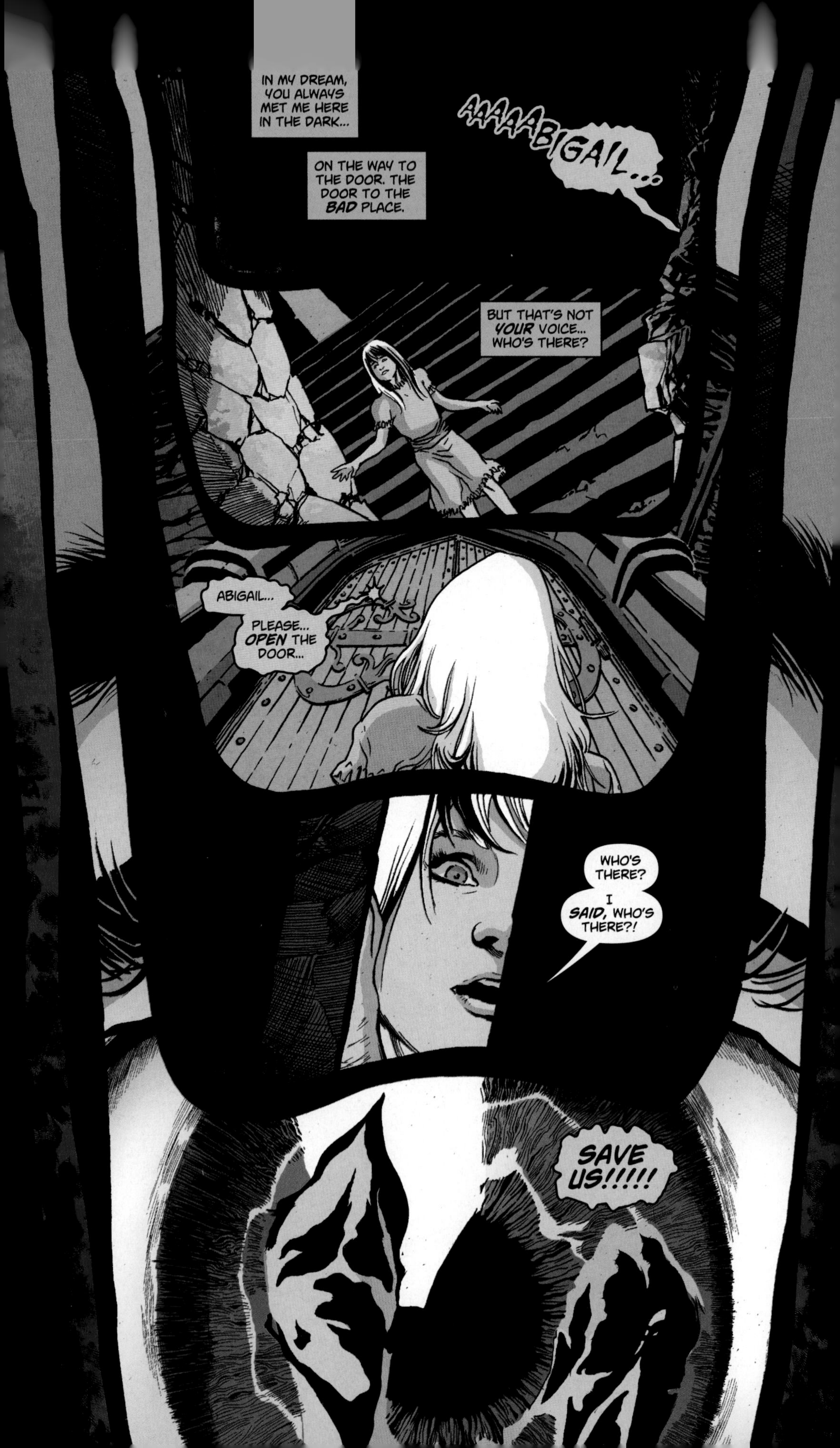
IN MY DREAM, YOU ALWAYS MET ME HERE IN THE DARK...
ON THE WAY TO THE DOOR. THE DOOR TO THE BAD PLACE.
AAAAABIGAIL...
BUT THAT'S NOT YOUR VOICE... WHO'S THERE?
ABIGAIL...
PLEASE... OPEN THE DOOR...
WHO'S THERE?
I SAID, WHO'S THERE?!
SAVE US!!!!!

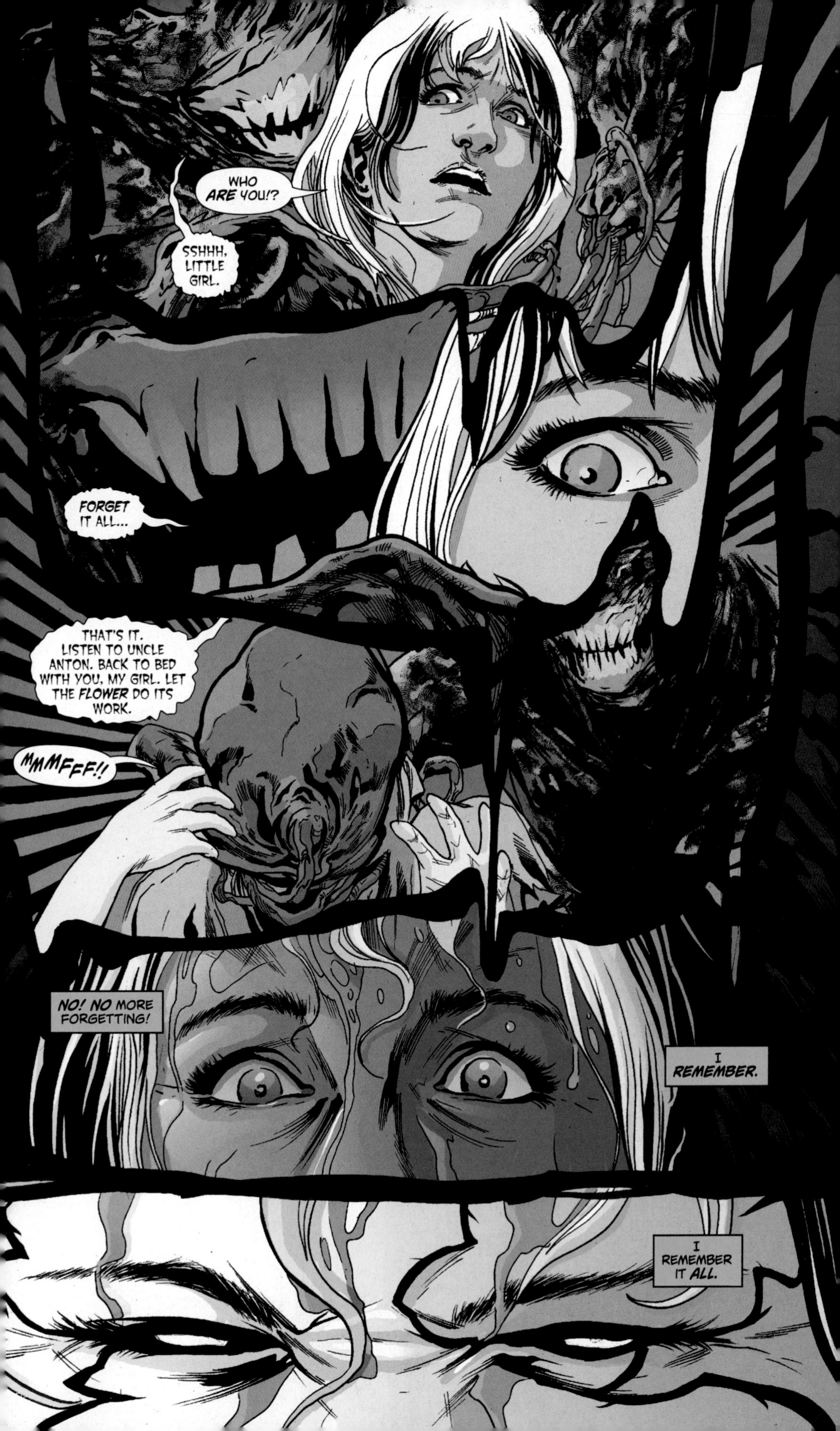
WHO ARE YOU!?
SSHHH, LITTLE GIRL.
FORGET IT ALL...
THAT'S IT. LISTEN TO UNCLE ANTON. BACK TO BED WITH YOU, MY GIRL. LET THE FLOWER DO ITS WORK.
MMMFFF!!
NO! NO MORE FORGETTING!
I REMEMBER.
I REMEMBER IT ALL.

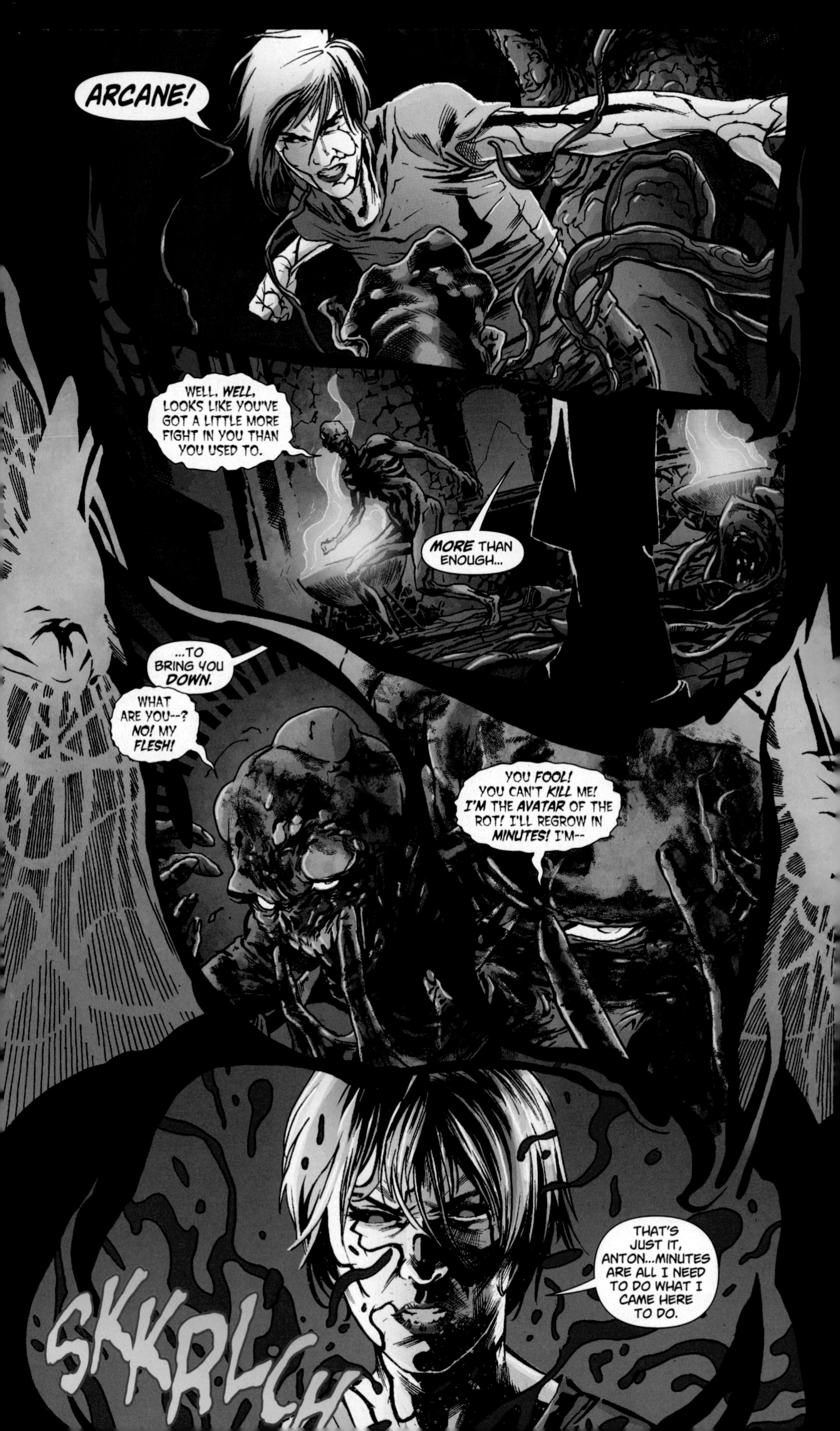
ARCANE!
WELL, WELL, LOOKS LIKE YOU'VE GOT A LITTLE MORE FIGHT IN YOU THAN YOU USED TO.
MORE THAN ENOUGH...
...TO BRING YOU DOWN.
WHAT ARE YOU--? NO! MY FLESH!
YOU FOOL! YOU CAN'T KILL ME! I'M THE AVATAR OF THE ROT! I'LL REGROW IN MINUTES! I'M--
THAT'S JUST IT, ANTON...MINUTES ARE ALL I NEED TO DO WHAT I CAME HERE TO DO.
SKKRLCH

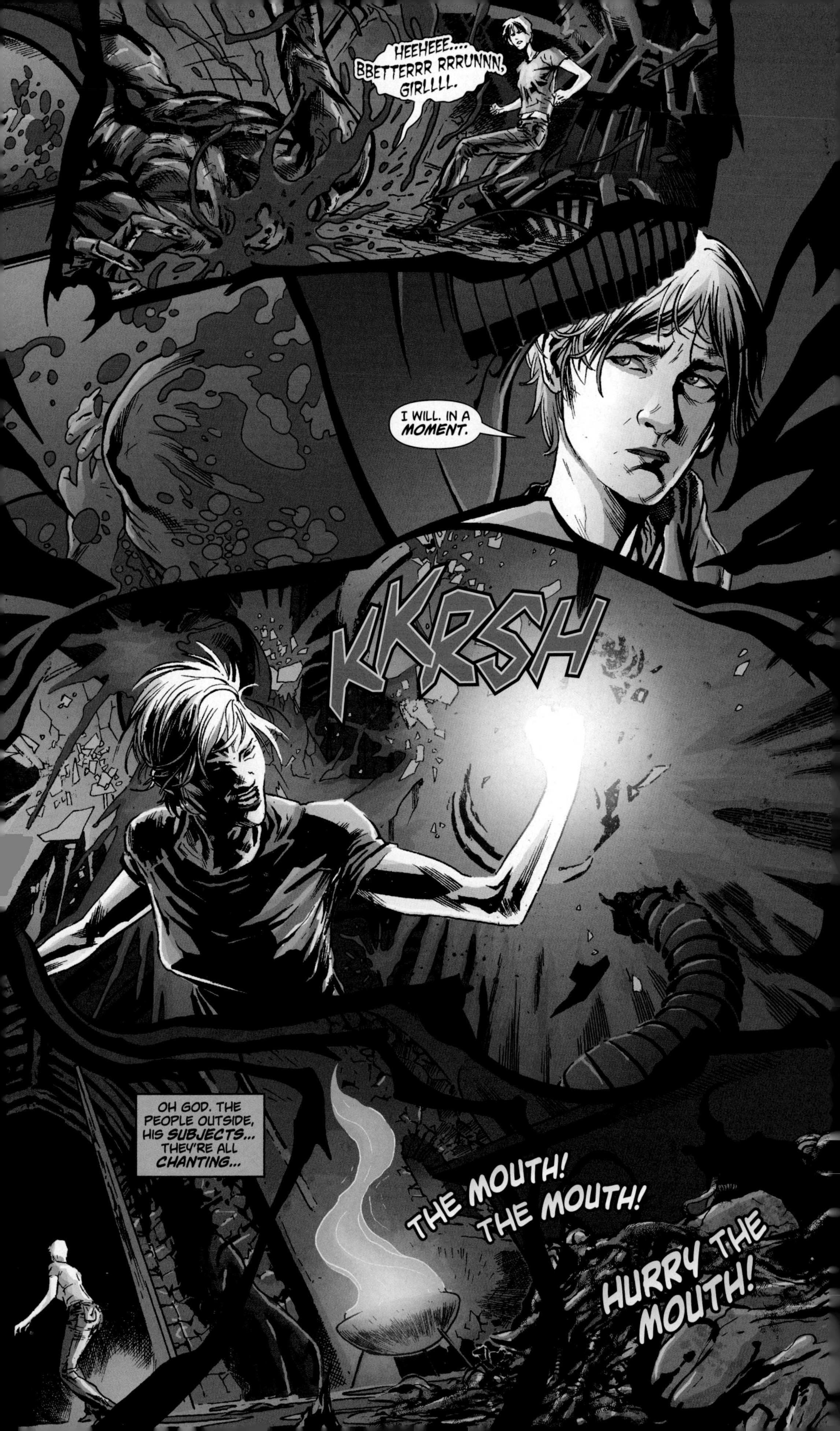
HEEHEEE.... BBETTERRR RRRUNNN, GIRLLLL.
I WILL. IN A MOMENT.
KKRSH
OH GOD. THE PEOPLE OUTSIDE, HIS SUBJECTS... THEY'RE ALL CHANTING...
THE MOUTH! THE MOUTH!
HURRY THE MOUTH!

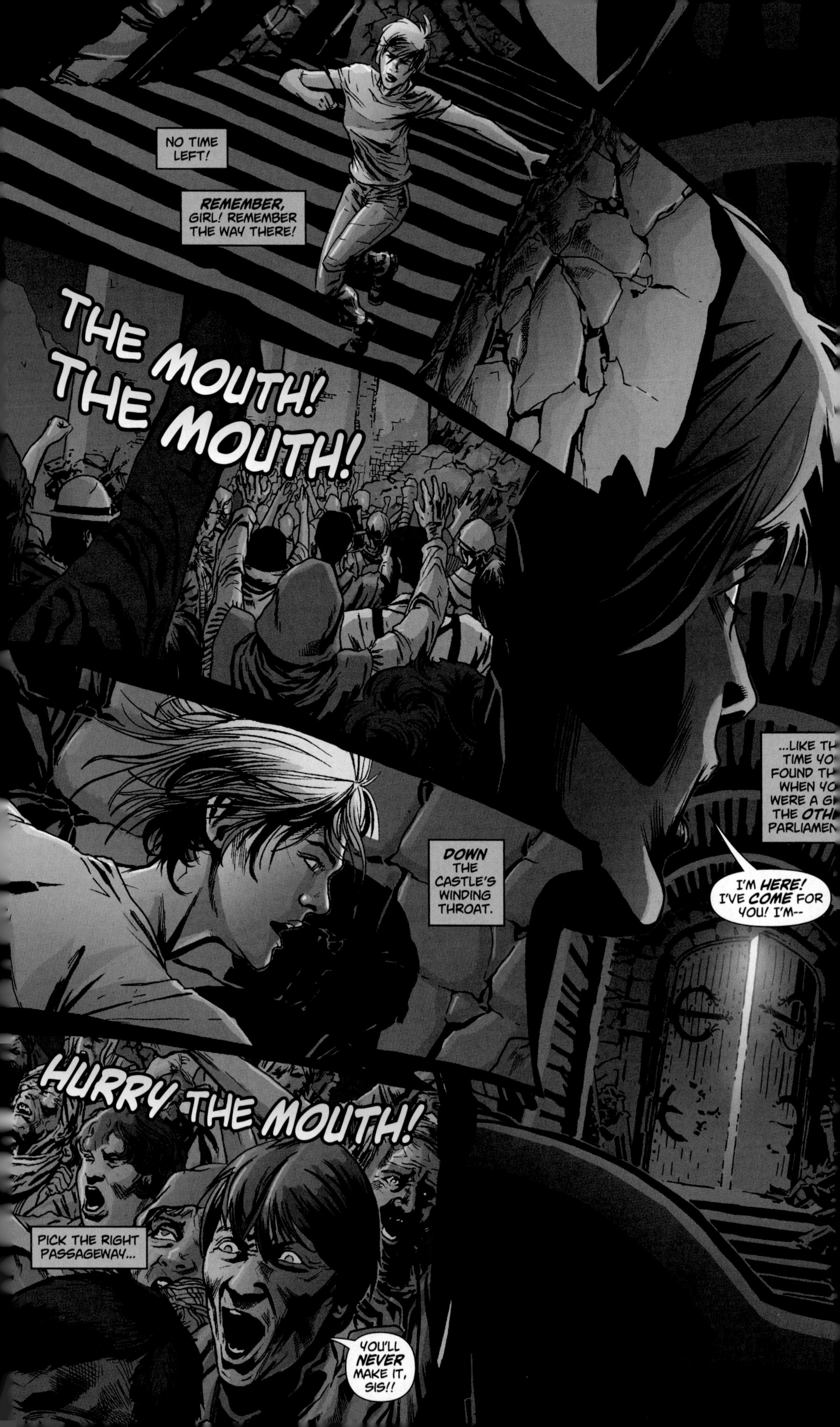
NO TIME LEFT!
REMEMBER, GIRL! REMEMBER THE WAY THERE!
THE MOUTH! THE MOUTH!
DOWN THE CASTLE'S WINDING THROAT.
...LIKE TH TIME YO FOUND TH WHEN YO WERE A GI THE OTH PARLIAMEN
I'M HERE! I'VE COME FOR YOU! I'M--
HURRY THE MOUTH!
PICK THE RIGHT PASSAGEWAY...
YOU'LL NEVER MAKE IT, SIS!!

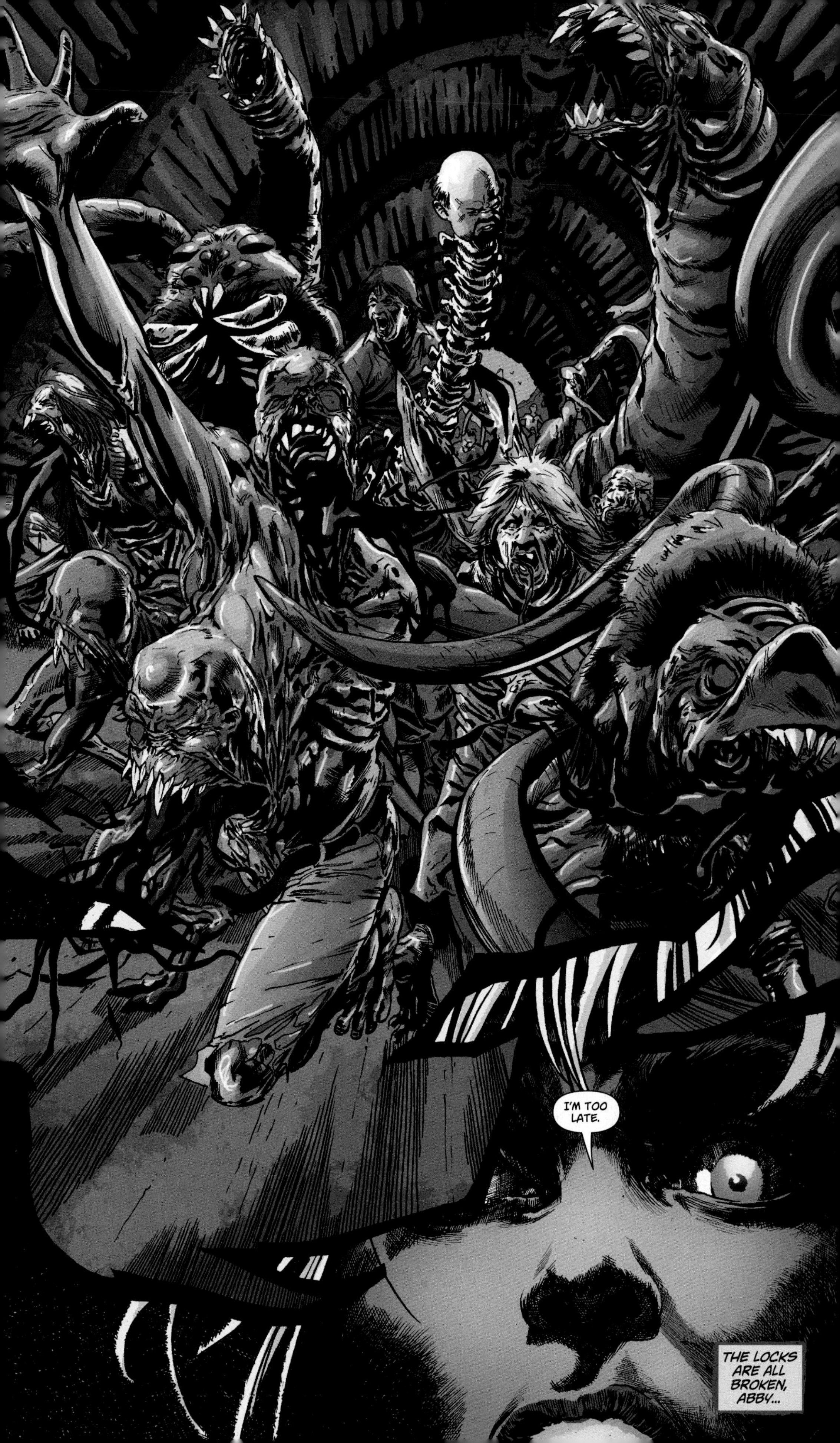
I'M TOO LATE.
THE LOCKS ARE ALL BROKEN, ABBY...

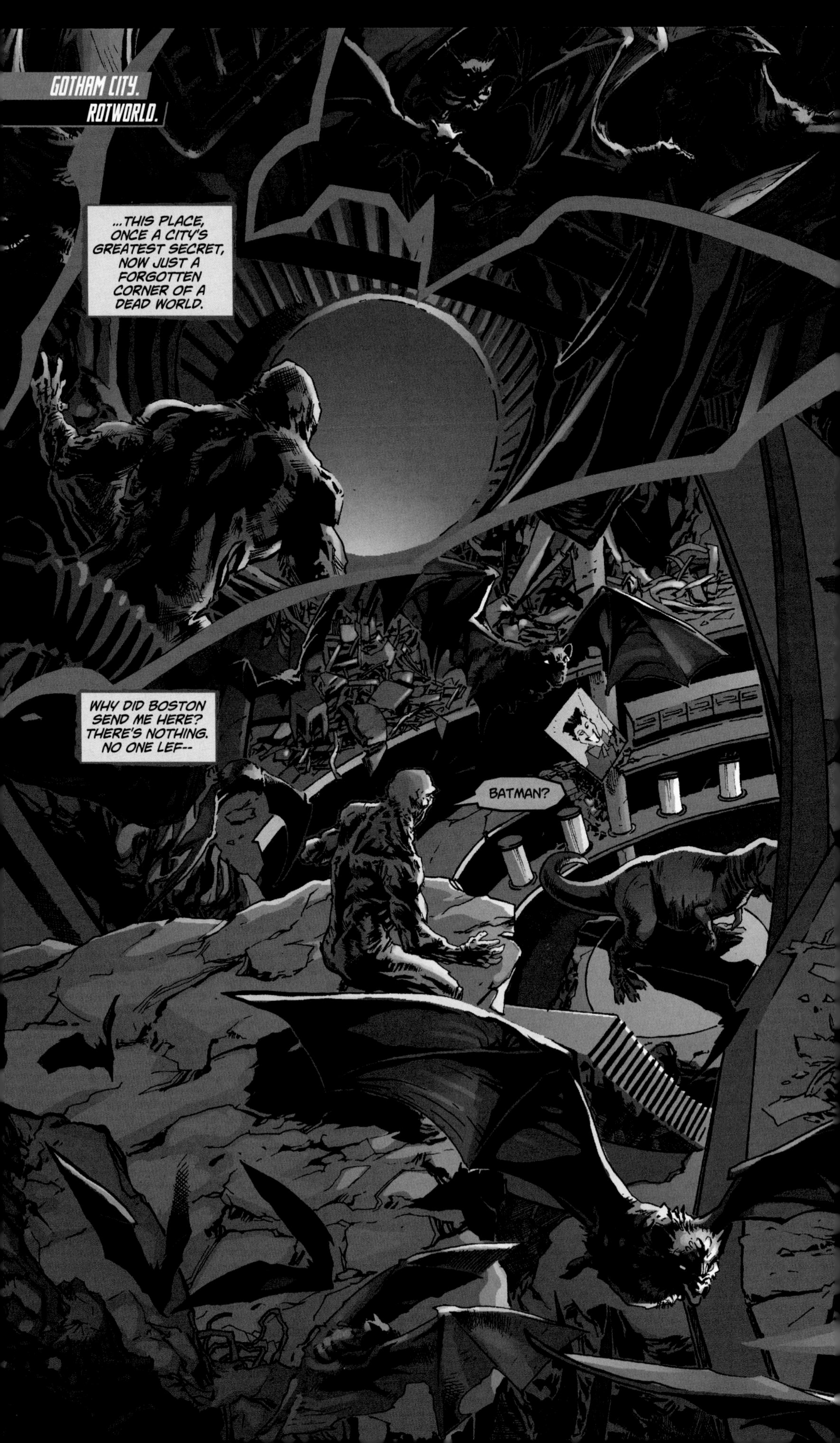
GOTHAM CITY.
ROTWORLD.
...THIS PLACE, ONCE A CITY'S GREATEST SECRET, NOW JUST A FORGOTTEN CORNER OF A DEAD WORLD.
WHY DID BOSTON SEND ME HERE? THERE'S NOTHING. NO ONE LEF--
BATMAN?

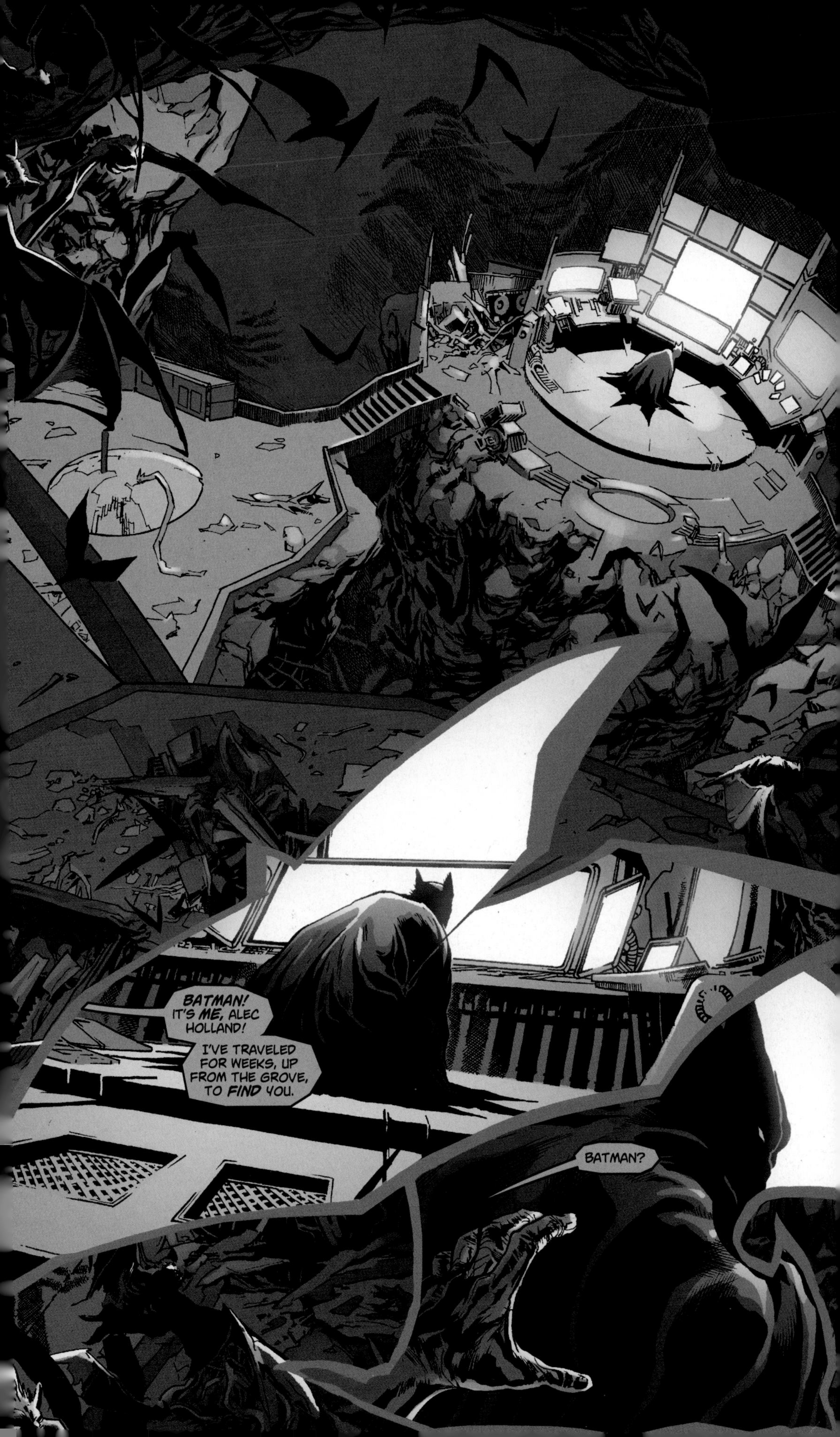
BATMAN! IT'S ME, ALEC HOLLAND!
I'VE TRAVELED FOR WEEKS, UP FROM THE GROVE, TO FIND YOU.
BATMAN?

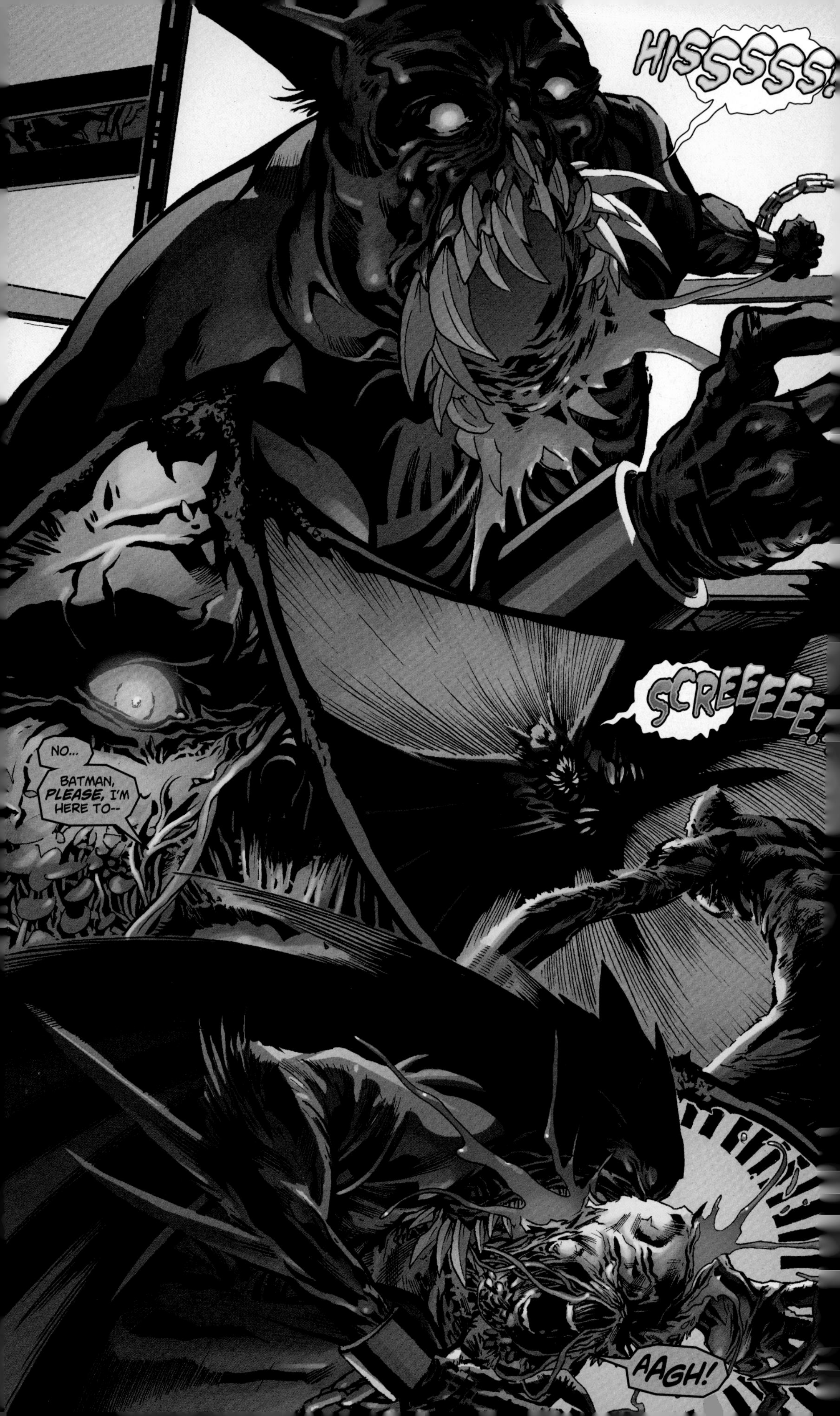
HISSSSS!
NO... BATMAN, PLEASE, I'M HERE TO--
SCREEEEEE!
AAGH!

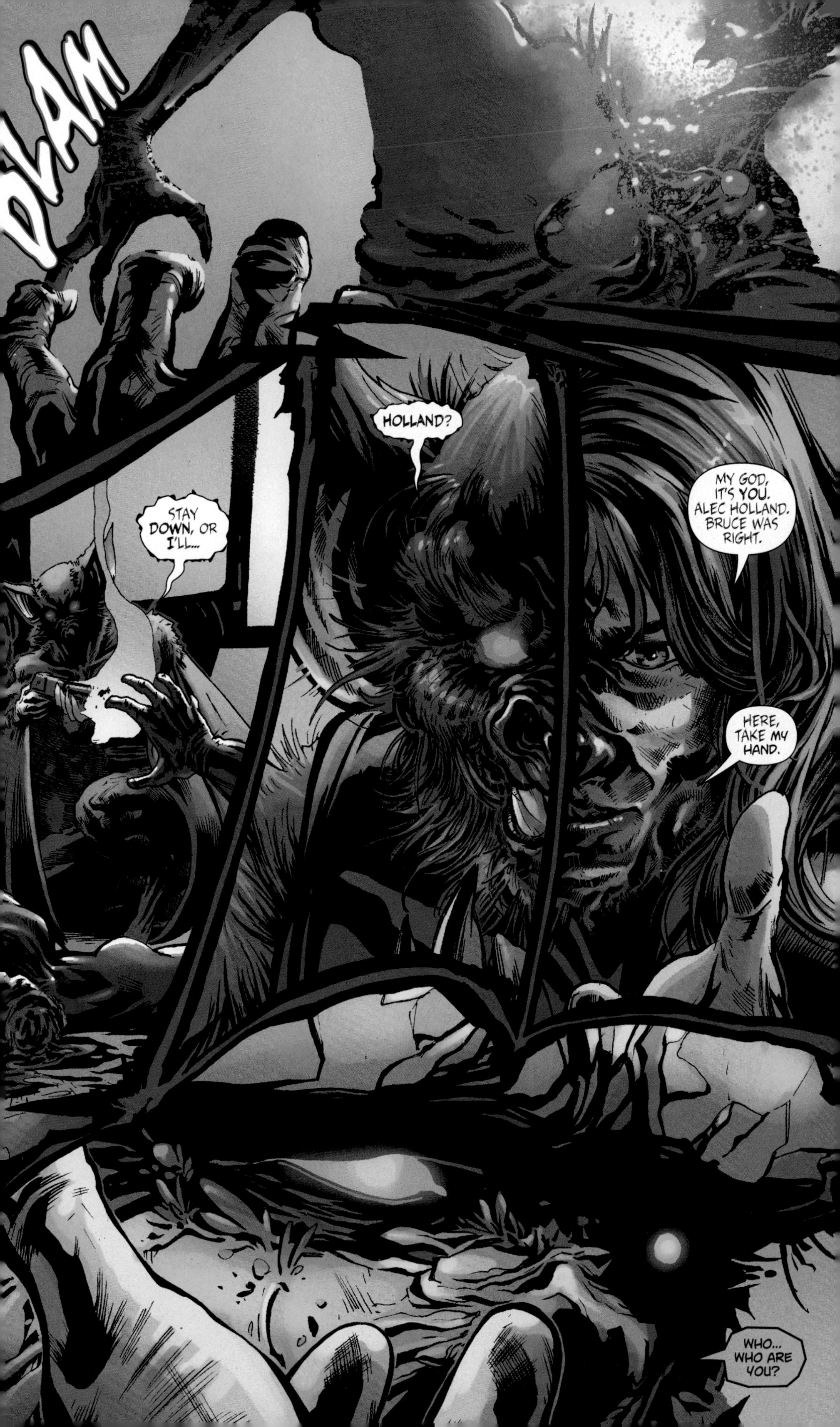
BLAM
HOLLAND?
STAY DOWN, OR I'LL...
MY GOD, IT'S YOU. ALEC HOLLAND. BRUCE WAS RIGHT.
HERE, TAKE MY HAND.
WHO... WHO ARE YOU?

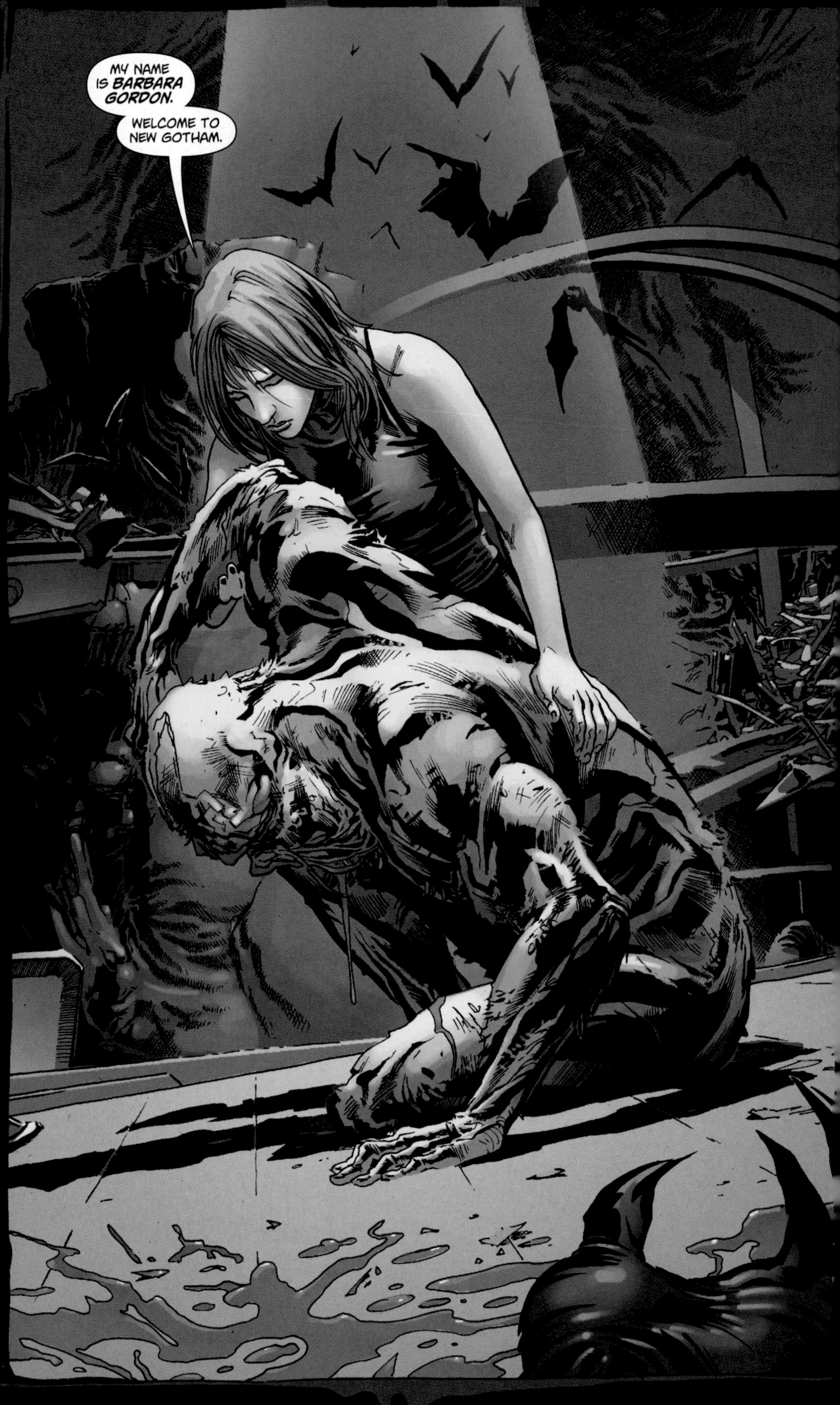
MY NAME IS BARBARA GORDON.
WELCOME TO NEW GOTHAM.

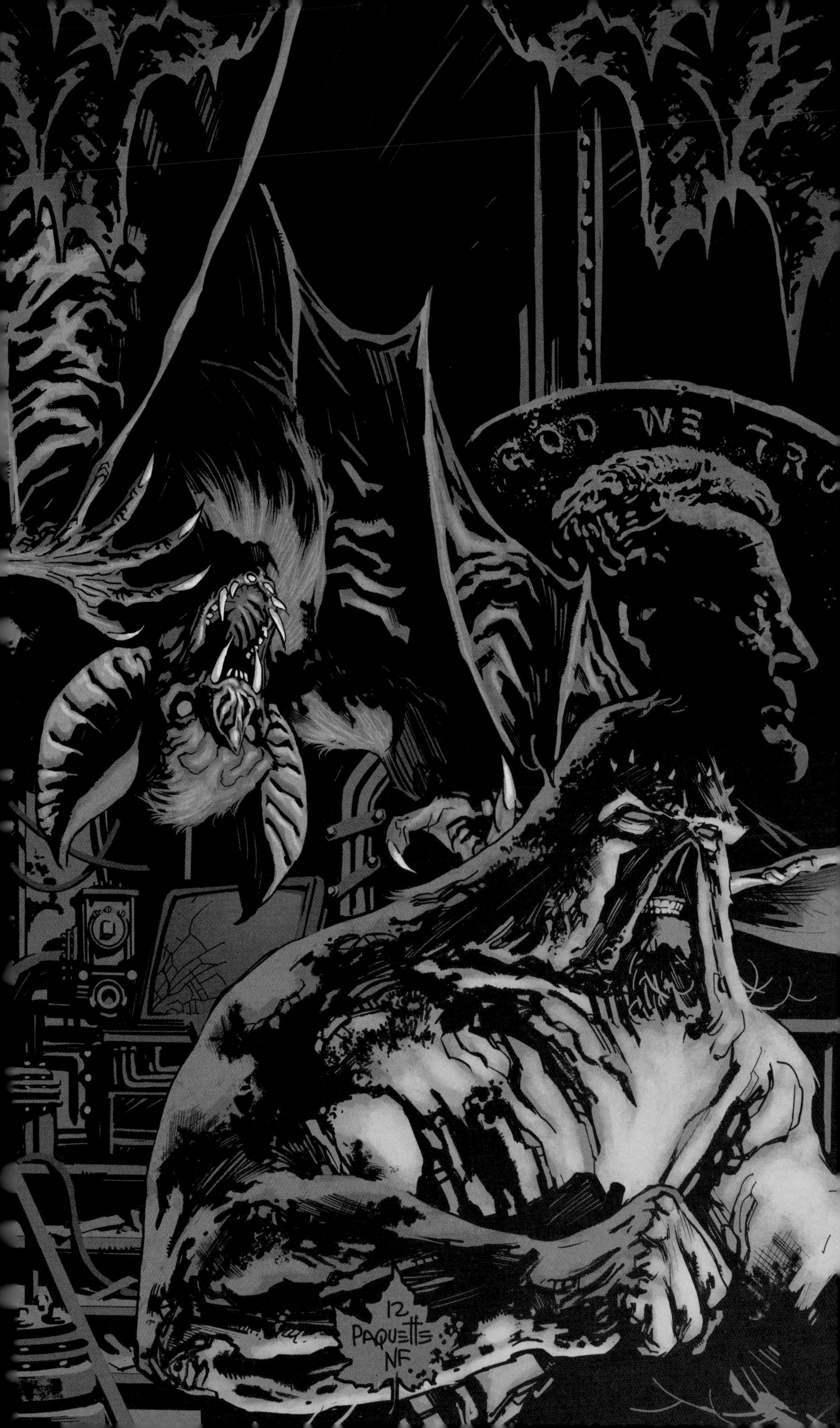
GOD WE TRU
12 PAQUETTE NF

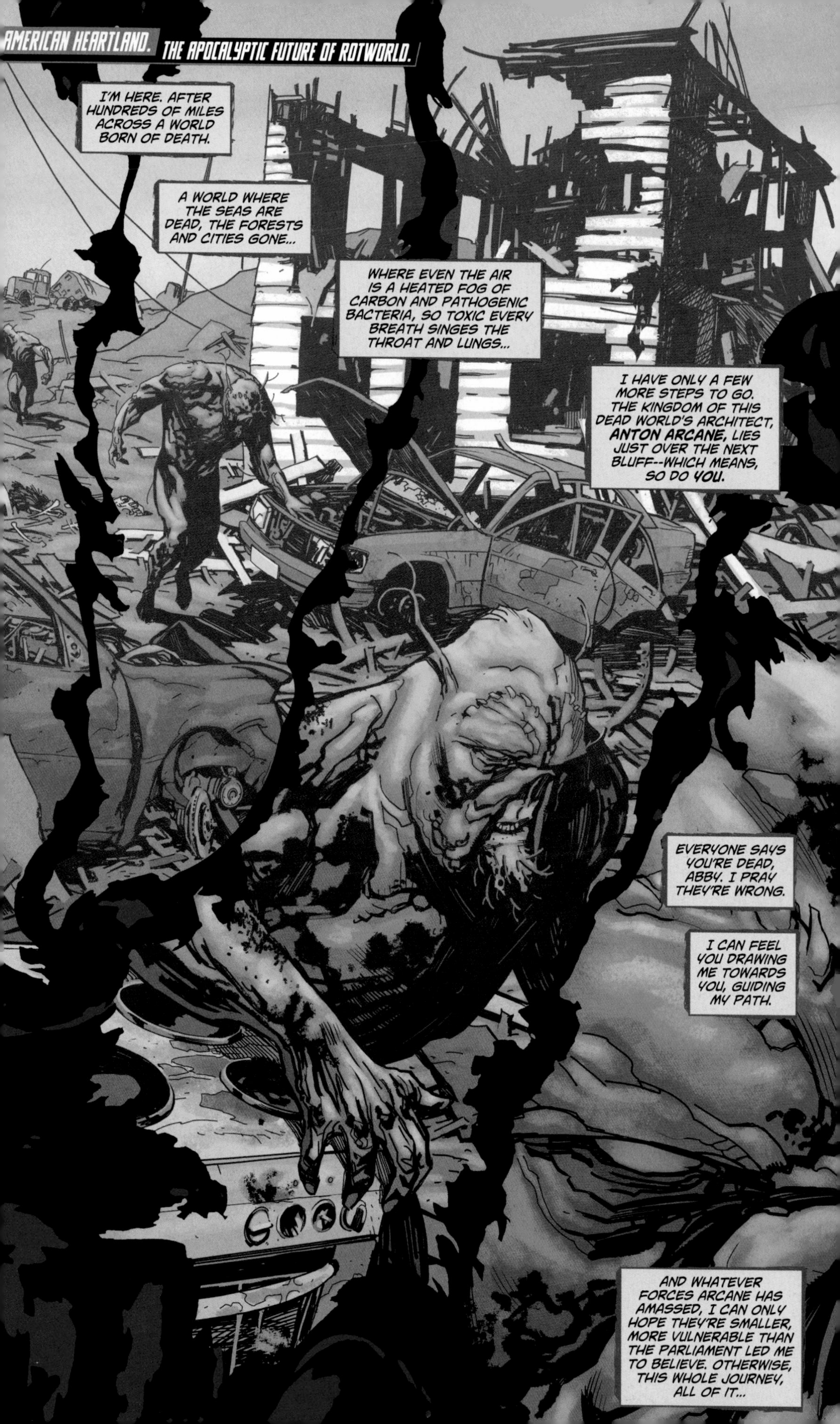
AMERICAN HEARTLAND.
THE APOCALYPTIC FUTURE OF ROTWORLD.
I'M HERE. AFTER HUNDREDS OF MILES ACROSS A WORLD BORN OF DEATH.
A WORLD WHERE THE SEAS ARE DEAD, THE FORESTS AND CITIES GONE...
WHERE EVEN THE AIR IS A HEATED FOG OF CARBON AND PATHOGENIC BACTERIA, SO TOXIC EVERY BREATH SINGES THE THROAT AND LUNGS...
I HAVE ONLY A FEW MORE STEPS TO GO. THE KINGDOM OF THIS DEAD WORLD'S ARCHITECT, ANTON ARCANE, LIES JUST OVER THE NEXT BLUFF--WHICH MEANS, SO DO YOU.
EVERYONE SAYS YOU'RE DEAD, ABBY. I PRAY THEY'RE WRONG.
I CAN FEEL YOU DRAWING ME TOWARDS YOU, GUIDING MY PATH.
AND WHATEVER FORCES ARCANE HAS AMASSED, I CAN ONLY HOPE THEY'RE SMALLER, MORE VULNERABLE THAN THE PARLIAMENT LED ME TO BELIEVE. OTHERWISE, THIS WHOLE JOURNEY, ALL OF IT...

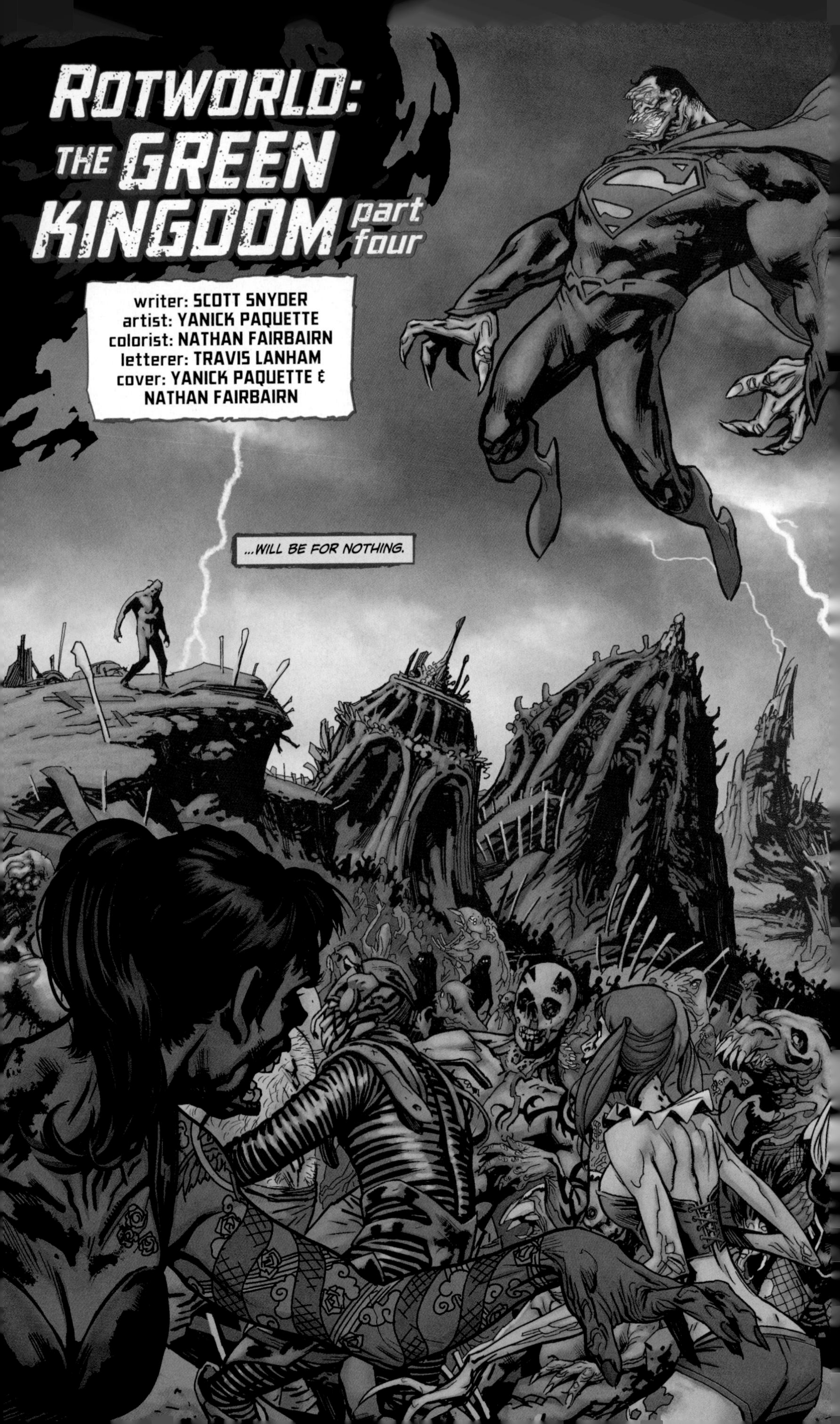
ROTWORLD: THE GREEN KINGDOM part four
writer: SCOTT SNYDER
artist: YANICK PAQUETTE
colorist: NATHAN FAIRBAIRN
letterer: TRAVIS LANHAM
cover: YANICK PAQUETTE & NATHAN FAIRBAIRN
...WILL BE FOR NOTHING.

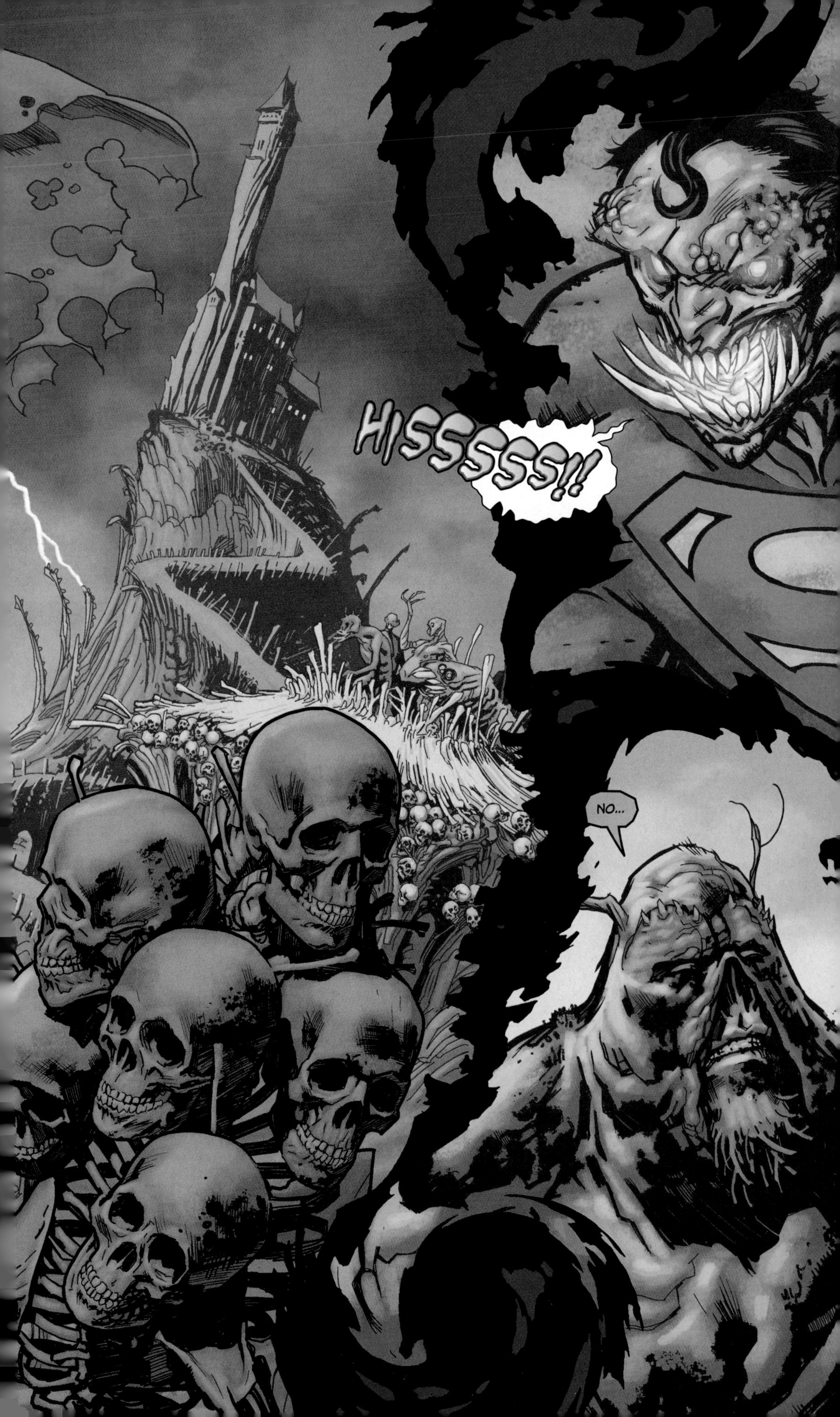
HISSSSSS!!
NO...

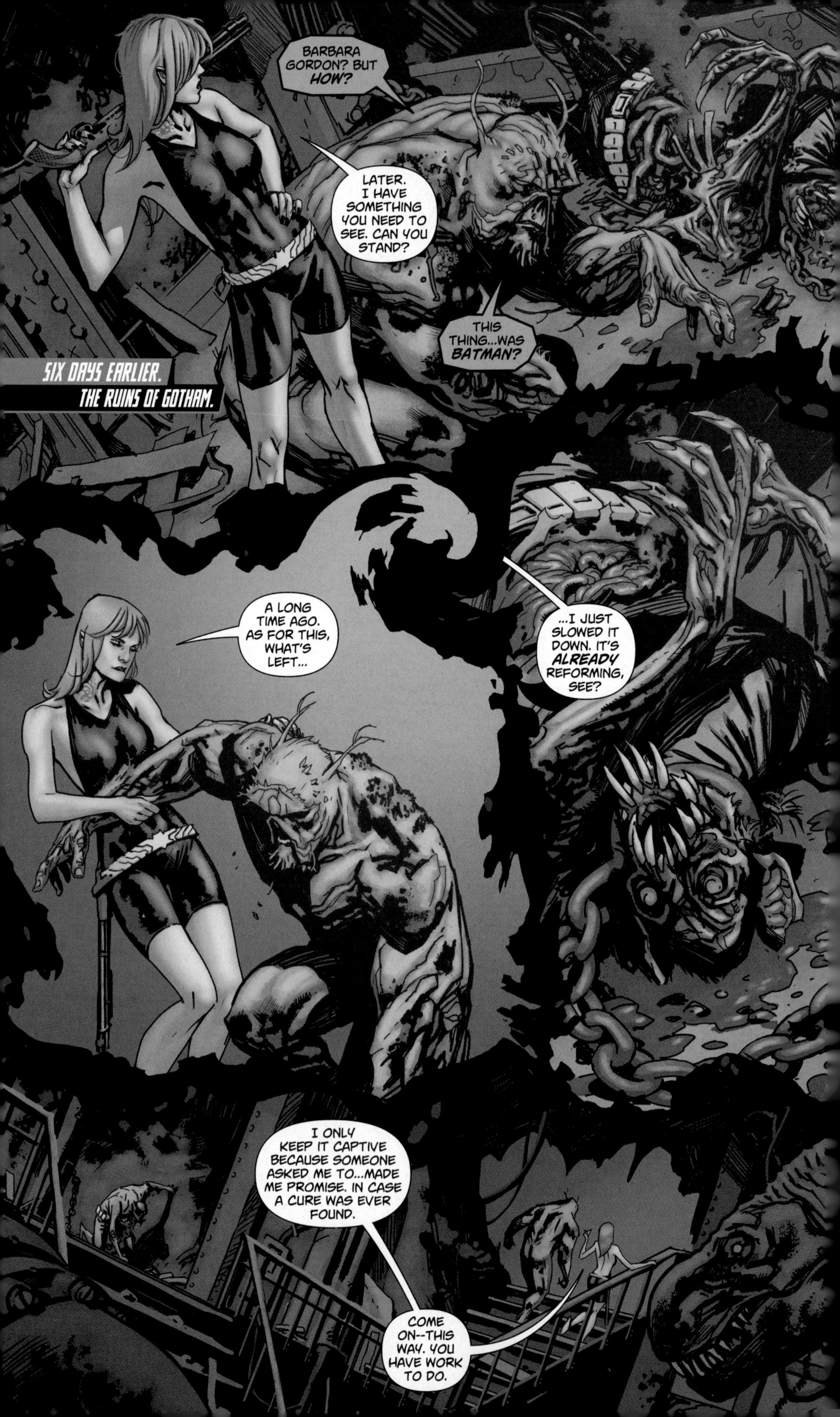
BARBARA GORDON? BUT HOW?
LATER. I HAVE SOMETHING YOU NEED TO SEE. CAN YOU STAND?
THIS THING...WAS BATMAN?
SIX DAYS EARLIER.
THE RUINS OF GOTHAM.
A LONG TIME AGO. AS FOR THIS, WHAT'S LEFT...
...I JUST SLOWED IT DOWN. IT'S ALREADY REFORMING, SEE?
I ONLY KEEP IT CAPTIVE BECAUSE SOMEONE ASKED ME TO...MADE ME PROMISE. IN CASE A CURE WAS EVER FOUND.
COME ON--THIS WAY. YOU HAVE WORK TO DO.

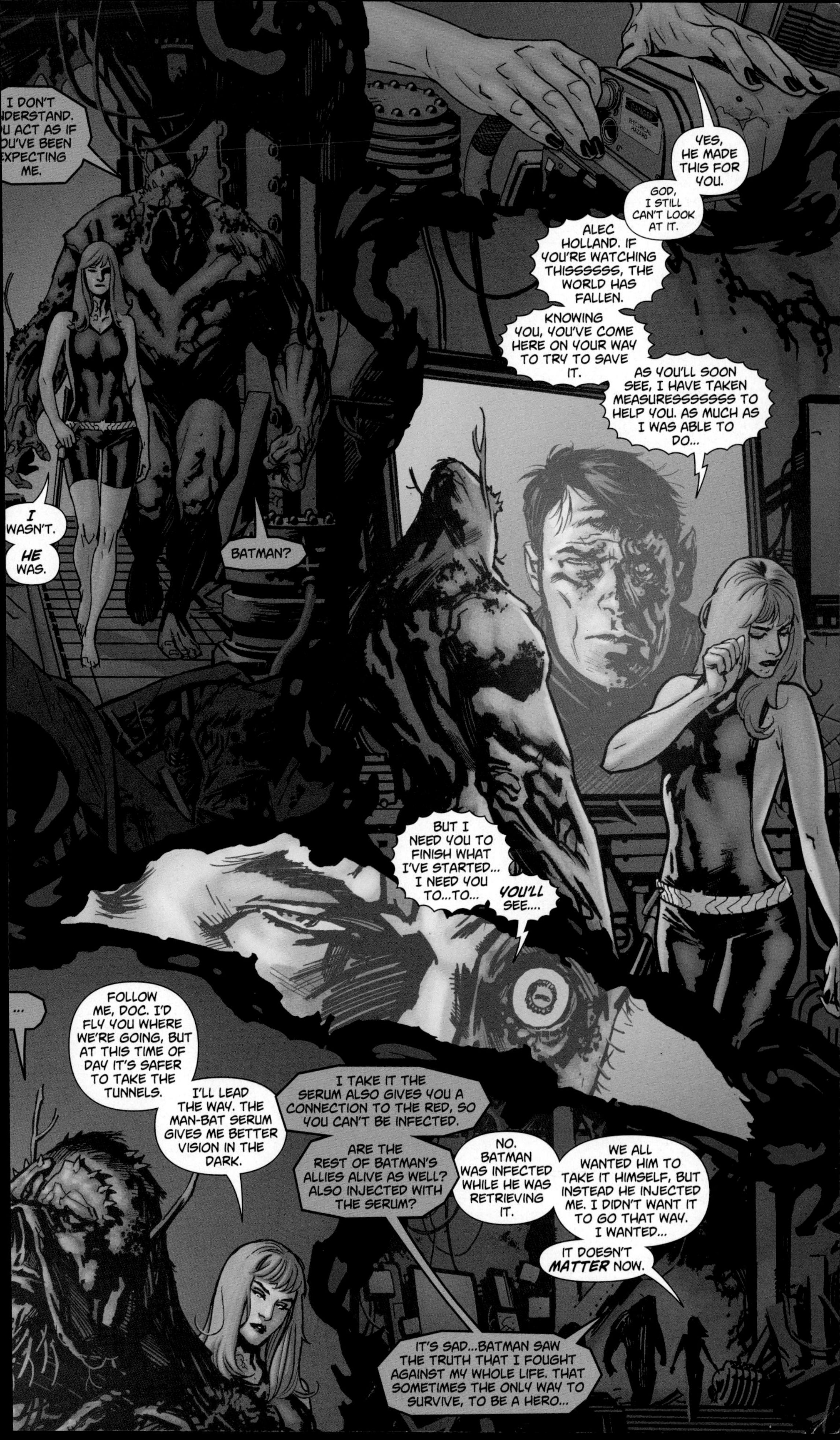
I DON'T
UNDERSTAND.
YOU ACT AS IF
YOU'VE BEEN
EXPECTING
ME.
YES,
HE MADE
THIS FOR
YOU.
GOD,
I STILL
CAN'T LOOK
AT IT.
ALEC HOLLAND. IF YOU'RE WATCHING THISSSSSS, THE WORLD HAS FALLEN.
KNOWING YOU, YOU'VE COME HERE ON YOUR WAY TO TRY TO SAVE IT.
AS YOU'LL SOON SEE, I HAVE TAKEN MEASURESSSSSSS TO HELP YOU. AS MUCH AS I WAS ABLE TO DO...
I WASN'T.
HE WAS.
BATMAN?
BUT I NEED YOU TO FINISH WHAT I'VE STARTED... I NEED YOU TO...TO...
YOU'LL SEE....
...
FOLLOW ME, DOC. I'D FLY YOU WHERE WE'RE GOING, BUT AT THIS TIME OF DAY IT'S SAFER TO TAKE THE TUNNELS.
I'LL LEAD THE WAY. THE MAN-BAT SERUM GIVES ME BETTER VISION IN THE DARK.
I TAKE IT THE SERUM ALSO GIVES YOU A CONNECTION TO THE RED, SO YOU CAN'T BE INFECTED.
ARE THE REST OF BATMAN'S ALLIES ALIVE AS WELL? ALSO INJECTED WITH THE SERUM?
NO. BATMAN WAS INFECTED WHILE HE WAS RETRIEVING IT.
WE ALL WANTED HIM TO TAKE IT HIMSELF, BUT INSTEAD HE INJECTED ME. I DIDN'T WANT IT TO GO THAT WAY. I WANTED...
IT DOESN'T MATTER NOW.
IT'S SAD...BATMAN SAW THE TRUTH THAT I FOUGHT AGAINST MY WHOLE LIFE. THAT SOMETIMES THE ONLY WAY TO SURVIVE, TO BE A HERO...

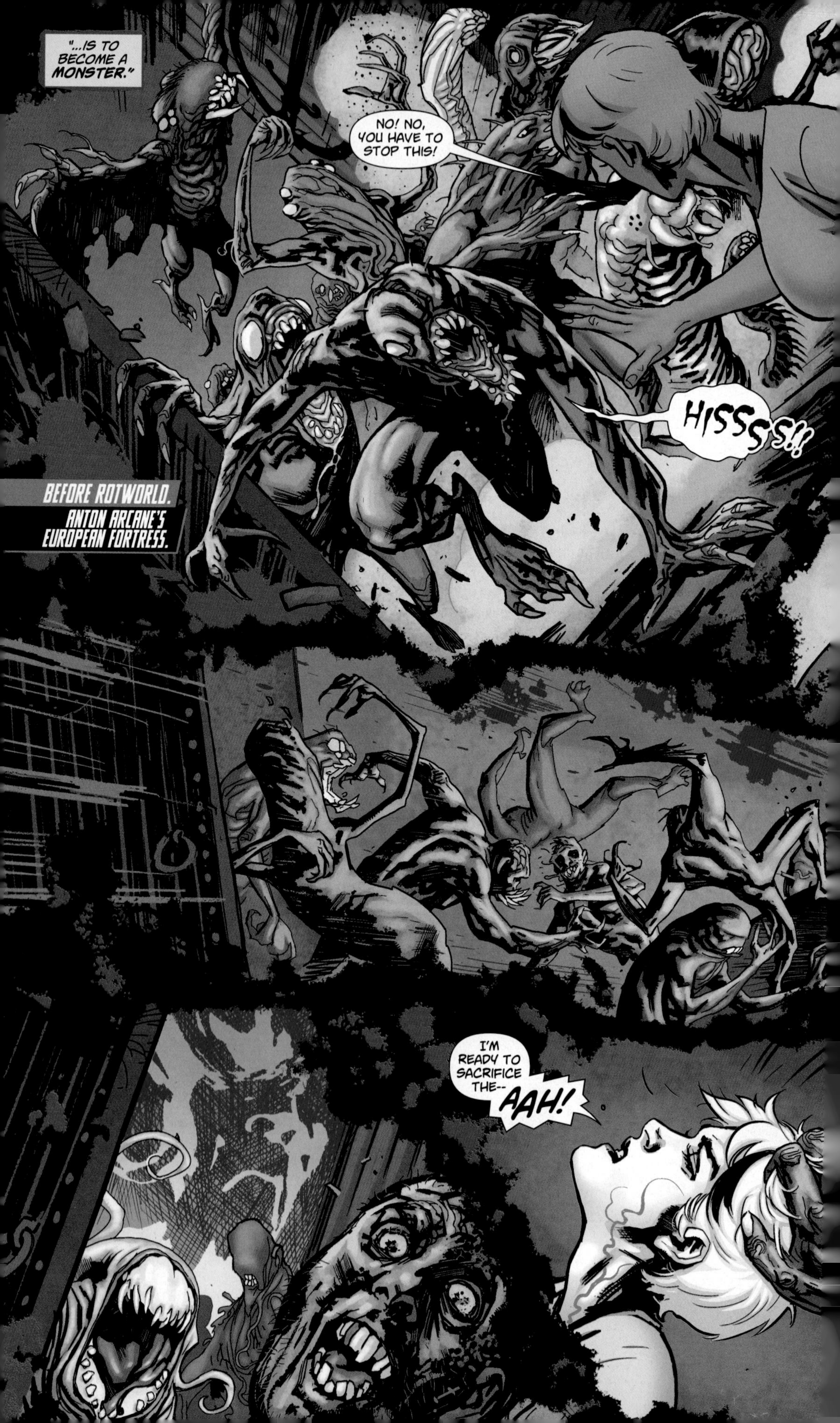
"...IS TO BECOME A MONSTER."
NO! NO, YOU HAVE TO STOP THIS!
HISSSS!!
BEFORE ROTWORLD.
ANTON ARCANE'S EUROPEAN FORTRESS.
I'M READY TO SACRIFICE THE--
AAH!

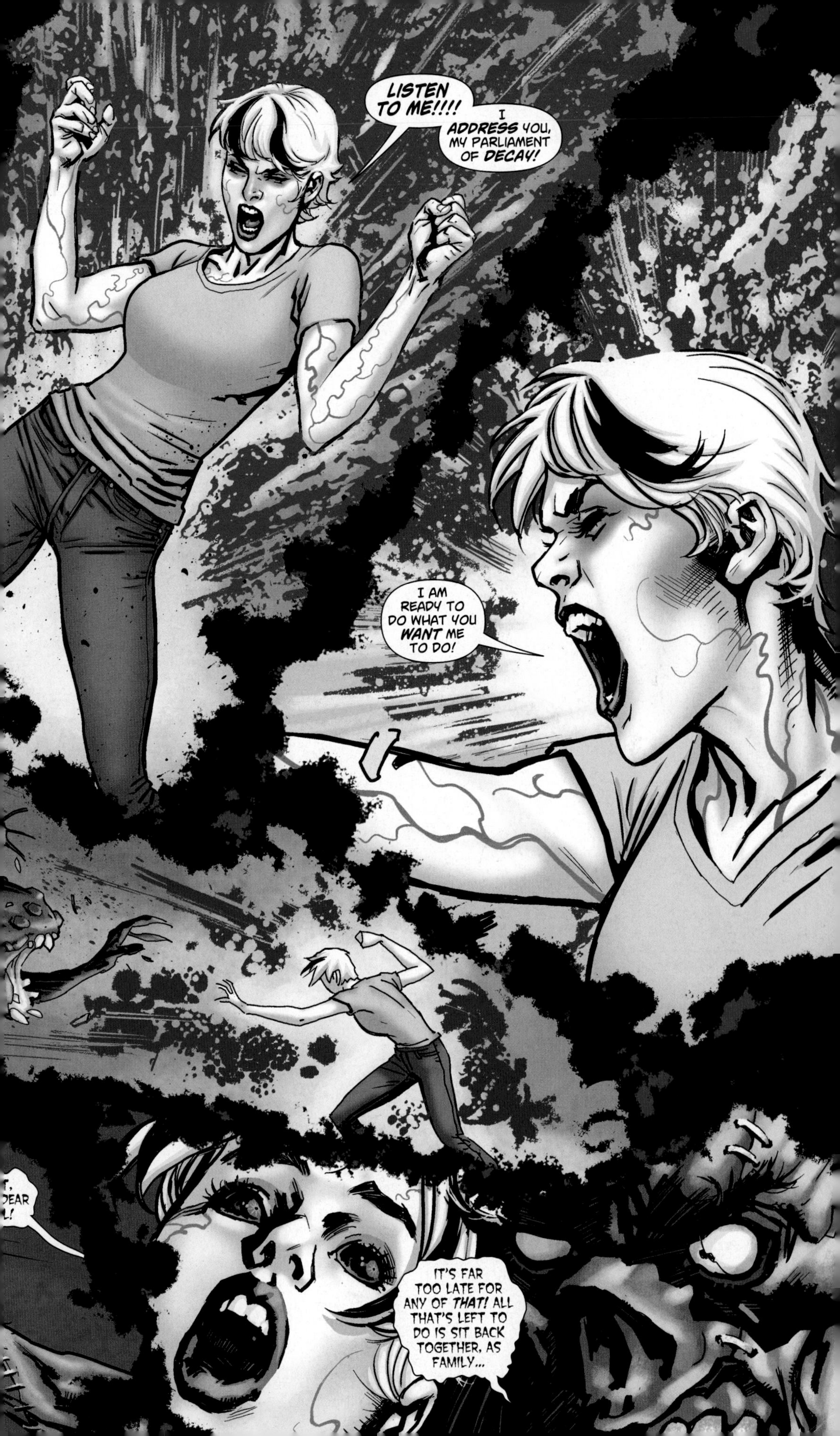
LISTEN TO ME!!!!
I ADDRESS YOU, MY PARLIAMENT OF DECAY!
I AM READY TO DO WHAT YOU WANT ME TO DO!
IT'S FAR TOO LATE FOR ANY OF THAT! ALL THAT'S LEFT TO DO IS SIT BACK TOGETHER, AS FAMILY...

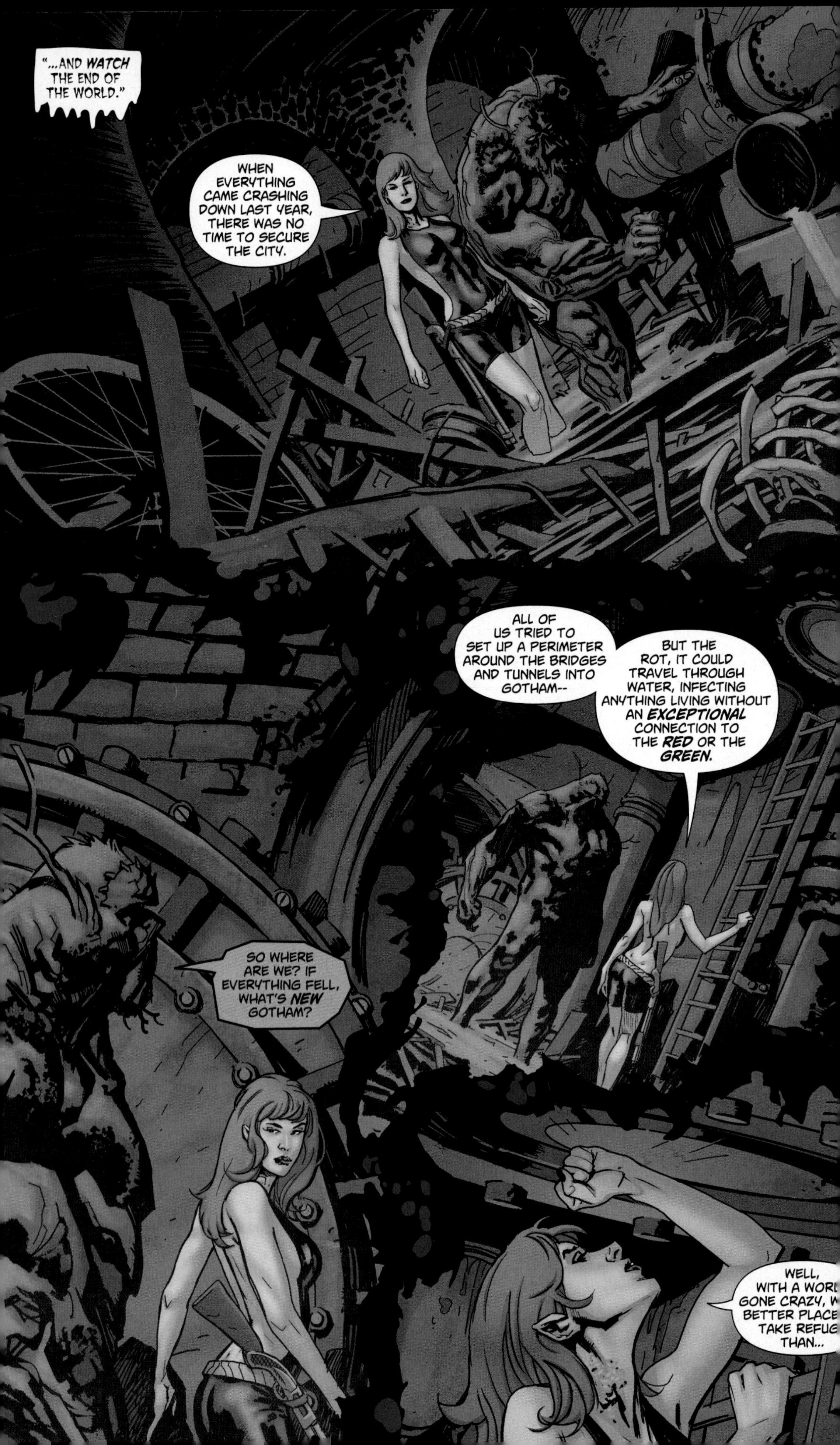
"...AND WATCH THE END OF THE WORLD."
WHEN EVERYTHING CAME CRASHING DOWN LAST YEAR, THERE WAS NO TIME TO SECURE THE CITY.
ALL OF US TRIED TO SET UP A PERIMETER AROUND THE BRIDGES AND TUNNELS INTO GOTHAM--
BUT THE ROT, IT COULD TRAVEL THROUGH WATER, INFECTING ANYTHING LIVING WITHOUT AN EXCEPTIONAL CONNECTION TO THE RED OR THE GREEN.
SO WHERE ARE WE? IF EVERYTHING FELL, WHAT'S NEW GOTHAM?
WELL, WITH A WORL GONE CRAZY, W BETTER PLACE TAKE REFUG THAN...

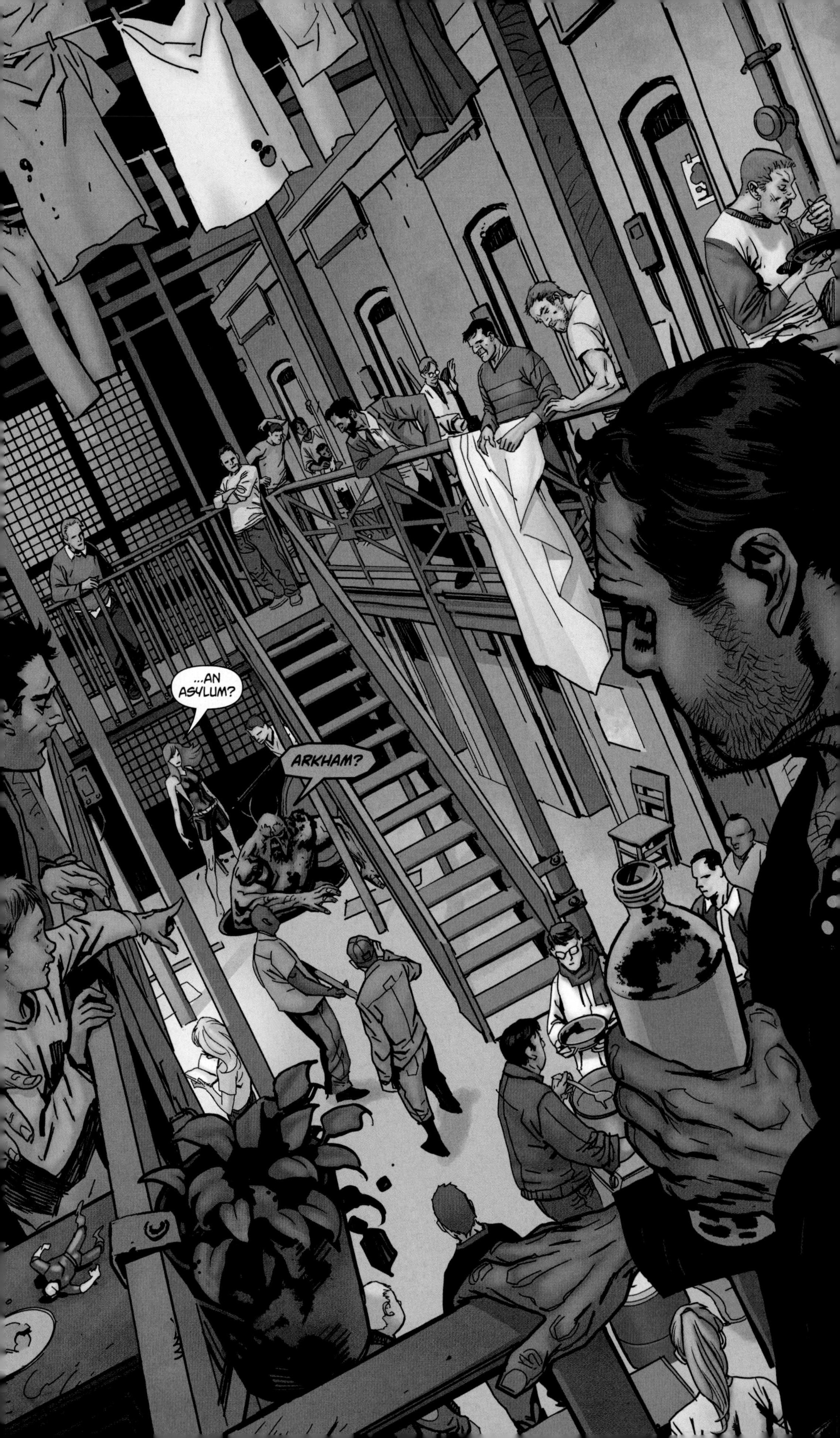
...AN ASYLUM?
ARKHAM?

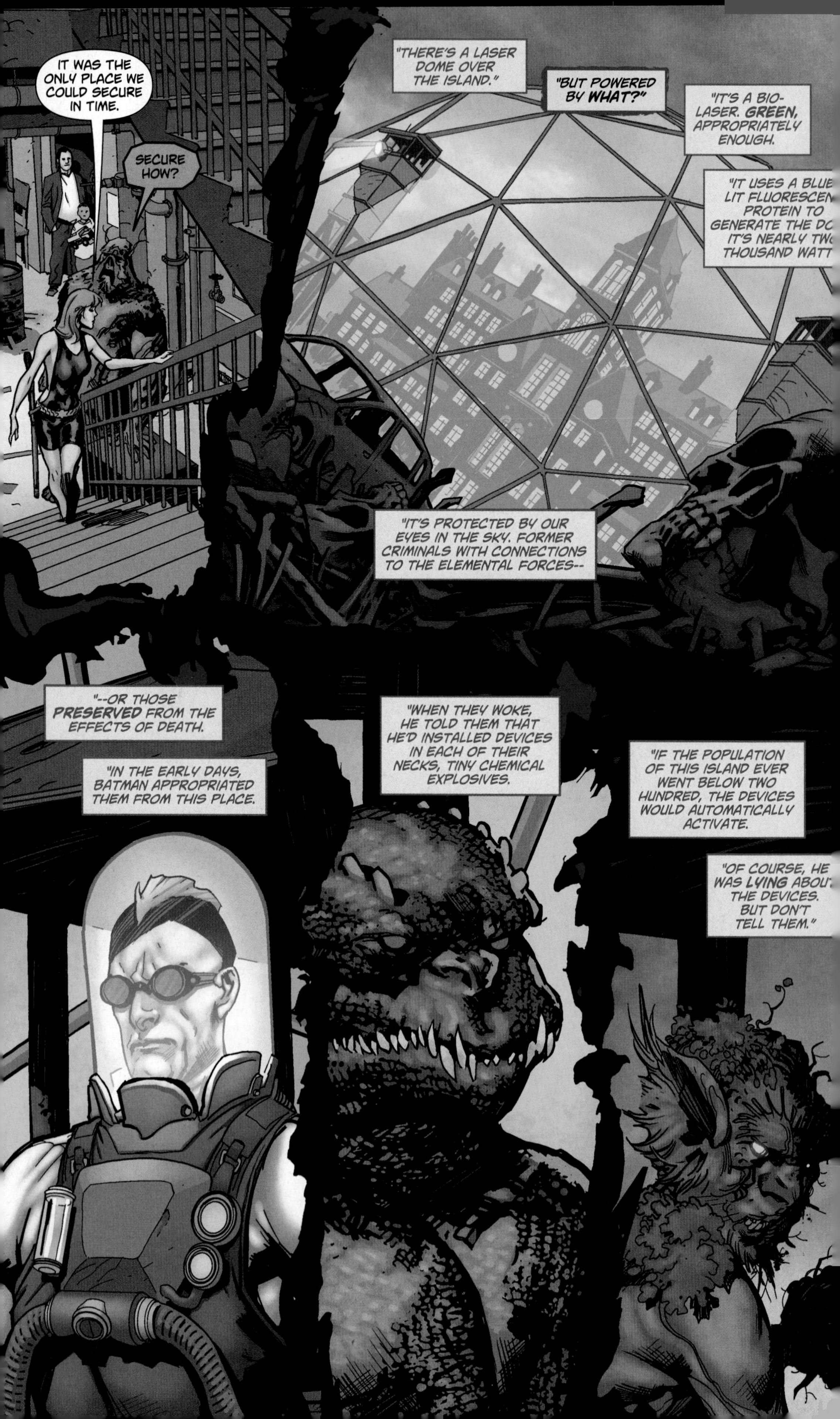

IT WAS THE ONLY PLACE WE COULD SECURE IN TIME.
SECURE HOW?
"THERE'S A LASER DOME OVER THE ISLAND."
"BUT POWERED BY WHAT?"
"IT'S A BIO-LASER. GREEN, APPROPRIATELY ENOUGH.
"IT USES A BLUE LIT FLUORESCEN PROTEIN TO GENERATE THE DO IT'S NEARLY TWO THOUSAND WATT
"IT'S PROTECTED BY OUR EYES IN THE SKY. FORMER CRIMINALS WITH CONNECTIONS TO THE ELEMENTAL FORCES--
"--OR THOSE PRESERVED FROM THE EFFECTS OF DEATH.
"IN THE EARLY DAYS, BATMAN APPROPRIATED THEM FROM THIS PLACE.
"WHEN THEY WOKE, HE TOLD THEM THAT HE'D INSTALLED DEVICES IN EACH OF THEIR NECKS, TINY CHEMICAL EXPLOSIVES.
"IF THE POPULATION OF THIS ISLAND EVER WENT BELOW TWO HUNDRED, THE DEVICES WOULD AUTOMATICALLY ACTIVATE.
"OF COURSE, HE WAS LYING ABOUT THE DEVICES. BUT DON'T TELL THEM."

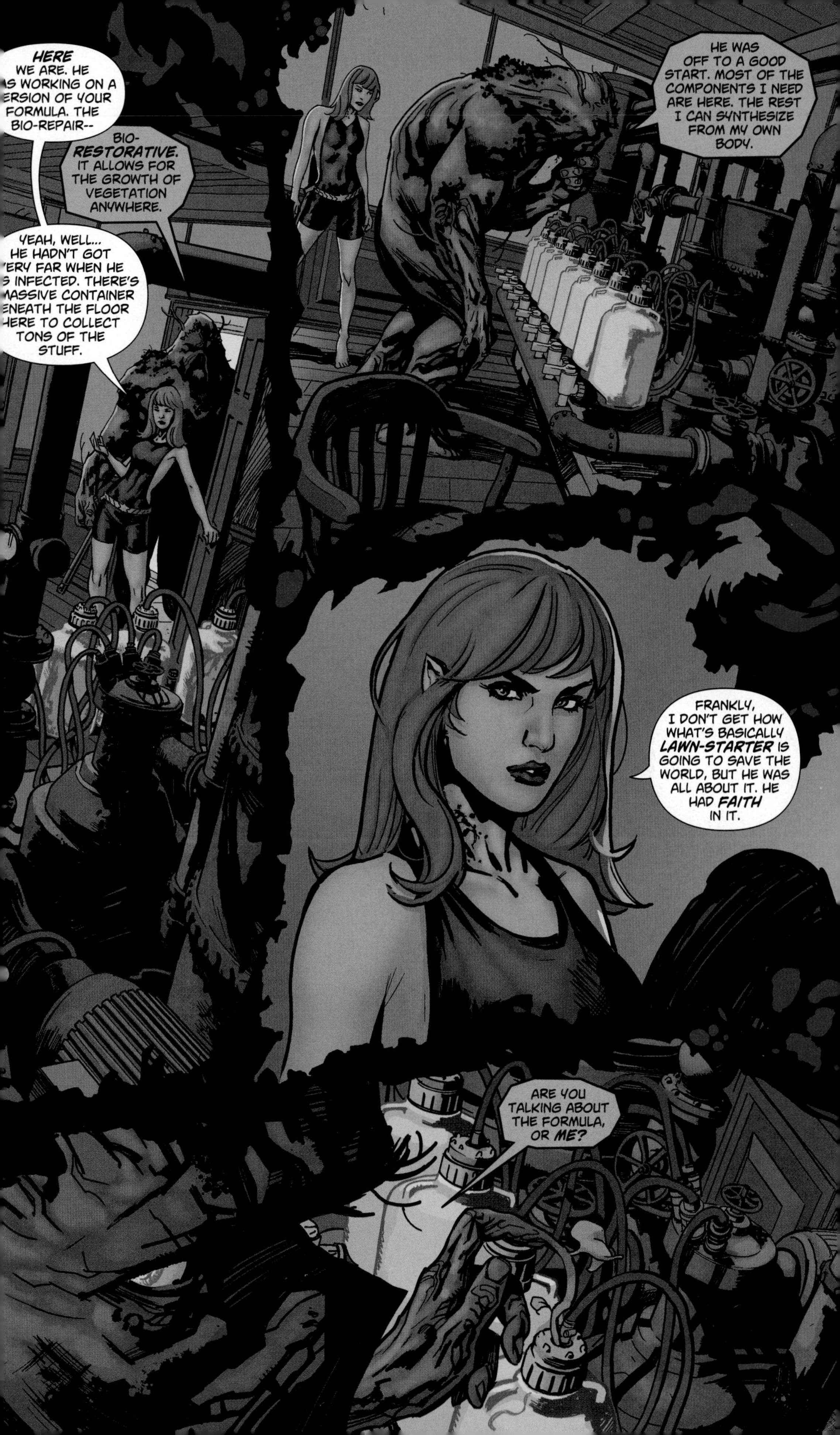
HERE WE ARE. HE AS WORKING ON A ERSION OF YOUR FORMULA. THE BIO-REPAIR--
BIO-RESTORATIVE. IT ALLOWS FOR THE GROWTH OF VEGETATION ANYWHERE.
YEAH, WELL... HE HADN'T GOT 'ERY FAR WHEN HE S INFECTED. THERE'S MASSIVE CONTAINER ENEATH THE FLOOR HERE TO COLLECT TONS OF THE STUFF.
HE WAS OFF TO A GOOD START. MOST OF THE COMPONENTS I NEED ARE HERE. THE REST I CAN SYNTHESIZE FROM MY OWN BODY.
FRANKLY, I DON'T GET HOW WHAT'S BASICALLY LAWN-STARTER IS GOING TO SAVE THE WORLD, BUT HE WAS ALL ABOUT IT. HE HAD FAITH IN IT.
ARE YOU TALKING ABOUT THE FORMULA, OR ME?

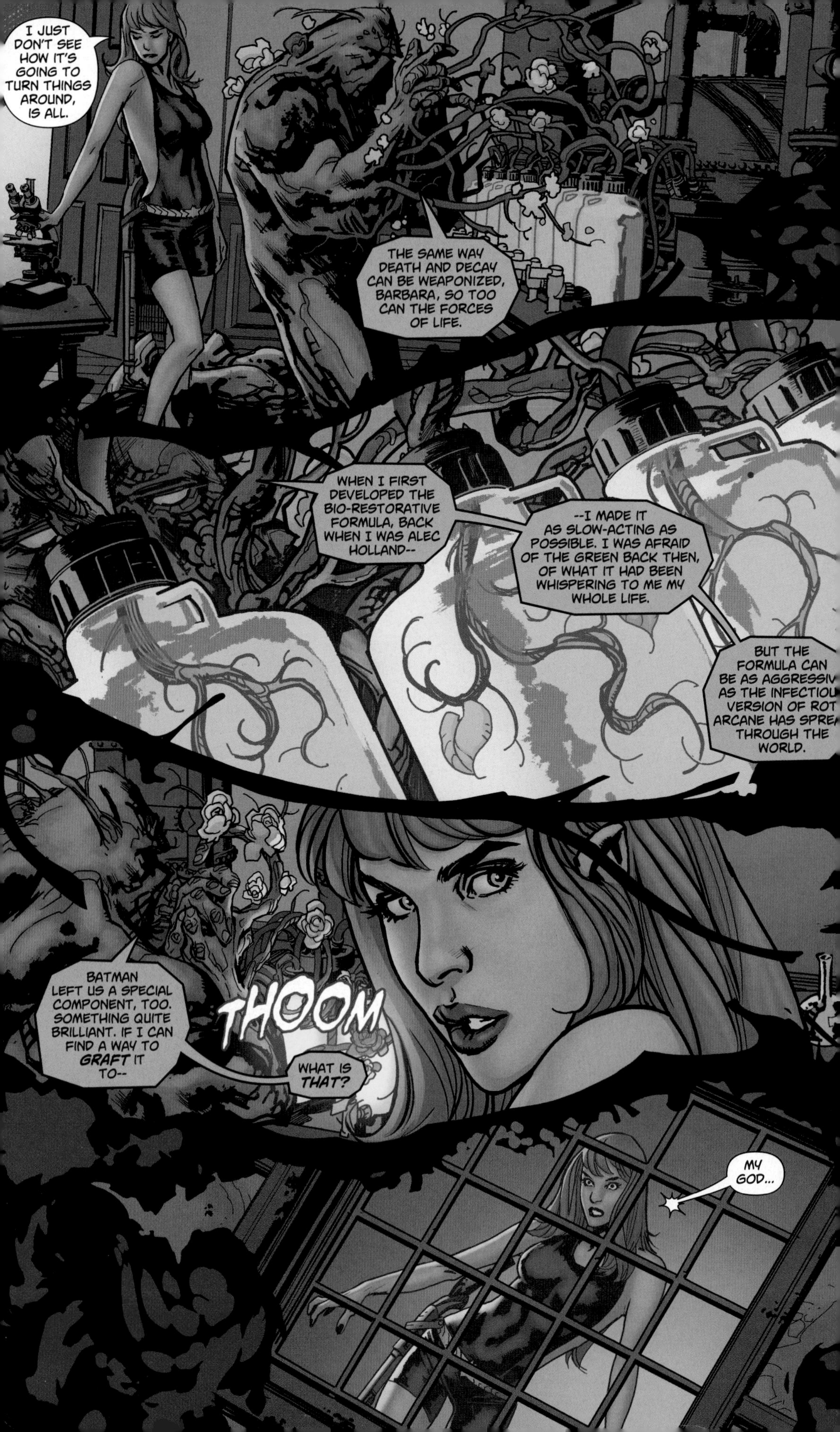
I JUST DON'T SEE HOW IT'S GOING TO TURN THINGS AROUND, IS ALL.
THE SAME WAY DEATH AND DECAY CAN BE WEAPONIZED, BARBARA, SO TOO CAN THE FORCES OF LIFE.
WHEN I FIRST DEVELOPED THE BIO-RESTORATIVE FORMULA, BACK WHEN I WAS ALEC HOLLAND--
--I MADE IT AS SLOW-ACTING AS POSSIBLE. I WAS AFRAID OF THE GREEN BACK THEN, OF WHAT IT HAD BEEN WHISPERING TO ME MY WHOLE LIFE.
BUT THE FORMULA CAN BE AS AGGRESSIV AS THE INFECTIOU VERSION OF ROT ARCANE HAS SPRE THROUGH THE WORLD.
BATMAN LEFT US A SPECIAL COMPONENT, TOO. SOMETHING QUITE BRILLIANT. IF I CAN FIND A WAY TO *GRAFT* IT TO--
THOOM
WHAT IS *THAT?*
MY GOD...

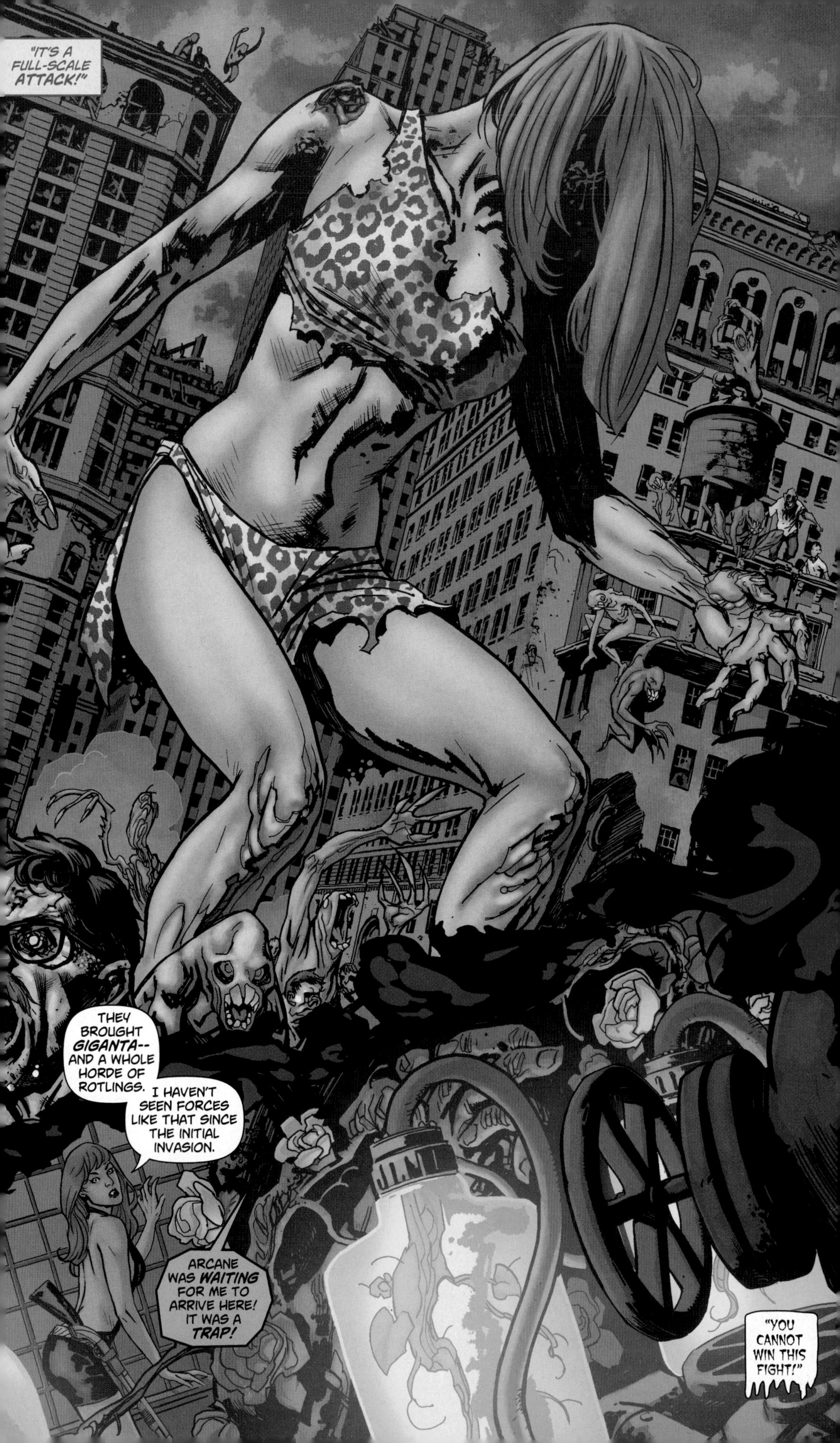
"IT'S A FULL-SCALE ATTACK!"
THEY BROUGHT GIGANTA-- AND A WHOLE HORDE OF ROTLINGS.
I HAVEN'T SEEN FORCES LIKE THAT SINCE THE INITIAL INVASION.
ARCANE WAS WAITING FOR ME TO ARRIVE HERE! IT WAS A TRAP!
"YOU CANNOT WIN THIS FIGHT!"

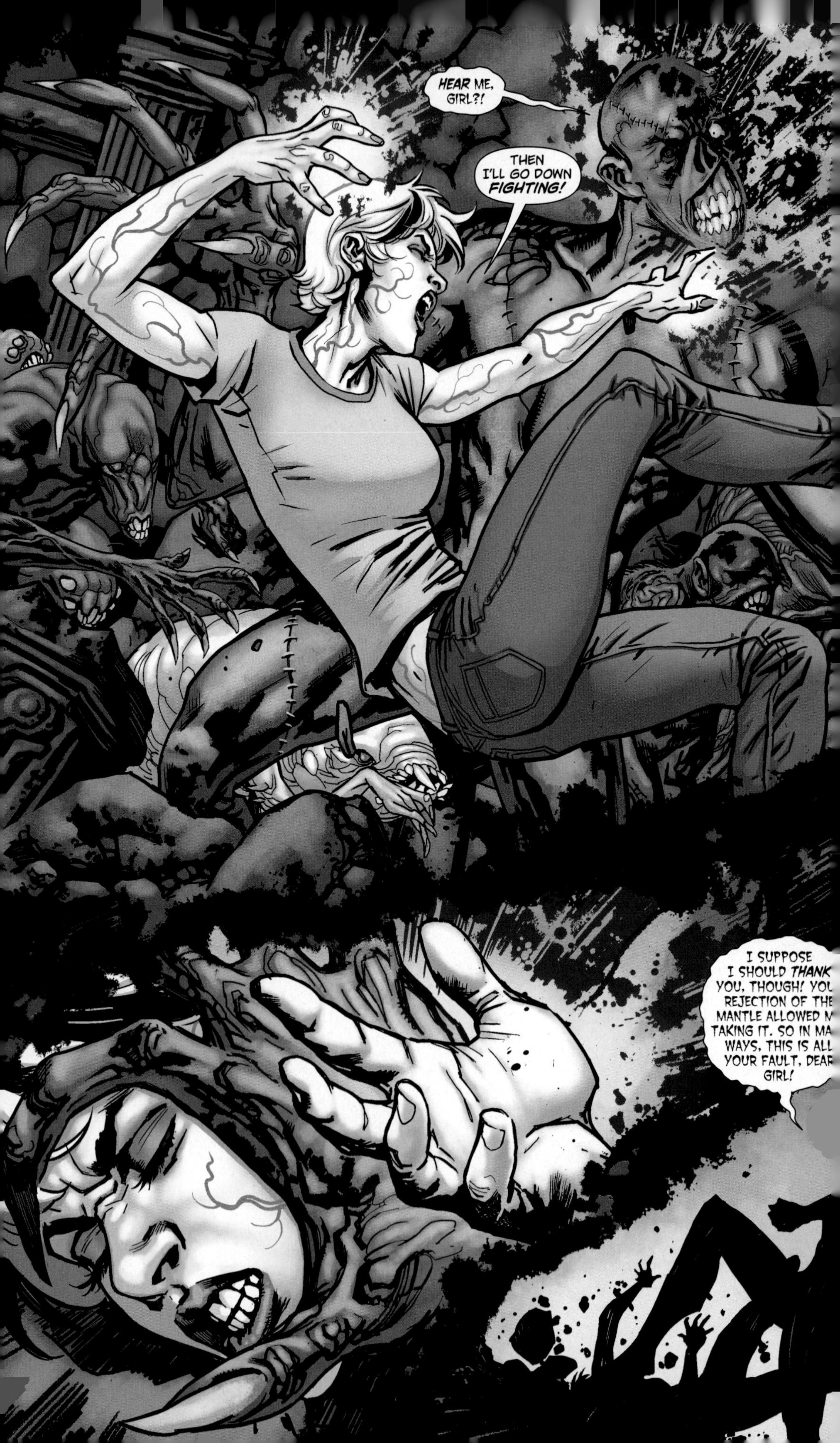
HEAR ME, GIRL?!
THEN I'LL GO DOWN FIGHTING!
I SUPPOSE I SHOULD THANK YOU, THOUGH! YOU REJECTION OF THE MANTLE ALLOWED M TAKING IT. SO IN MA WAYS, THIS IS ALL YOUR FAULT, DEAR GIRL!

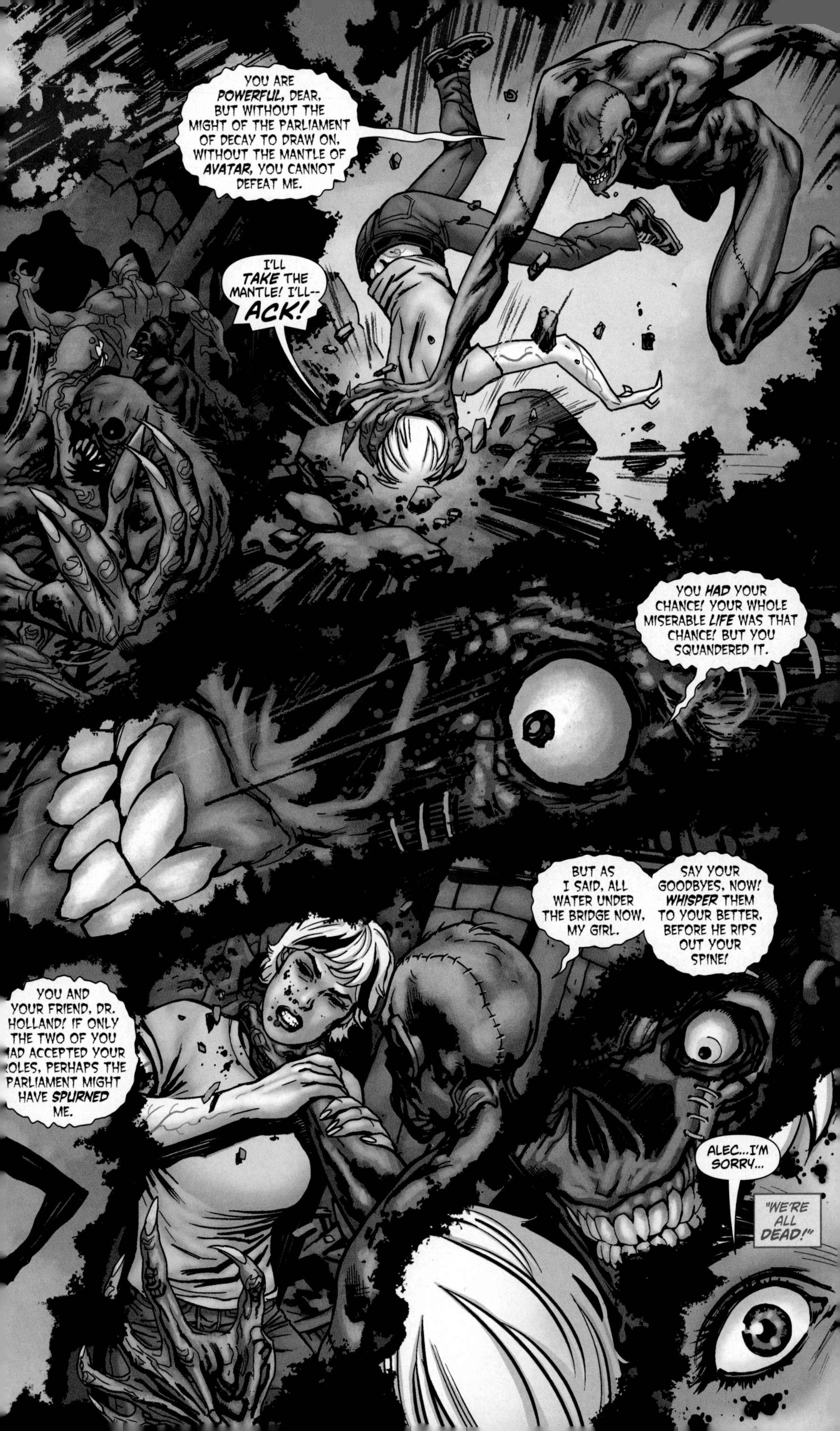
YOU ARE POWERFUL, DEAR, BUT WITHOUT THE MIGHT OF THE PARLIAMENT OF DECAY TO DRAW ON, WITHOUT THE MANTLE OF AVATAR, YOU CANNOT DEFEAT ME.
I'LL TAKE THE MANTLE! I'LL-- ACK!
YOU HAD YOUR CHANCE! YOUR WHOLE MISERABLE LIFE WAS THAT CHANCE! BUT YOU SQUANDERED IT.
YOU AND YOUR FRIEND, DR. HOLLAND! IF ONLY THE TWO OF YOU HAD ACCEPTED YOUR ROLES, PERHAPS THE PARLIAMENT MIGHT HAVE SPURNED ME.
BUT AS I SAID, ALL WATER UNDER THE BRIDGE NOW, MY GIRL.
SAY YOUR GOODBYES, NOW! WHISPER THEM TO YOUR BETTER, BEFORE HE RIPS OUT YOUR SPINE!
ALEC...I'M SORRY...
"WE'RE ALL DEAD!"

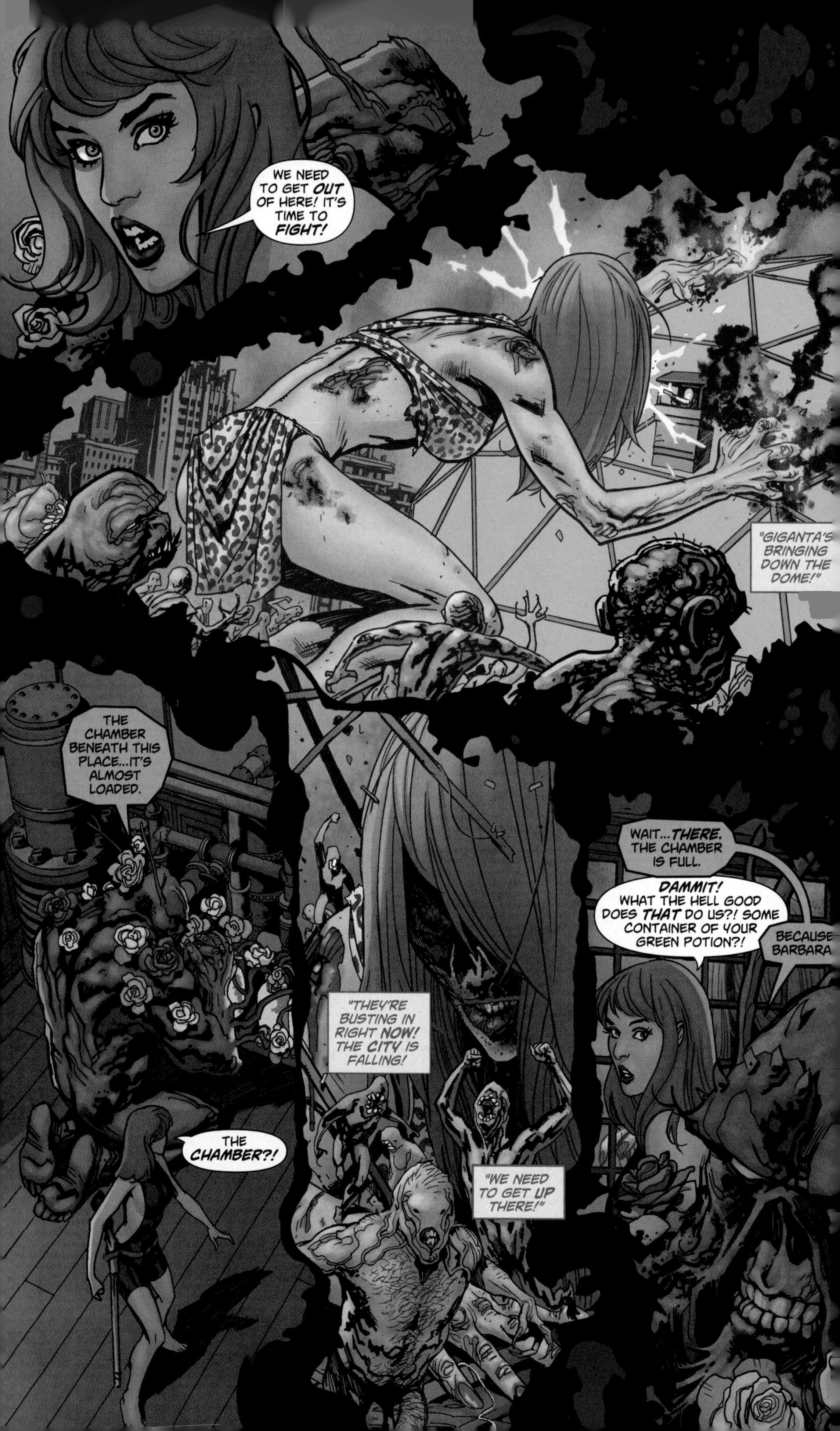

WE NEED TO GET OUT OF HERE! IT'S TIME TO FIGHT!
"GIGANTA'S BRINGING DOWN THE DOME!"
THE CHAMBER BENEATH THIS PLACE...IT'S ALMOST LOADED.
WAIT...THERE. THE CHAMBER IS FULL.
DAMMIT! WHAT THE HELL GOOD DOES THAT DO US?! SOME CONTAINER OF YOUR GREEN POTION?!
BECAUSE BARBARA
"THEY'RE BUSTING IN RIGHT NOW! THE CITY IS FALLING!
THE CHAMBER?!
"WE NEED TO GET UP THERE!"

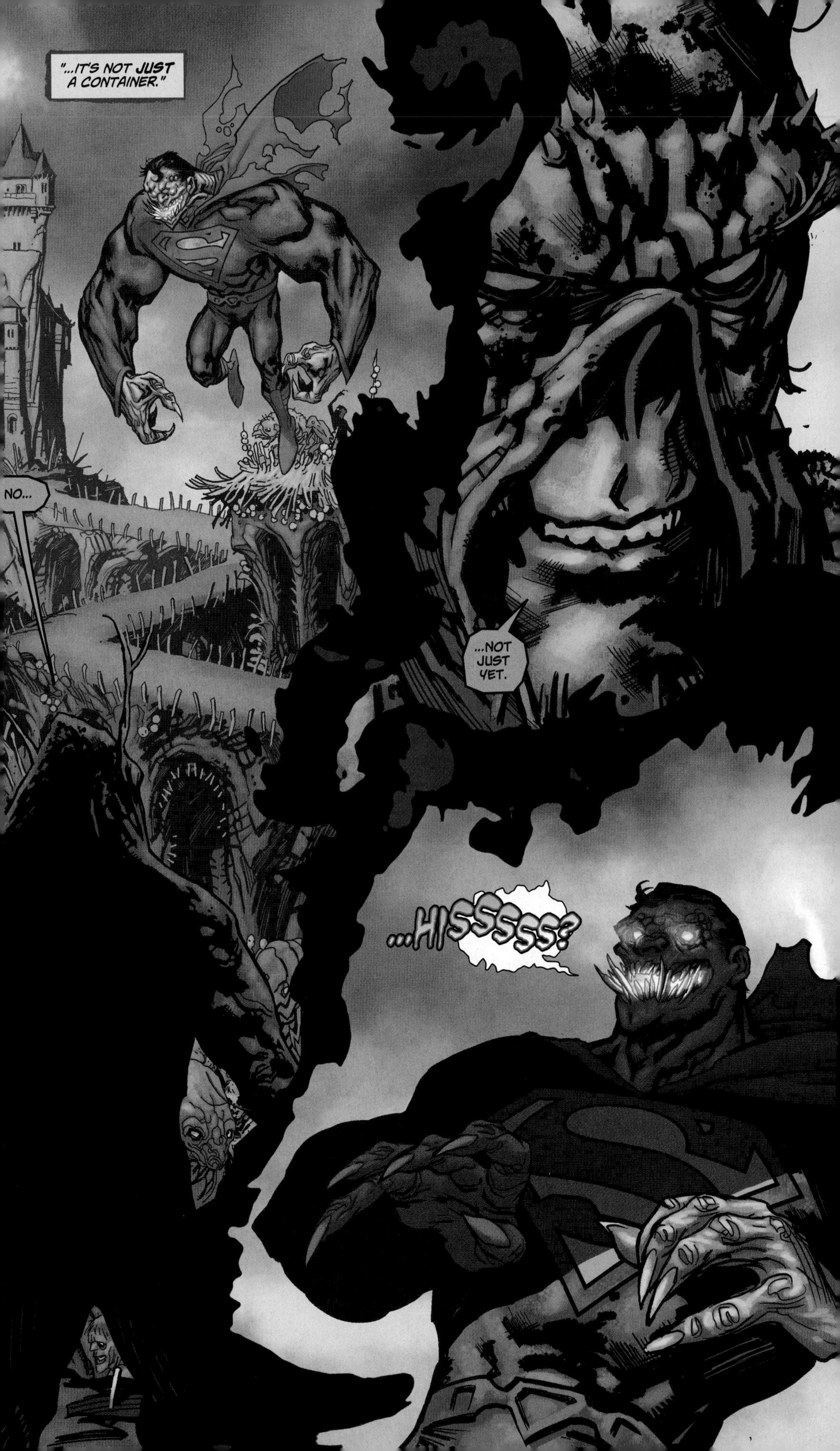
"...IT'S NOT JUST A CONTAINER."
NO...
...NOT JUST YET.
...HISSSSS?

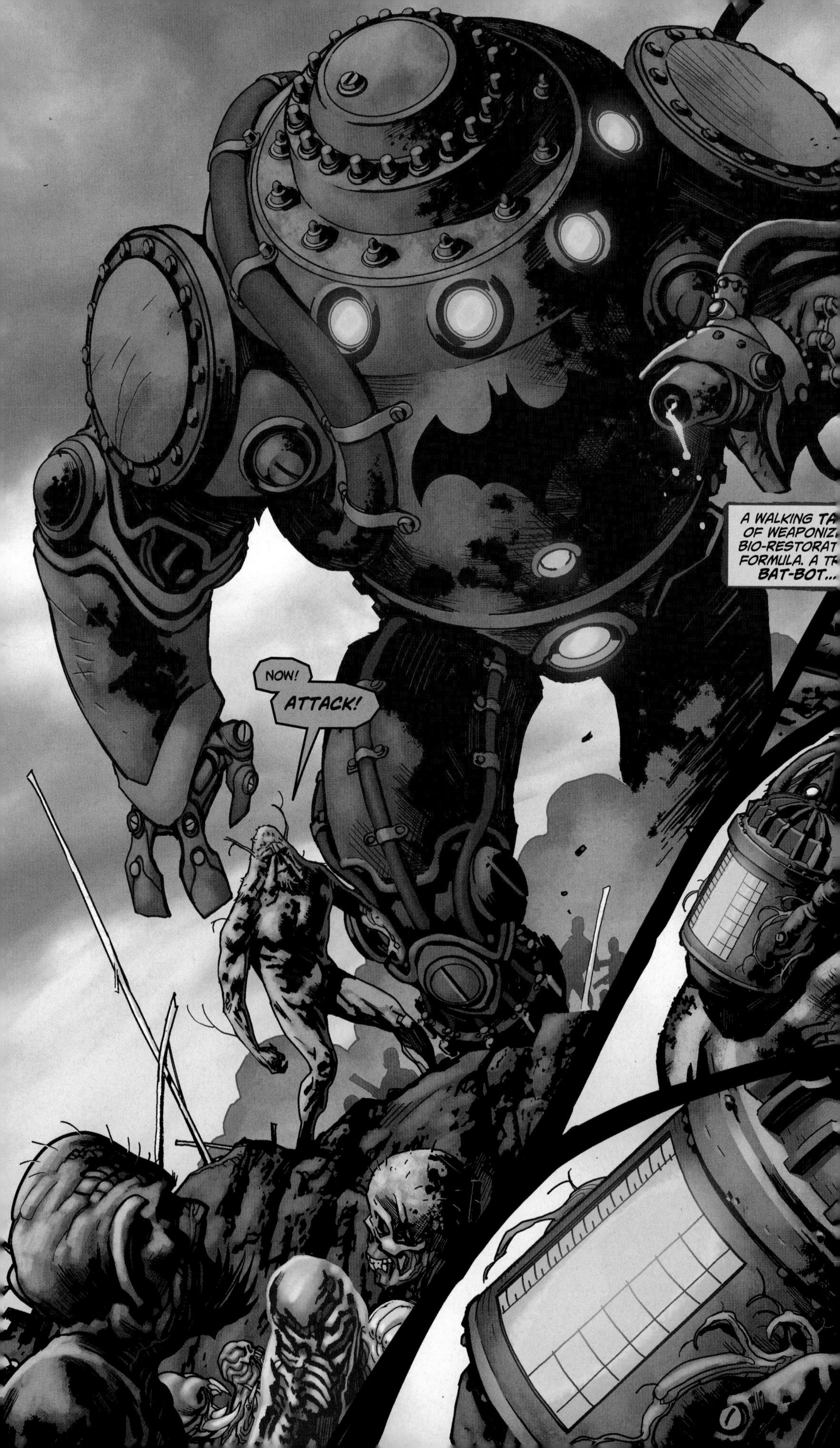
A WALKING TA
OF WEAPONIZ
BIO-RESTORAT
FORMULA. A TR
BAT-BOT...
NOW!
ATTACK!

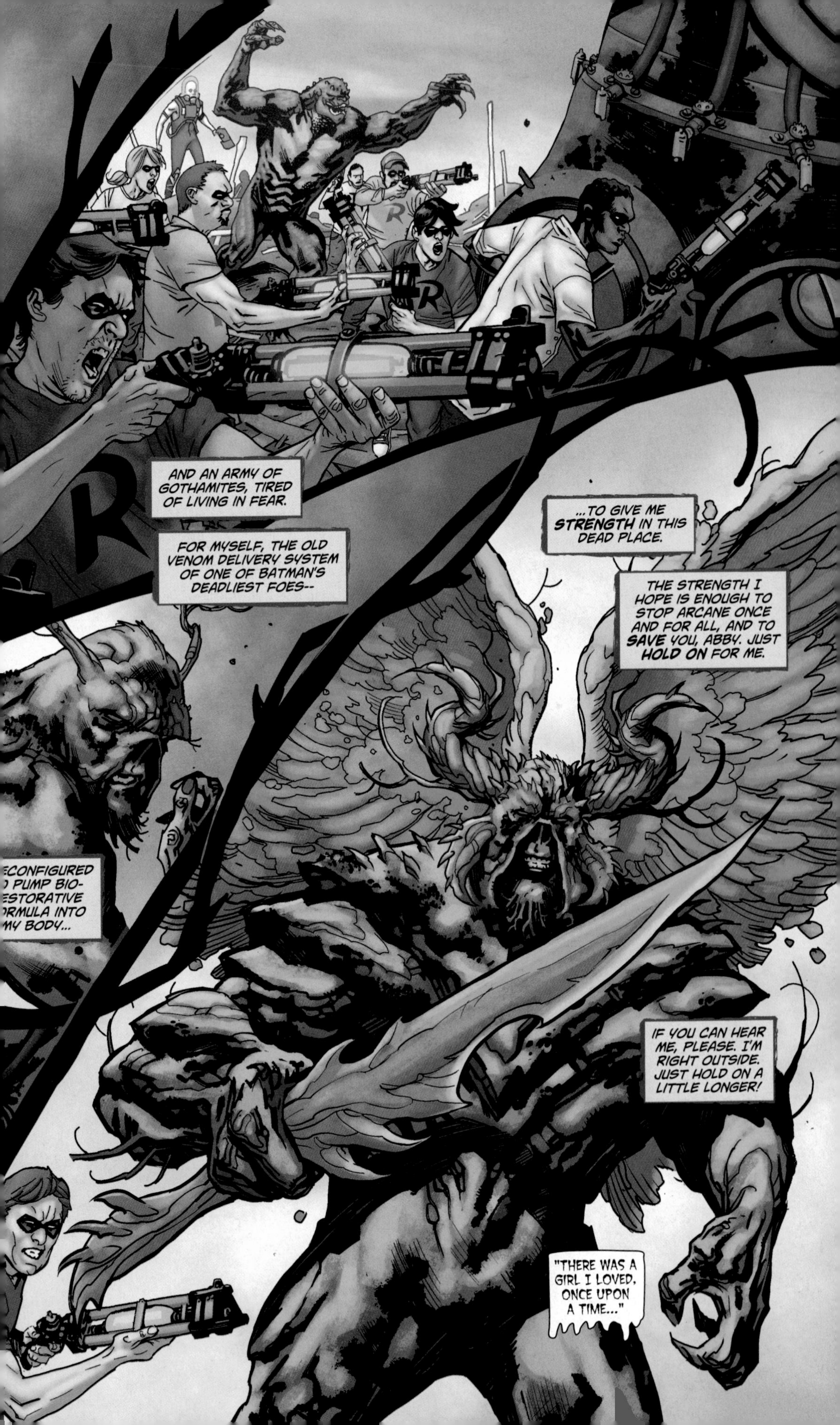
AND AN ARMY OF GOTHAMITES, TIRED OF LIVING IN FEAR.
FOR MYSELF, THE OLD VENOM DELIVERY SYSTEM OF ONE OF BATMAN'S DEADLIEST FOES--
ECONFIGURED O PUMP BIO- ESTORATIVE ORMULA INTO MY BODY...
...TO GIVE ME STRENGTH IN THIS DEAD PLACE.
THE STRENGTH I HOPE IS ENOUGH TO STOP ARCANE ONCE AND FOR ALL, AND TO SAVE YOU, ABBY. JUST HOLD ON FOR ME.
IF YOU CAN HEAR ME, PLEASE. I'M RIGHT OUTSIDE. JUST HOLD ON A LITTLE LONGER!
"THERE WAS A GIRL I LOVED, ONCE UPON A TIME..."

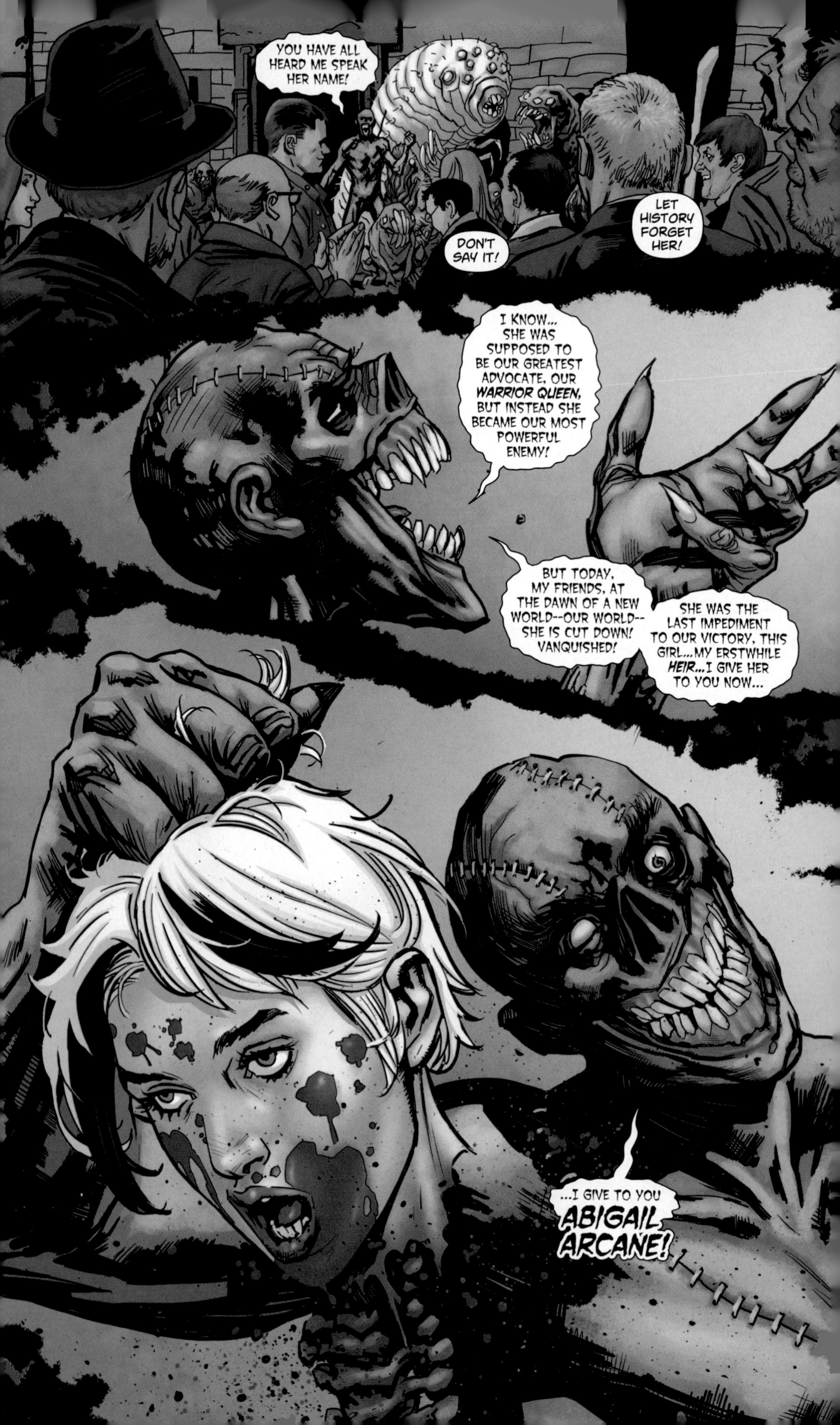
YOU HAVE ALL HEARD ME SPEAK HER NAME!
DON'T SAY IT!
LET HISTORY FORGET HER!
I KNOW... SHE WAS SUPPOSED TO BE OUR GREATEST ADVOCATE, OUR WARRIOR QUEEN, BUT INSTEAD SHE BECAME OUR MOST POWERFUL ENEMY!
BUT TODAY, MY FRIENDS, AT THE DAWN OF A NEW WORLD--OUR WORLD--SHE IS CUT DOWN! VANQUISHED!
SHE WAS THE LAST IMPEDIMENT TO OUR VICTORY, THIS GIRL...MY ERSTWHILE HEIR...I GIVE HER TO YOU NOW...
...I GIVE TO YOU ABIGAIL ARCANE!

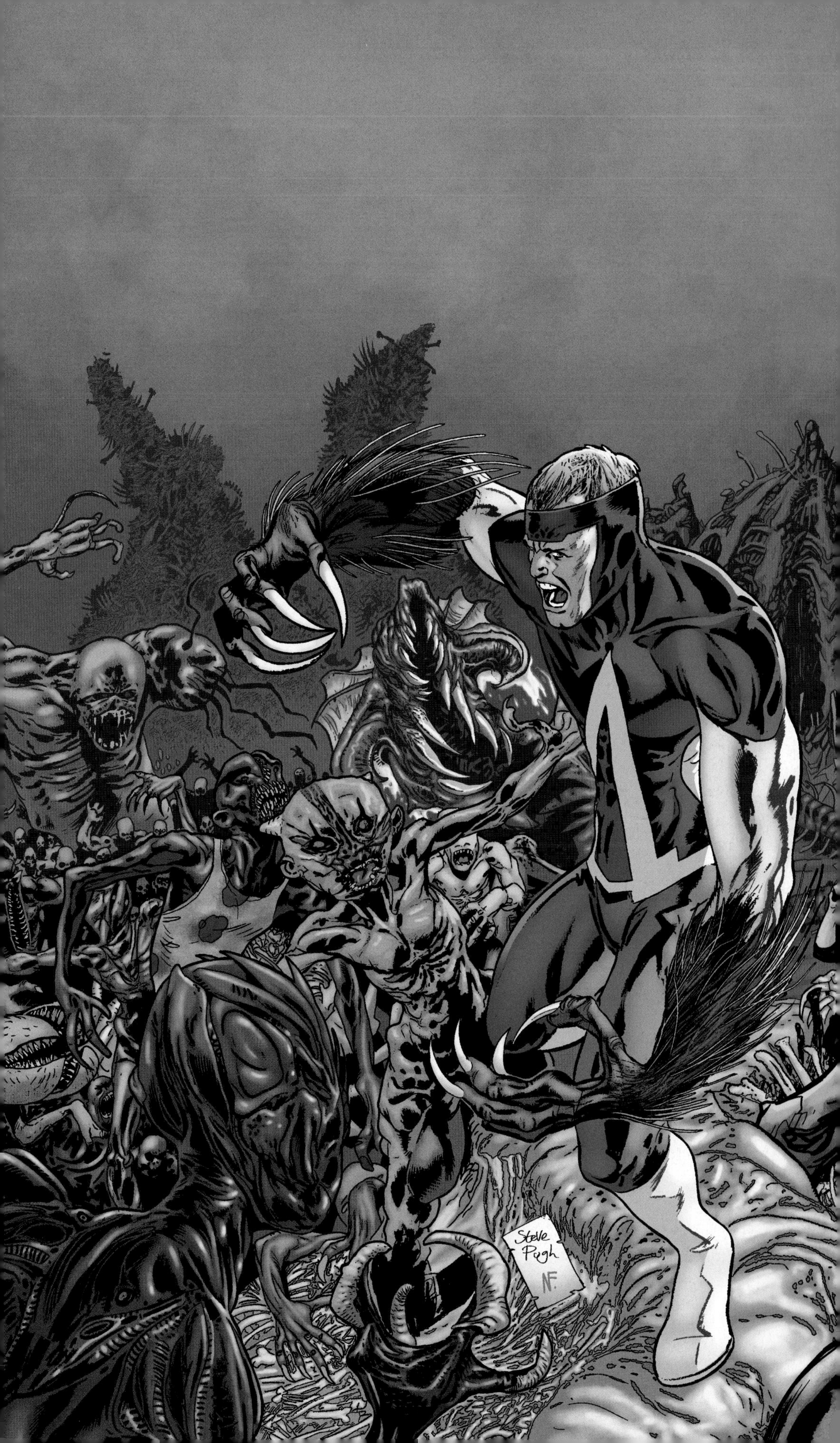
Steve Pugh
NF.

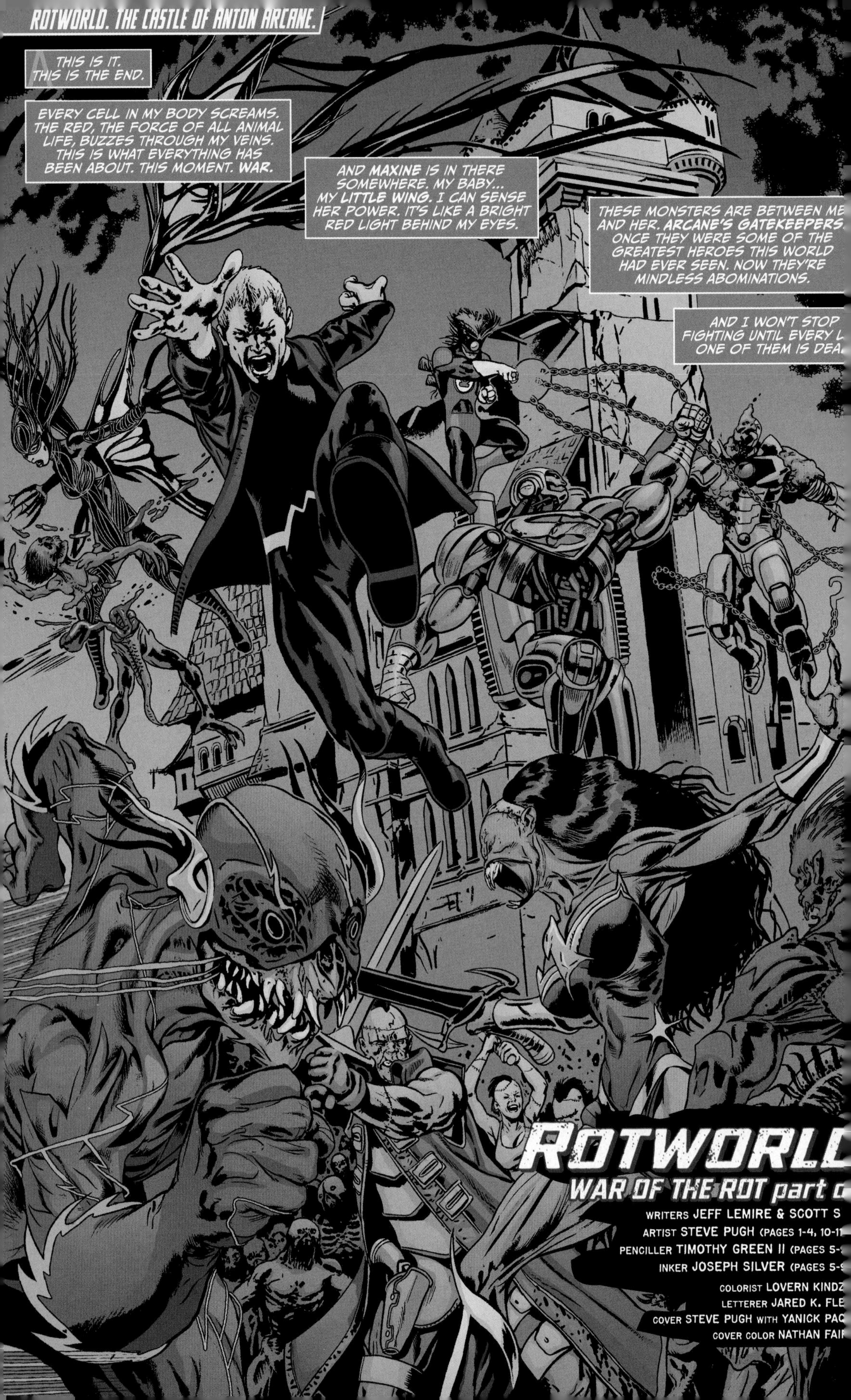
ROTWORLD. THE CASTLE OF ANTON ARCANE.
THIS IS IT. THIS IS THE END.
EVERY CELL IN MY BODY SCREAMS. THE RED, THE FORCE OF ALL ANIMAL LIFE, BUZZES THROUGH MY VEINS. THIS IS WHAT EVERYTHING HAS BEEN ABOUT. THIS MOMENT. WAR.
AND MAXINE IS IN THERE SOMEWHERE. MY BABY... MY LITTLE WING. I CAN SENSE HER POWER. IT'S LIKE A BRIGHT RED LIGHT BEHIND MY EYES.
THESE MONSTERS ARE BETWEEN ME AND HER. ARCANE'S GATEKEEPERS. ONCE THEY WERE SOME OF THE GREATEST HEROES THIS WORLD HAD EVER SEEN. NOW THEY'RE MINDLESS ABOMINATIONS.
AND I WON'T STOP FIGHTING UNTIL EVERY L ONE OF THEM IS DEA
ROTWORLD
WAR OF THE ROT part
WRITERS JEFF LEMIRE & SCOTT S
ARTIST STEVE PUGH (PAGES 1-4, 10-1
PENCILLER TIMOTHY GREEN II (PAGES 5-
INKER JOSEPH SILVER (PAGES 5-
COLORIST LOVERN KINDZ
LETTERER JARED K. FLE
COVER STEVE PUGH WITH YANICK PAC
COVER COLOR NATHAN FAIR

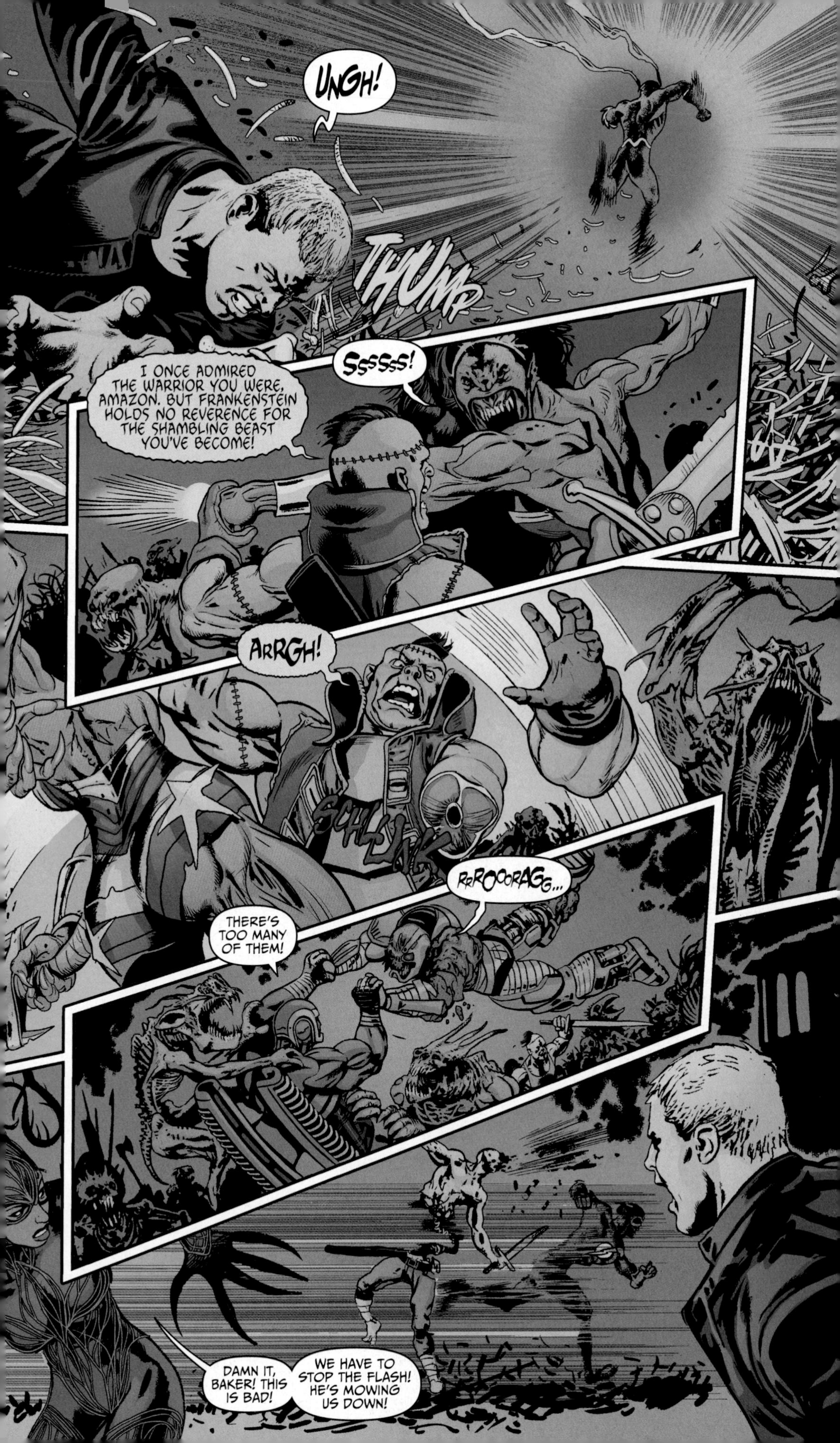
UNGH!
THUMP
I ONCE ADMIRED THE WARRIOR YOU WERE, AMAZON. BUT FRANKENSTEIN HOLDS NO REVERENCE FOR THE SHAMBLING BEAST YOU'VE BECOME!
SSSSSS!
ARRGH!
SCHLINK
RRROOORAGG...
THERE'S TOO MANY OF THEM!
DAMN IT, BAKER! THIS IS BAD!
WE HAVE TO STOP THE FLASH! HE'S MOWING US DOWN!

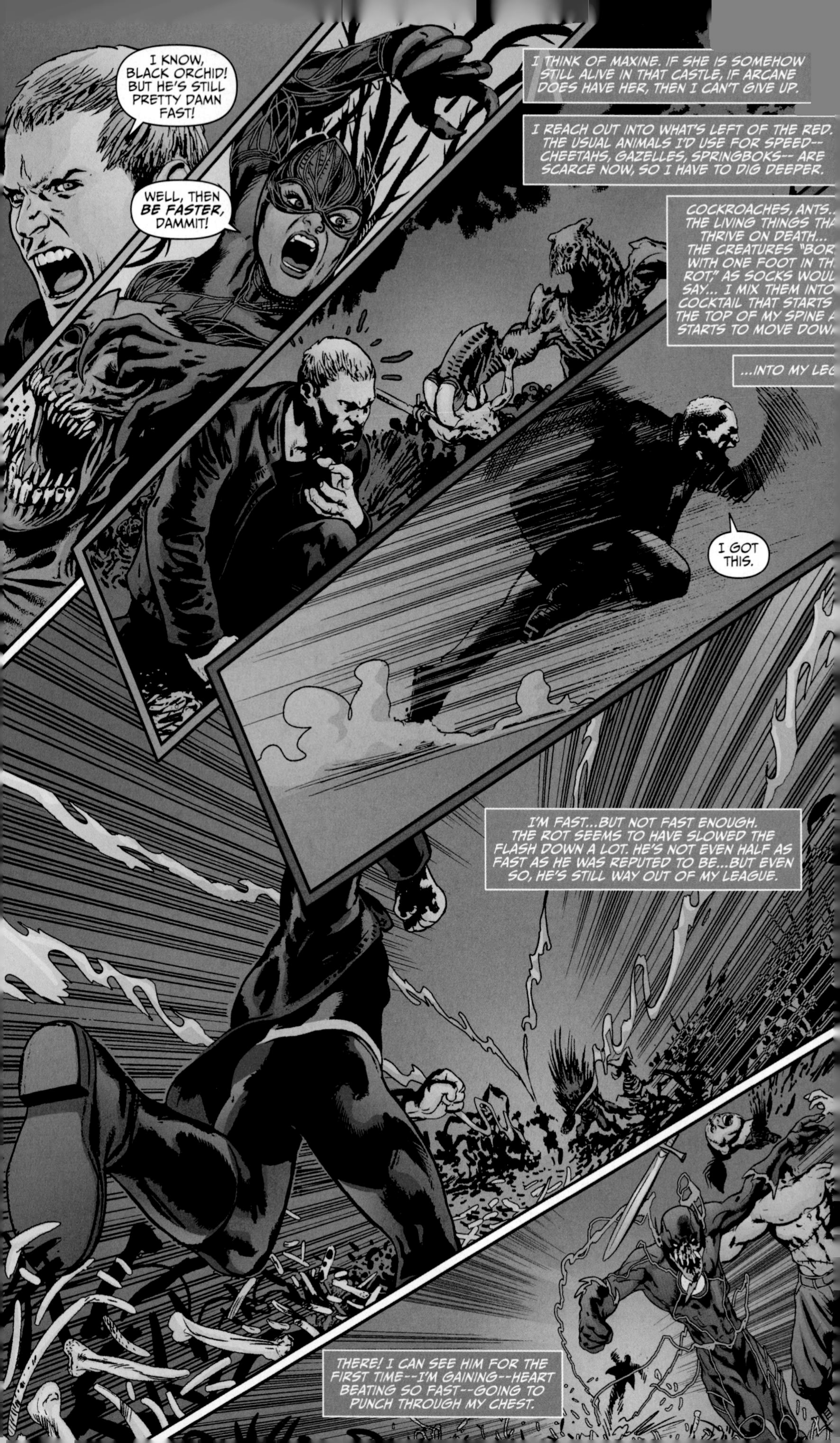

I KNOW, BLACK ORCHID! BUT HE'S STILL PRETTY DAMN FAST!
WELL, THEN BE FASTER, DAMMIT!
I THINK OF MAXINE. IF SHE IS SOMEHOW STILL ALIVE IN THAT CASTLE, IF ARCANE DOES HAVE HER, THEN I CAN'T GIVE UP.
I REACH OUT INTO WHAT'S LEFT OF THE RED. THE USUAL ANIMALS I'D USE FOR SPEED-- CHEETAHS, GAZELLES, SPRINGBOKS-- ARE SCARCE NOW, SO I HAVE TO DIG DEEPER.
COCKROACHES, ANTS... THE LIVING THINGS THA THRIVE ON DEATH... THE CREATURES "BOR WITH ONE FOOT IN TH ROT," AS SOCKS WOUL SAY... I MIX THEM INTO COCKTAIL THAT STARTS THE TOP OF MY SPINE A STARTS TO MOVE DOW
...INTO MY LEG
I GOT THIS.
I'M FAST...BUT NOT FAST ENOUGH. THE ROT SEEMS TO HAVE SLOWED THE FLASH DOWN A LOT. HE'S NOT EVEN HALF AS FAST AS HE WAS REPUTED TO BE...BUT EVEN SO, HE'S STILL WAY OUT OF MY LEAGUE.
THERE! I CAN SEE HIM FOR THE FIRST TIME--I'M GAINING--HEART BEATING SO FAST--GOING TO PUNCH THROUGH MY CHEST.

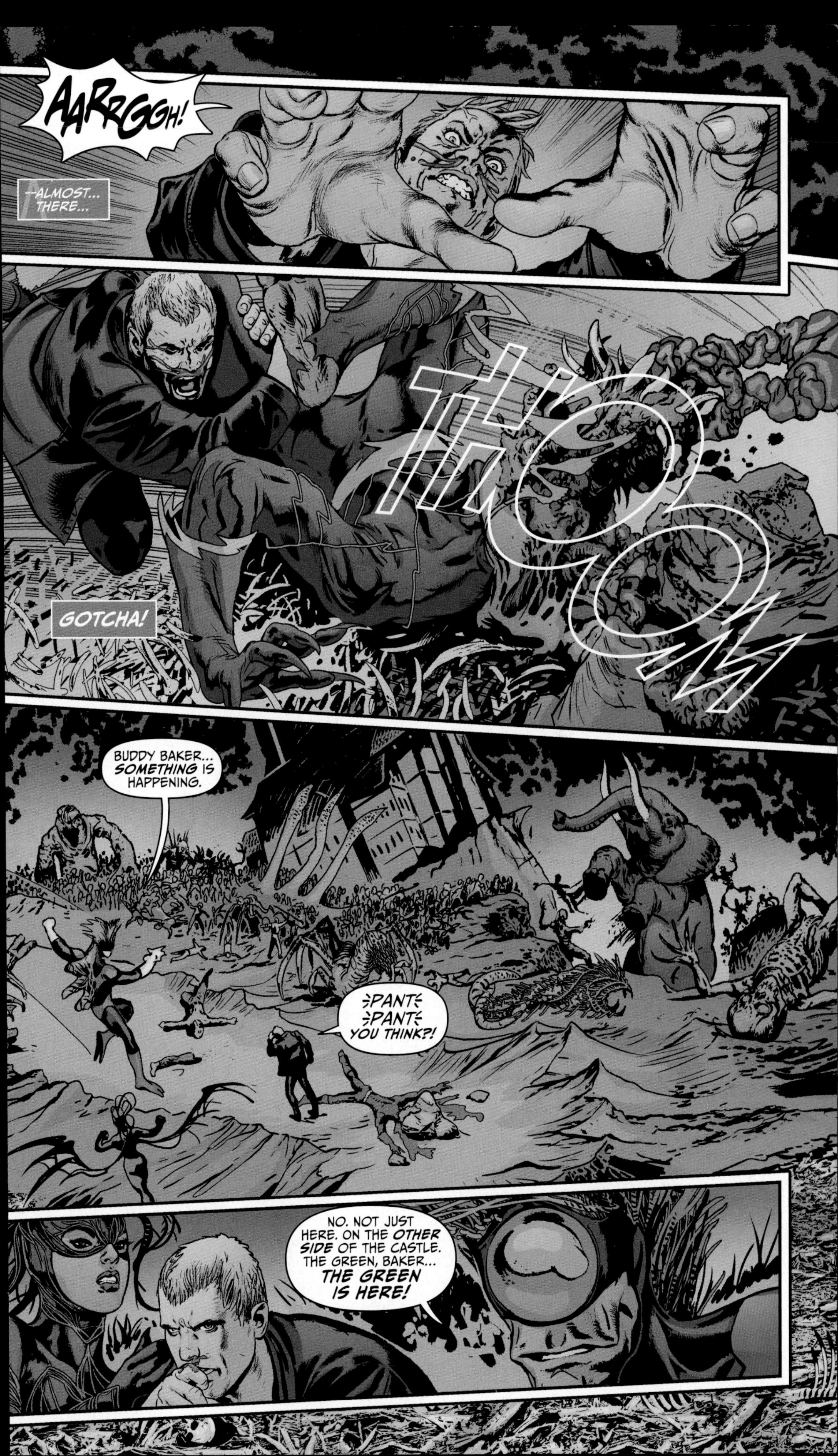

AARRGGH!
--ALMOST... THERE...
GOTCHA!
THOOM
BUDDY BAKER... SOMETHING IS HAPPENING.
PANT PANT YOU THINK?!
NO. NOT JUST HERE. ON THE OTHER SIDE OF THE CASTLE. THE GREEN, BAKER... THE GREEN IS HERE!

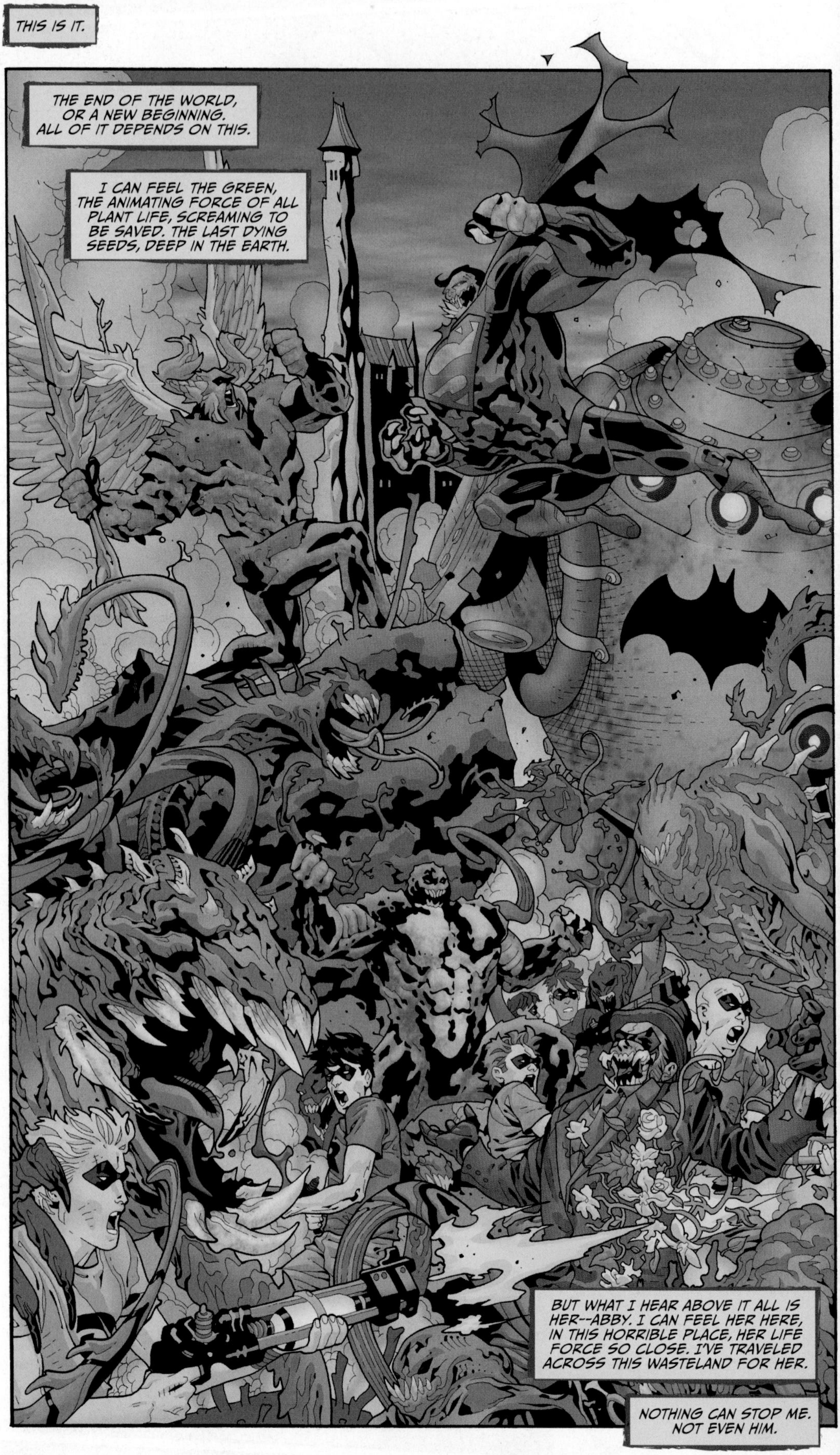
THIS IS IT.
THE END OF THE WORLD, OR A NEW BEGINNING. ALL OF IT DEPENDS ON THIS.
I CAN FEEL THE GREEN, THE ANIMATING FORCE OF ALL PLANT LIFE, SCREAMING TO BE SAVED. THE LAST DYING SEEDS, DEEP IN THE EARTH.
BUT WHAT I HEAR ABOVE IT ALL IS HER--ABBY. I CAN FEEL HER HERE, IN THIS HORRIBLE PLACE, HER LIFE FORCE SO CLOSE. I'VE TRAVELED ACROSS THIS WASTELAND FOR HER.
NOTHING CAN STOP ME. NOT EVEN HIM.

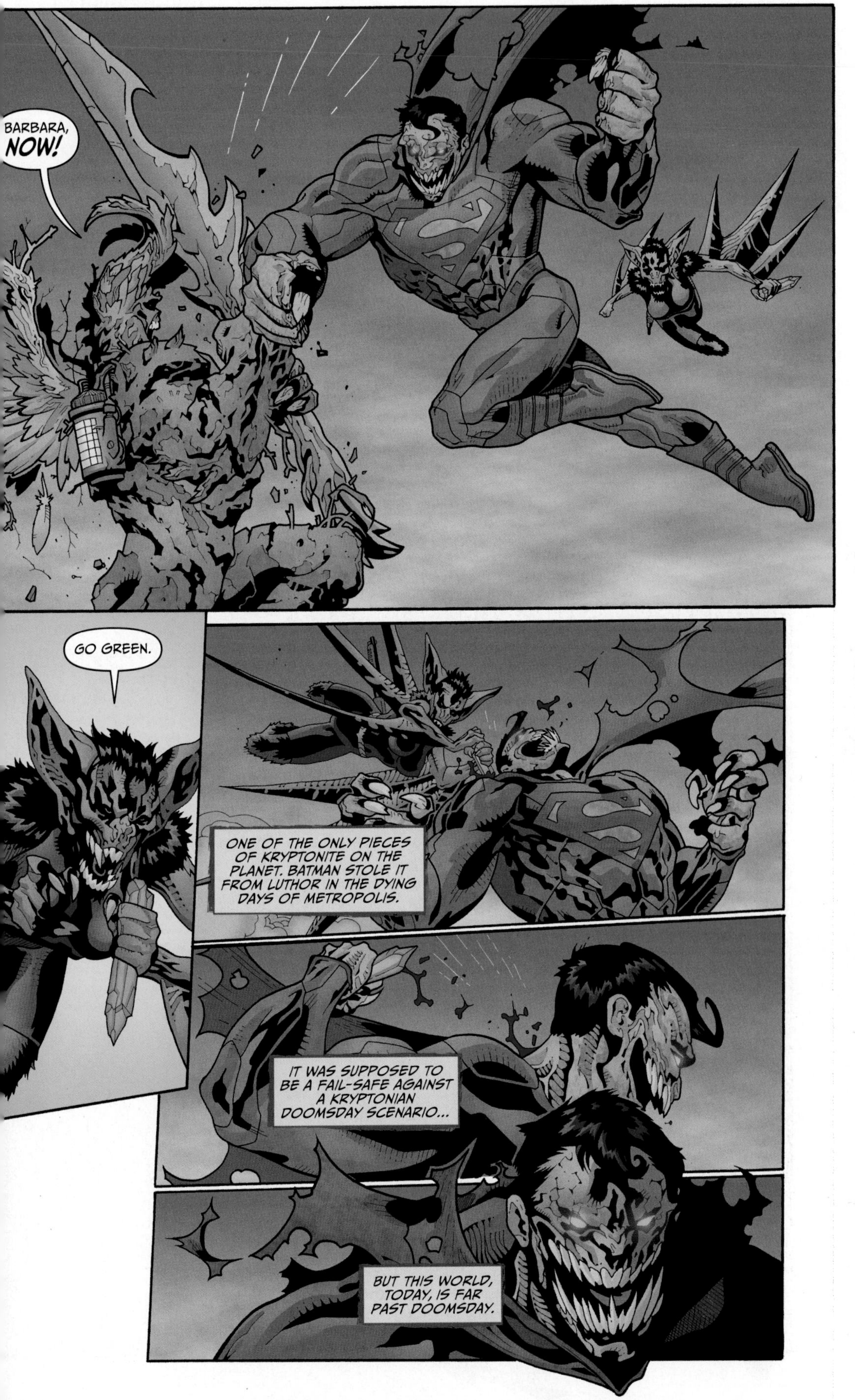
BARBARA, NOW!
GO GREEN.
ONE OF THE ONLY PIECES OF KRYPTONITE ON THE PLANET. BATMAN STOLE IT FROM LUTHOR IN THE DYING DAYS OF METROPOLIS.
IT WAS SUPPOSED TO BE A FAIL-SAFE AGAINST A KRYPTONIAN DOOMSDAY SCENARIO...
BUT THIS WORLD, TODAY, IS FAR PAST DOOMSDAY.

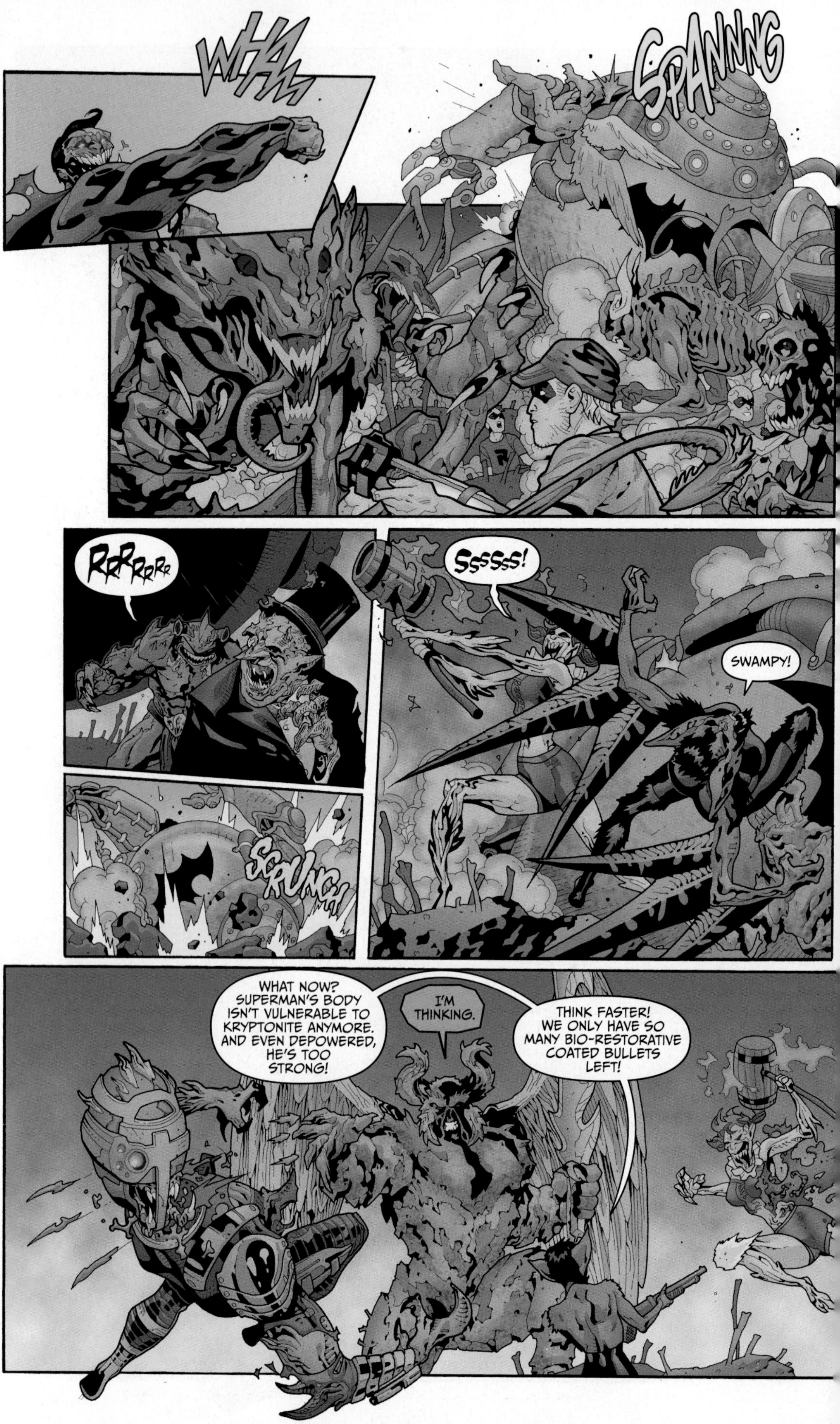
WHAM
SPANNNG
RRRRRRR
SSSSSS!
SWAMPY!
SCRUNCH
WHAT NOW? SUPERMAN'S BODY ISN'T VULNERABLE TO KRYPTONITE ANYMORE. AND EVEN DEPOWERED, HE'S TOO STRONG!
I'M THINKING.
THINK FASTER! WE ONLY HAVE SO MANY BIO-RESTORATIVE COATED BULLETS LEFT!

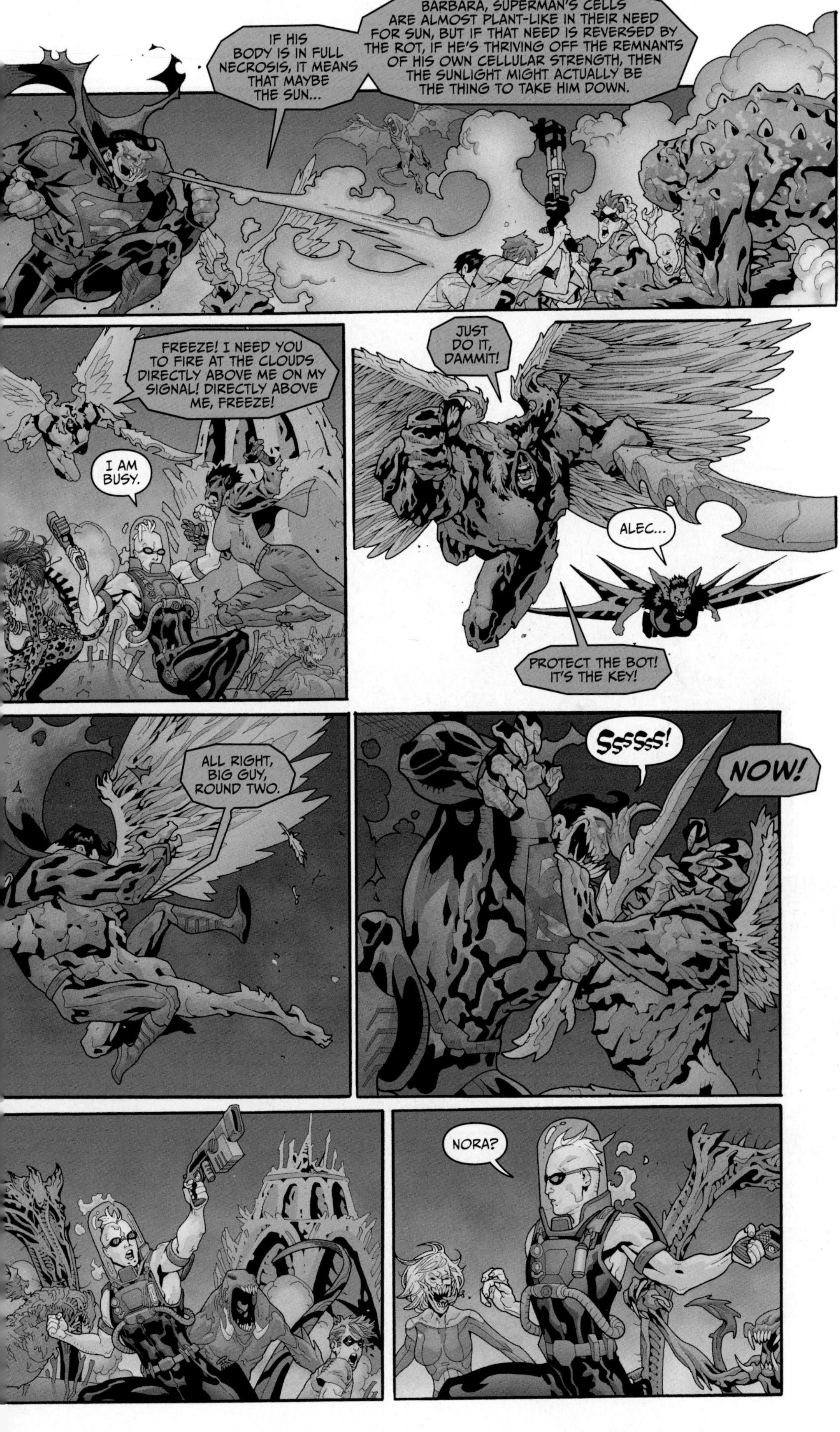
IF HIS BODY IS IN FULL NECROSIS, IT MEANS THAT MAYBE THE SUN...
BARBARA, SUPERMAN'S CELLS ARE ALMOST PLANT-LIKE IN THEIR NEED FOR SUN, BUT IF THAT NEED IS REVERSED BY THE ROT, IF HE'S THRIVING OFF THE REMNANTS OF HIS OWN CELLULAR STRENGTH, THEN THE SUNLIGHT MIGHT ACTUALLY BE THE THING TO TAKE HIM DOWN.
FREEZE! I NEED YOU TO FIRE AT THE CLOUDS DIRECTLY ABOVE ME ON MY SIGNAL! DIRECTLY ABOVE ME, FREEZE!
I AM BUSY.
JUST DO IT, DAMMIT!
ALEC...
PROTECT THE BOT! IT'S THE KEY!
ALL RIGHT, BIG GUY, ROUND TWO.
SSSSSS!
NOW!
NORA?

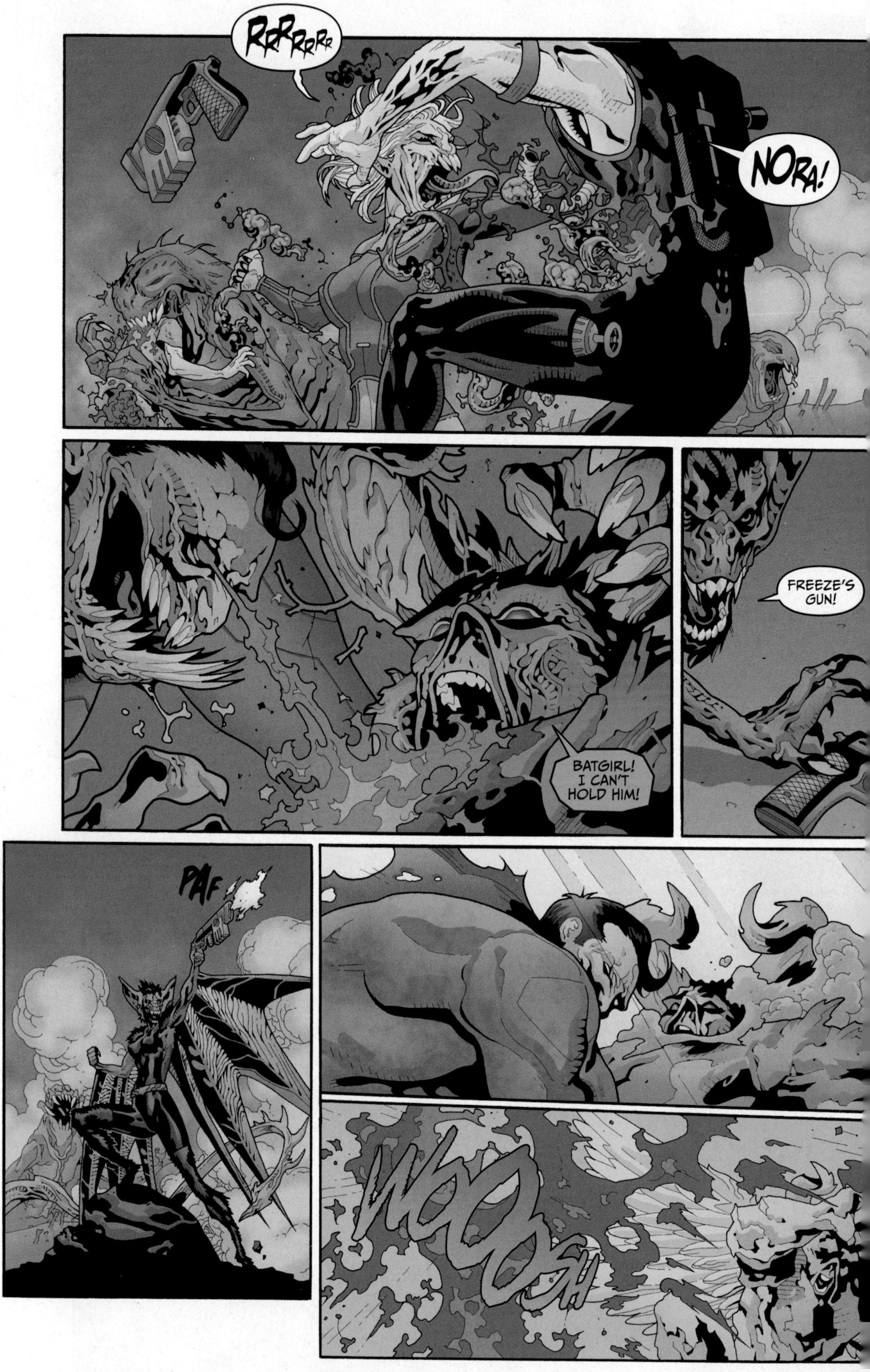
RRRRRRR
NORA!
FREEZE'S GUN!
BATGIRL! I CAN'T HOLD HIM!
PAF
WOOOSH

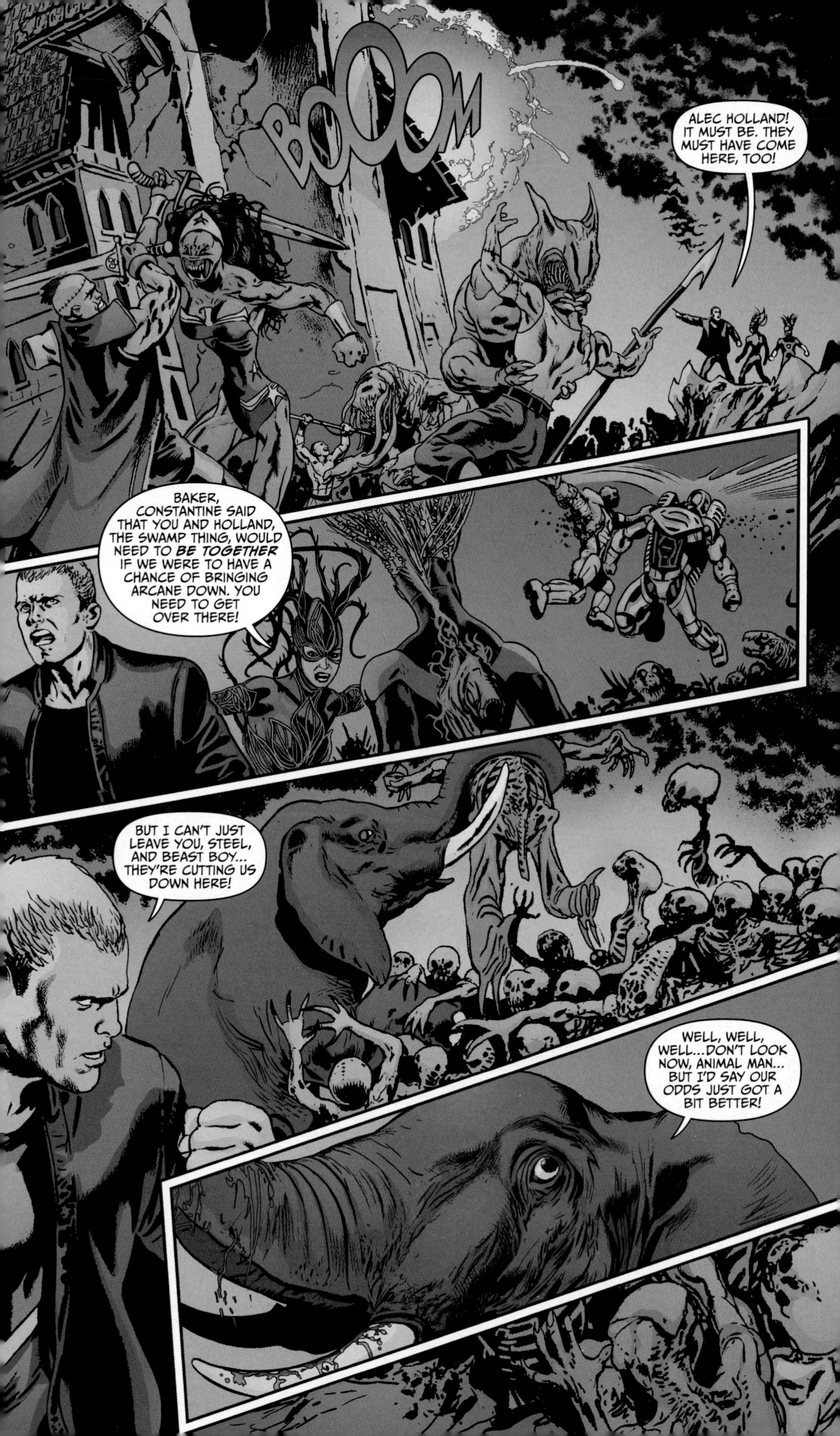
BOOOOM
ALEC HOLLAND! IT MUST BE. THEY MUST HAVE COME HERE, TOO!
BAKER, CONSTANTINE SAID THAT YOU AND HOLLAND, THE SWAMP THING, WOULD NEED TO BE TOGETHER IF WE WERE TO HAVE A CHANCE OF BRINGING ARCANE DOWN. YOU NEED TO GET OVER THERE!
BUT I CAN'T JUST LEAVE YOU, STEEL, AND BEAST BOY... THEY'RE CUTTING US DOWN HERE!
WELL, WELL, WELL...DON'T LOOK NOW, ANIMAL MAN... BUT I'D SAY OUR ODDS JUST GOT A BIT BETTER!

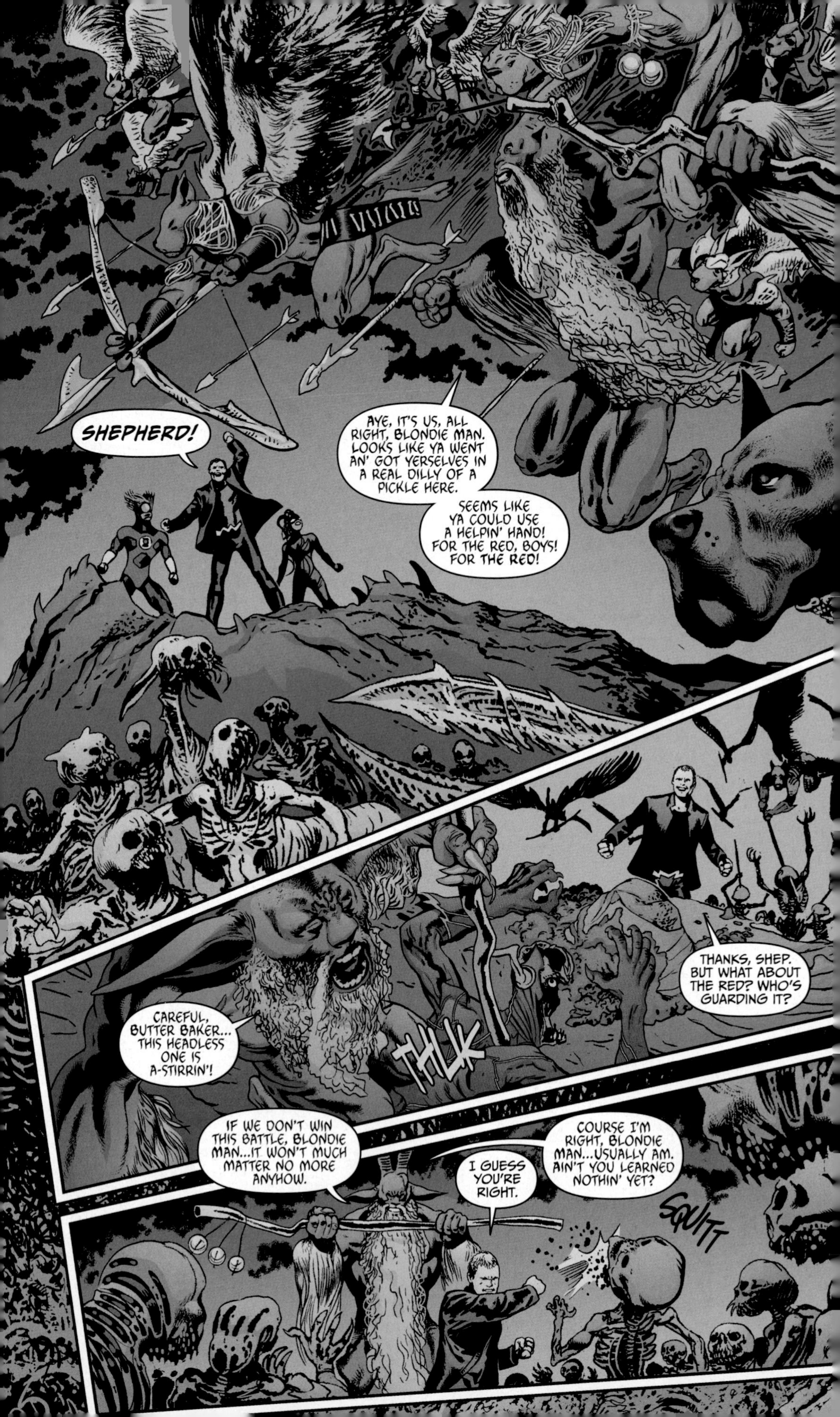
SHEPHERD!
AYE, IT'S US, ALL RIGHT, BLONDIE MAN. LOOKS LIKE YA WENT AN' GOT YERSELVES IN A REAL DILLY OF A PICKLE HERE.
SEEMS LIKE YA COULD USE A HELPIN' HAND! FOR THE RED, BOYS! FOR THE RED!
THANKS, SHEP. BUT WHAT ABOUT THE RED? WHO'S GUARDING IT?
CAREFUL, BUTTER BAKER... THIS HEADLESS ONE IS A-STIRRIN'!
THUK
IF WE DON'T WIN THIS BATTLE, BLONDIE MAN...IT WON'T MUCH MATTER NO MORE ANYHOW.
I GUESS YOU'RE RIGHT.
COURSE I'M RIGHT, BLONDIE MAN...USUALLY AM. AIN'T YOU LEARNED NOTHIN' YET?
SQUITT

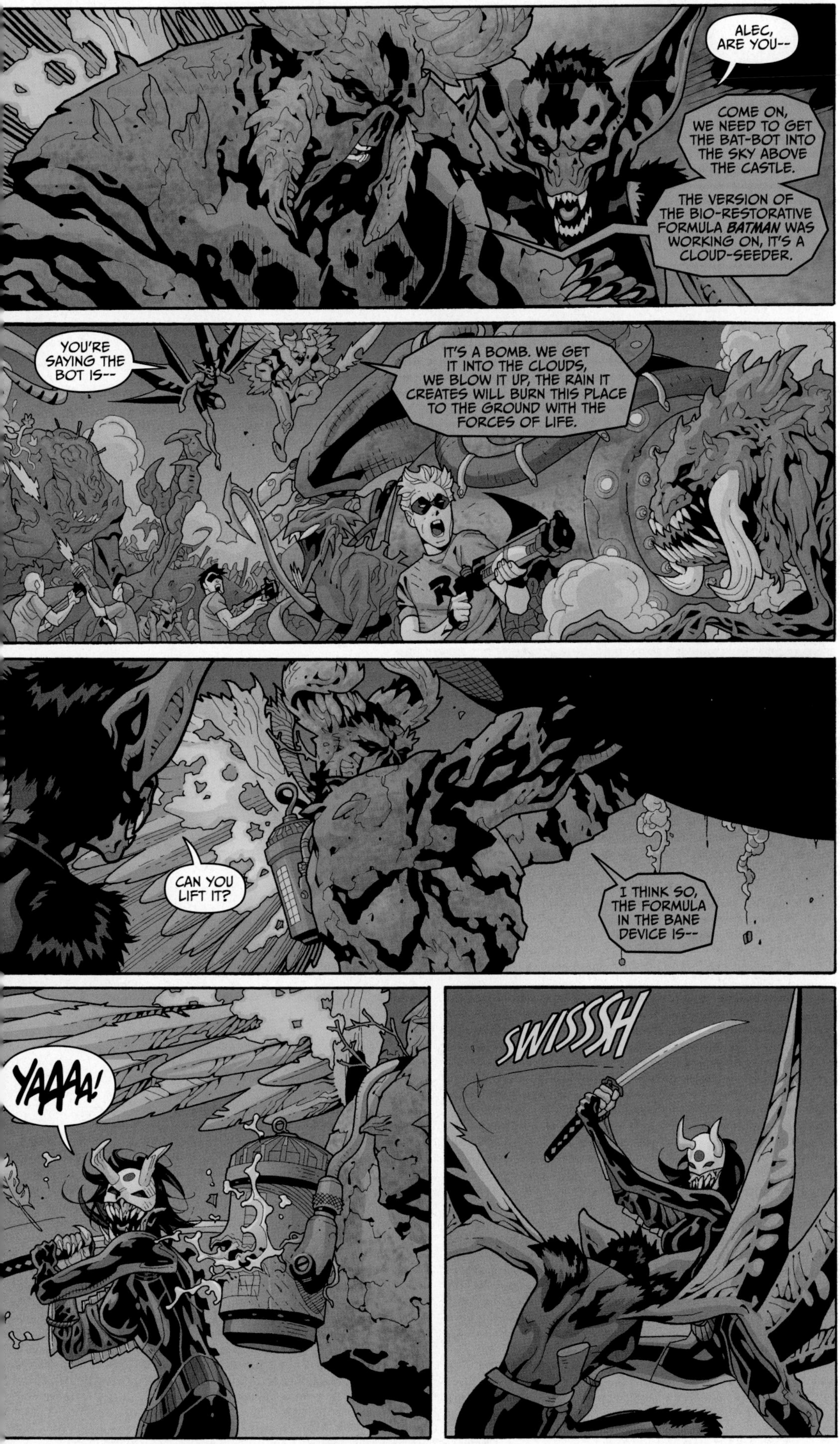
ALEC, ARE YOU--
COME ON, WE NEED TO GET THE BAT-BOT INTO THE SKY ABOVE THE CASTLE.
THE VERSION OF THE BIO-RESTORATIVE FORMULA BATMAN WAS WORKING ON, IT'S A CLOUD-SEEDER.
YOU'RE SAYING THE BOT IS--
IT'S A BOMB. WE GET IT INTO THE CLOUDS, WE BLOW IT UP, THE RAIN IT CREATES WILL BURN THIS PLACE TO THE GROUND WITH THE FORCES OF LIFE.
CAN YOU LIFT IT?
I THINK SO, THE FORMULA IN THE BANE DEVICE IS--
YAAAA!
SWISSSH

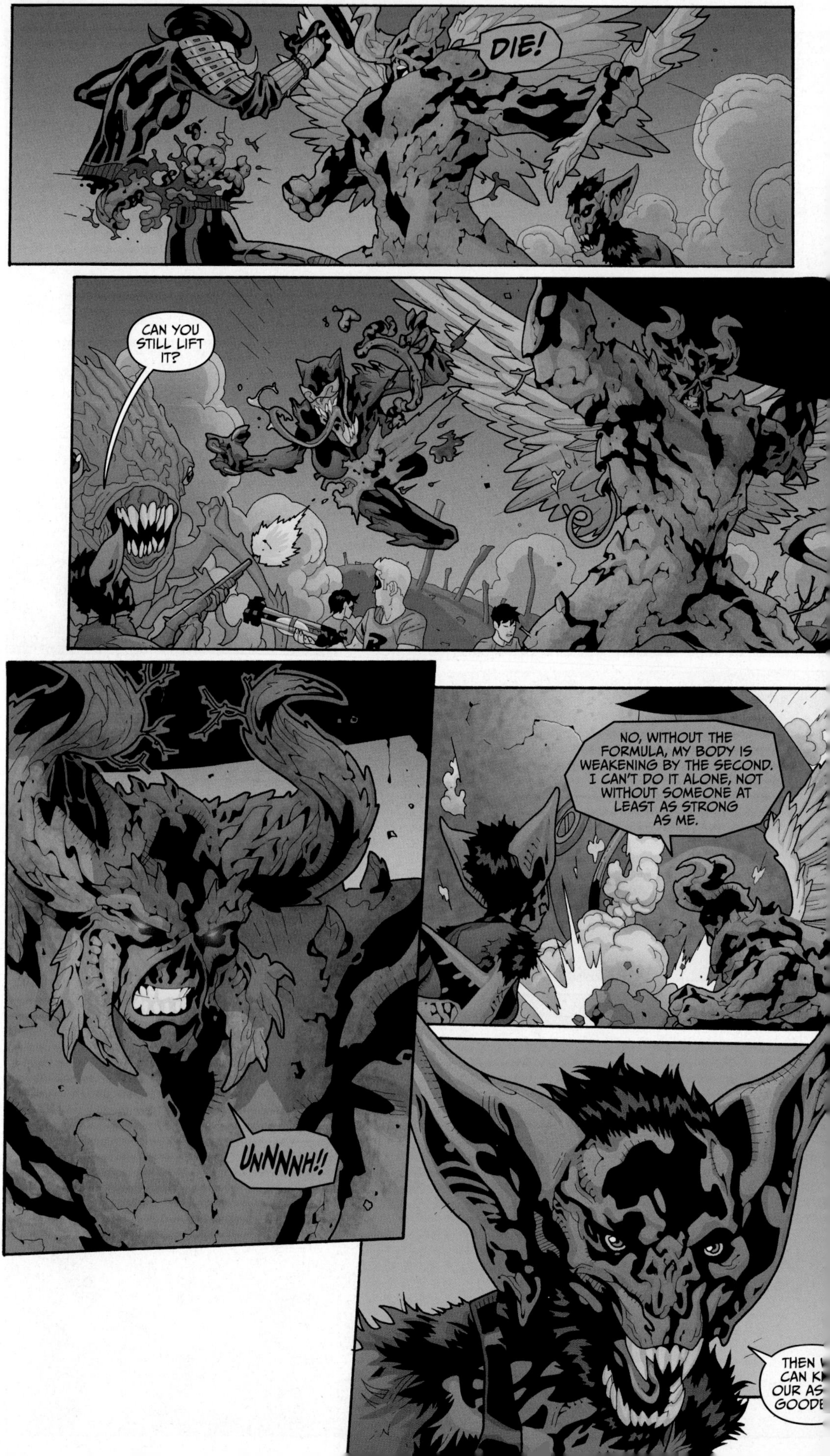
DIE!
CAN YOU STILL LIFT IT?
UNNNNH!!
NO, WITHOUT THE FORMULA, MY BODY IS WEAKENING BY THE SECOND. I CAN'T DO IT ALONE, NOT WITHOUT SOMEONE AT LEAST AS STRONG AS ME.
THEN

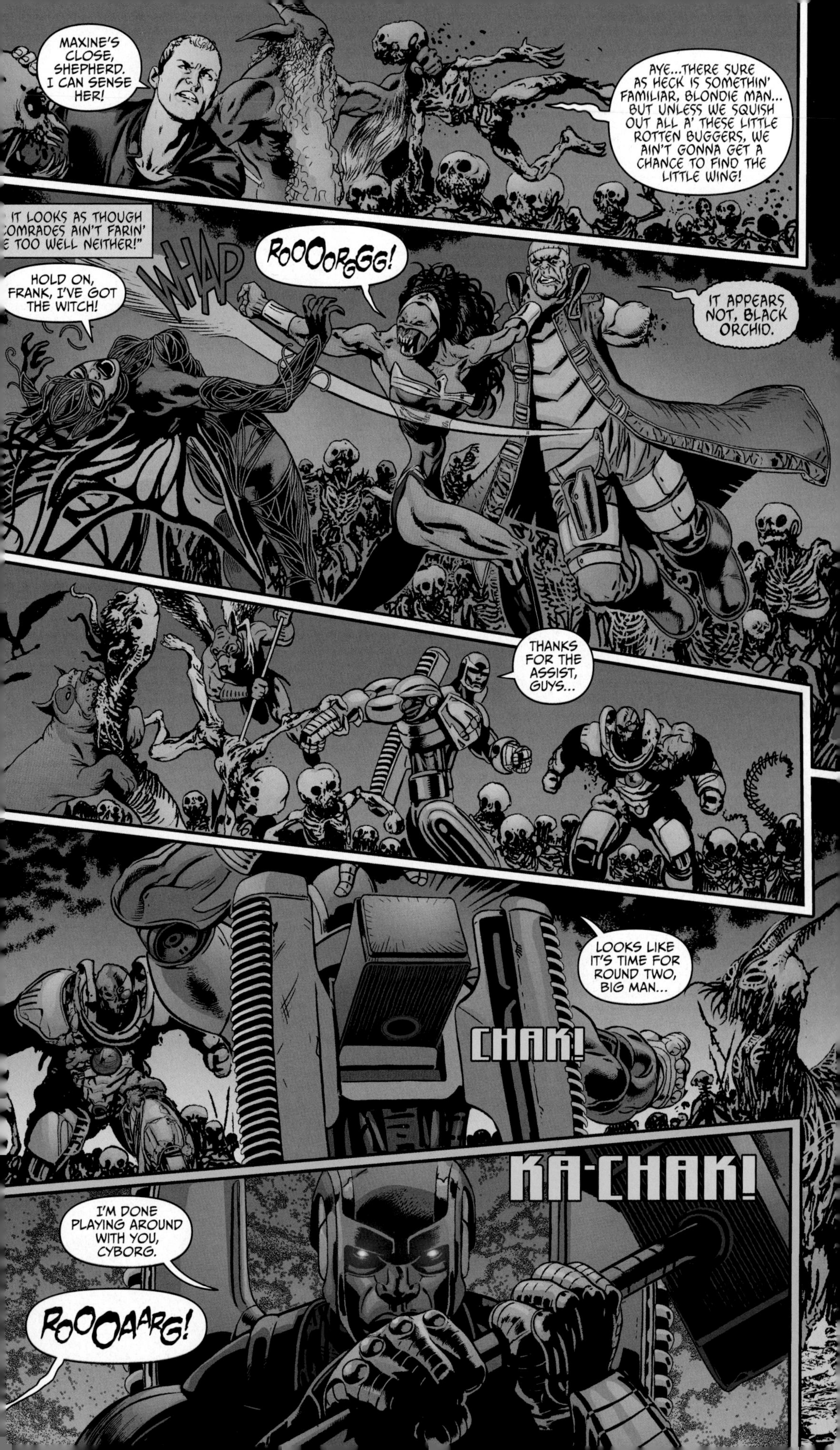
MAXINE'S CLOSE, SHEPHERD. I CAN SENSE HER!
AYE...THERE SURE AS HECK IS SOMETHIN' FAMILIAR, BLONDIE MAN... BUT UNLESS WE SQUISH OUT ALL A' THESE LITTLE ROTTEN BUGGERS, WE AIN'T GONNA GET A CHANCE TO FIND THE LITTLE WING!
IT LOOKS AS THOUGH COMRADES AIN'T FARIN' TOO WELL NEITHER!"
WHAP
ROOOORGGG!
HOLD ON, FRANK, I'VE GOT THE WITCH!
IT APPEARS NOT, BLACK ORCHID.
THANKS FOR THE ASSIST, GUYS...
LOOKS LIKE IT'S TIME FOR ROUND TWO, BIG MAN...
CHAK!
KA-CHAK!
I'M DONE PLAYING AROUND WITH YOU, CYBORG.
ROOOAARG!

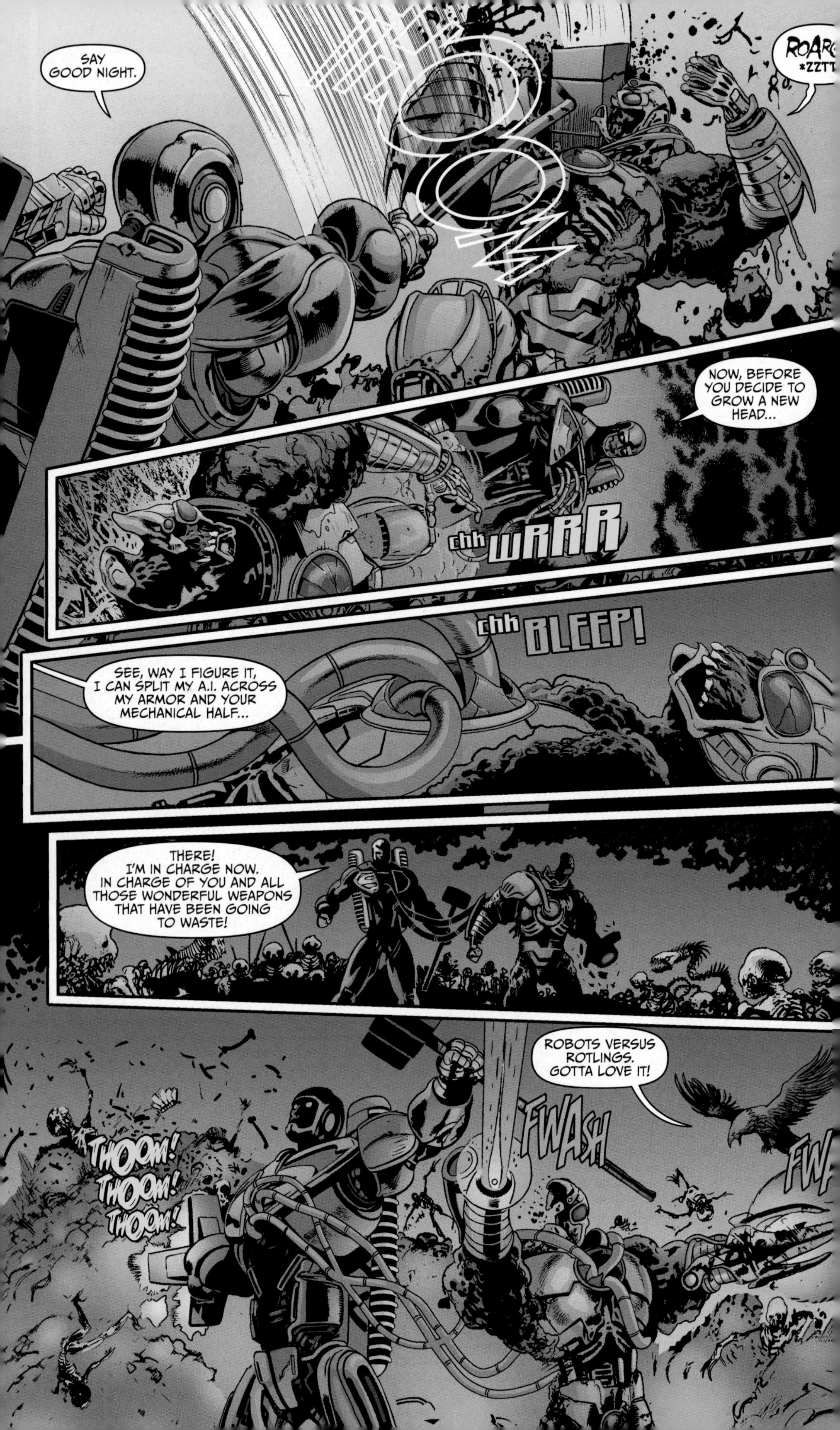
SAY GOOD NIGHT.
BOOOM
ROAR
*ZZTT
NOW, BEFORE YOU DECIDE TO GROW A NEW HEAD...
chk WRRR
chk BLEEP!
SEE, WAY I FIGURE IT, I CAN SPLIT MY A.I. ACROSS MY ARMOR AND YOUR MECHANICAL HALF...
THERE! I'M IN CHARGE NOW. IN CHARGE OF YOU AND ALL THOSE WONDERFUL WEAPONS THAT HAVE BEEN GOING TO WASTE!
ROBOTS VERSUS ROTLINGS. GOTTA LOVE IT!
THOOM! THOOM! THOOM!
FWASH

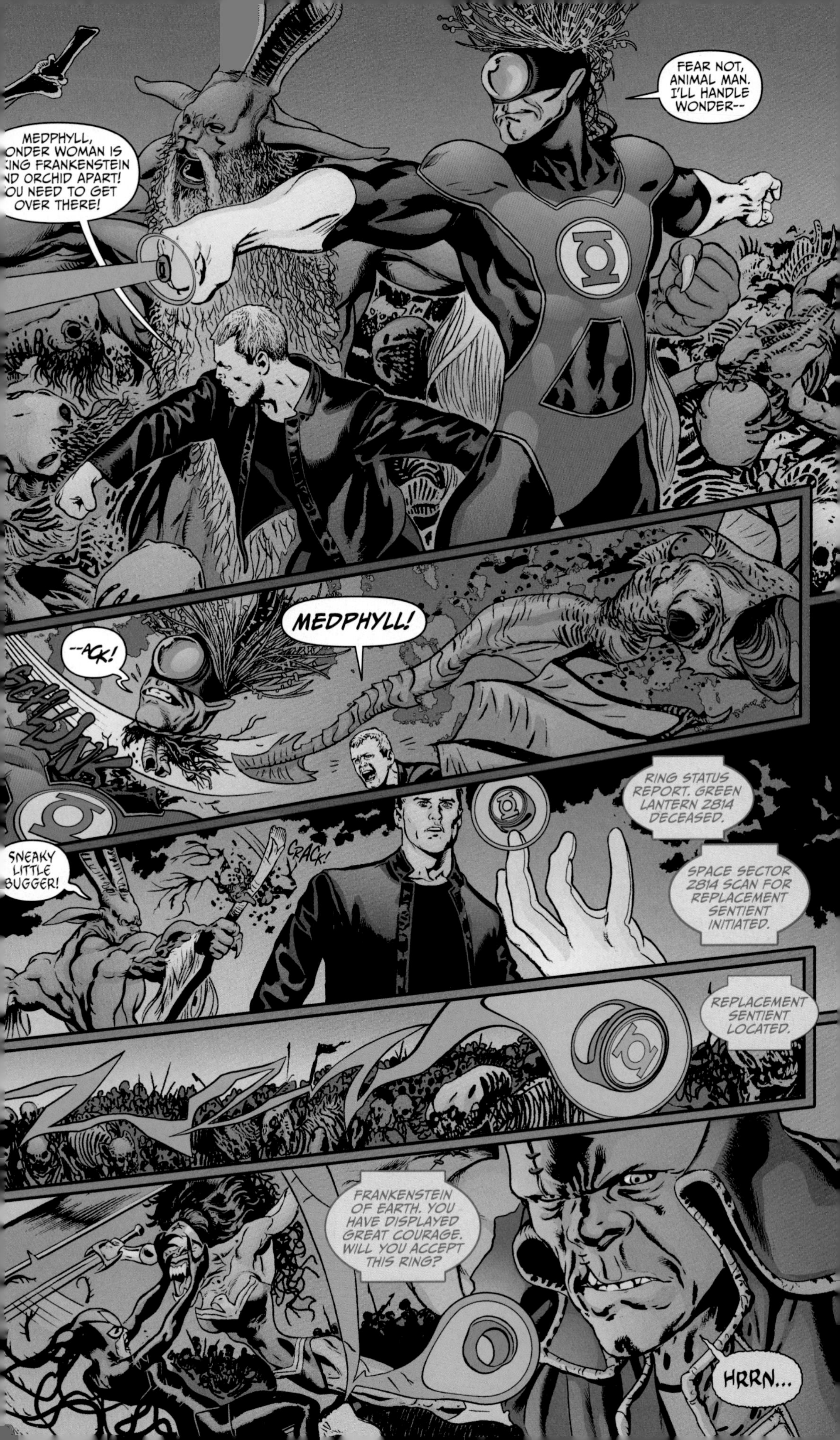
MEDPHYLL, ONDER WOMAN IS KING FRANKENSTEIN ND ORCHID APART! OU NEED TO GET OVER THERE!
FEAR NOT, ANIMAL MAN. I'LL HANDLE WONDER--
--ACK!
MEDPHYLL!
RING STATUS REPORT. GREEN LANTERN 2814 DECEASED.
SNEAKY LITTLE BUGGER!
CRACK!
SPACE SECTOR 2814 SCAN FOR REPLACEMENT SENTIENT INITIATED.
REPLACEMENT SENTIENT LOCATED.
FRANKENSTEIN OF EARTH. YOU HAVE DISPLAYED GREAT COURAGE. WILL YOU ACCEPT THIS RING?
HRRN...

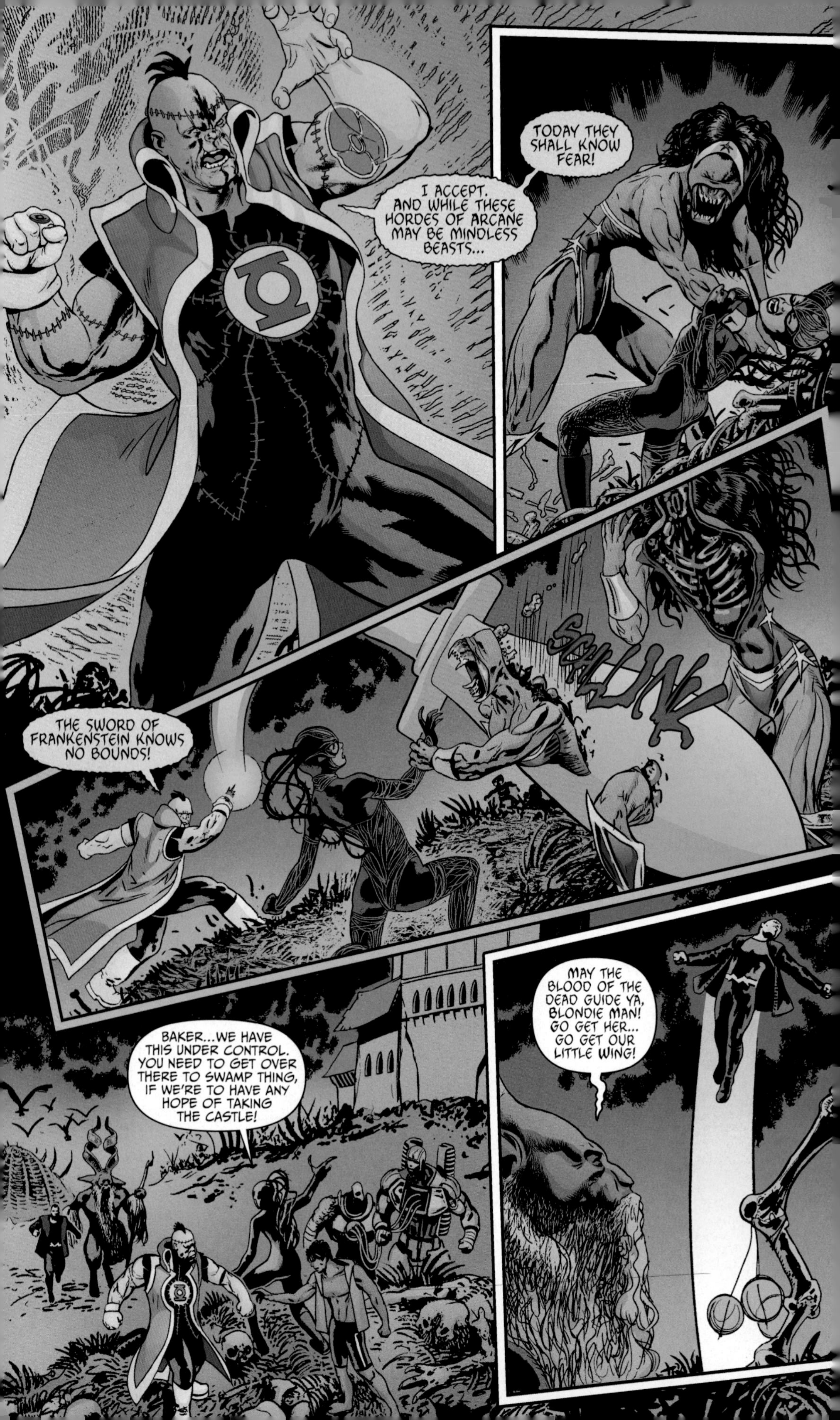
I ACCEPT. AND WHILE THESE HORDES OF ARCANE MAY BE MINDLESS BEASTS...
TODAY THEY SHALL KNOW FEAR!
SCHLINK
THE SWORD OF FRANKENSTEIN KNOWS NO BOUNDS!
BAKER...WE HAVE THIS UNDER CONTROL. YOU NEED TO GET OVER THERE TO SWAMP THING, IF WE'RE TO HAVE ANY HOPE OF TAKING THE CASTLE!
MAY THE BLOOD OF THE DEAD GUIDE YA, BLONDIE MAN! GO GET HER... GO GET OUR LITTLE WING!

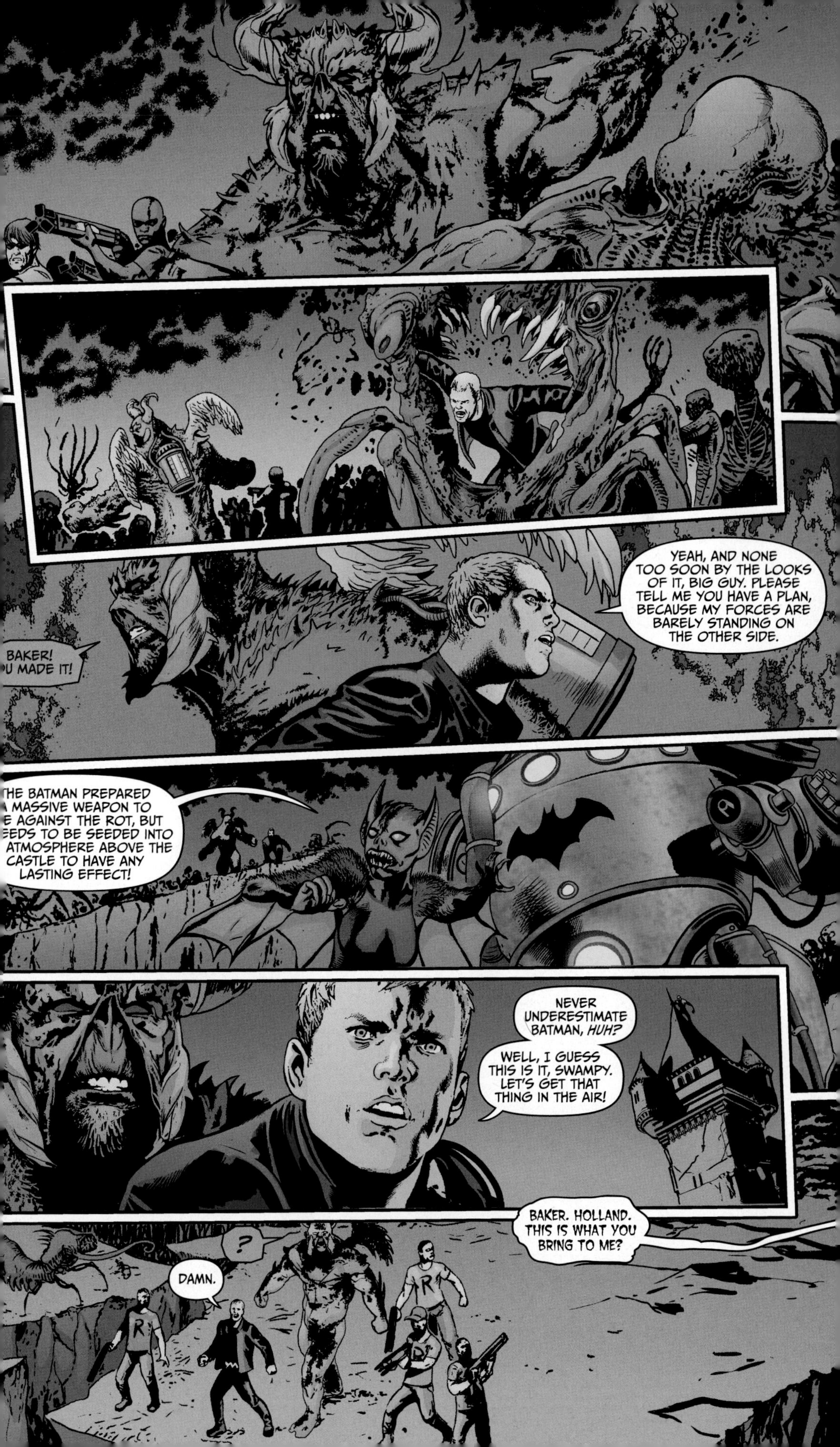
BAKER! U MADE IT!
YEAH, AND NONE TOO SOON BY THE LOOKS OF IT, BIG GUY. PLEASE TELL ME YOU HAVE A PLAN, BECAUSE MY FORCES ARE BARELY STANDING ON THE OTHER SIDE.
THE BATMAN PREPARED A MASSIVE WEAPON TO E AGAINST THE ROT, BUT EEDS TO BE SEEDED INTO ATMOSPHERE ABOVE THE CASTLE TO HAVE ANY LASTING EFFECT!
NEVER UNDERESTIMATE BATMAN, *HUH?*
WELL, I GUESS THIS IS IT, SWAMPY. LET'S GET THAT THING IN THE AIR!
BAKER. HOLLAND. THIS IS WHAT YOU BRING TO ME?
?
DAMN.

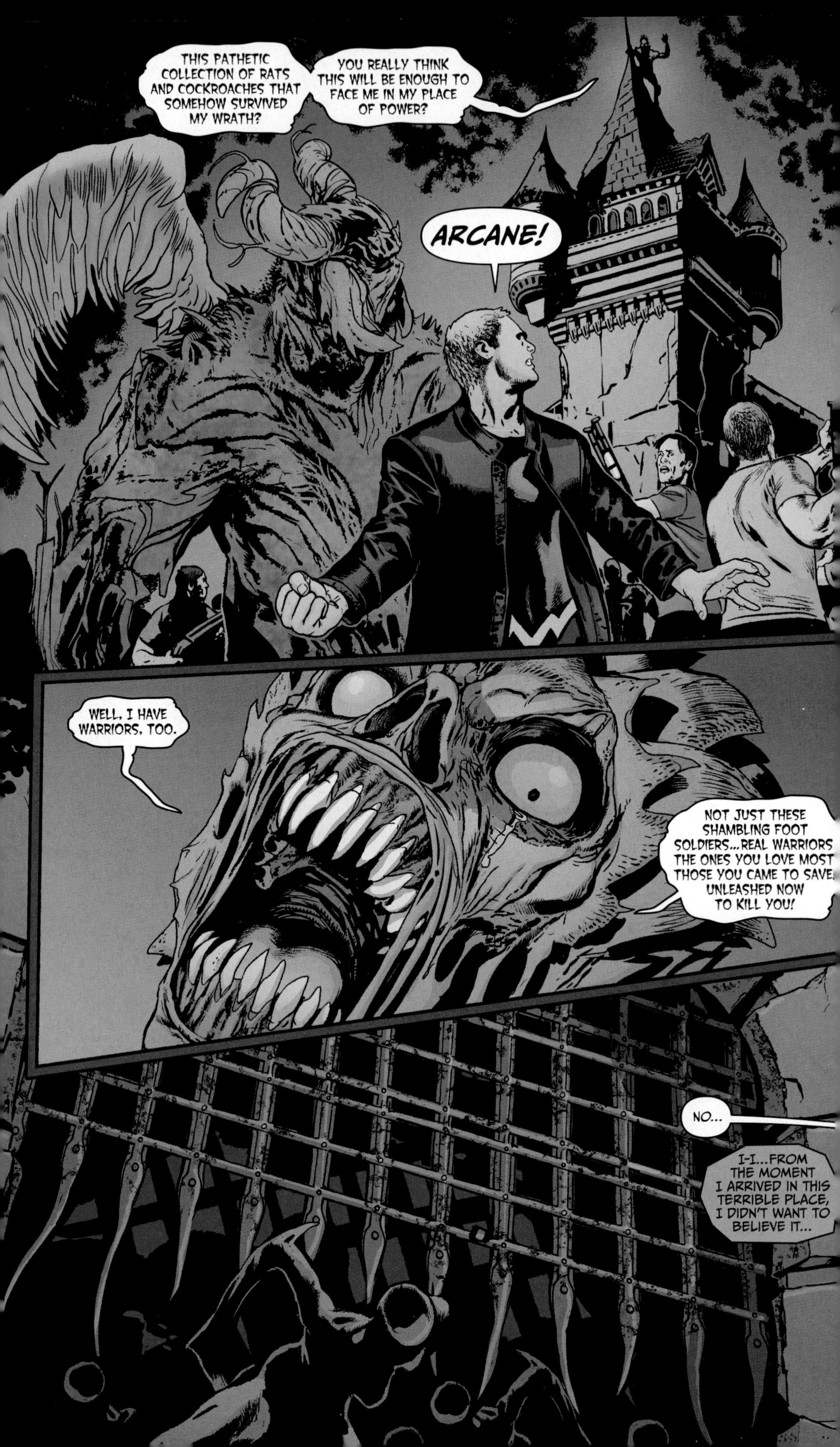
THIS PATHETIC COLLECTION OF RATS AND COCKROACHES THAT SOMEHOW SURVIVED MY WRATH?
YOU REALLY THINK THIS WILL BE ENOUGH TO FACE ME IN MY PLACE OF POWER?
ARCANE!
WELL, I HAVE WARRIORS, TOO.
NOT JUST THESE SHAMBLING FOOT SOLDIERS...REAL WARRIORS THE ONES YOU LOVE MOST THOSE YOU CAME TO SAVE UNLEASHED NOW TO KILL YOU!
NO...
I-I...FROM THE MOMENT I ARRIVED IN THIS TERRIBLE PLACE, I DIDN'T WANT TO BELIEVE IT...

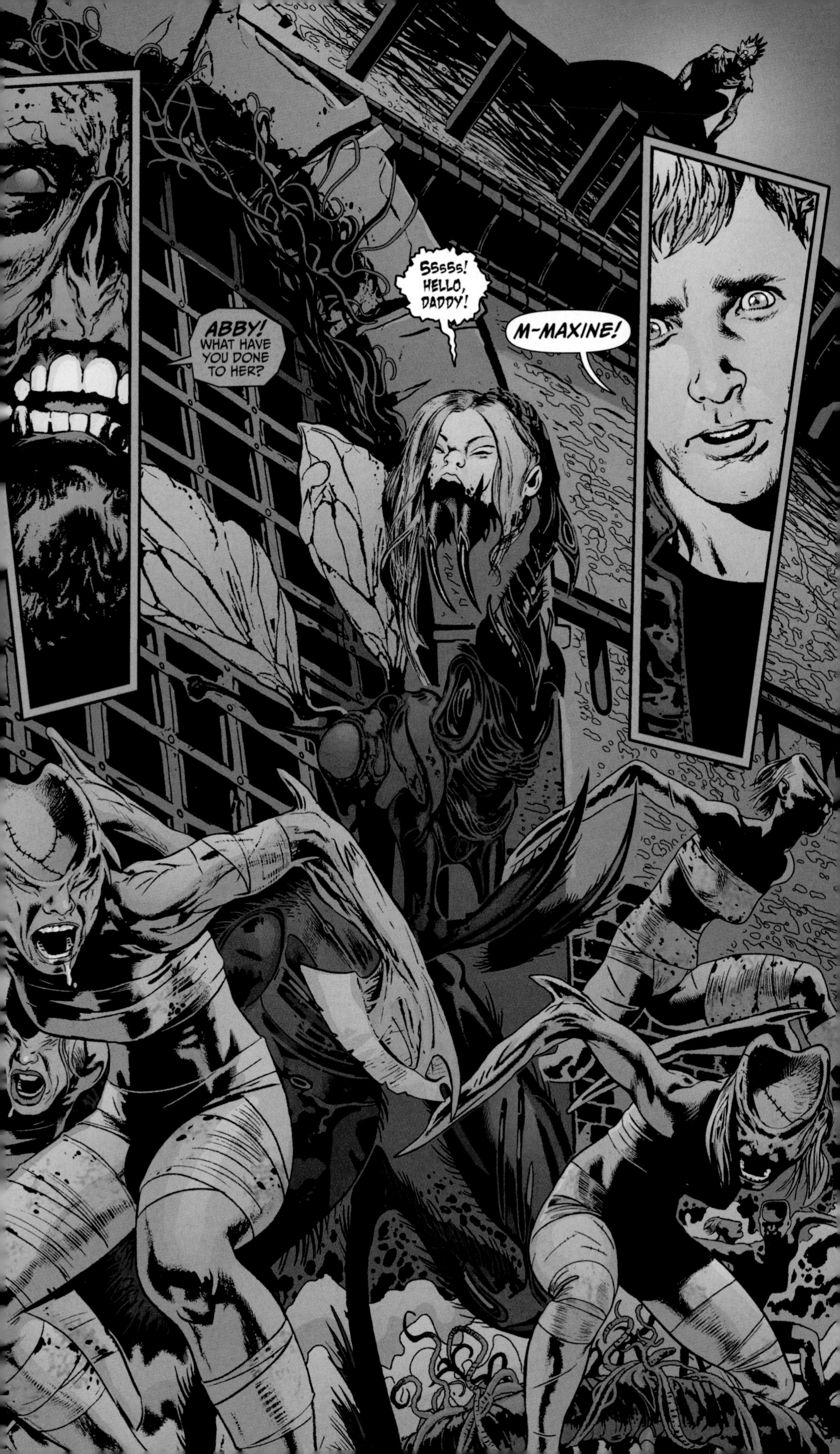
ABBY! WHAT HAVE YOU DONE TO HER?
Sssss! HELLO, DADDY!
M-MAXINE!

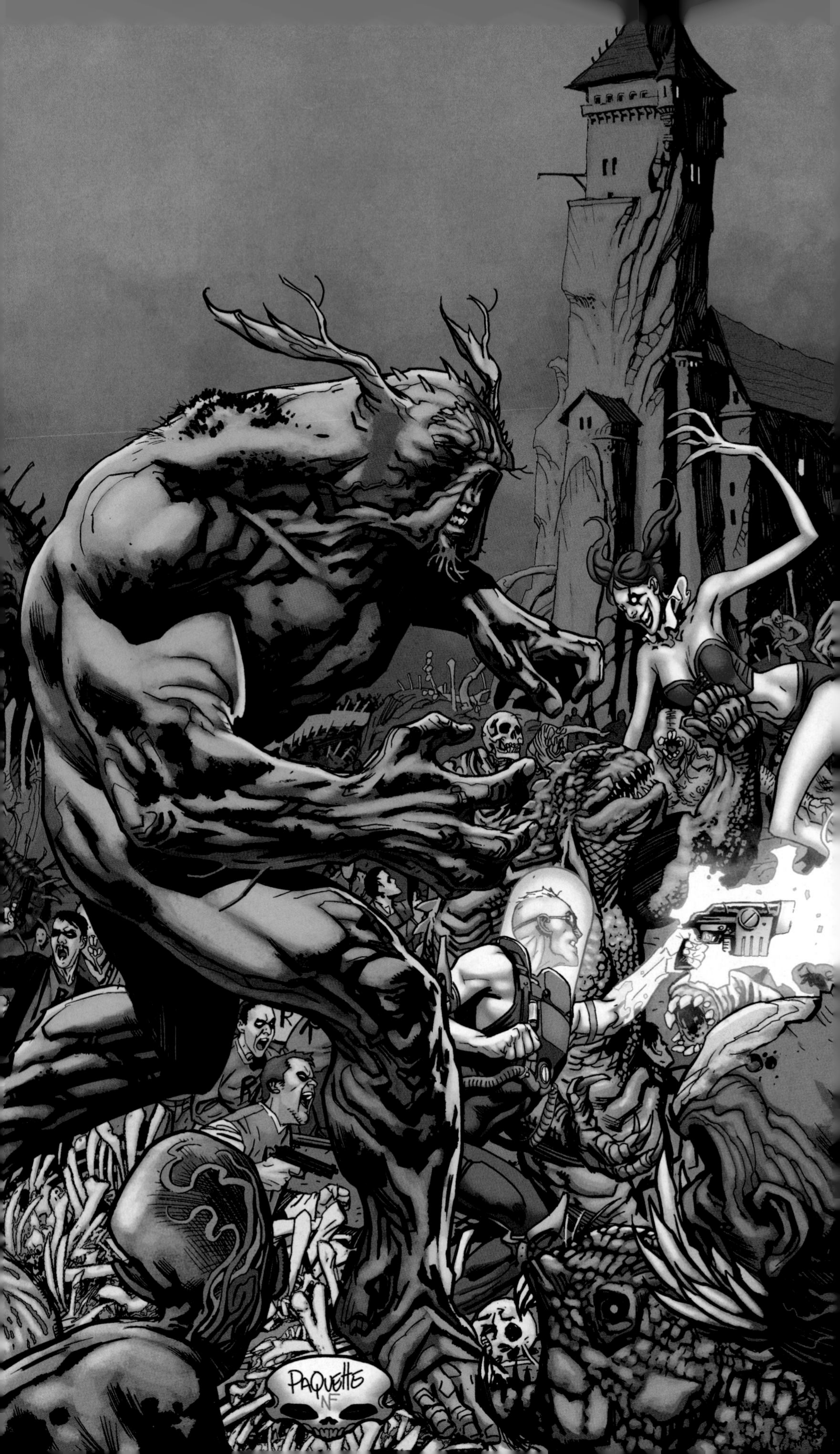
PAQUETTE
NF

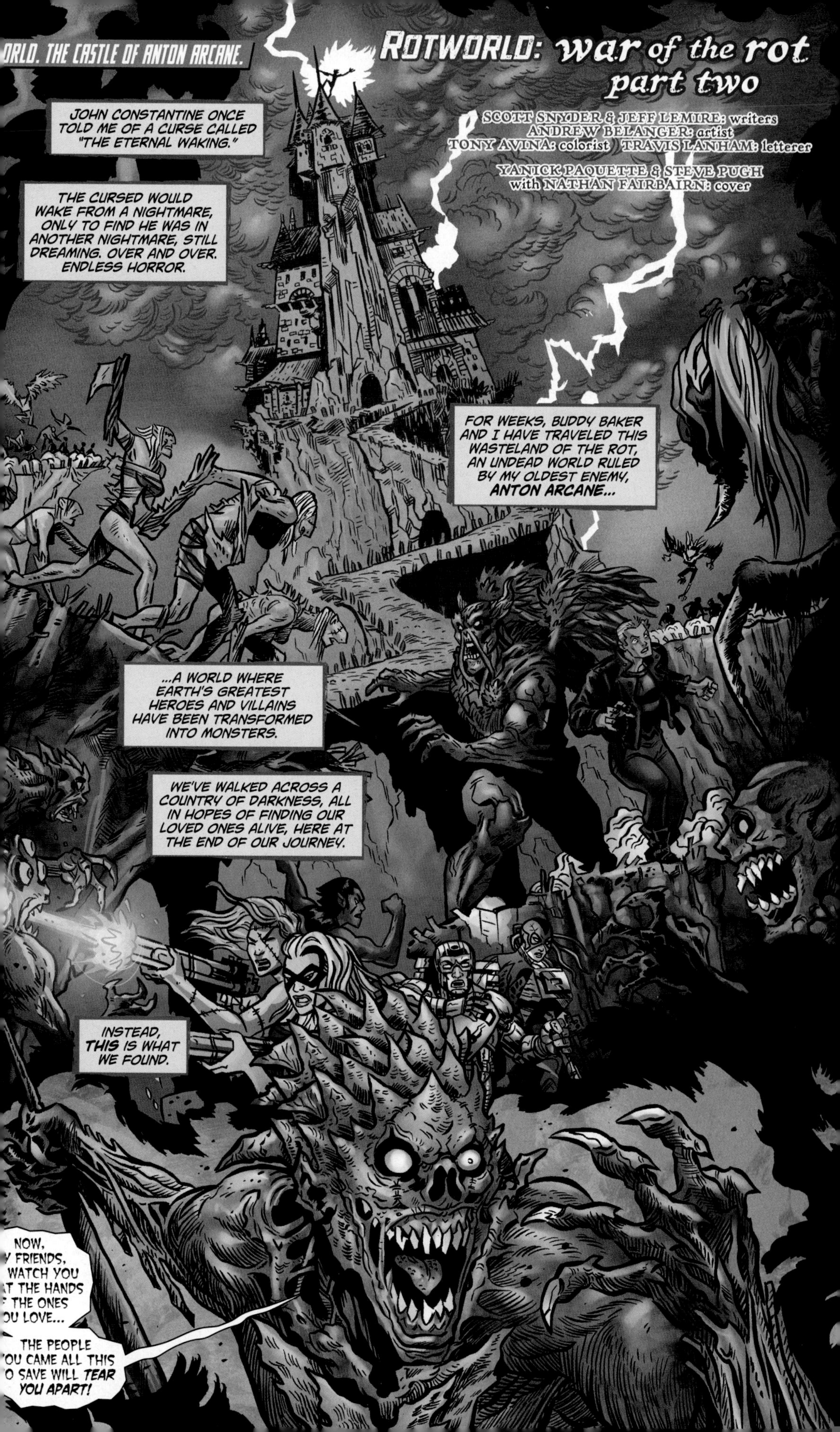

ORLD. THE CASTLE OF ANTON ARCANE.
ROTWORLD: war of the rot part two
SCOTT SNYDER & JEFF LEMIRE: writers
ANDREW BELANGER: artist
TONY AVINA: colorist TRAVIS LANHAM: letterer
YANICK PAQUETTE & STEVE PUGH with NATHAN FAIRBAIRN: cover
JOHN CONSTANTINE ONCE TOLD ME OF A CURSE CALLED "THE ETERNAL WAKING."
THE CURSED WOULD WAKE FROM A NIGHTMARE, ONLY TO FIND HE WAS IN ANOTHER NIGHTMARE, STILL DREAMING. OVER AND OVER. ENDLESS HORROR.
FOR WEEKS, BUDDY BAKER AND I HAVE TRAVELED THIS WASTELAND OF THE ROT, AN UNDEAD WORLD RULED BY MY OLDEST ENEMY, ANTON ARCANE...
...A WORLD WHERE EARTH'S GREATEST HEROES AND VILLAINS HAVE BEEN TRANSFORMED INTO MONSTERS.
WE'VE WALKED ACROSS A COUNTRY OF DARKNESS, ALL IN HOPES OF FINDING OUR LOVED ONES ALIVE, HERE AT THE END OF OUR JOURNEY.
INSTEAD, THIS IS WHAT WE FOUND.
NOW, Y FRIENDS, WATCH YOU T THE HANDS F THE ONES OU LOVE...
THE PEOPLE OU CAME ALL THIS O SAVE WILL TEAR YOU APART!

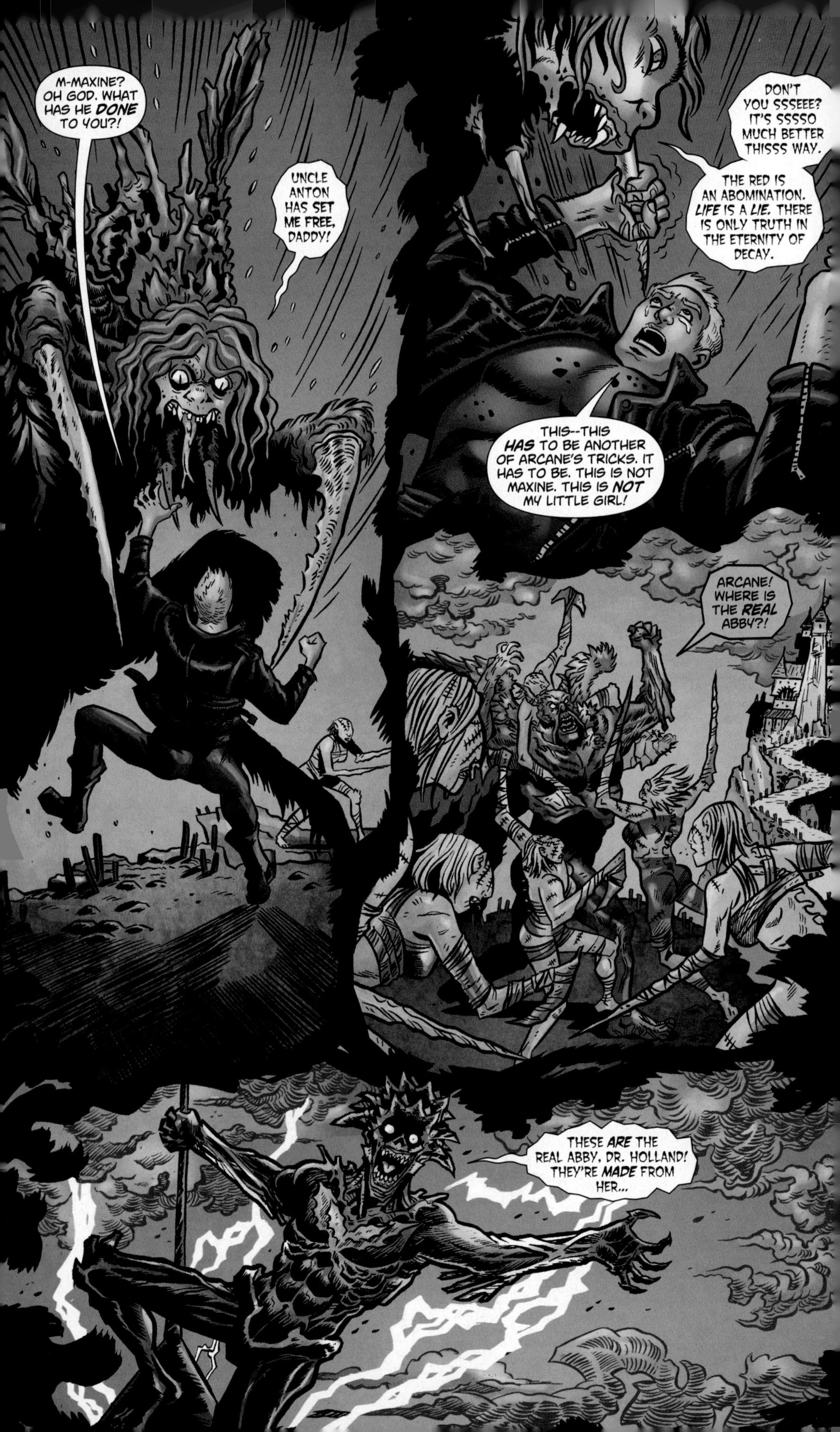
M-MAXINE? OH GOD. WHAT HAS HE DONE TO YOU?!
UNCLE ANTON HAS SET ME FREE, DADDY!
DON'T YOU SSSEEE? IT'S SSSSO MUCH BETTER THISSS WAY.
THE RED IS AN ABOMINATION. LIFE IS A LIE. THERE IS ONLY TRUTH IN THE ETERNITY OF DECAY.
THIS--THIS HAS TO BE ANOTHER OF ARCANE'S TRICKS. IT HAS TO BE. THIS IS NOT MAXINE. THIS IS NOT MY LITTLE GIRL!
ARCANE! WHERE IS THE REAL ABBY?!
THESE ARE THE REAL ABBY, DR. HOLLAND! THEY'RE MADE FROM HER...

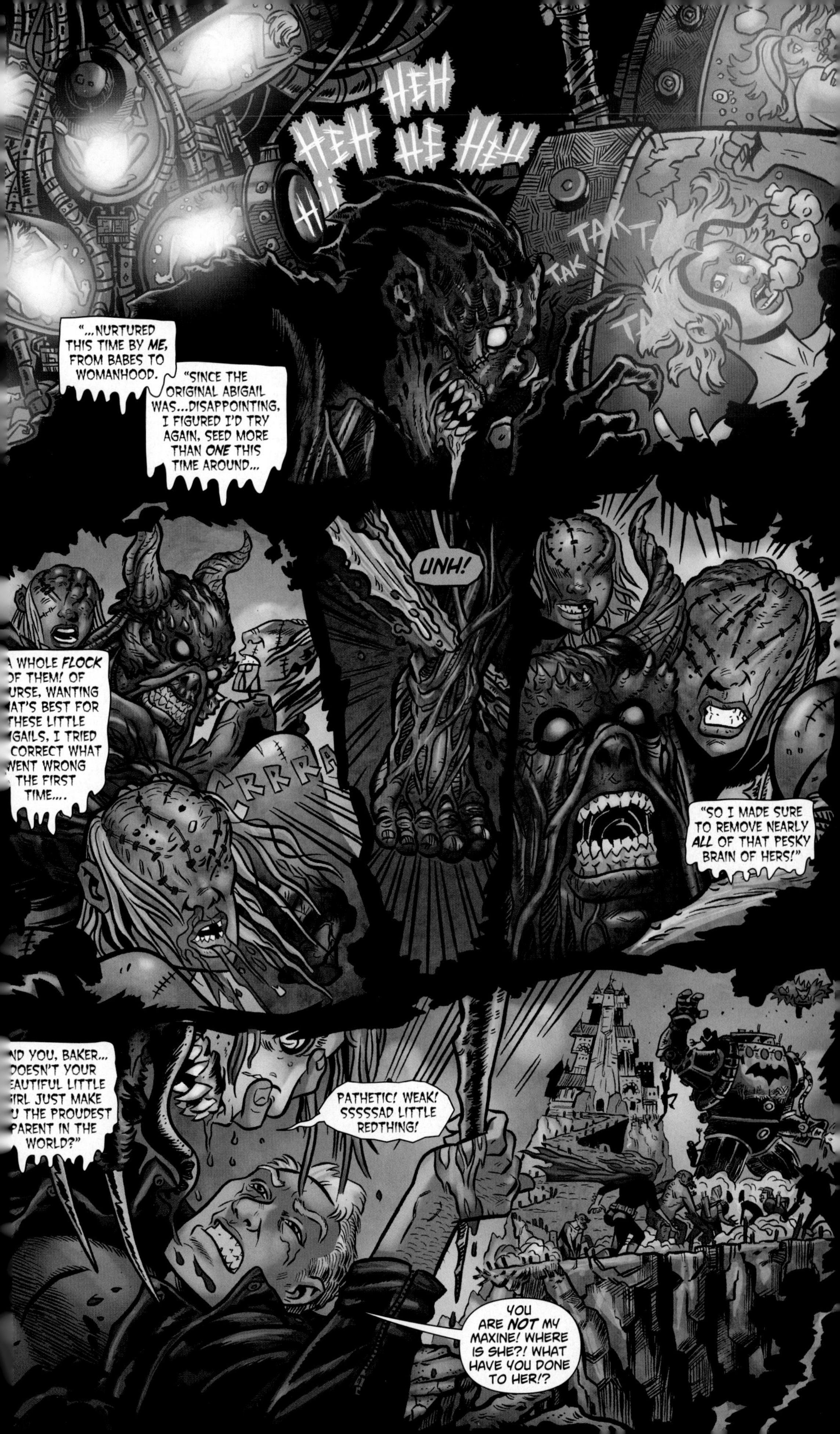
HEH HEH
HEH HE HEH
TAK TAK TAK
"...NURTURED THIS TIME BY *ME*, FROM BABES TO WOMANHOOD.
"SINCE THE ORIGINAL ABIGAIL WAS...DISAPPOINTING, I FIGURED I'D TRY AGAIN, SEED MORE THAN *ONE* THIS TIME AROUND...
A WHOLE *FLOCK*
OF THEM! OF
URSE, WANTING
AT'S BEST FOR
THESE LITTLE
IGAILS, I TRIED
CORRECT WHAT
WENT WRONG
THE FIRST
TIME....
CRRRRA
UNH!
"SO I MADE SURE TO REMOVE NEARLY *ALL* OF THAT PESKY BRAIN OF HERS!"
ND YOU, BAKER...
DOESN'T YOUR
EAUTIFUL LITTLE
IRL JUST MAKE
U THE PROUDEST
PARENT IN THE
WORLD?"
PATHETIC! WEAK! SSSSSAD LITTLE REDTHING!
YOU ARE *NOT* MY MAXINE! WHERE IS SHE?! WHAT HAVE YOU DONE TO HER!?

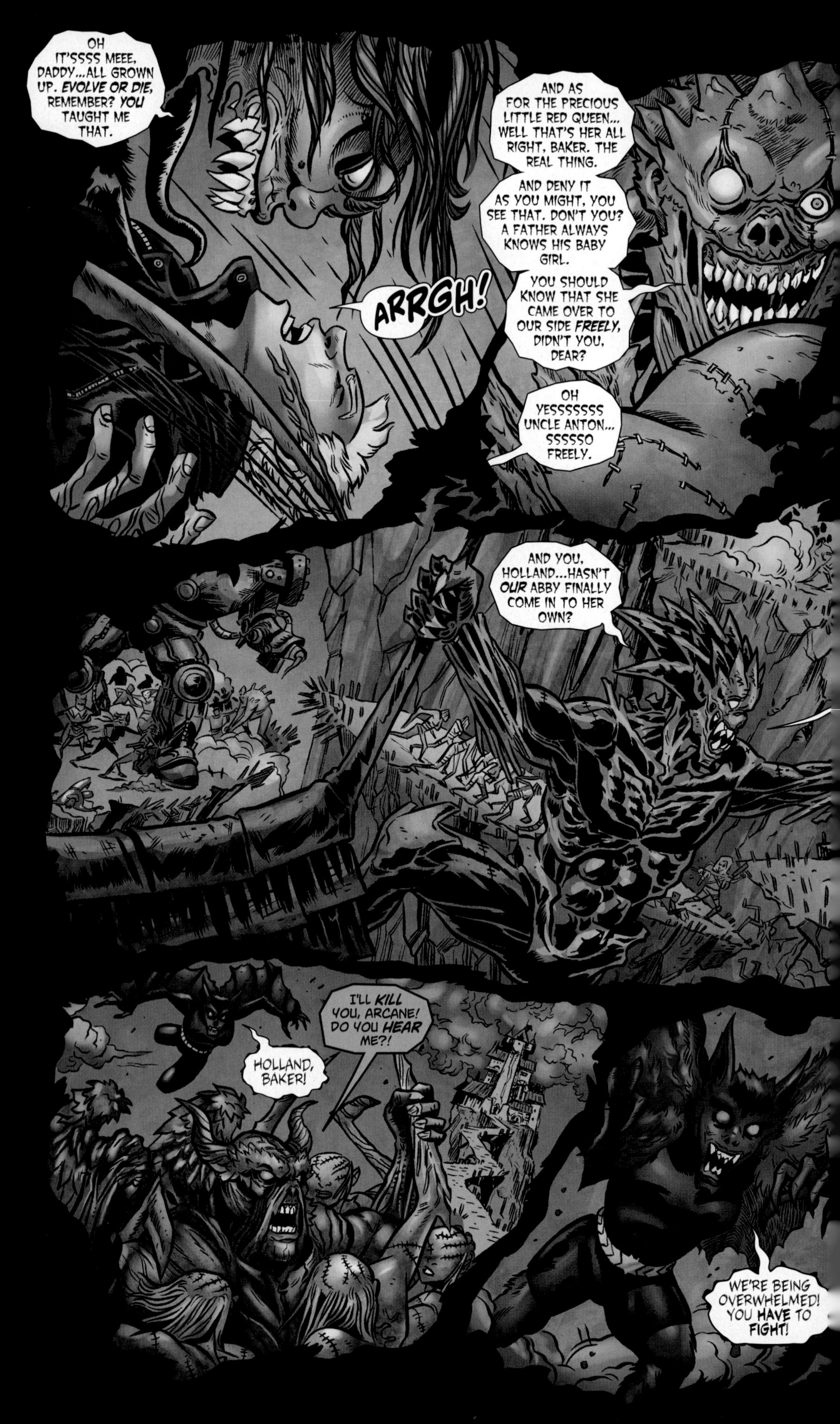
OH IT'SSSS MEEE, DADDY...ALL GROWN UP. EVOLVE OR DIE, REMEMBER? YOU TAUGHT ME THAT.
ARRGH!
AND AS FOR THE PRECIOUS LITTLE RED QUEEN... WELL THAT'S HER ALL RIGHT, BAKER. THE REAL THING.
AND DENY IT AS YOU MIGHT, YOU SEE THAT. DON'T YOU? A FATHER ALWAYS KNOWS HIS BABY GIRL.
YOU SHOULD KNOW THAT SHE CAME OVER TO OUR SIDE FREELY, DIDN'T YOU, DEAR?
OH YESSSSSSS UNCLE ANTON... SSSSSO FREELY.
AND YOU, HOLLAND...HASN'T OUR ABBY FINALLY COME IN TO HER OWN?
HOLLAND, BAKER!
I'LL KILL YOU, ARCANE! DO YOU HEAR ME?!
WE'RE BEING OVERWHELMED! YOU HAVE TO FIGHT!

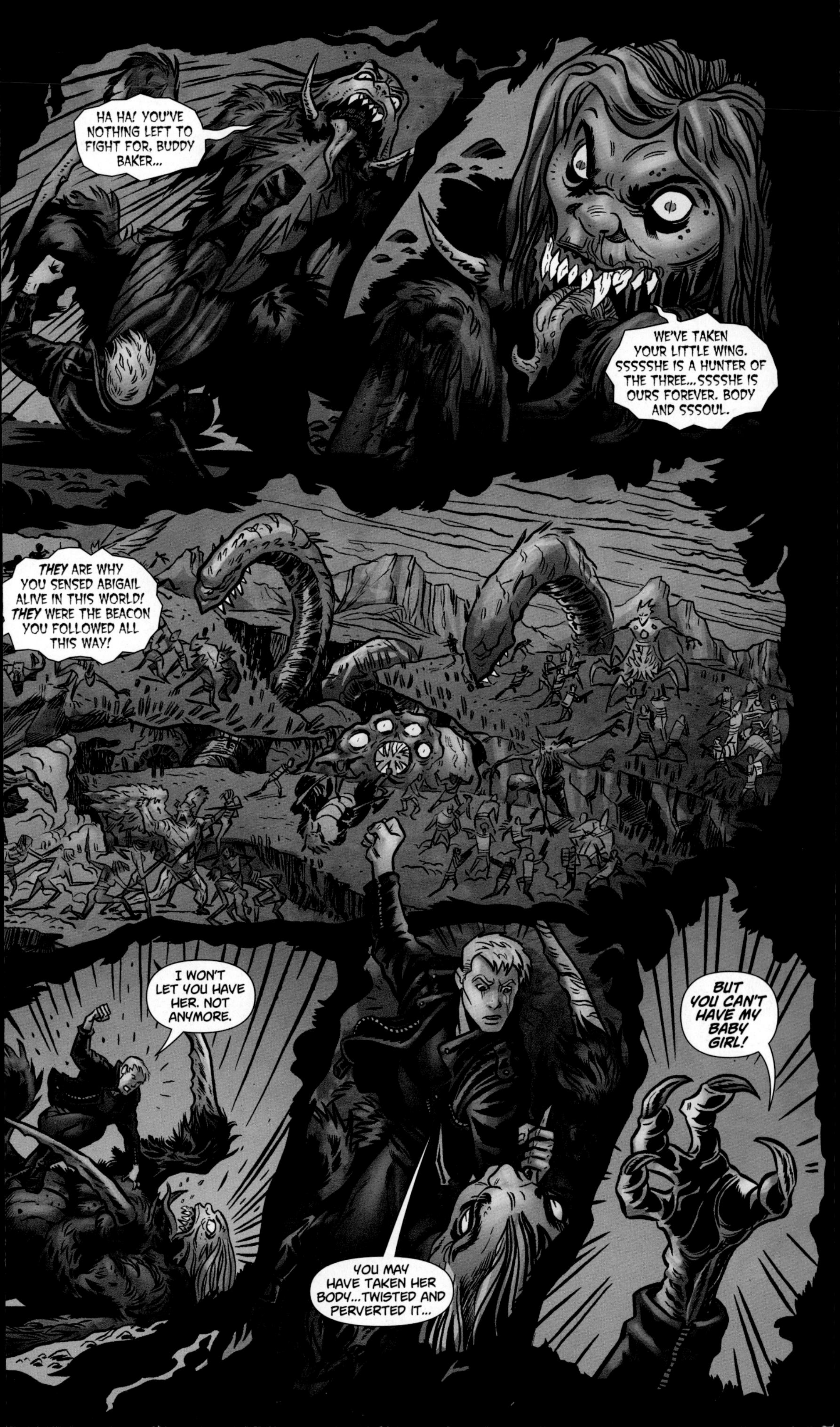
HA HA! YOU'VE NOTHING LEFT TO FIGHT FOR, BUDDY BAKER...
WE'VE TAKEN YOUR LITTLE WING. SSSSSHE IS A HUNTER OF THE THREE... SSSSHE IS OURS FOREVER. BODY AND SSSOUL.
THEY ARE WHY YOU SENSED ABIGAIL ALIVE IN THIS WORLD! *THEY* WERE THE BEACON YOU FOLLOWED ALL THIS WAY!
I WON'T LET YOU HAVE HER. NOT ANYMORE.
YOU MAY HAVE TAKEN HER BODY... TWISTED AND PERVERTED IT...
BUT YOU CAN'T HAVE MY BABY GIRL!

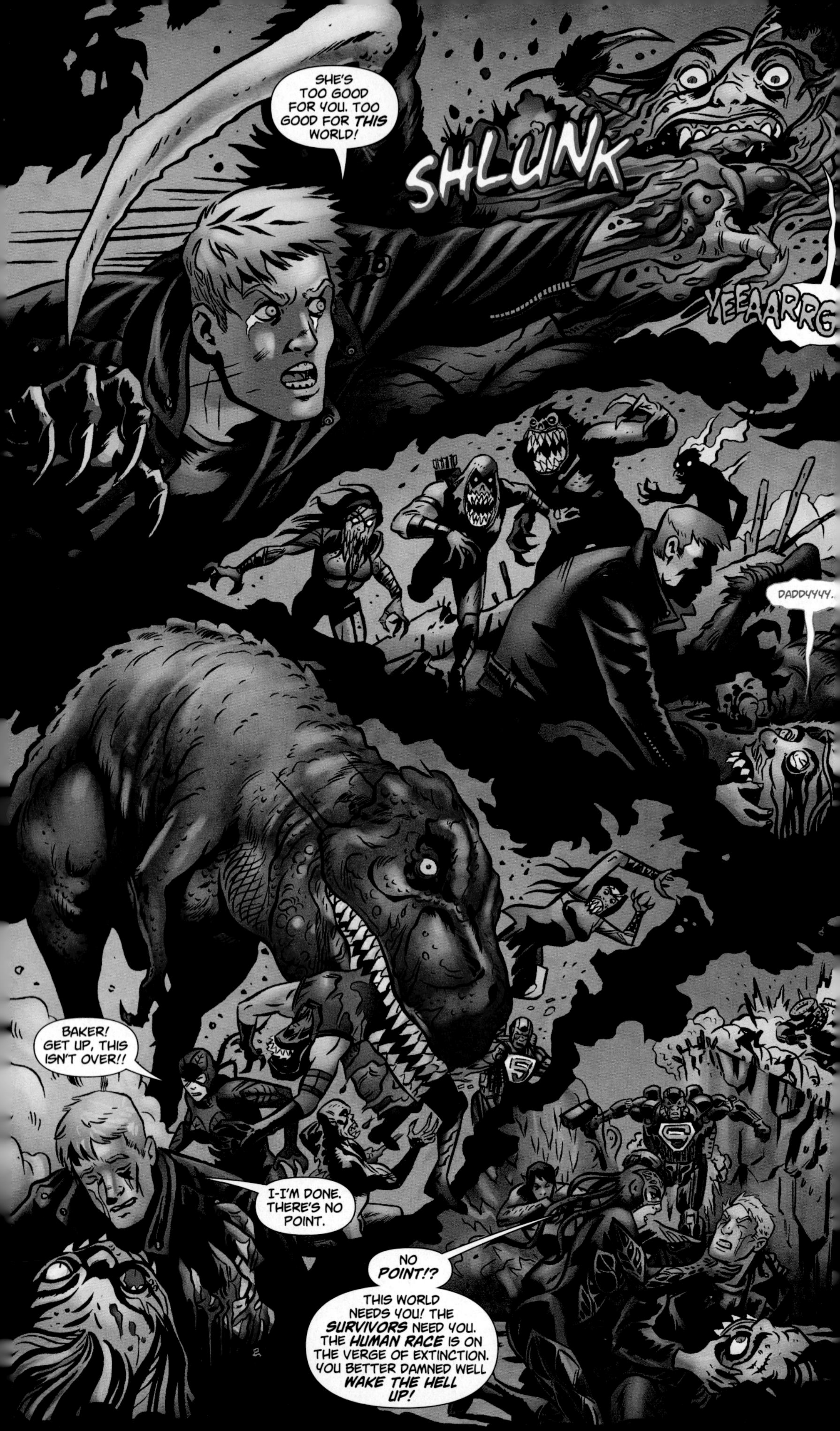
SHE'S TOO GOOD FOR YOU. TOO GOOD FOR THIS WORLD!
SHLUNK
YEEAARRG
DADDYYYY..
BAKER! GET UP, THIS ISN'T OVER!!
I-I'M DONE. THERE'S NO POINT.
NO POINT!?
THIS WORLD NEEDS YOU! THE SURVIVORS NEED YOU. THE HUMAN RACE IS ON THE VERGE OF EXTINCTION. YOU BETTER DAMNED WELL WAKE THE HELL UP!

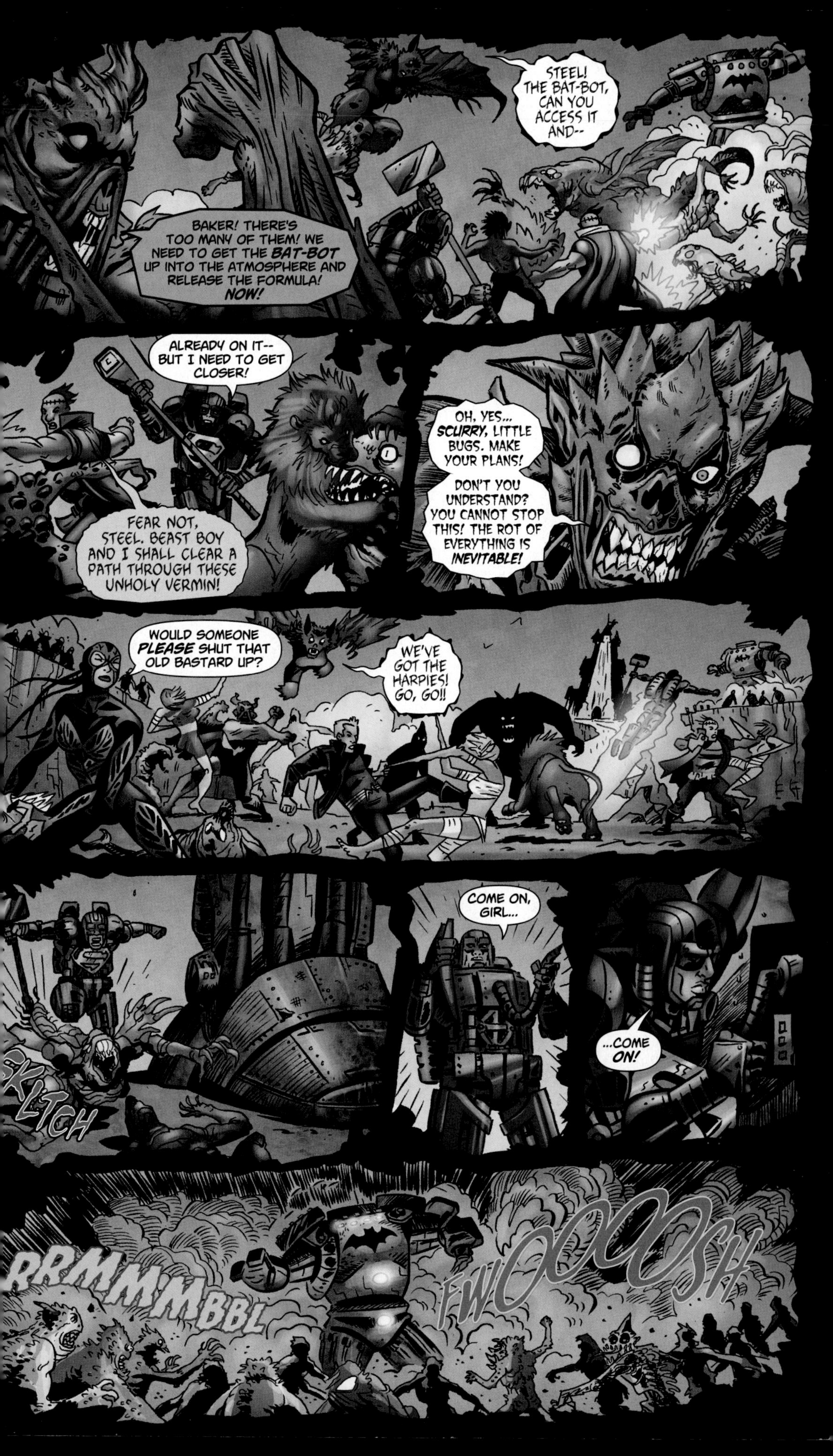
STEEL! THE BAT-BOT, CAN YOU ACCESS IT AND--
BAKER! THERE'S TOO MANY OF THEM! WE NEED TO GET THE BAT-BOT UP INTO THE ATMOSPHERE AND RELEASE THE FORMULA! NOW!
ALREADY ON IT-- BUT I NEED TO GET CLOSER!
FEAR NOT, STEEL. BEAST BOY AND I SHALL CLEAR A PATH THROUGH THESE UNHOLY VERMIN!
OH, YES... SCURRY, LITTLE BUGS. MAKE YOUR PLANS!
DON'T YOU UNDERSTAND? YOU CANNOT STOP THIS! THE ROT OF EVERYTHING IS INEVITABLE!
WOULD SOMEONE PLEASE SHUT THAT OLD BASTARD UP?
WE'VE GOT THE HARPIES! GO, GO!!
SKLITCH
COME ON, GIRL...
...COME ON!
RRMMMMBBL
FWOOOOSH

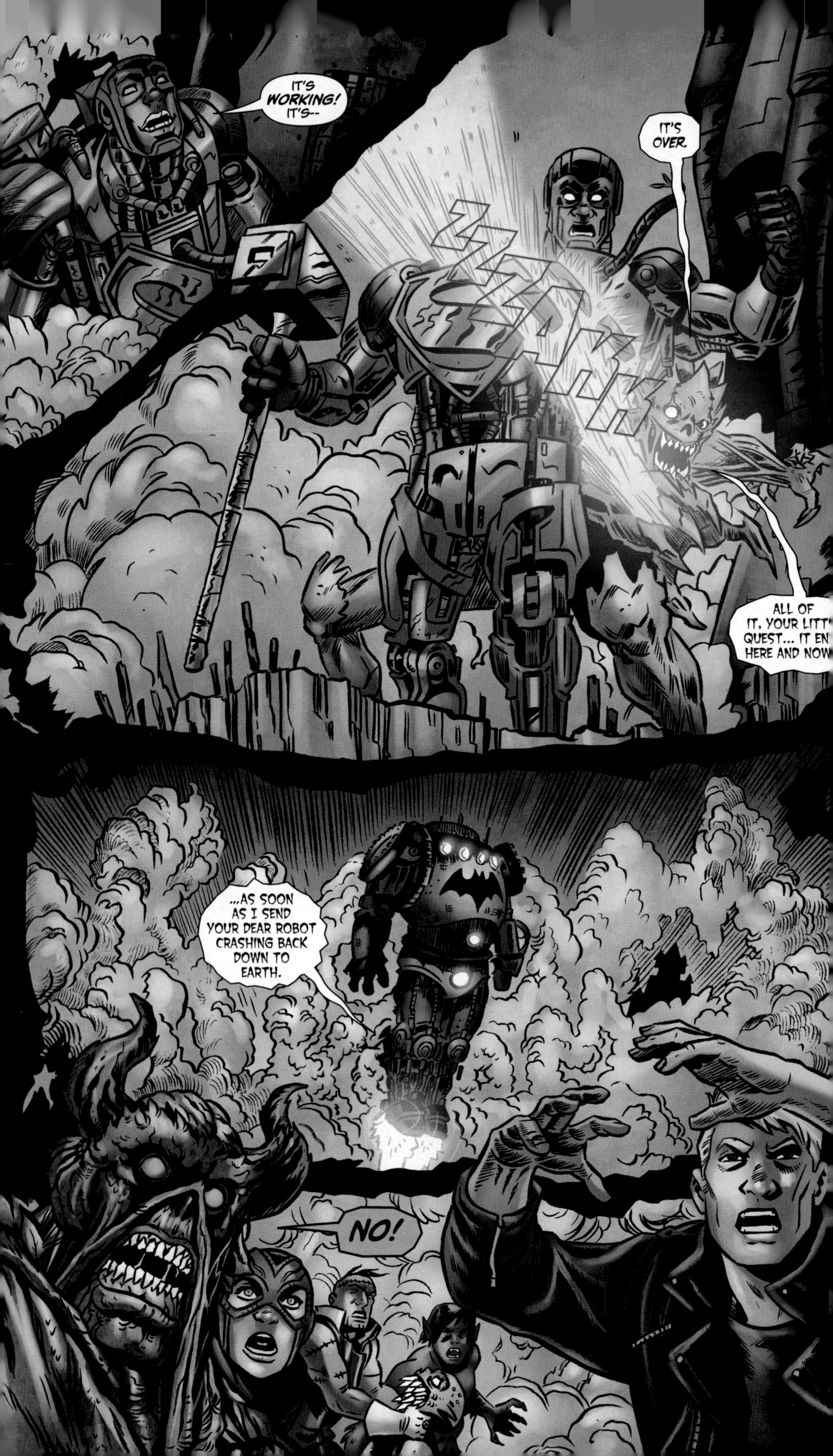
IT'S WORKING! IT'S--
IT'S OVER.
ALL OF IT. YOUR LITT QUEST... IT EN HERE AND NOW
...AS SOON AS I SEND YOUR DEAR ROBOT CRASHING BACK DOWN TO EARTH.
NO!

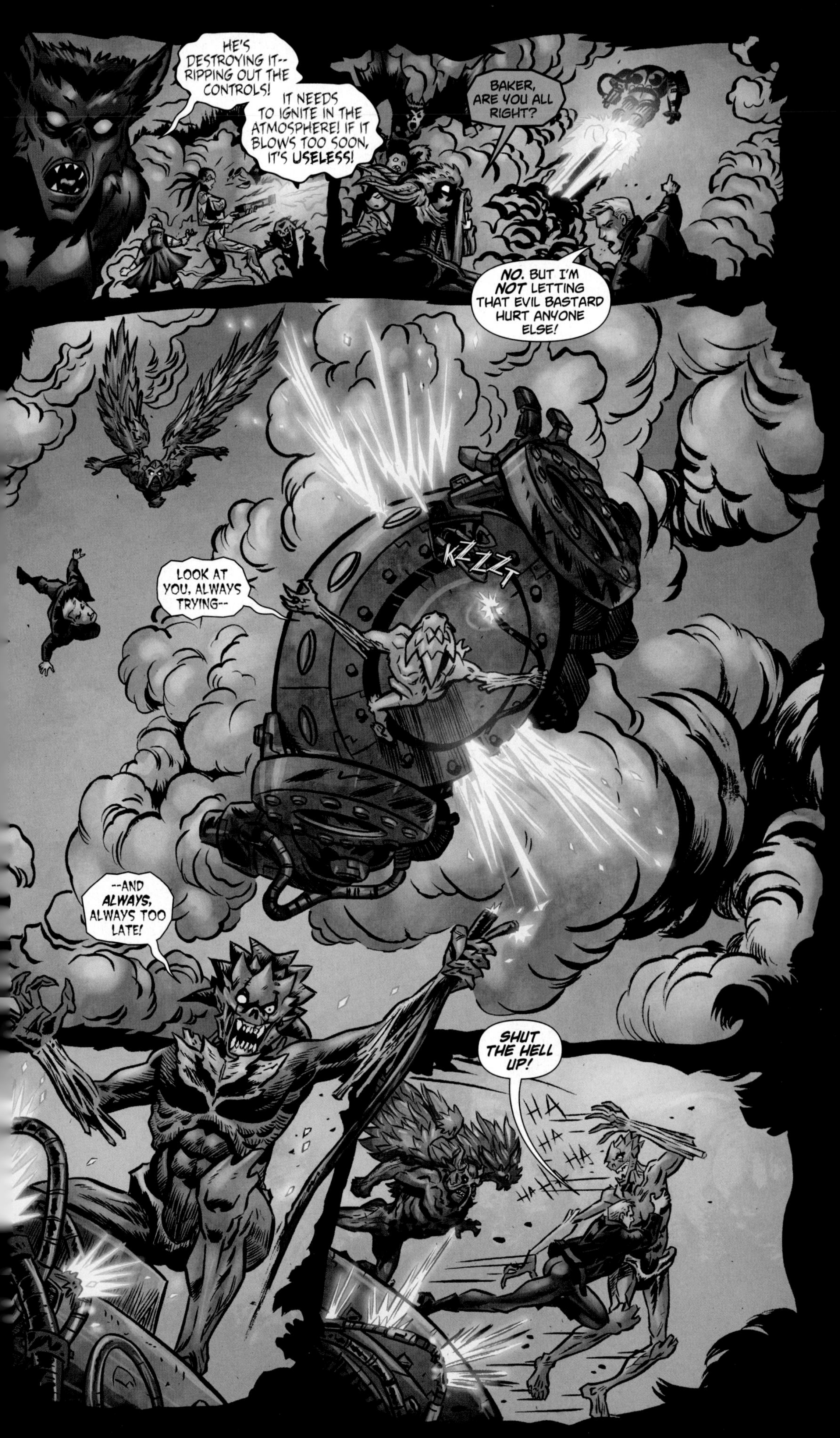
HE'S DESTROYING IT--RIPPING OUT THE CONTROLS!
IT NEEDS TO IGNITE IN THE ATMOSPHERE! IF IT BLOWS TOO SOON, IT'S **USELESS!**
BAKER, ARE YOU ALL RIGHT?
NO. BUT I'M ***NOT*** LETTING THAT EVIL BASTARD HURT ANYONE ELSE!
KZZZT
LOOK AT YOU, ALWAYS TRYING--
--AND ***ALWAYS,*** ALWAYS TOO LATE!
SHUT THE HELL UP!
HA HA HA HA
HA HA

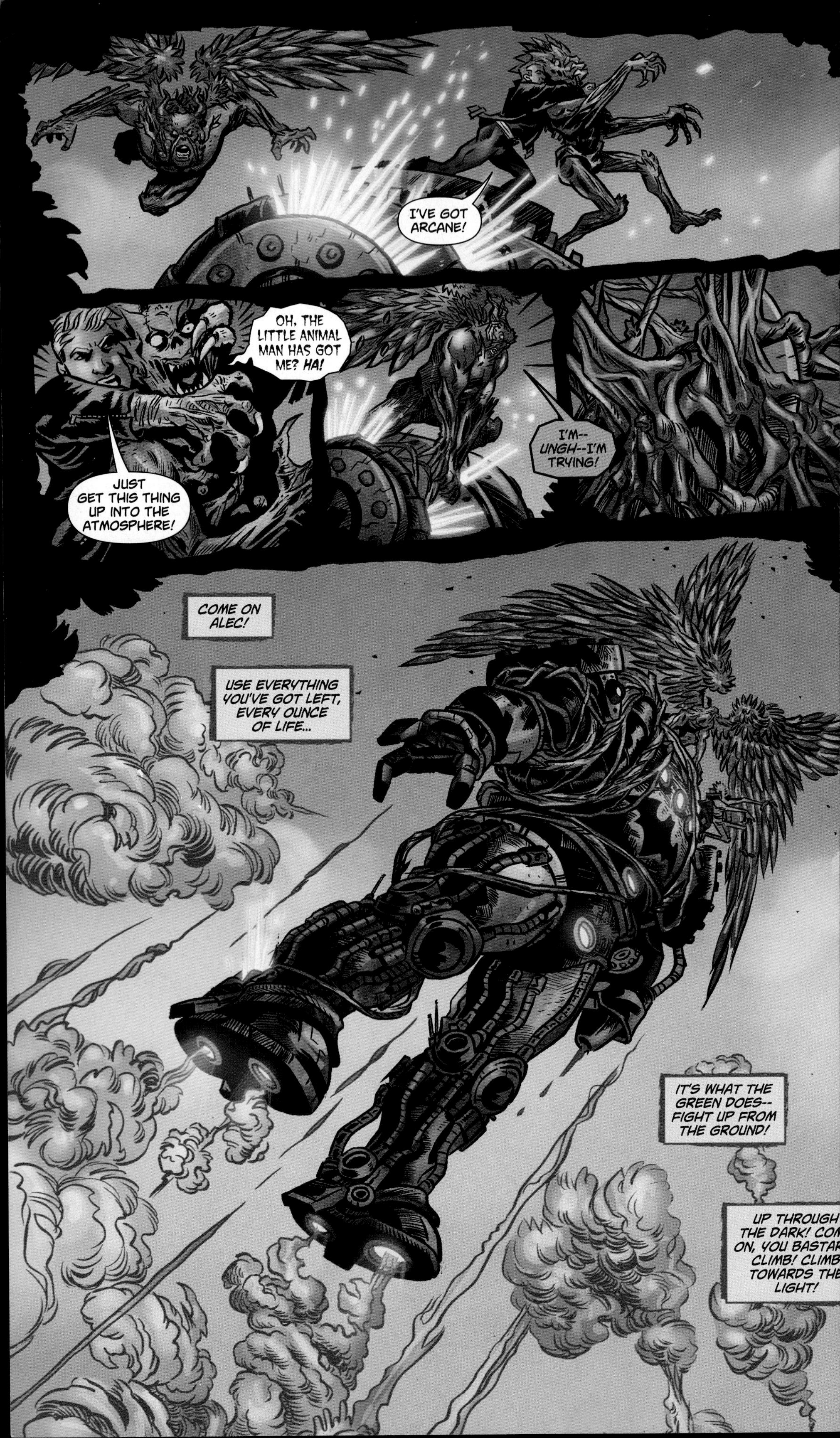
I'VE GOT ARCANE!
OH, THE LITTLE ANIMAL MAN HAS GOT ME? HA!
JUST GET THIS THING UP INTO THE ATMOSPHERE!
I'M-- UNGH--I'M TRYING!
COME ON ALEC!
USE EVERYTHING YOU'VE GOT LEFT, EVERY OUNCE OF LIFE...
IT'S WHAT THE GREEN DOES-- FIGHT UP FROM THE GROUND!

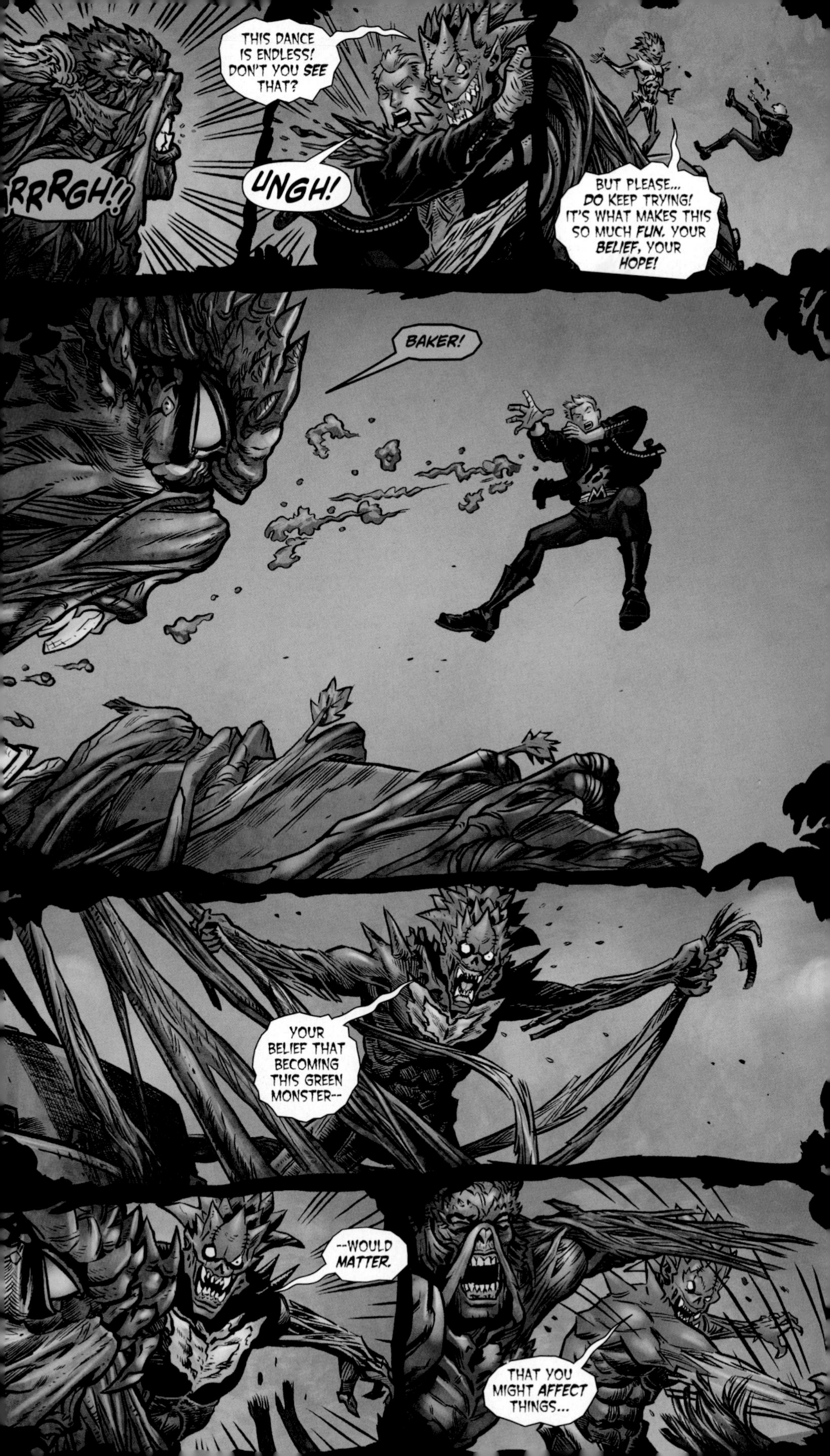
ARRRGH!!
THIS DANCE IS ENDLESS! DON'T YOU SEE THAT?
UNGH!
BUT PLEASE... DO KEEP TRYING! IT'S WHAT MAKES THIS SO MUCH FUN. YOUR BELIEF, YOUR HOPE!
BAKER!
YOUR BELIEF THAT BECOMING THIS GREEN MONSTER--
--WOULD MATTER.
THAT YOU MIGHT AFFECT THINGS...

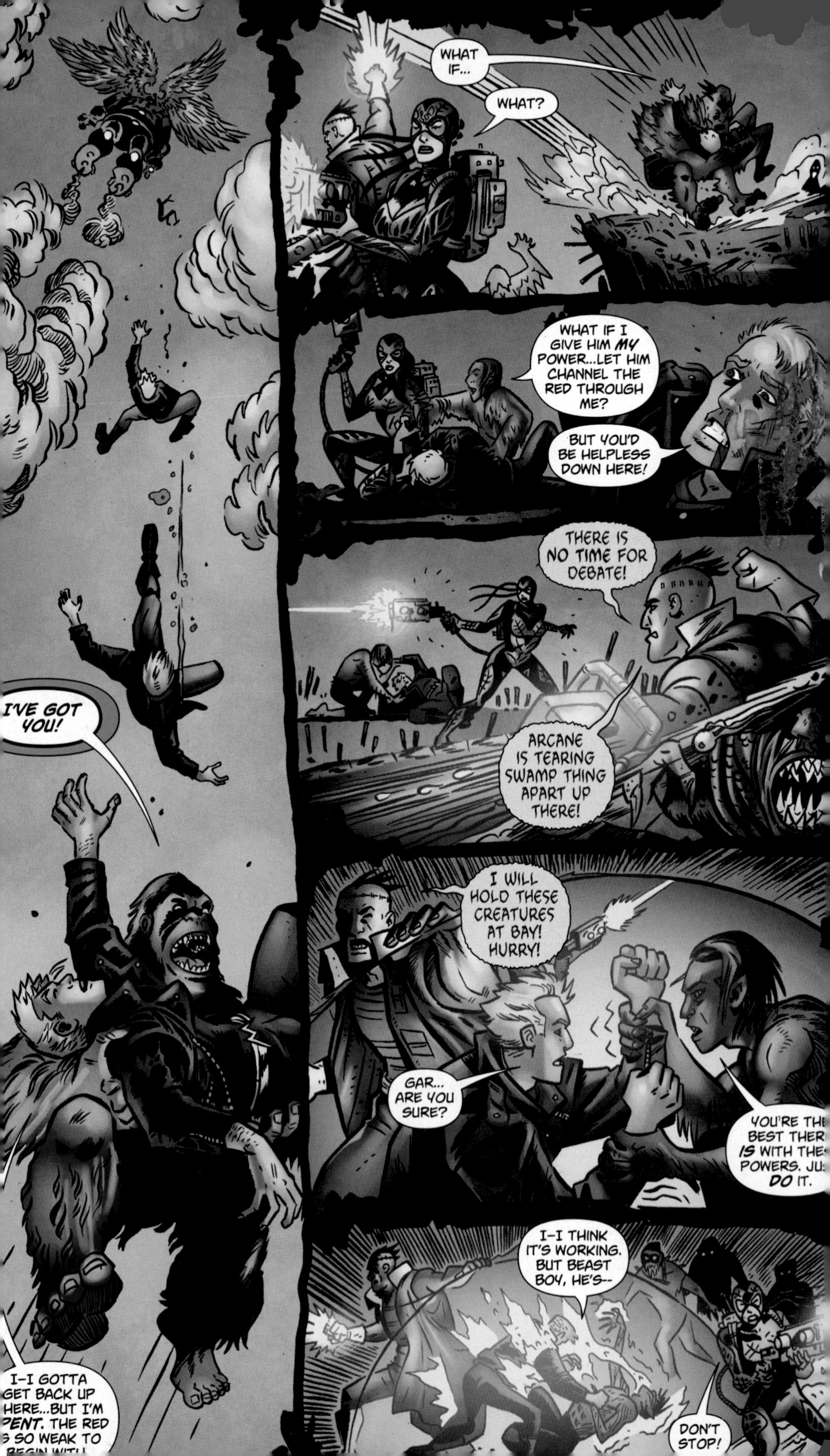
I'VE GOT YOU!
I–I GOTTA GET BACK UP HERE...BUT I'M PENT. THE RED S SO WEAK TO
WHAT IF...
WHAT?
WHAT IF I GIVE HIM MY POWER...LET HIM CHANNEL THE RED THROUGH ME?
BUT YOU'D BE HELPLESS DOWN HERE!
THERE IS NO TIME FOR DEBATE!
ARCANE IS TEARING SWAMP THING APART UP THERE!
I WILL HOLD THESE CREATURES AT BAY! HURRY!
GAR... ARE YOU SURE?
YOU'RE THE BEST THER IS WITH THE POWERS. JU DO IT.
I–I THINK IT'S WORKING. BUT BEAST BOY, HE'S--
DON'T STOP!

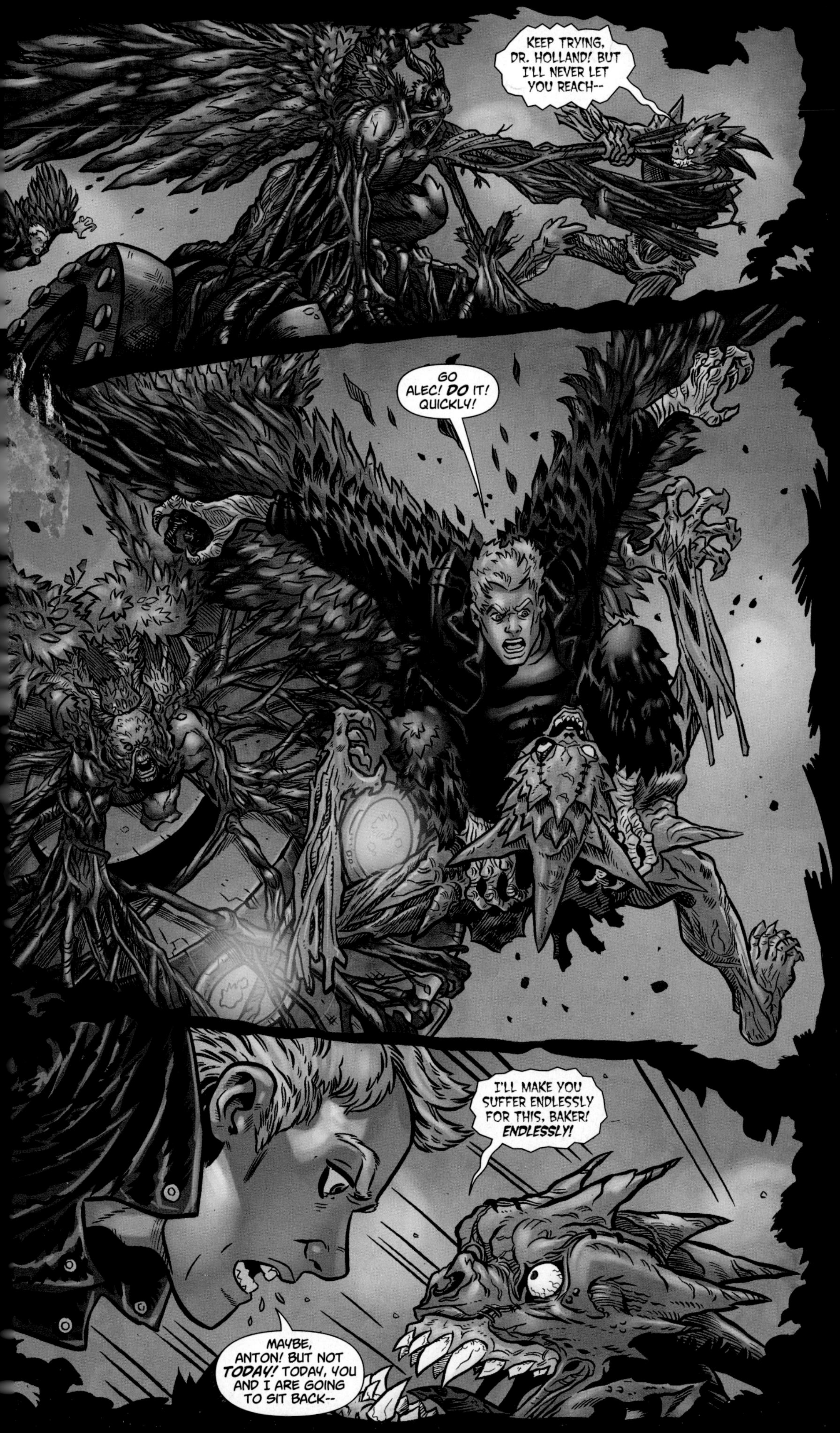
KEEP TRYING, DR. HOLLAND! BUT I'LL NEVER LET YOU REACH--
GO ALEC! DO IT! QUICKLY!
I'LL MAKE YOU SUFFER ENDLESSLY FOR THIS, BAKER! ENDLESSLY!
MAYBE, ANTON! BUT NOT TODAY! TODAY, YOU AND I ARE GOING TO SIT BACK--

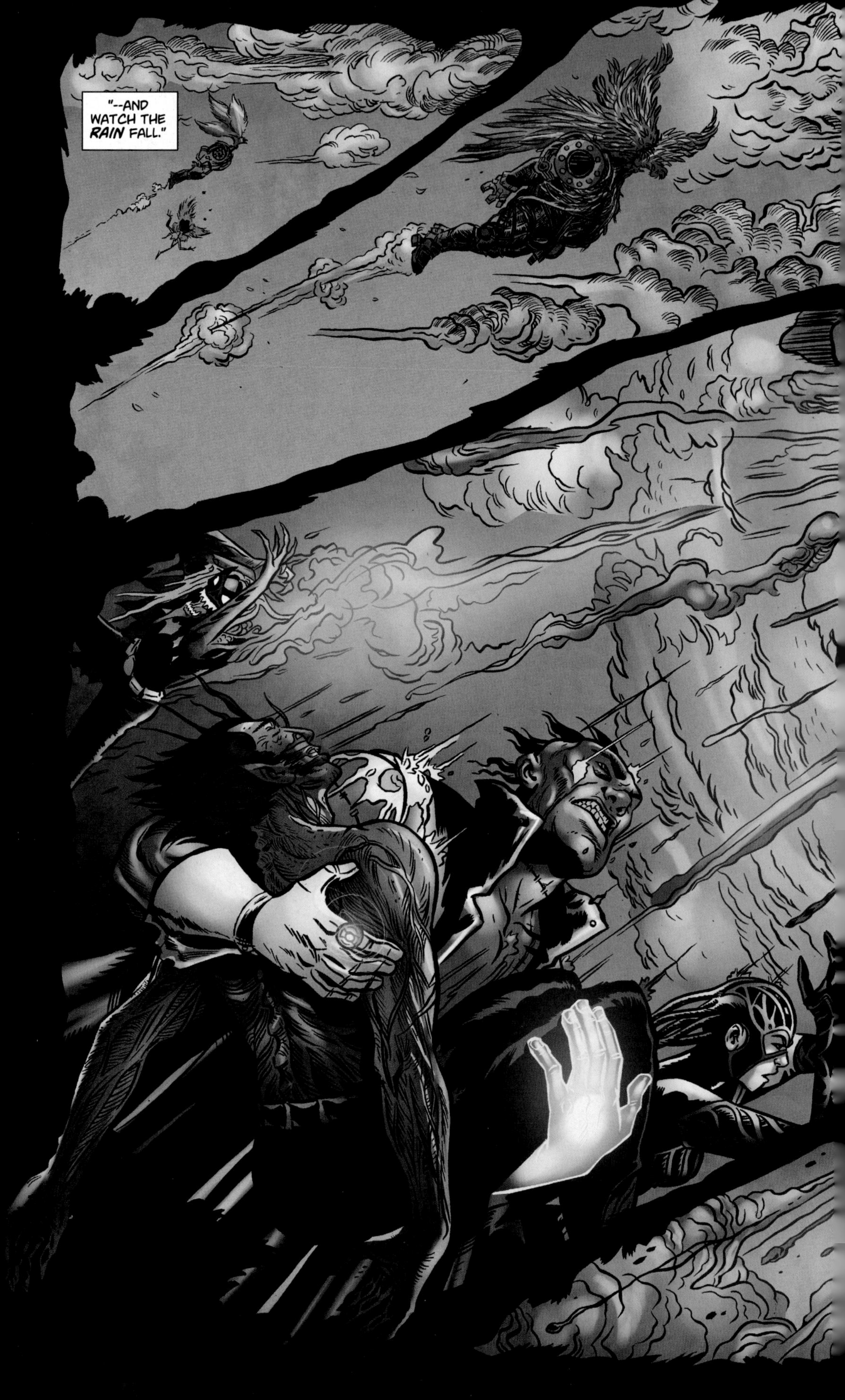
"--AND WATCH THE RAIN FALL."

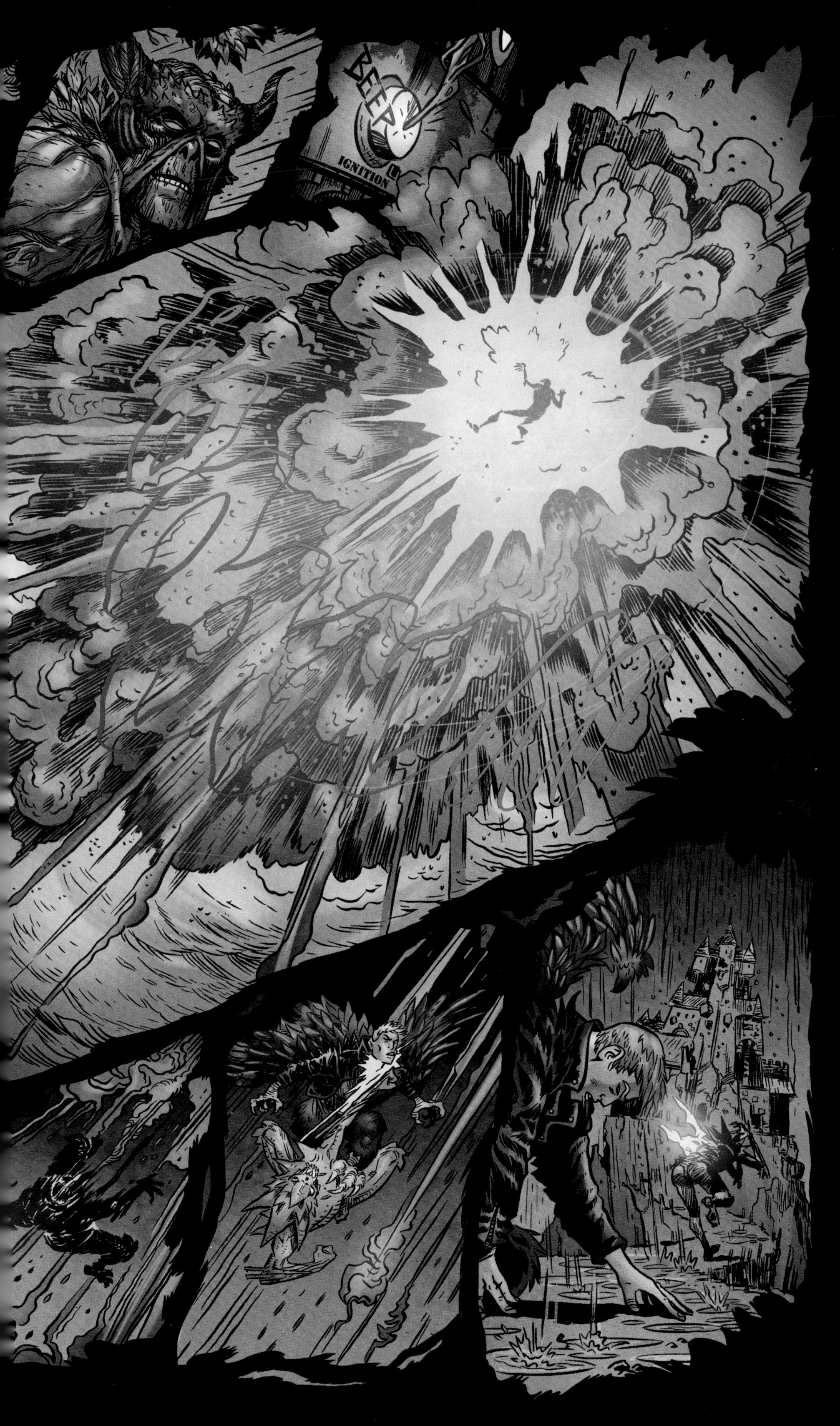
BEEP
IGNITION

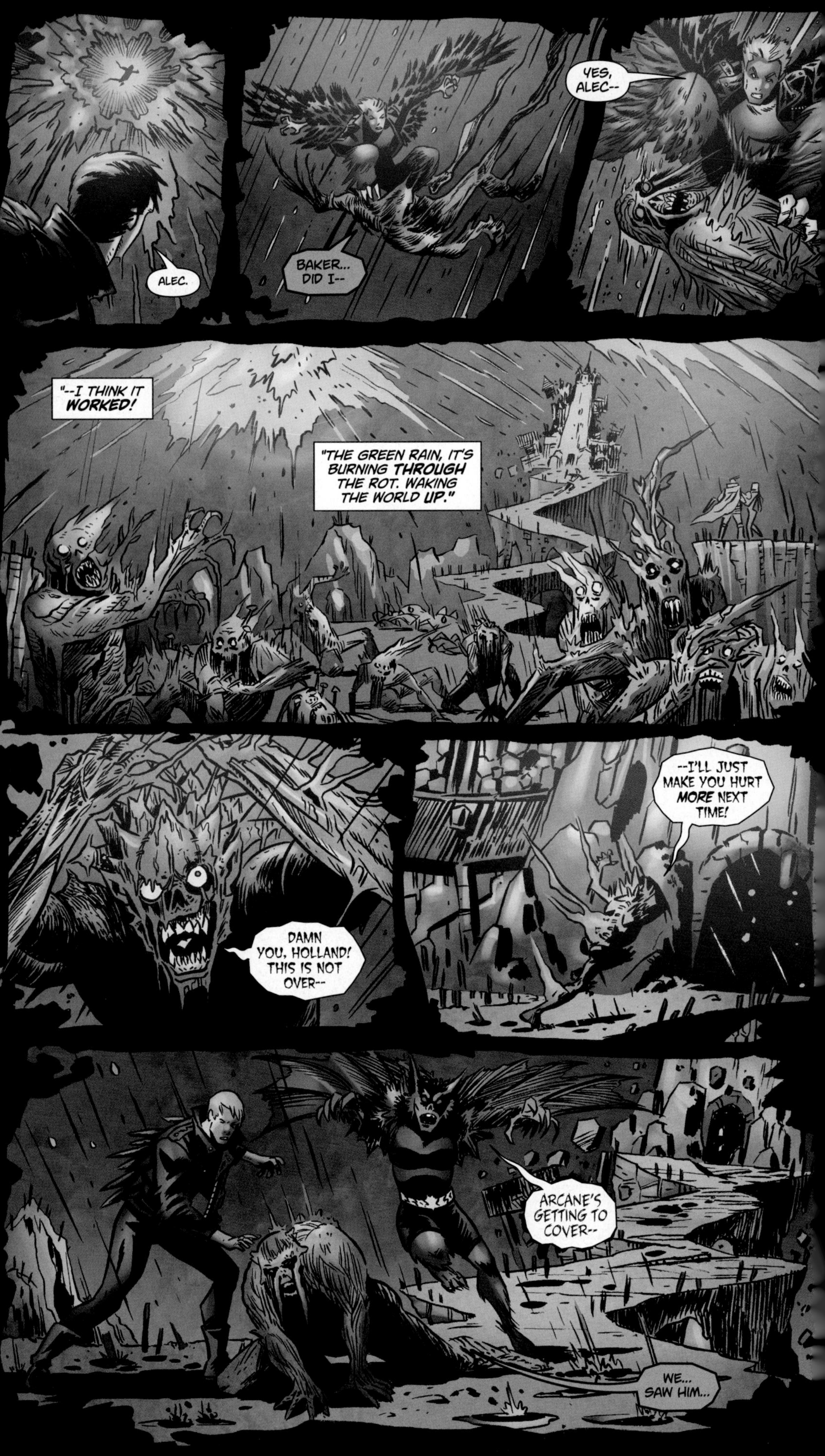
ALEC.
BAKER... DID I--
YES, ALEC--
"--I THINK IT WORKED!
"THE GREEN RAIN, IT'S BURNING THROUGH THE ROT. WAKING THE WORLD UP."
DAMN YOU, HOLLAND! THIS IS NOT OVER--
--I'LL JUST MAKE YOU HURT MORE NEXT TIME!
ARCANE'S GETTING TO COVER--
WE... SAW HIM...

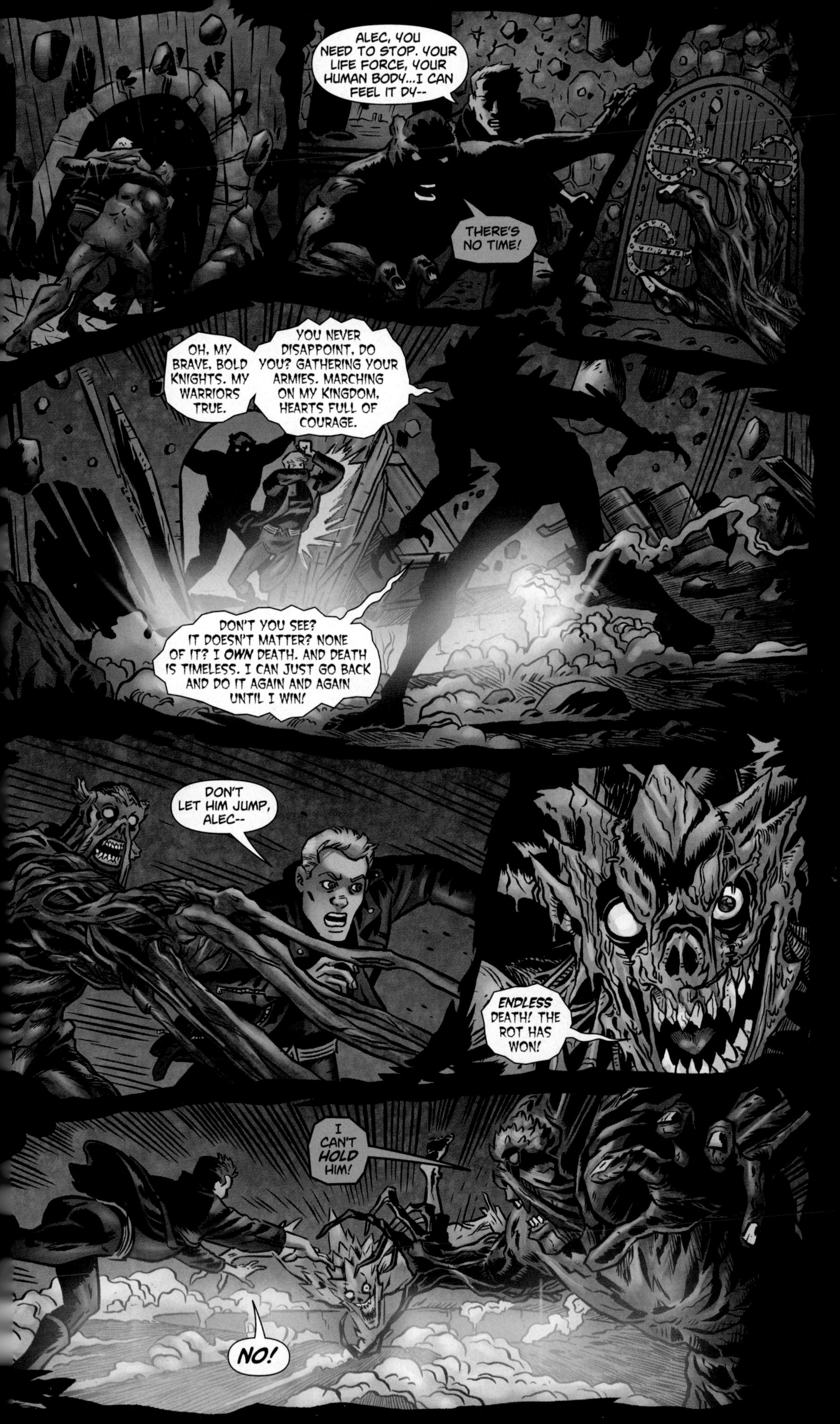
ALEC, YOU NEED TO STOP. YOUR LIFE FORCE, YOUR HUMAN BODY...I CAN FEEL IT DY--
THERE'S NO TIME!
OH, MY BRAVE, BOLD KNIGHTS. MY WARRIORS TRUE.
YOU NEVER DISAPPOINT, DO YOU? GATHERING YOUR ARMIES. MARCHING ON MY KINGDOM, HEARTS FULL OF COURAGE.
DON'T YOU SEE? IT DOESN'T MATTER? NONE OF IT? I *OWN* DEATH. AND DEATH IS TIMELESS. I CAN JUST GO BACK AND DO IT AGAIN AND AGAIN UNTIL I WIN!
DON'T LET HIM JUMP, ALEC--
ENDLESS DEATH! THE ROT HAS WON!
I CAN'T *HOLD* HIM!
NO!

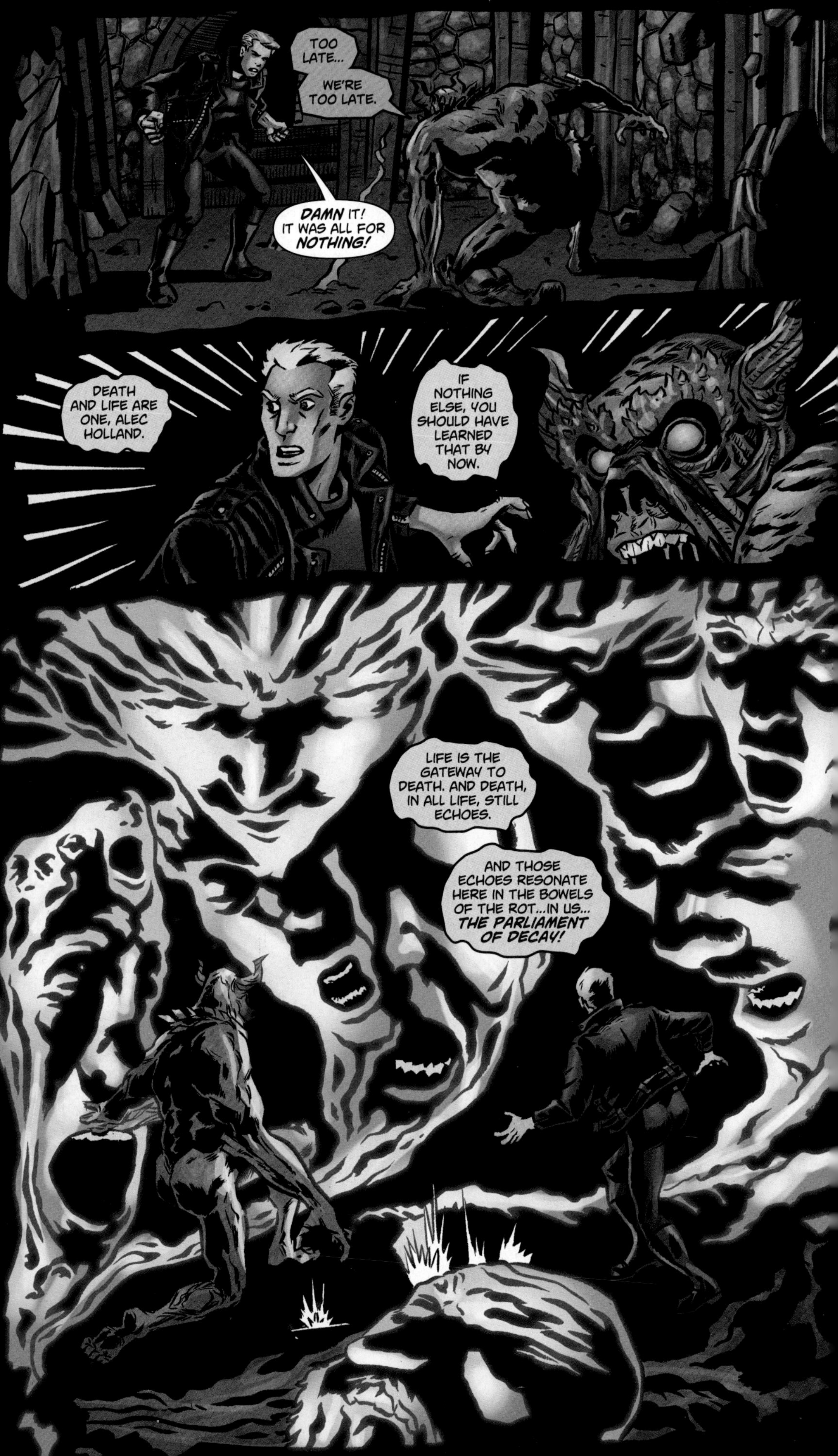
TOO LATE...
WE'RE TOO LATE.
DAMN IT! IT WAS ALL FOR NOTHING!
DEATH AND LIFE ARE ONE, ALEC HOLLAND.
IF NOTHING ELSE, YOU SHOULD HAVE LEARNED THAT BY NOW.
LIFE IS THE GATEWAY TO DEATH. AND DEATH, IN ALL LIFE, STILL ECHOES.
AND THOSE ECHOES RESONATE HERE IN THE BOWELS OF THE ROT...IN US... THE PARLIAMENT OF DECAY!

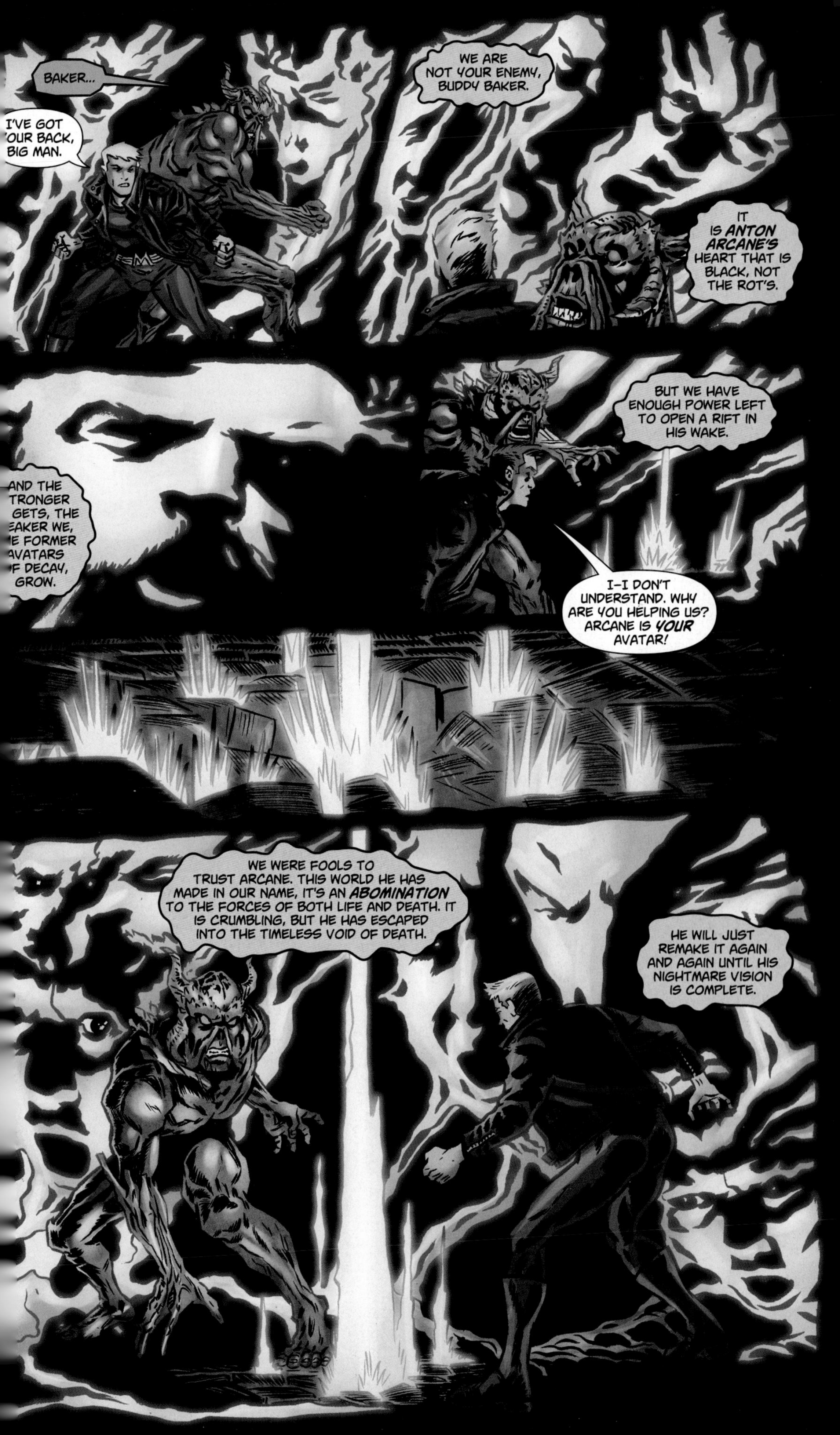
BAKER...
I'VE GOT YOUR BACK, BIG MAN.
WE ARE NOT YOUR ENEMY, BUDDY BAKER.
IT IS ANTON ARCANE'S HEART THAT IS BLACK, NOT THE ROT'S.
AND THE TRONGER GETS, THE EAKER WE, E FORMER AVATARS OF DECAY, GROW.
BUT WE HAVE ENOUGH POWER LEFT TO OPEN A RIFT IN HIS WAKE.
I-I DON'T UNDERSTAND. WHY ARE YOU HELPING US? ARCANE IS YOUR AVATAR!
WE WERE FOOLS TO TRUST ARCANE. THIS WORLD HE HAS MADE IN OUR NAME, IT'S AN ABOMINATION TO THE FORCES OF BOTH LIFE AND DEATH. IT IS CRUMBLING, BUT HE HAS ESCAPED INTO THE TIMELESS VOID OF DEATH.
HE WILL JUST REMAKE IT AGAIN AND AGAIN UNTIL HIS NIGHTMARE VISION IS COMPLETE.

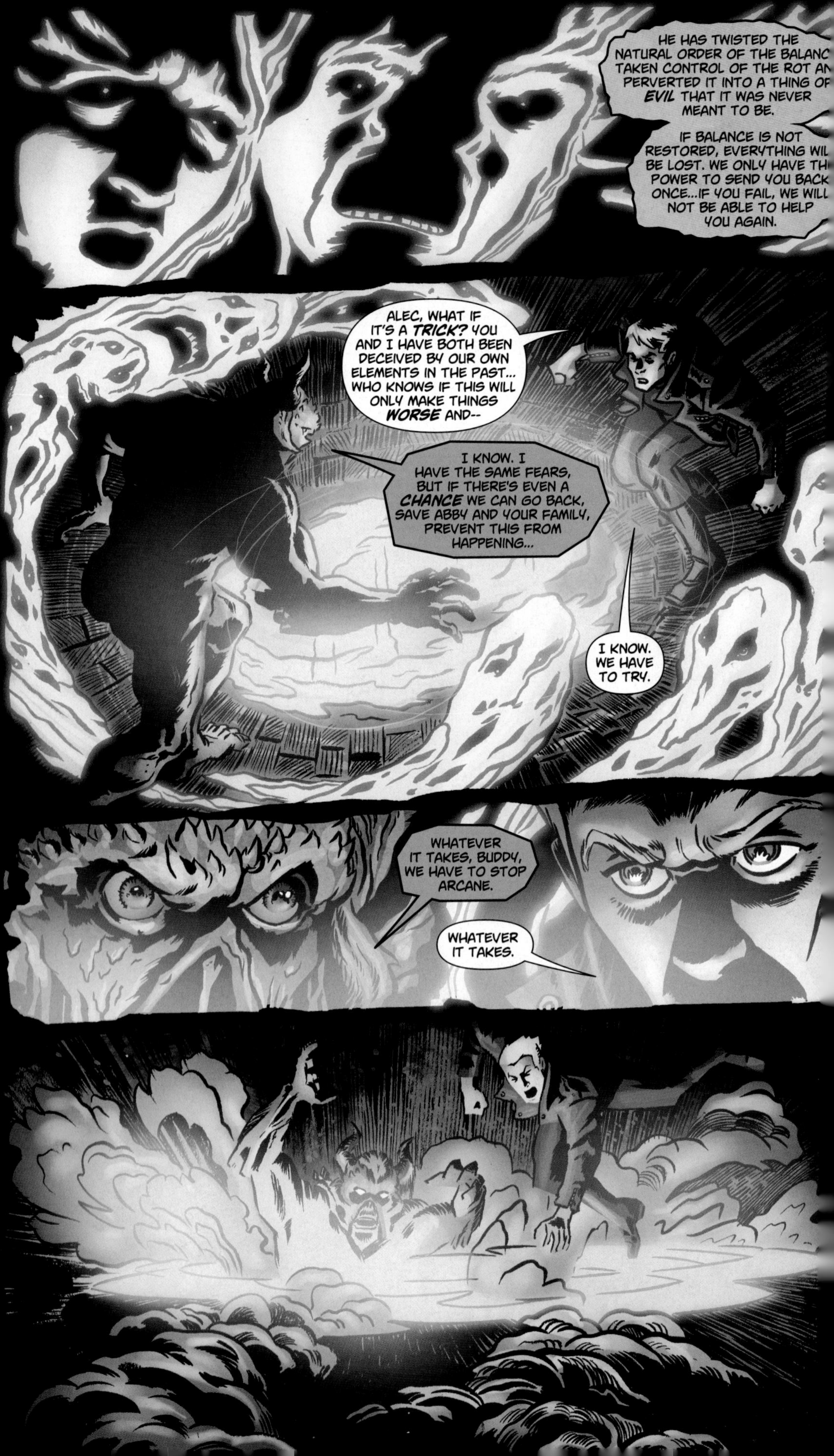
HE HAS TWISTED THE NATURAL ORDER OF THE BALANC TAKEN CONTROL OF THE ROT AN PERVERTED IT INTO A THING OF EVIL THAT IT WAS NEVER MEANT TO BE.
IF BALANCE IS NOT RESTORED, EVERYTHING WIL BE LOST. WE ONLY HAVE TH POWER TO SEND YOU BACK ONCE...IF YOU FAIL, WE WILL NOT BE ABLE TO HELP YOU AGAIN.
ALEC, WHAT IF IT'S A TRICK? YOU AND I HAVE BOTH BEEN DECEIVED BY OUR OWN ELEMENTS IN THE PAST... WHO KNOWS IF THIS WILL ONLY MAKE THINGS WORSE AND--
I KNOW. I HAVE THE SAME FEARS, BUT IF THERE'S EVEN A CHANCE WE CAN GO BACK, SAVE ABBY AND YOUR FAMILY, PREVENT THIS FROM HAPPENING...
I KNOW. WE HAVE TO TRY.
WHATEVER IT TAKES, BUDDY, WE HAVE TO STOP ARCANE.
WHATEVER IT TAKES.

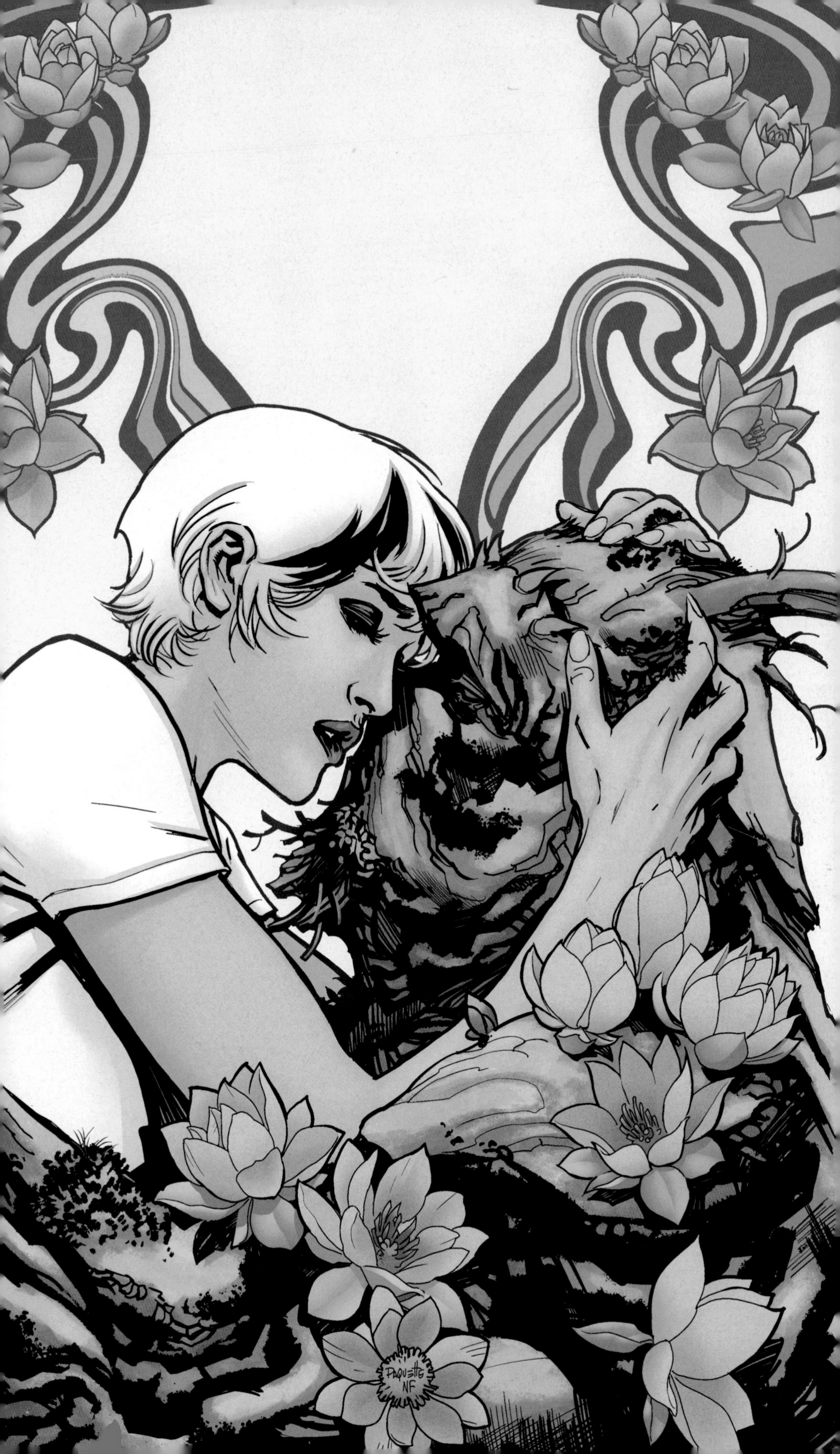
PAQUETTE
NF

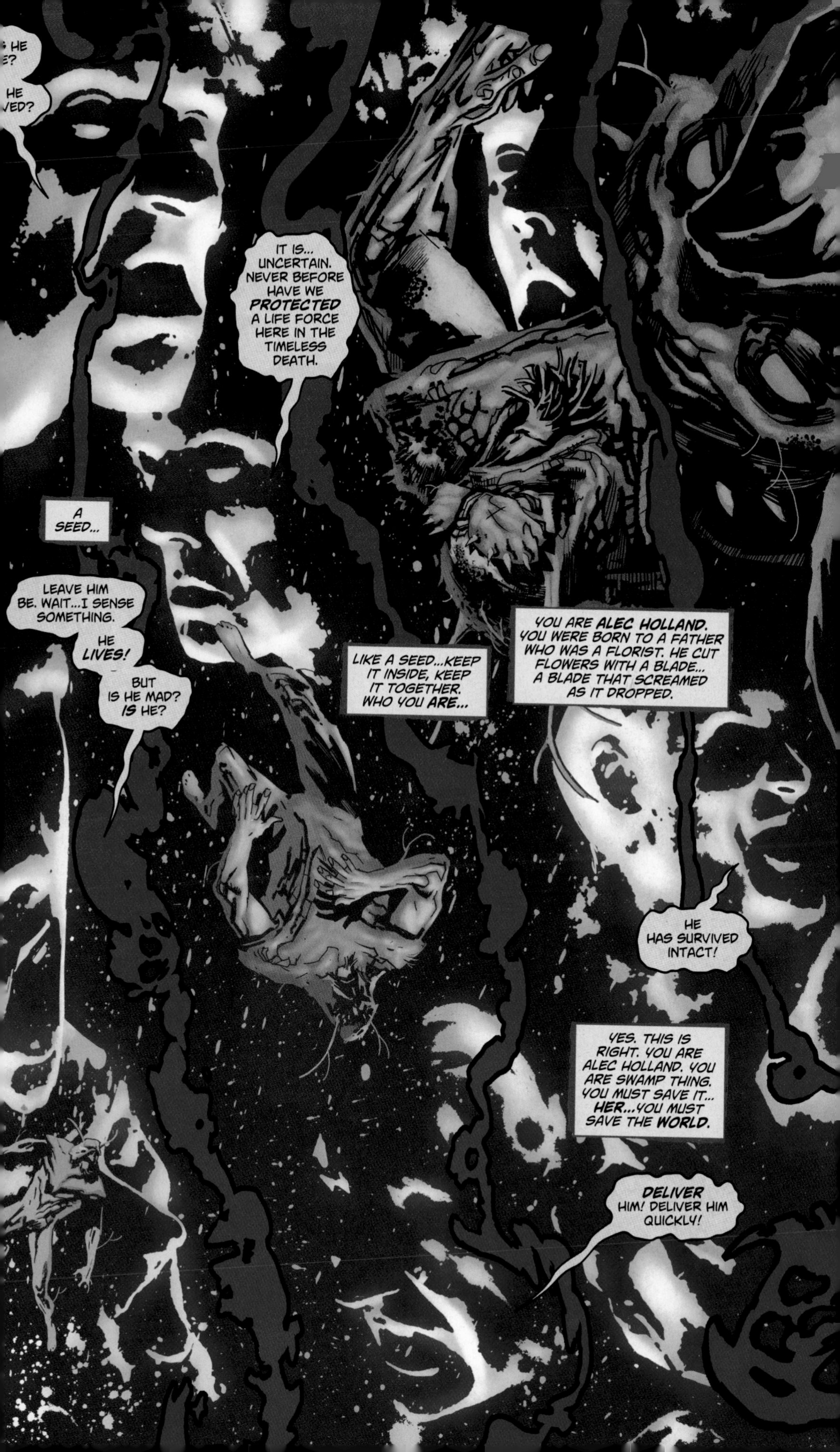
IT IS... UNCERTAIN. NEVER BEFORE HAVE WE PROTECTED A LIFE FORCE HERE IN THE TIMELESS DEATH.
A SEED...
LEAVE HIM BE. WAIT...I SENSE SOMETHING.
HE LIVES!
BUT IS HE MAD? IS HE?
LIKE A SEED...KEEP IT INSIDE, KEEP IT TOGETHER. WHO YOU ARE...
YOU ARE ALEC HOLLAND. YOU WERE BORN TO A FATHER WHO WAS A FLORIST. HE CUT FLOWERS WITH A BLADE... A BLADE THAT SCREAMED AS IT DROPPED.
HE HAS SURVIVED INTACT!
YES. THIS IS RIGHT. YOU ARE ALEC HOLLAND. YOU ARE SWAMP THING. YOU MUST SAVE IT... HER...YOU MUST SAVE THE WORLD.
DELIVER HIM! DELIVER HIM QUICKLY!

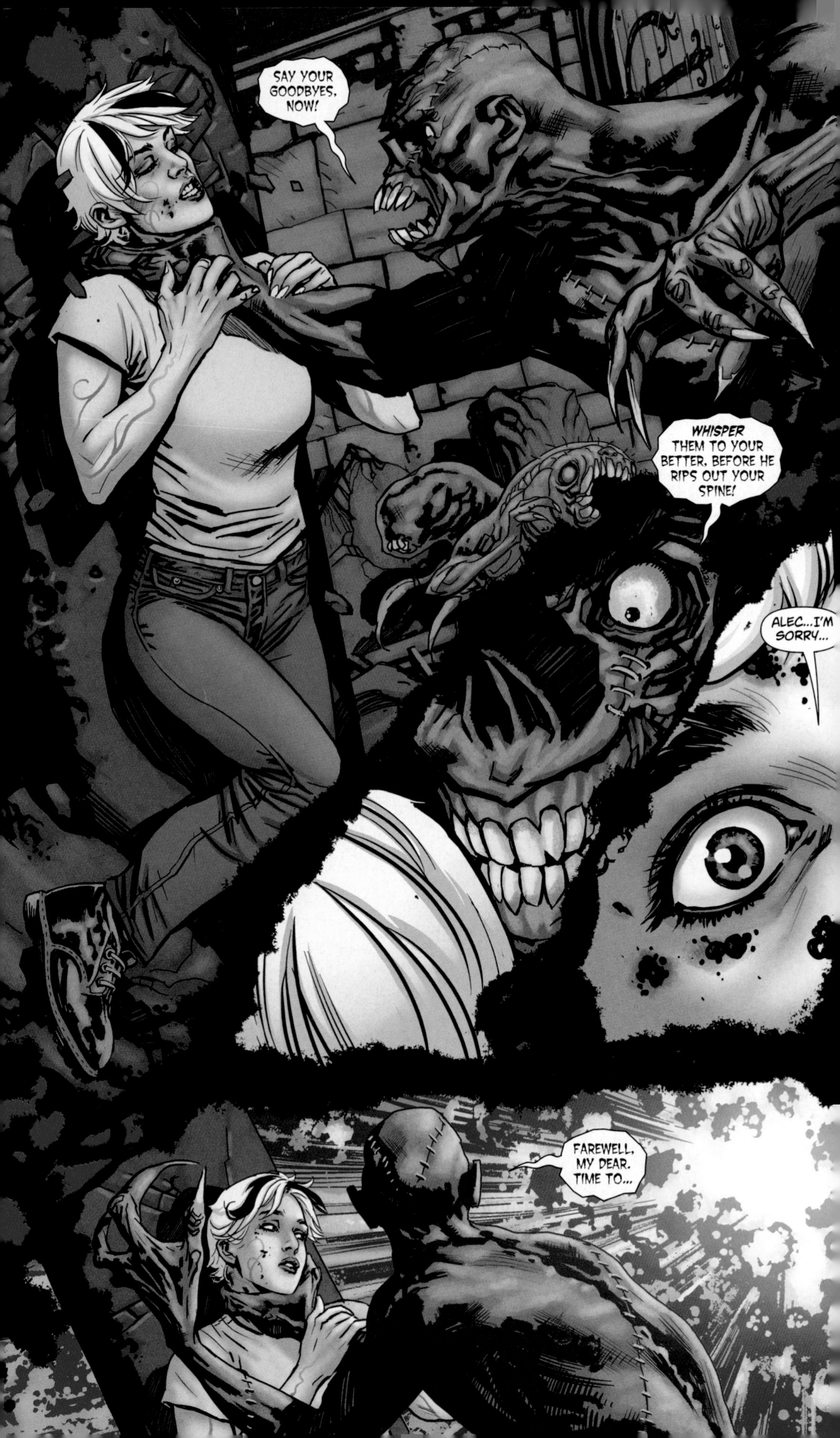
SAY YOUR GOODBYES, NOW!
WHISPER THEM TO YOUR BETTER, BEFORE HE RIPS OUT YOUR SPINE!
ALEC...I'M SORRY...
FAREWELL, MY DEAR. TIME TO...

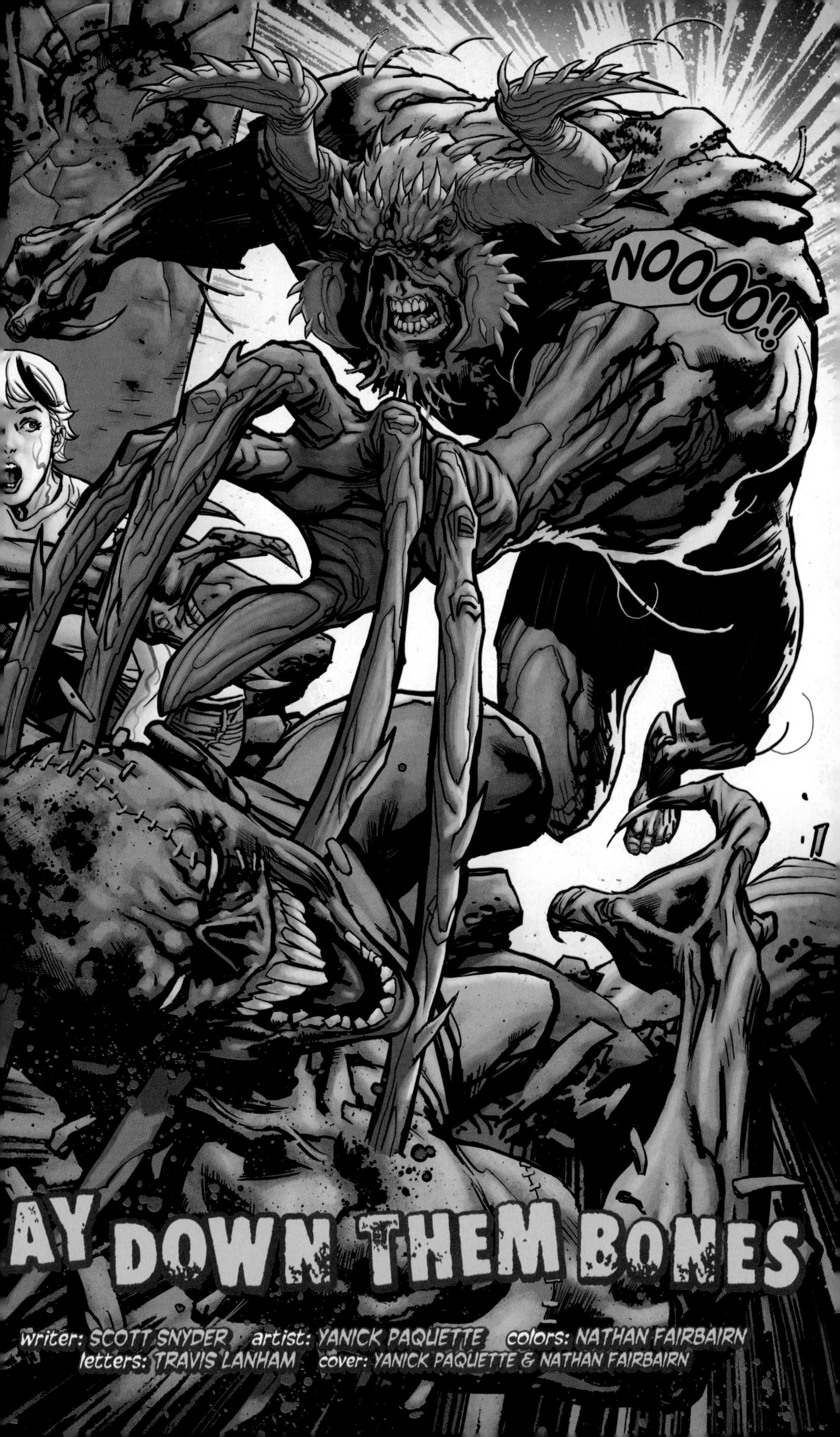
NOOOO!!
AY DOWN THEM BONES
writer: SCOTT SNYDER artist: YANICK PAQUETTE colors: NATHAN FAIRBAIRN
letters: TRAVIS LANHAM cover: YANICK PAQUETTE & NATHAN FAIRBAIRN

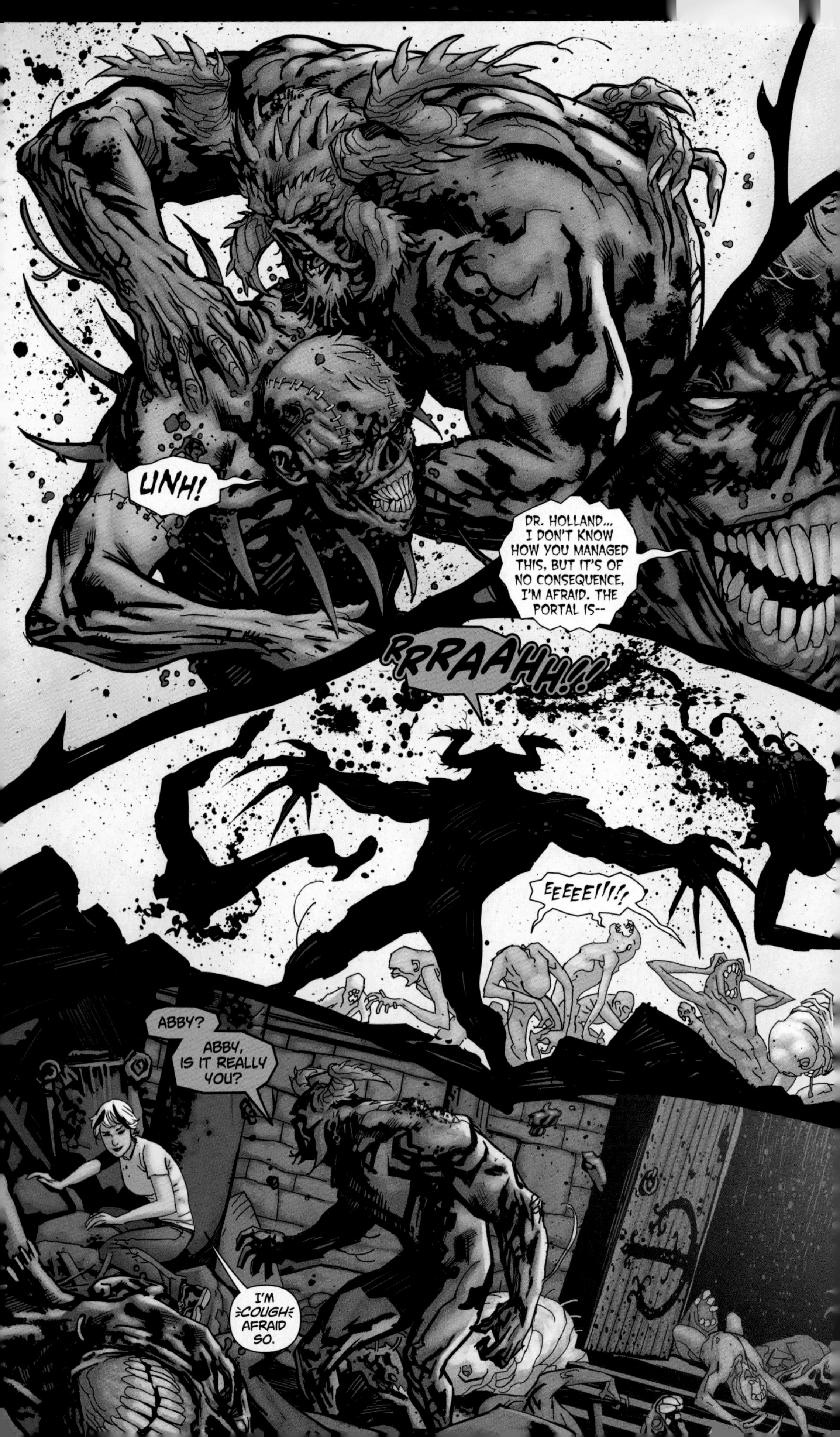
UNH!
DR. HOLLAND... I DON'T KNOW HOW YOU MANAGED THIS, BUT IT'S OF NO CONSEQUENCE, I'M AFRAID. THE PORTAL IS--
RRRAAHHH!!!
EEEEE!!!!!
ABBY?
ABBY, IS IT REALLY YOU?
I'M *COUGH* AFRAID SO.

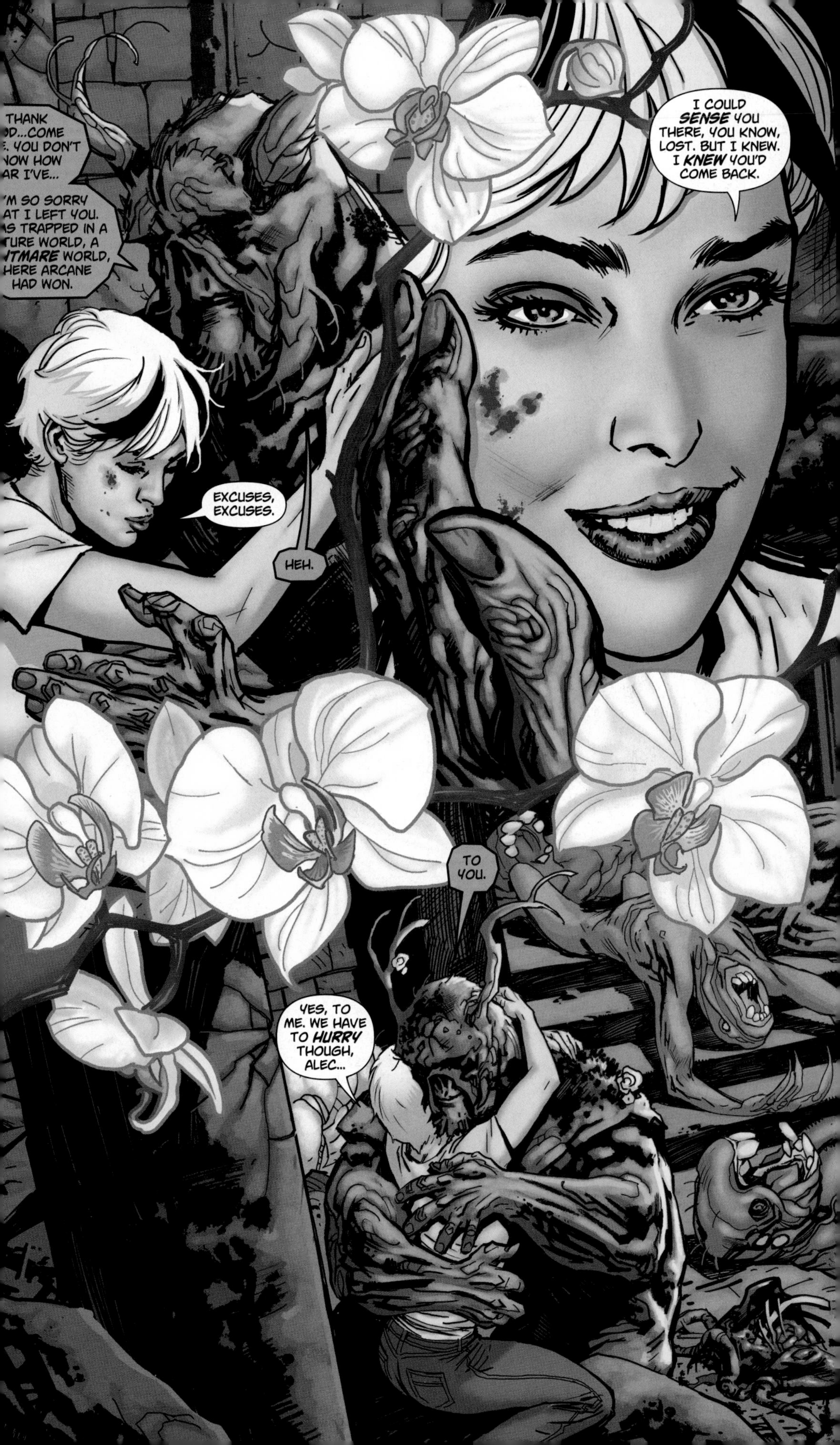
THANK
OD...COME
E. YOU DON'T
NOW HOW
AR I'VE...
'M SO SORRY
AT I LEFT YOU.
S TRAPPED IN A
TURE WORLD, A
ITMARE WORLD,
HERE ARCANE
HAD WON.
I COULD SENSE YOU THERE, YOU KNOW, LOST. BUT I KNEW. I KNEW YOU'D COME BACK.
EXCUSES, EXCUSES.
HEH.
TO YOU.
YES, TO ME. WE HAVE TO HURRY THOUGH, ALEC...

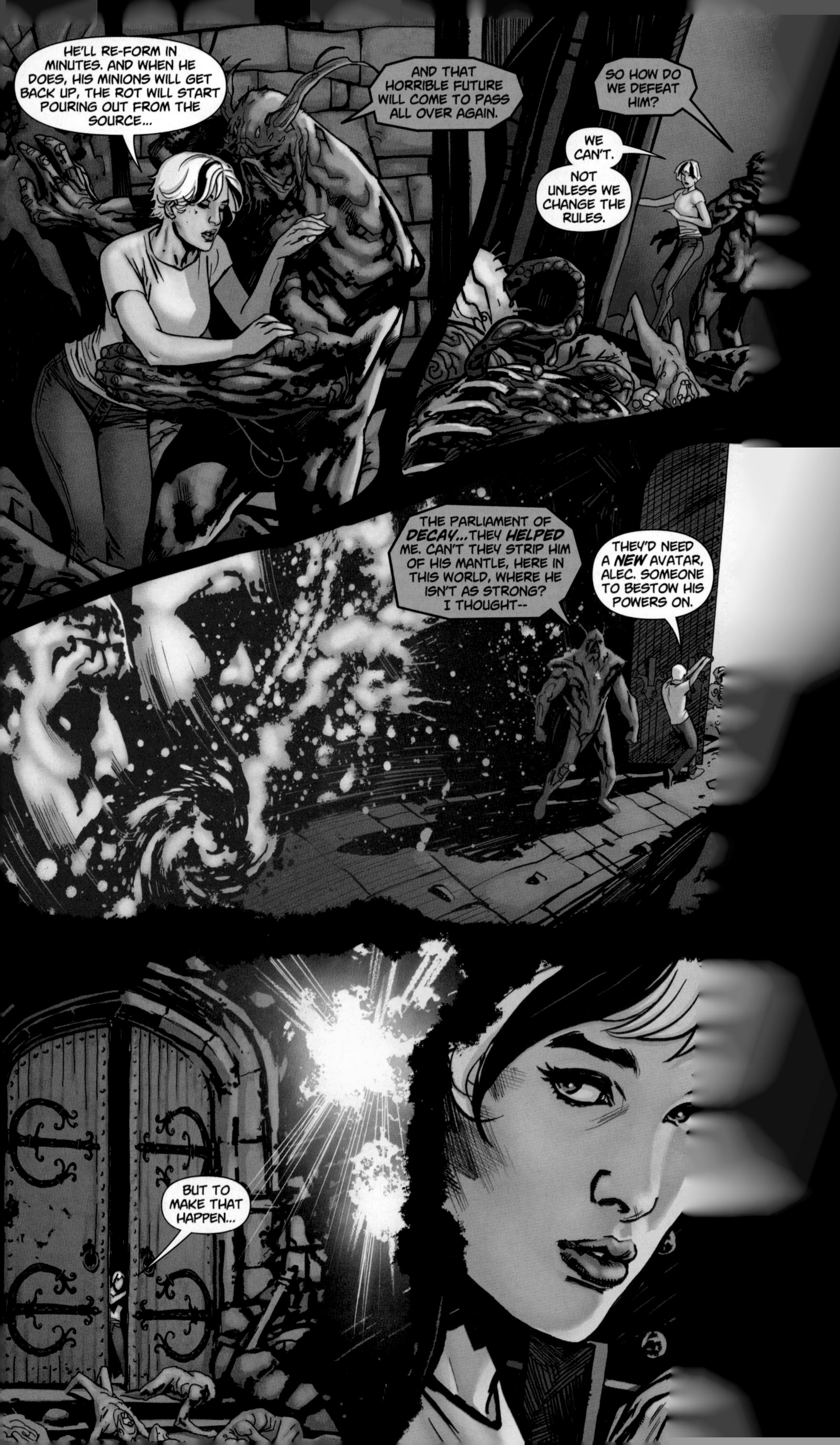
HE'LL RE-FORM IN MINUTES. AND WHEN HE DOES, HIS MINIONS WILL GET BACK UP, THE ROT WILL START POURING OUT FROM THE SOURCE...
AND THAT HORRIBLE FUTURE WILL COME TO PASS ALL OVER AGAIN.
SO HOW DO WE DEFEAT HIM?
WE CAN'T.
NOT UNLESS WE CHANGE THE RULES.
THE PARLIAMENT OF DECAY...THEY HELPED ME. CAN'T THEY STRIP HIM OF HIS MANTLE, HERE IN THIS WORLD, WHERE HE ISN'T AS STRONG? I THOUGHT--
THEY'D NEED A NEW AVATAR, ALEC. SOMEONE TO BESTOW HIS POWERS ON.
BUT TO MAKE THAT HAPPEN...

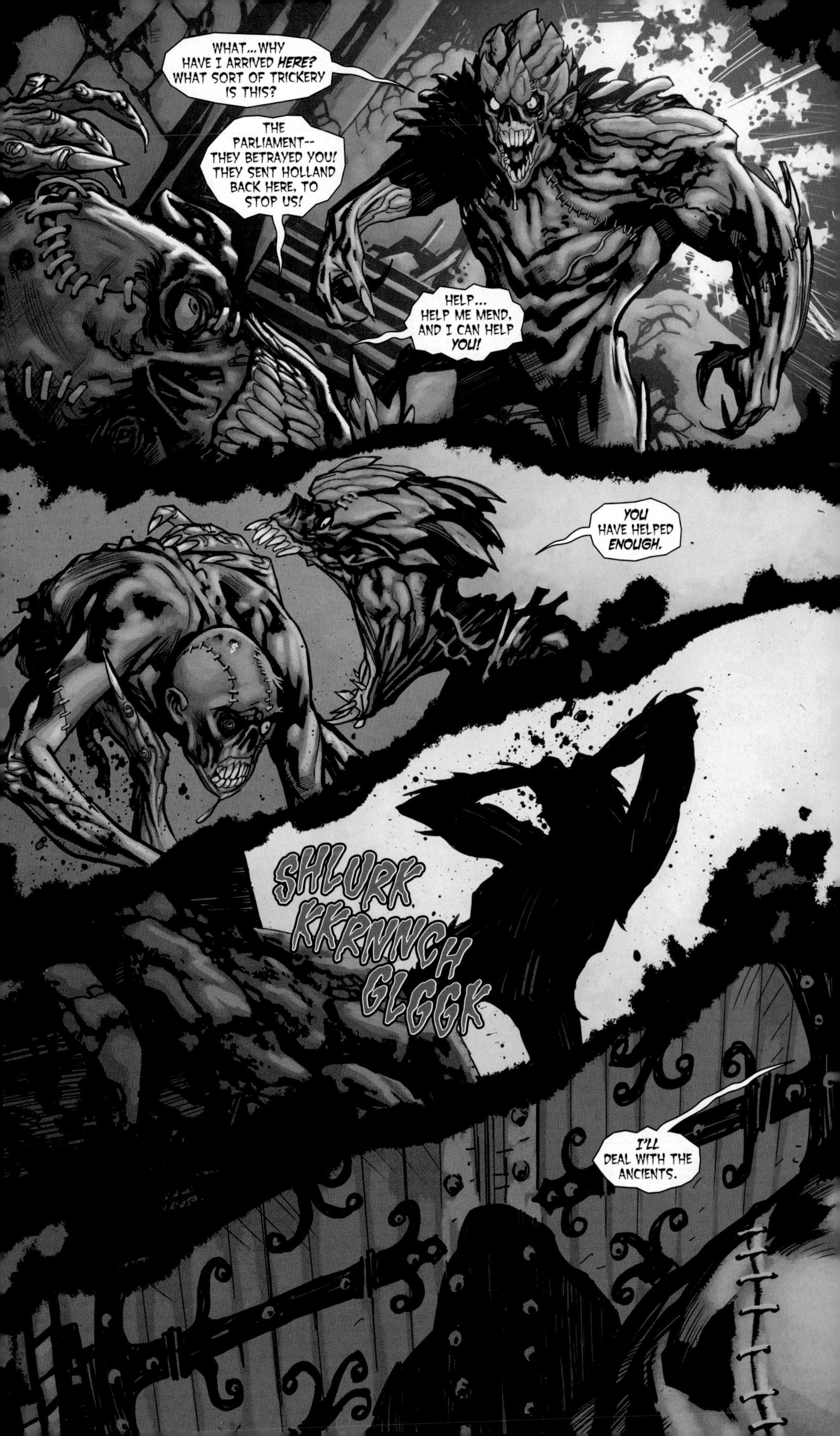
WHAT...WHY HAVE I ARRIVED HERE? WHAT SORT OF TRICKERY IS THIS?
THE PARLIAMENT-- THEY BETRAYED YOU! THEY SENT HOLLAND BACK HERE, TO STOP US!
HELP... HELP ME MEND, AND I CAN HELP YOU!
YOU HAVE HELPED ENOUGH.
SHLURK KKRNNCH GLGGK
I'LL DEAL WITH THE ANCIENTS.

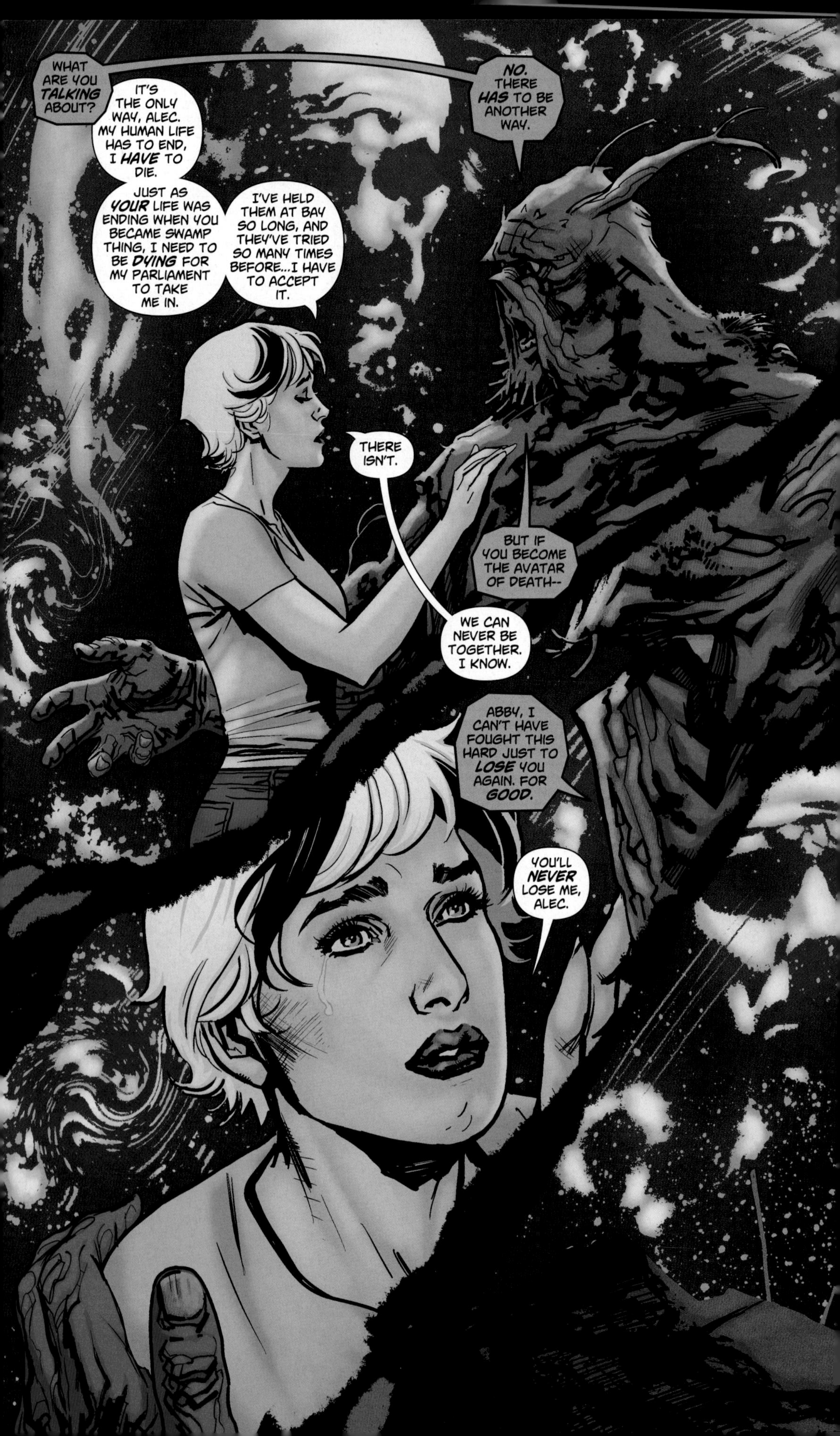

WHAT ARE YOU TALKING ABOUT?
NO. THERE HAS TO BE ANOTHER WAY.
IT'S THE ONLY WAY, ALEC. MY HUMAN LIFE HAS TO END, I HAVE TO DIE.
JUST AS YOUR LIFE WAS ENDING WHEN YOU BECAME SWAMP THING, I NEED TO BE DYING FOR MY PARLIAMENT TO TAKE ME IN.
I'VE HELD THEM AT BAY SO LONG, AND THEY'VE TRIED SO MANY TIMES BEFORE...I HAVE TO ACCEPT IT.
THERE ISN'T.
BUT IF YOU BECOME THE AVATAR OF DEATH--
WE CAN NEVER BE TOGETHER. I KNOW.
ABBY, I CAN'T HAVE FOUGHT THIS HARD JUST TO LOSE YOU AGAIN. FOR GOOD.
YOU'LL NEVER LOSE ME, ALEC.

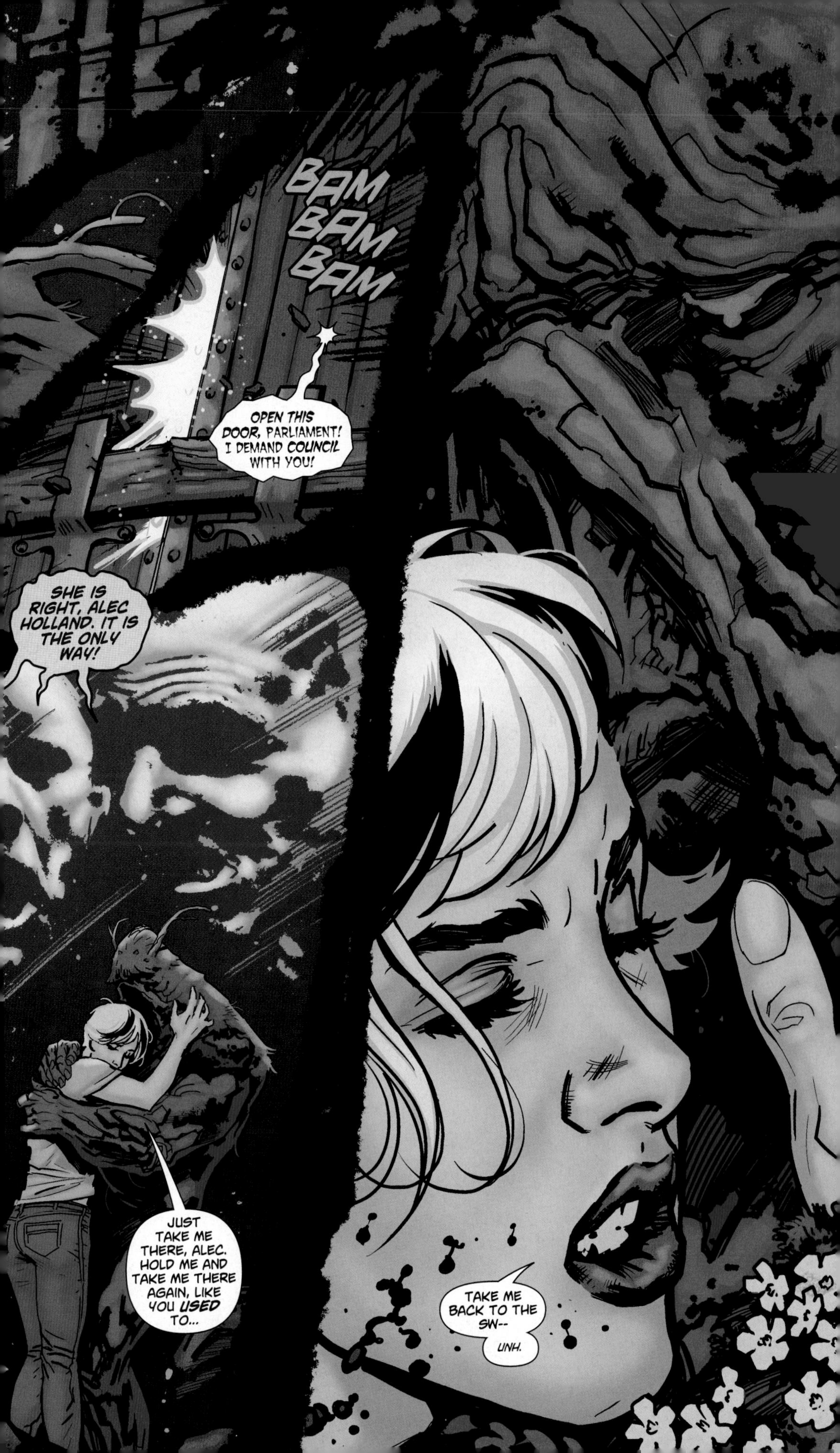
BAM BAM BAM
OPEN THIS DOOR, PARLIAMENT! I DEMAND COUNCIL WITH YOU!
SHE IS RIGHT, ALEC HOLLAND. IT IS THE ONLY WAY!
JUST TAKE ME THERE, ALEC. HOLD ME AND TAKE ME THERE AGAIN, LIKE YOU USED TO...
TAKE ME BACK TO THE SW--
UNH.

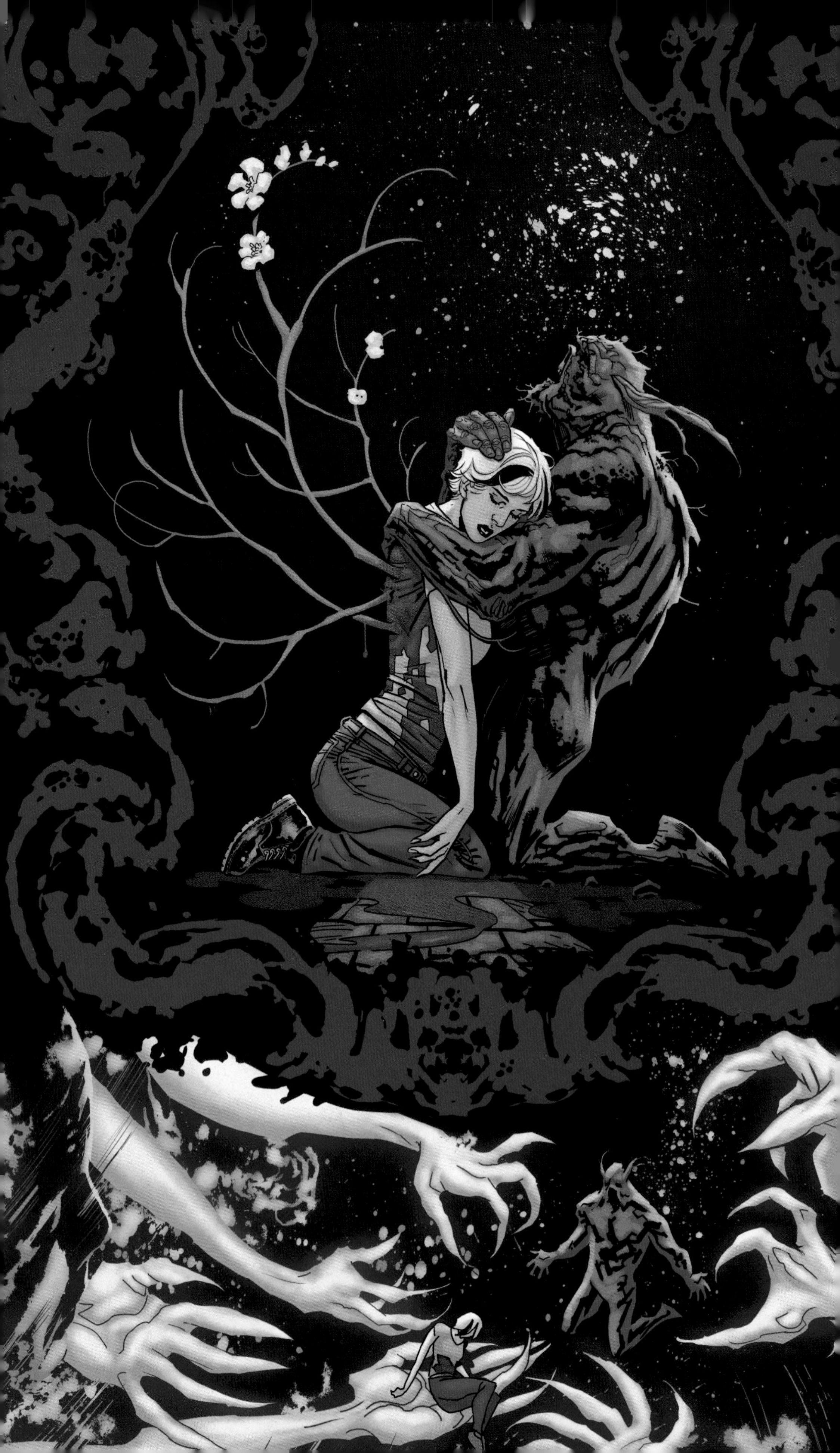

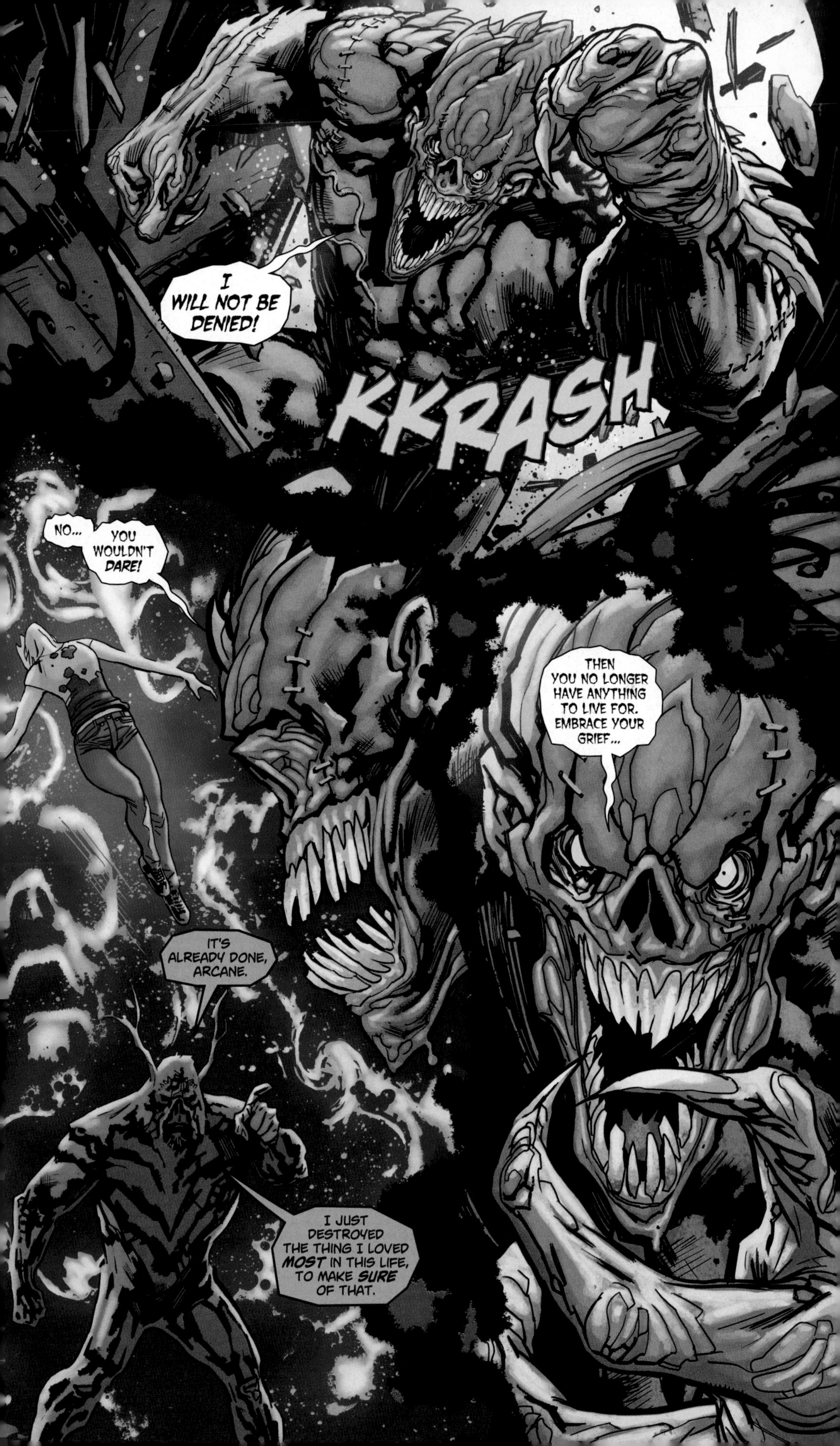
I WILL NOT BE DENIED!
KKRASH
NO...
YOU WOULDN'T DARE!
THEN YOU NO LONGER HAVE ANYTHING TO LIVE FOR. EMBRACE YOUR GRIEF...
IT'S ALREADY DONE, ARCANE.
I JUST DESTROYED THE THING I LOVED MOST IN THIS LIFE, TO MAKE SURE OF THAT.

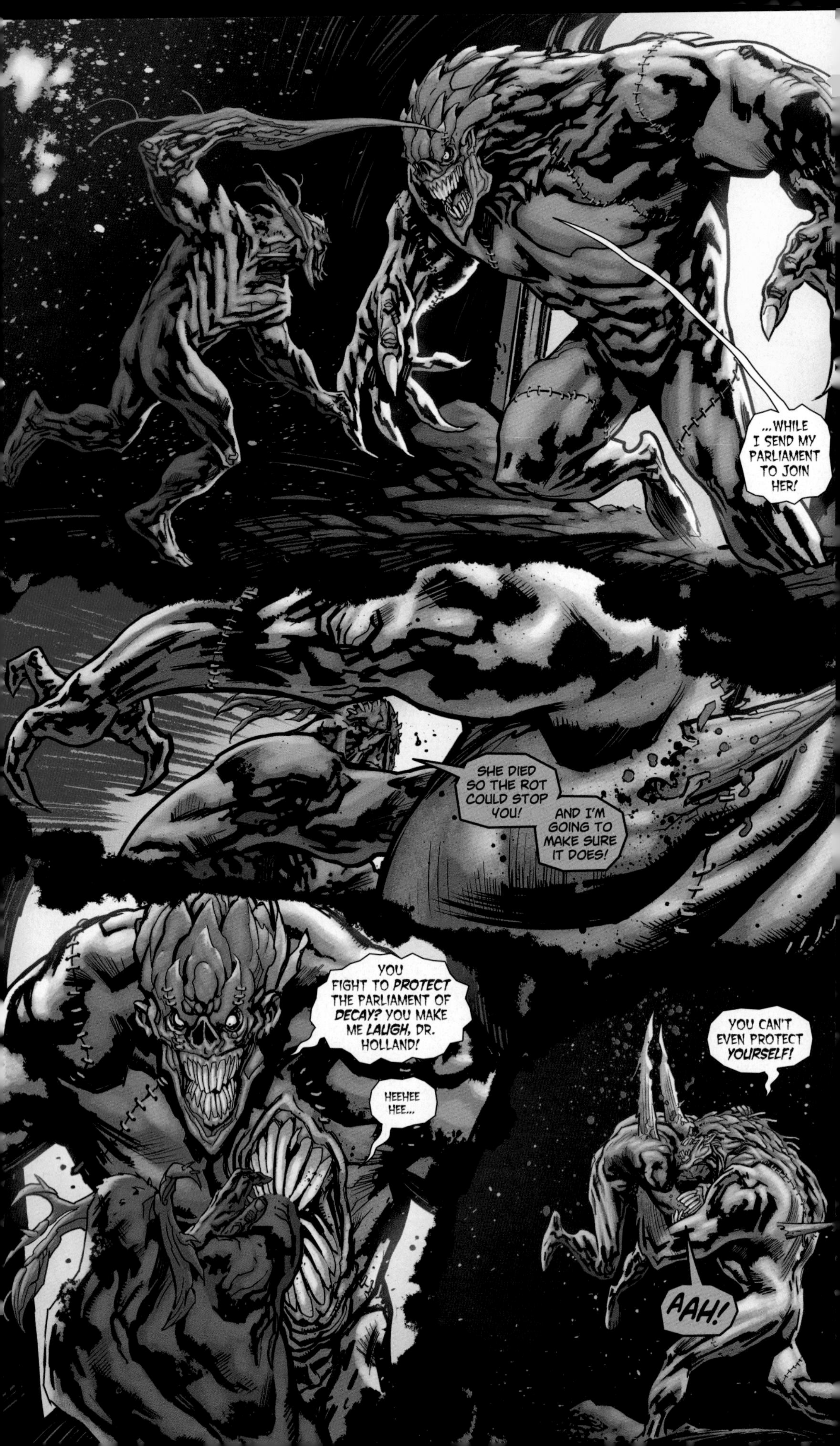
...WHILE I SEND MY PARLIAMENT TO JOIN HER!
SHE DIED SO THE ROT COULD STOP YOU!
AND I'M GOING TO MAKE SURE IT DOES!
YOU FIGHT TO PROTECT THE PARLIAMENT OF DECAY? YOU MAKE ME LAUGH, DR. HOLLAND!
HEEHEE HEE...
YOU CAN'T EVEN PROTECT YOURSELF!
AAH!

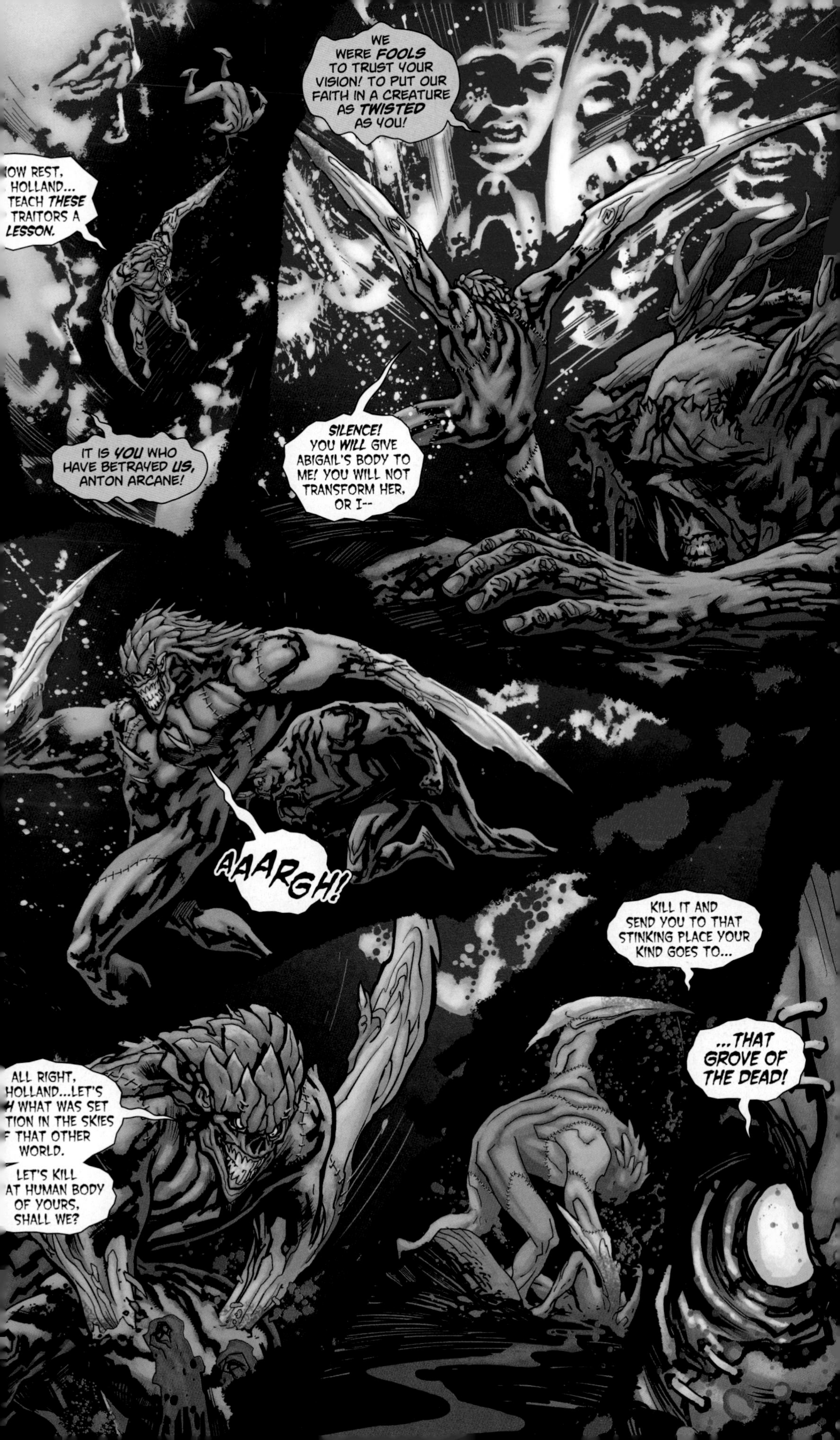
WE WERE FOOLS TO TRUST YOUR VISION! TO PUT OUR FAITH IN A CREATURE AS TWISTED AS YOU!
OW REST, HOLLAND... TEACH THESE TRAITORS A LESSON.
IT IS YOU WHO HAVE BETRAYED US, ANTON ARCANE!
SILENCE! YOU WILL GIVE ABIGAIL'S BODY TO ME! YOU WILL NOT TRANSFORM HER, OR I--
AAARGH!
KILL IT AND SEND YOU TO THAT STINKING PLACE YOUR KIND GOES TO...
...THAT GROVE OF THE DEAD!
ALL RIGHT, HOLLAND...LET'S H WHAT WAS SET TION IN THE SKIES THAT OTHER WORLD.
LET'S KILL AT HUMAN BODY OF YOURS, SHALL WE?

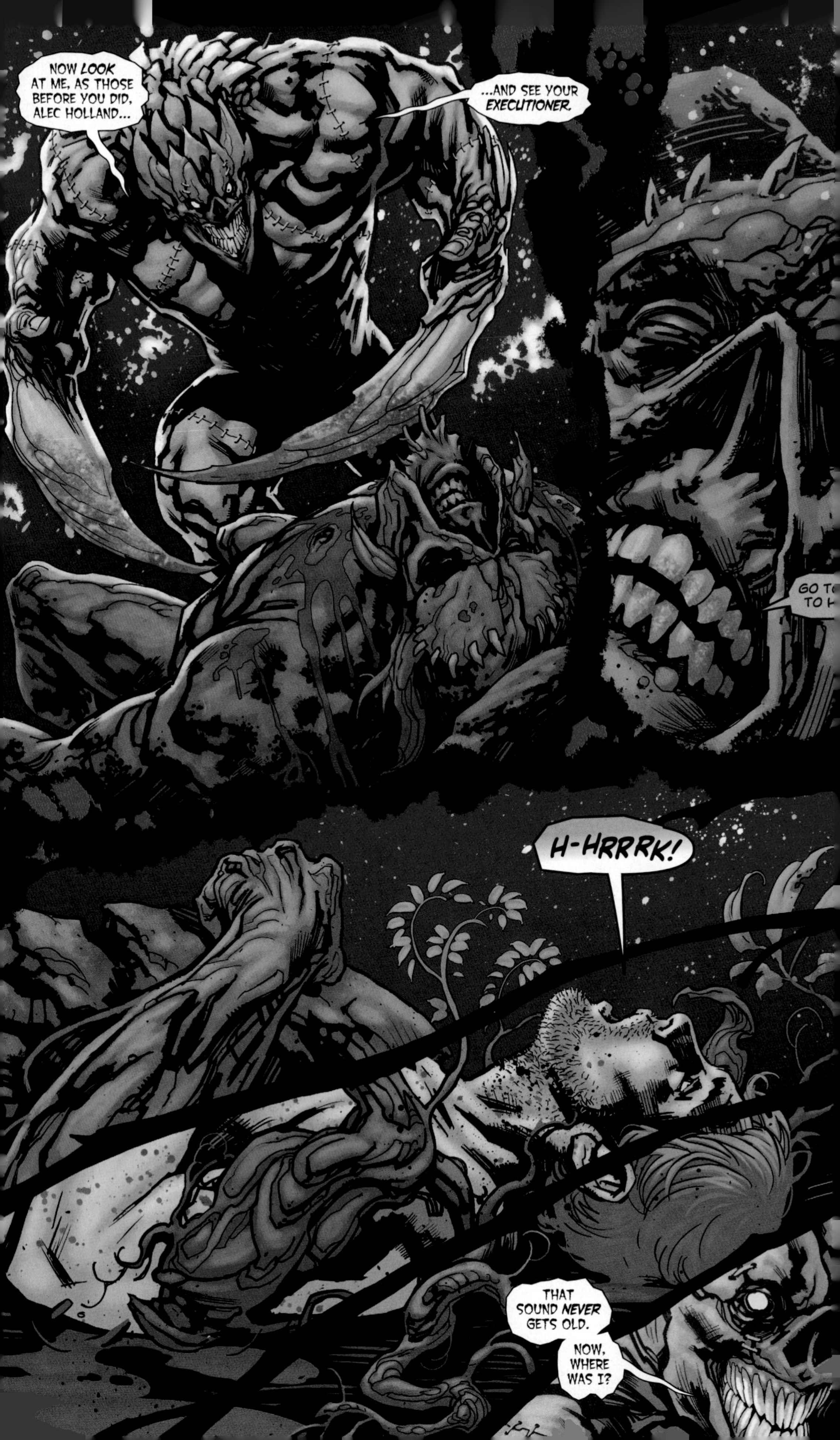
NOW *LOOK* AT ME, AS THOSE BEFORE YOU DID, ALEC HOLLAND...
...AND SEE YOUR *EXECUTIONER.*
H-HRRRK!
THAT SOUND *NEVER* GETS OLD.
NOW, WHERE WAS I?

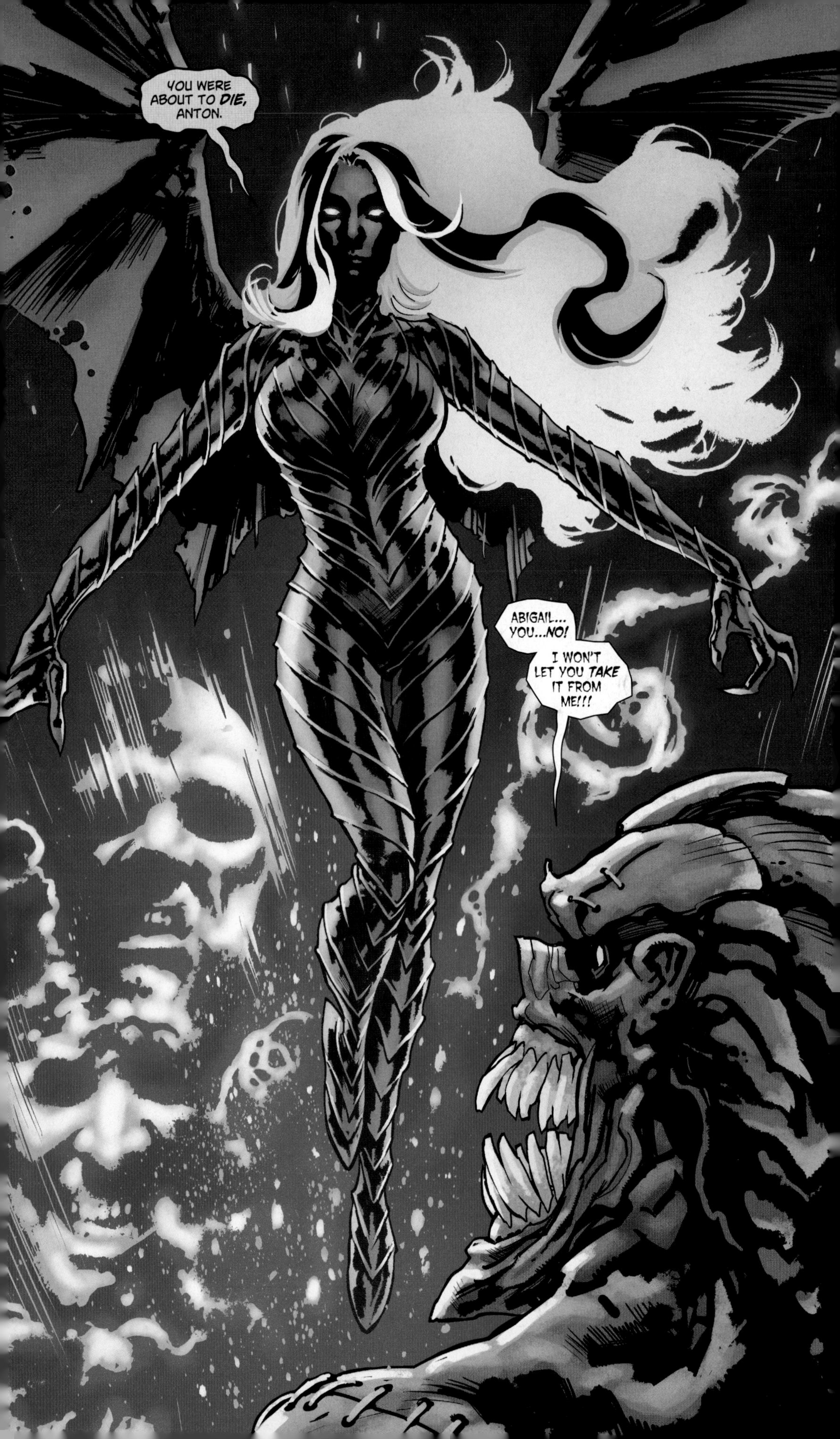
YOU WERE ABOUT TO DIE, ANTON.
ABIGAIL... YOU...NO!
I WON'T LET YOU TAKE IT FROM ME!!!

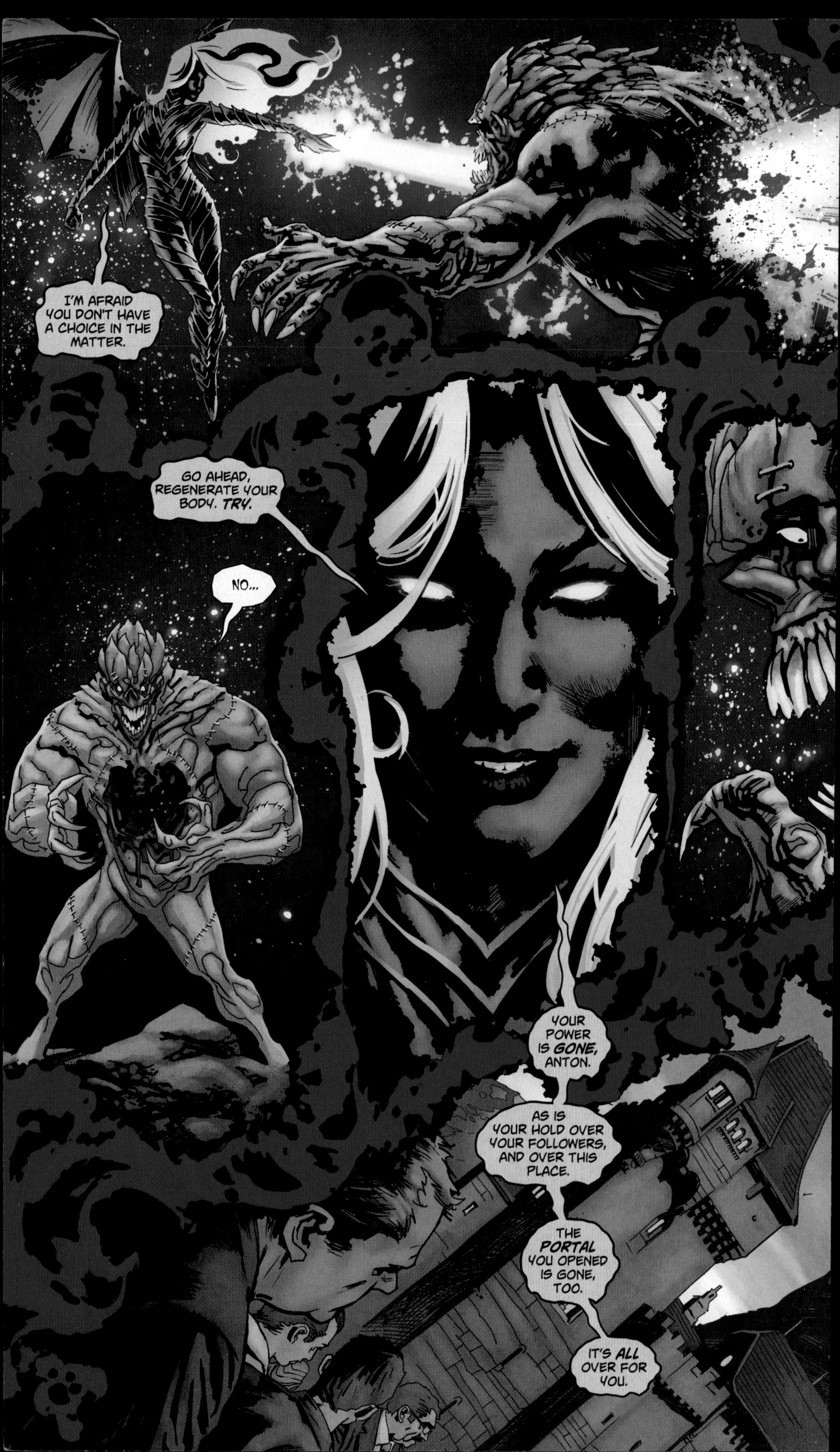
I'M AFRAID YOU DON'T HAVE A CHOICE IN THE MATTER.
GO AHEAD, REGENERATE YOUR BODY. TRY.
NO...
YOUR POWER IS GONE, ANTON.
AS IS YOUR HOLD OVER YOUR FOLLOWERS, AND OVER THIS PLACE.
THE PORTAL YOU OPENED IS GONE, TOO.
IT'S ALL OVER FOR YOU.

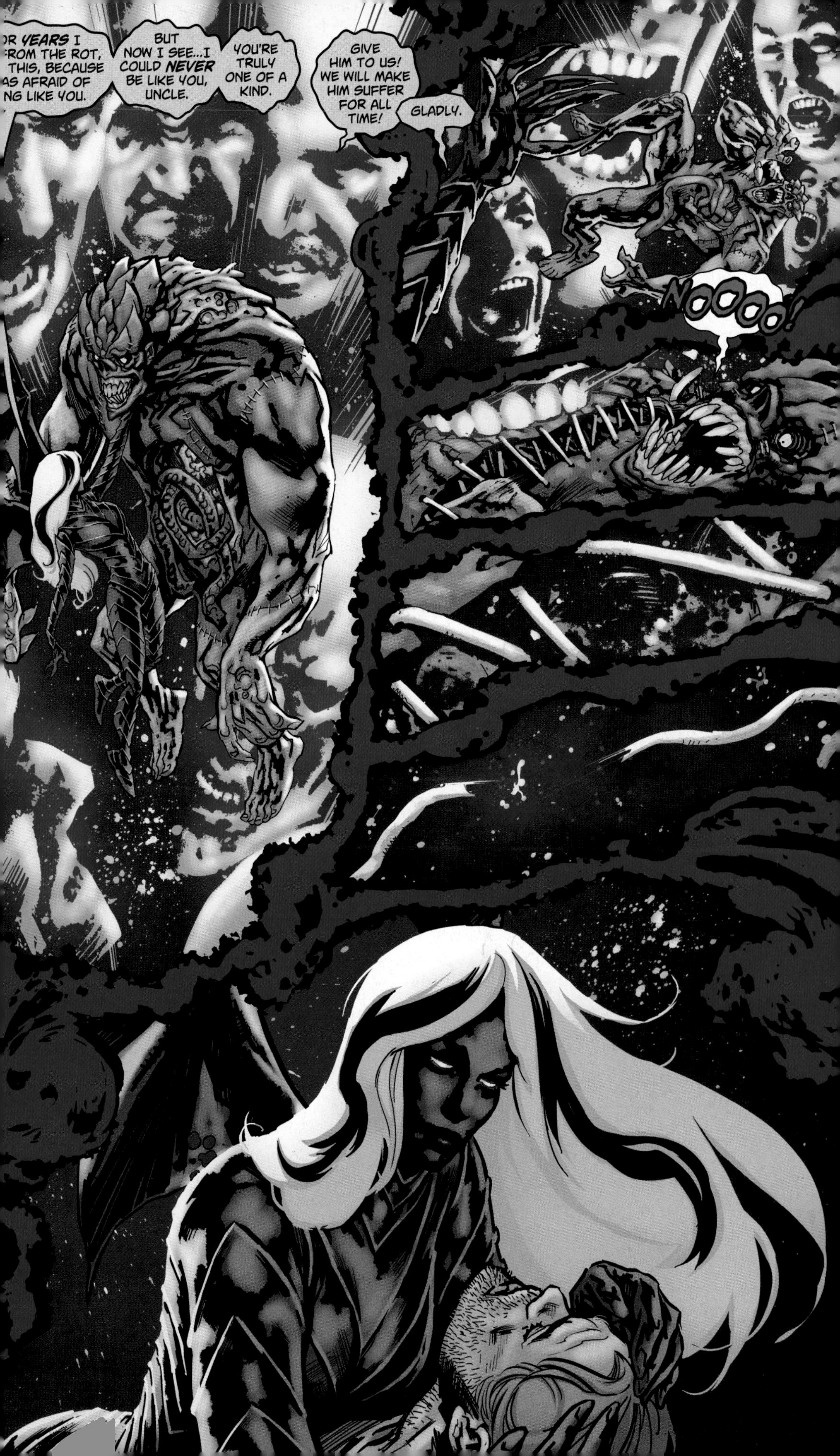

OR YEARS I FROM THE ROT, THIS, BECAUSE AS AFRAID OF NG LIKE YOU.
BUT NOW I SEE...I COULD NEVER BE LIKE YOU, UNCLE.
YOU'RE TRULY ONE OF A KIND.
GIVE HIM TO US! WE WILL MAKE HIM SUFFER FOR ALL TIME!
GLADLY.
NOOOOO!

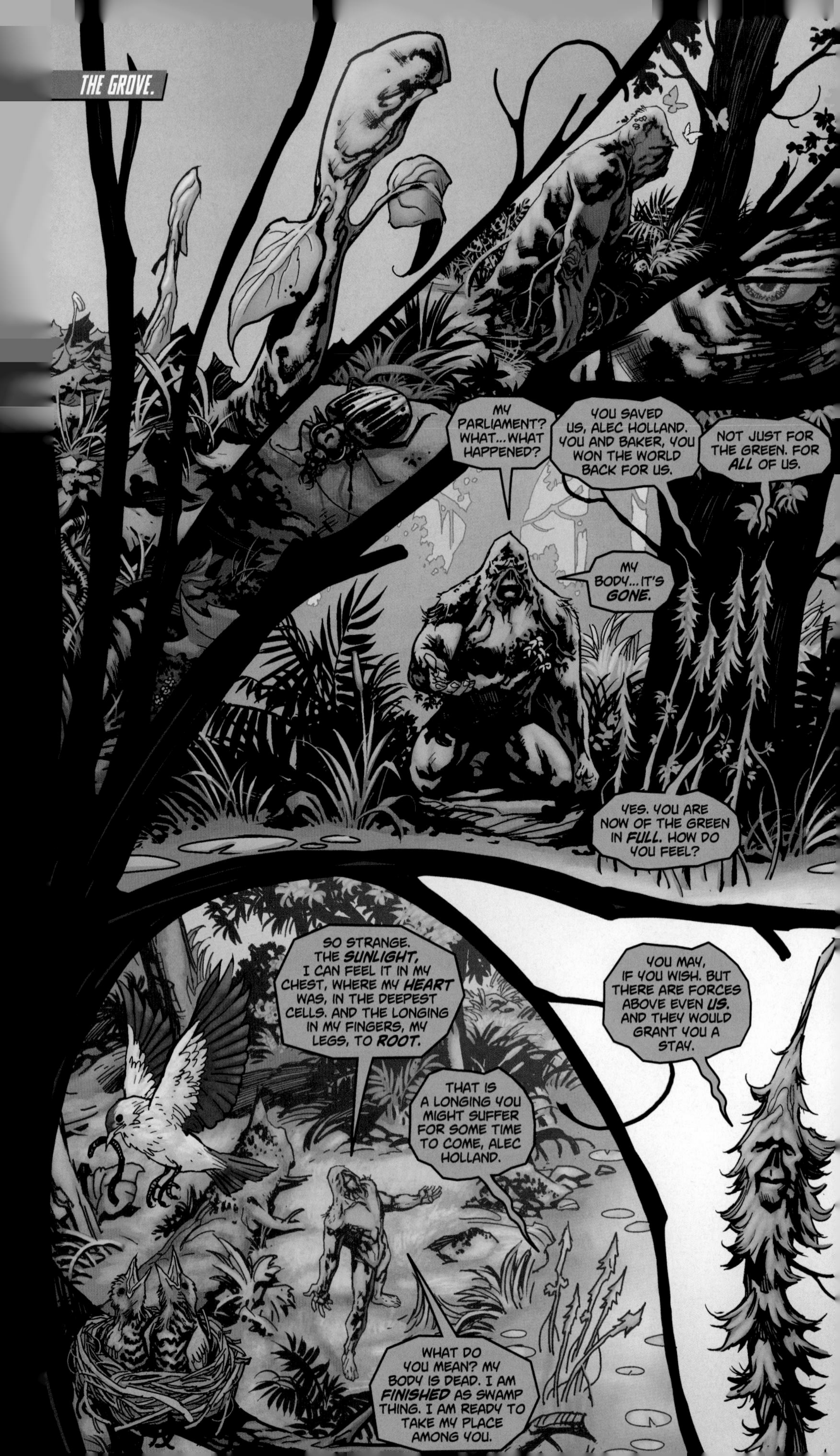
THE GROVE.
MY PARLIAMENT? WHAT...WHAT HAPPENED?
YOU SAVED US, ALEC HOLLAND. YOU AND BAKER, YOU WON THE WORLD BACK FOR US.
NOT JUST FOR THE GREEN. FOR ALL OF US.
MY BODY...IT'S GONE.
YES. YOU ARE NOW OF THE GREEN IN FULL. HOW DO YOU FEEL?
SO STRANGE. THE SUNLIGHT, I CAN FEEL IT IN MY CHEST, WHERE MY HEART WAS, IN THE DEEPEST CELLS. AND THE LONGING IN MY FINGERS, MY LEGS, TO ROOT.
THAT IS A LONGING YOU MIGHT SUFFER FOR SOME TIME TO COME, ALEC HOLLAND.
WHAT DO YOU MEAN? MY BODY IS DEAD. I AM FINISHED AS SWAMP THING. I AM READY TO TAKE MY PLACE AMONG YOU.
YOU MAY, IF YOU WISH. BUT THERE ARE FORCES ABOVE EVEN US. AND THEY WOULD GRANT YOU A STAY.

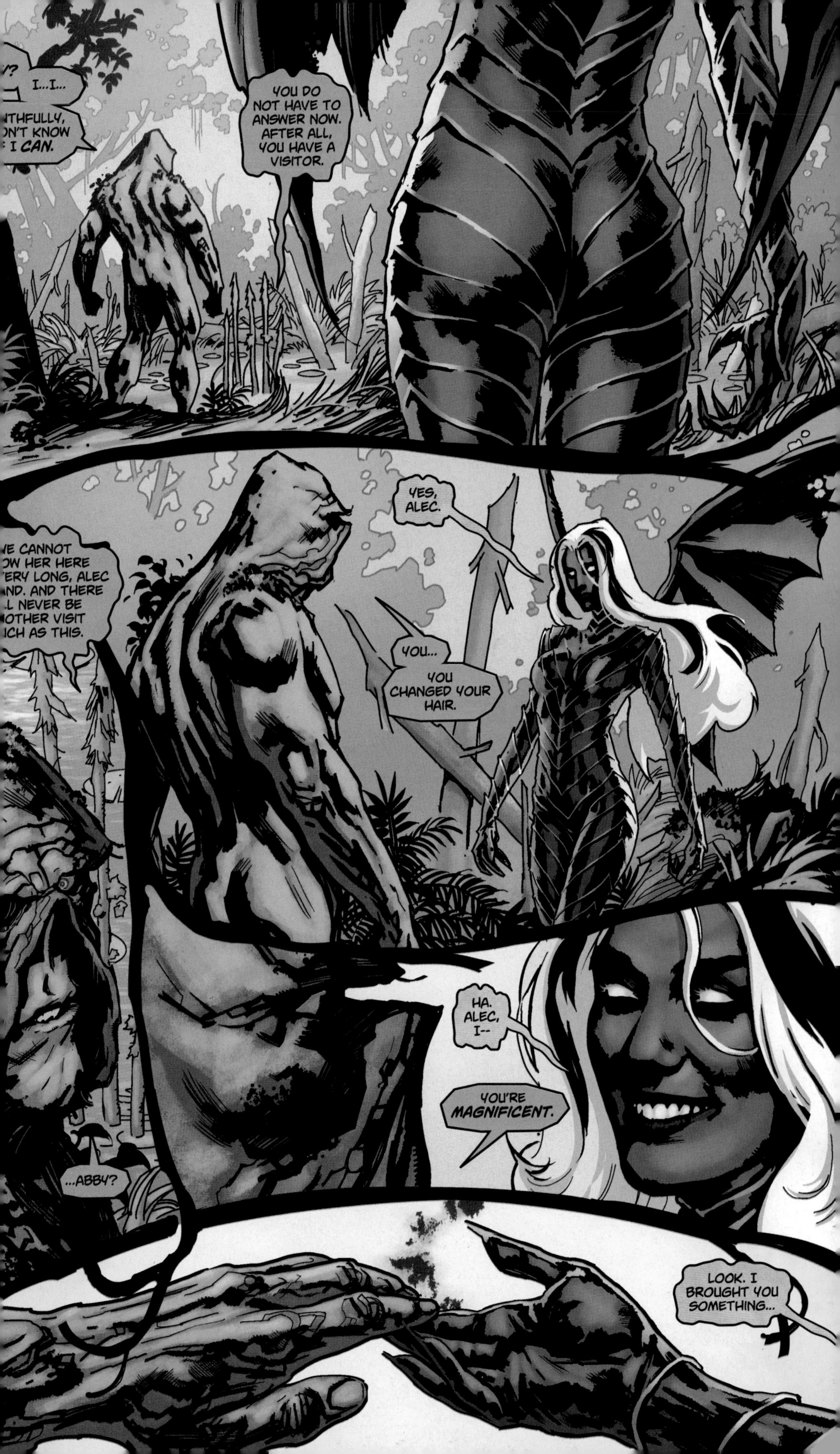

I...I...
NTHFULLY, N'T KNOW I CAN.
YOU DO NOT HAVE TO ANSWER NOW. AFTER ALL, YOU HAVE A VISITOR.
E CANNOT OW HER HERE ERY LONG, ALEC ND. AND THERE L NEVER BE OTHER VISIT ICH AS THIS.
YES, ALEC.
YOU...
YOU CHANGED YOUR HAIR.
...ABBY?
HA. ALEC, I--
YOU'RE MAGNIFICENT.
LOOK. I BROUGHT YOU SOMETHING...

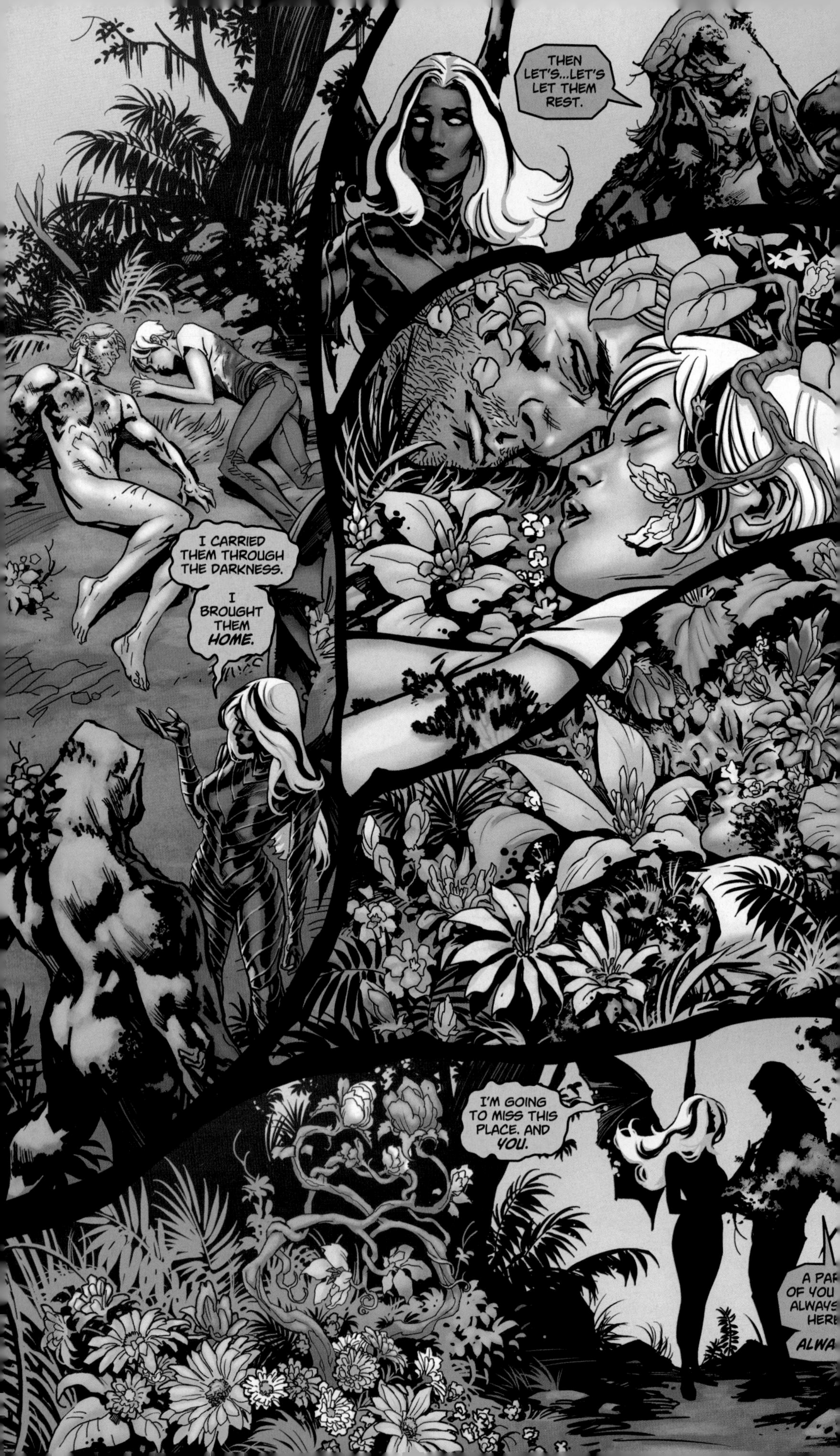
THEN LET'S...LET'S LET THEM REST.
I CARRIED THEM THROUGH THE DARKNESS.
I BROUGHT THEM *HOME*.
I'M GOING TO MISS THIS PLACE. AND *YOU*.

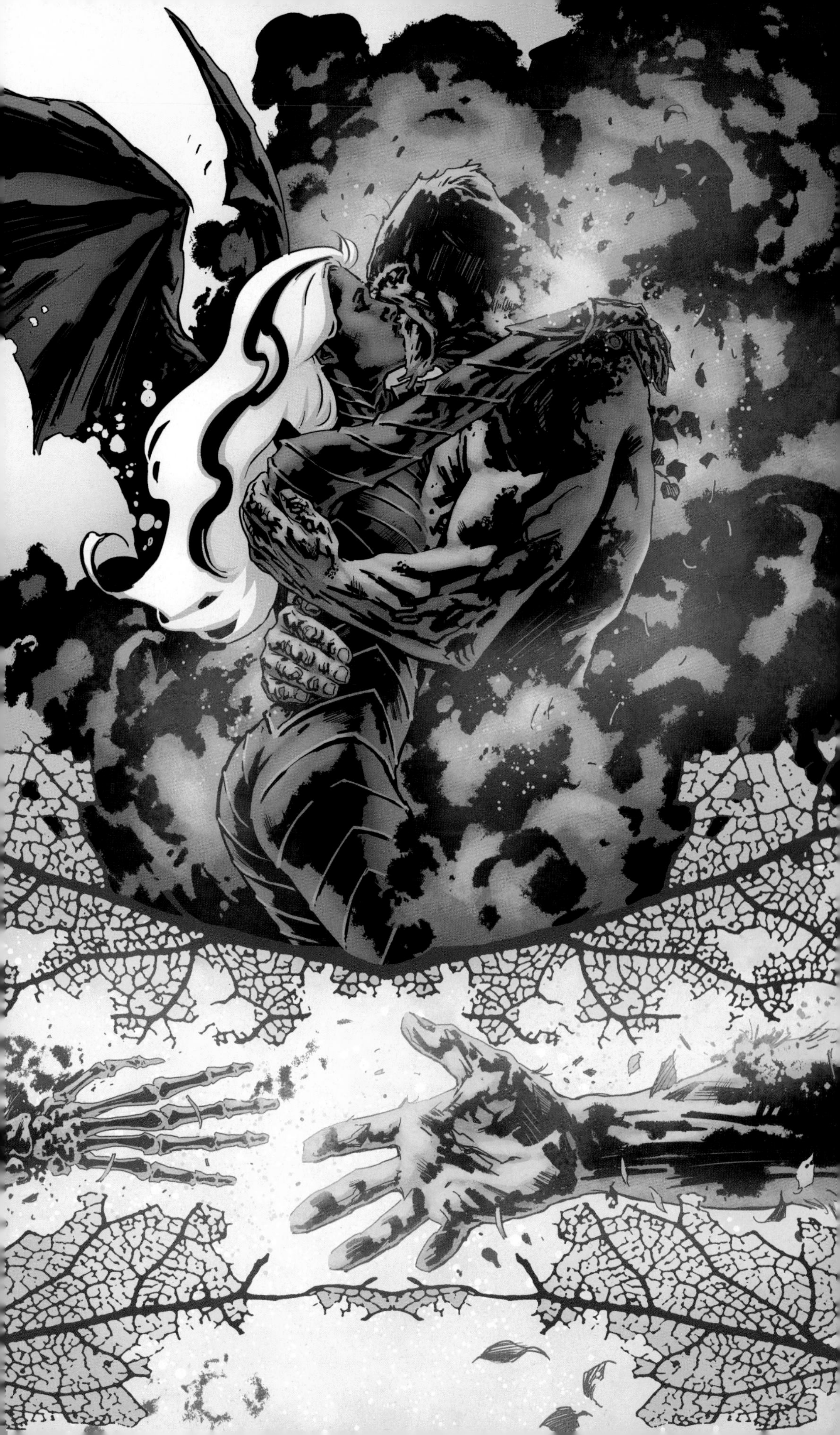

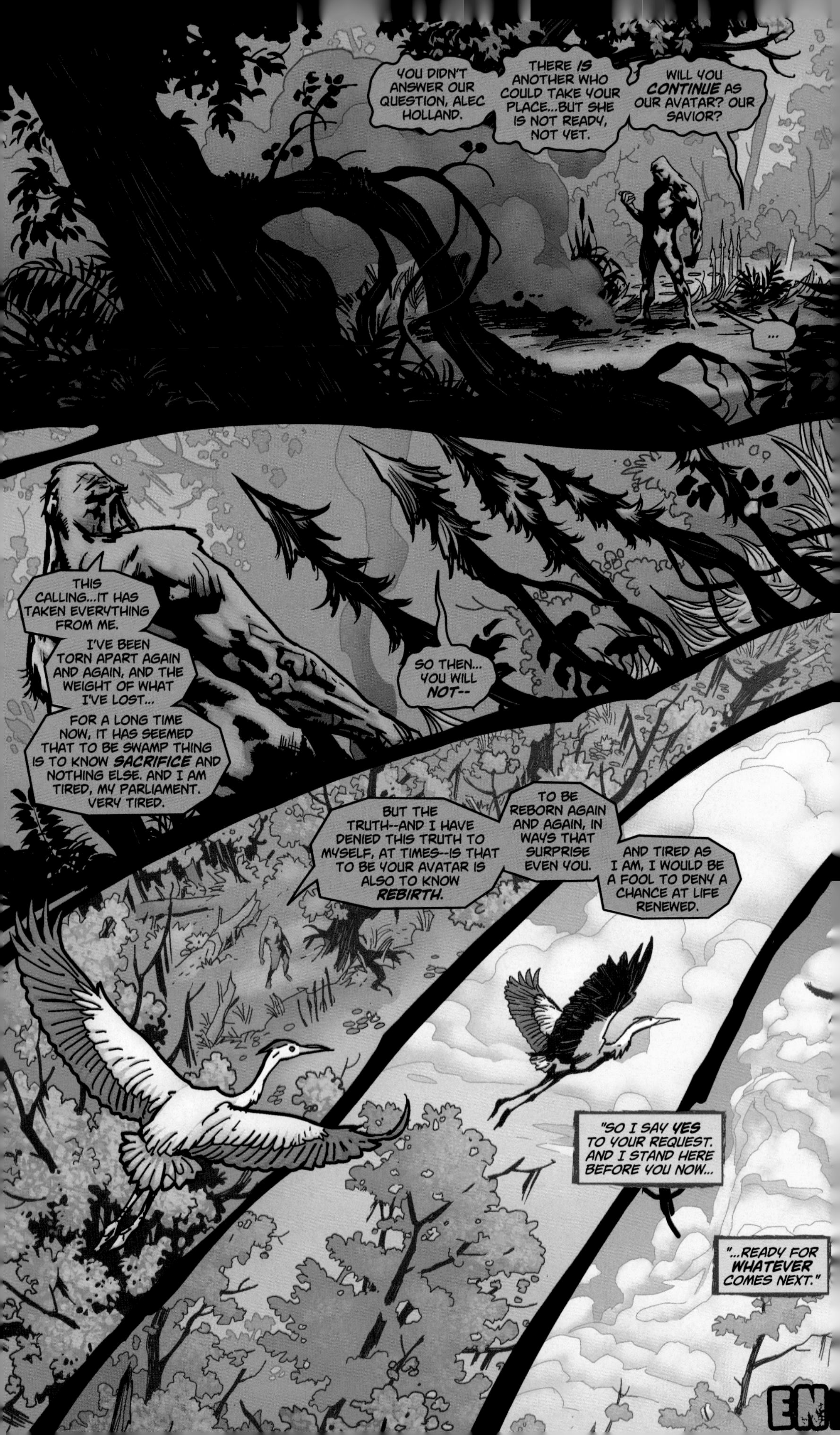
YOU DIDN'T ANSWER OUR QUESTION, ALEC HOLLAND.
THERE *IS* ANOTHER WHO COULD TAKE YOUR PLACE...BUT SHE IS NOT READY, NOT YET.
WILL YOU *CONTINUE* AS OUR AVATAR? OUR SAVIOR?
...
THIS CALLING...IT HAS TAKEN EVERYTHING FROM ME.
I'VE BEEN TORN APART AGAIN AND AGAIN, AND THE WEIGHT OF WHAT I'VE LOST...
FOR A LONG TIME NOW, IT HAS SEEMED THAT TO BE SWAMP THING IS TO KNOW *SACRIFICE* AND NOTHING ELSE. AND I AM TIRED, MY PARLIAMENT. VERY TIRED.
SO THEN... YOU WILL *NOT*--
BUT THE TRUTH--AND I HAVE DENIED THIS TRUTH TO MYSELF, AT TIMES--IS THAT TO BE YOUR AVATAR IS ALSO TO KNOW *REBIRTH*.
TO BE REBORN AGAIN AND AGAIN, IN WAYS THAT SURPRISE EVEN YOU.
AND TIRED AS I AM, I WOULD BE A FOOL TO DENY A CHANCE AT LIFE RENEWED.
"SO I SAY *YES* TO YOUR REQUEST. AND I STAND HERE BEFORE YOU NOW...
"...READY FOR *WHATEVER* COMES NEXT."

SWAMP THING
COVER SKETCHES AND DESIGNS

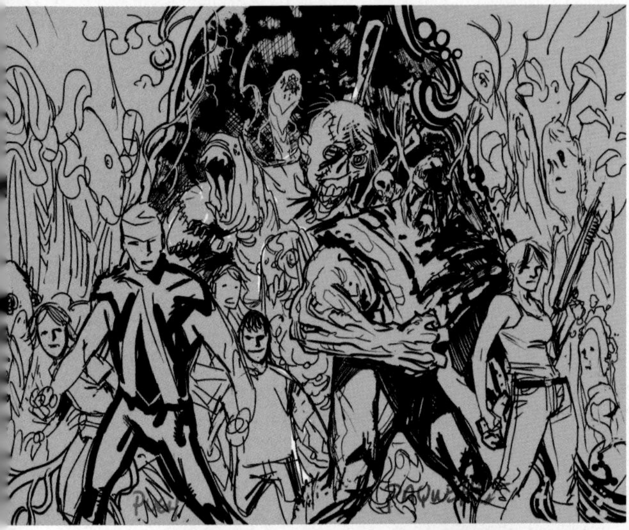

SWAMP THING #12 and ANIMAL MAN #12 combined cover design by Yanick Paquette & Steve Pugh

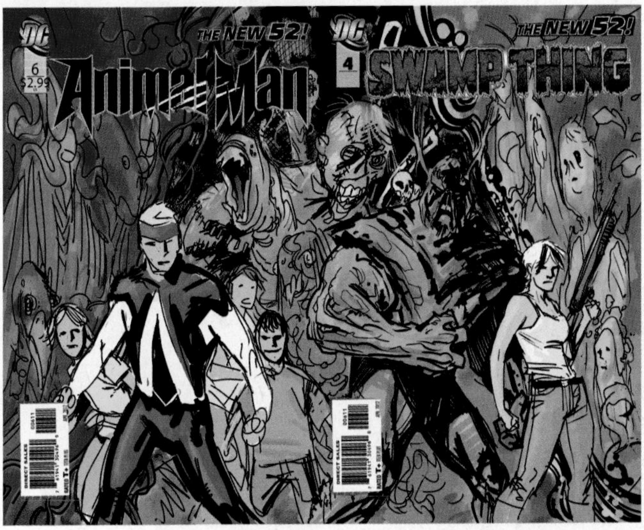
THE NEW 52!
6
$2.99
Animal Man
THE NEW 52!
4
SWAMP THING

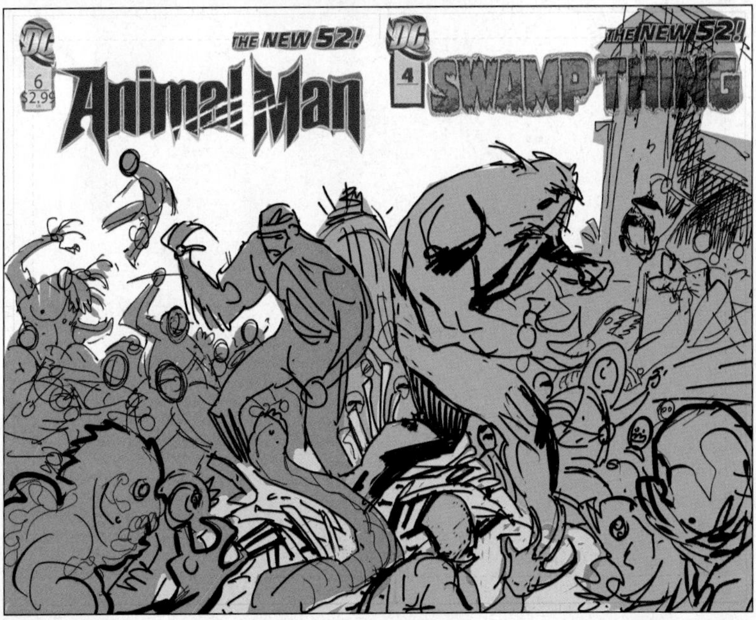
THE NEW 52!
6
$2.99
Animal Man
THE NEW 52!
4
SWAMP THING

SWAMP THING #17 and ANIMAL MAN #17 combined cover design by Yanick Paquette & Steve Pugh

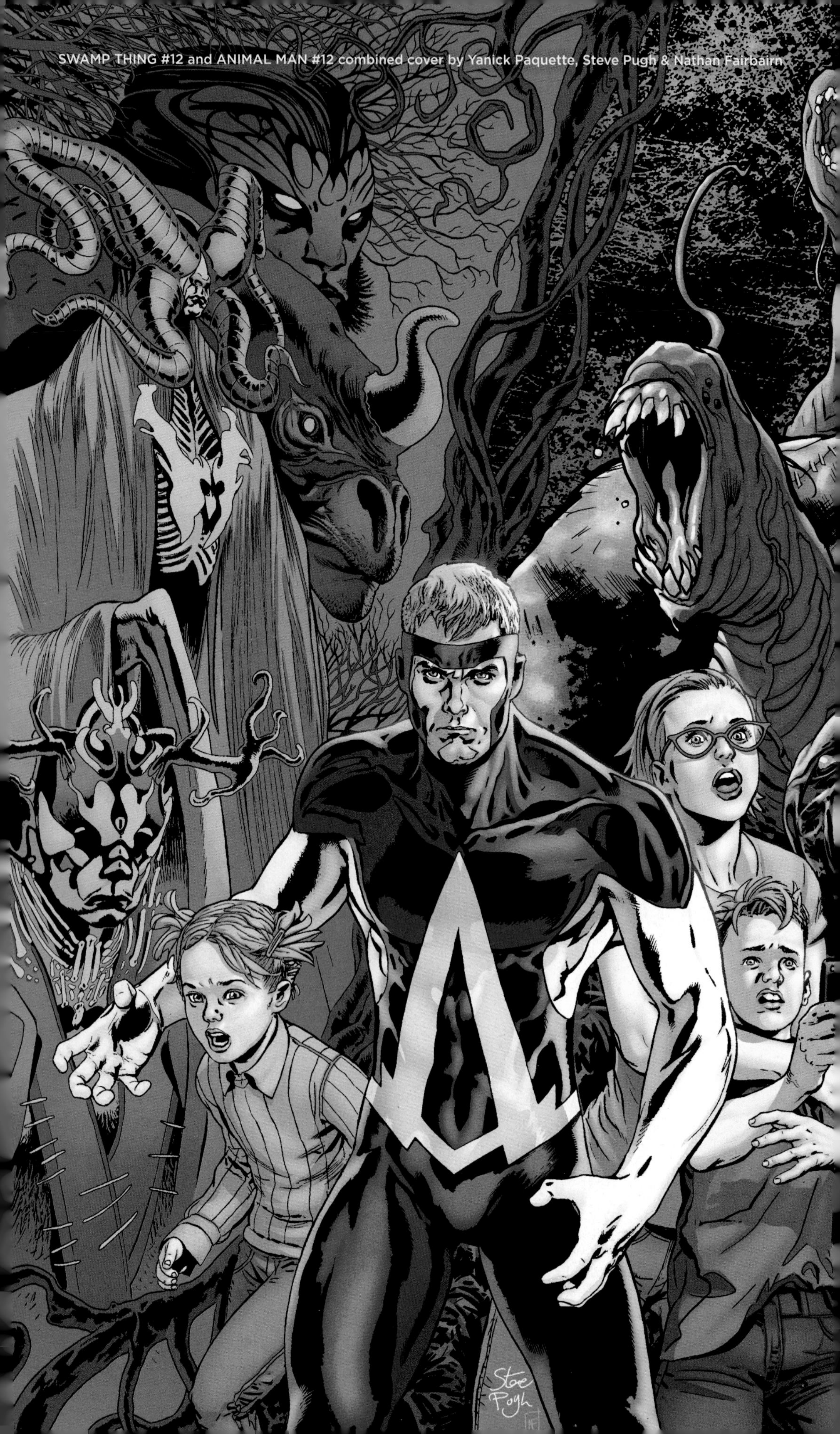

SWAMP THING #12 and ANIMAL MAN #12 combined cover by Yanick Paquette, Steve Pugh & Nathan Fairbairn

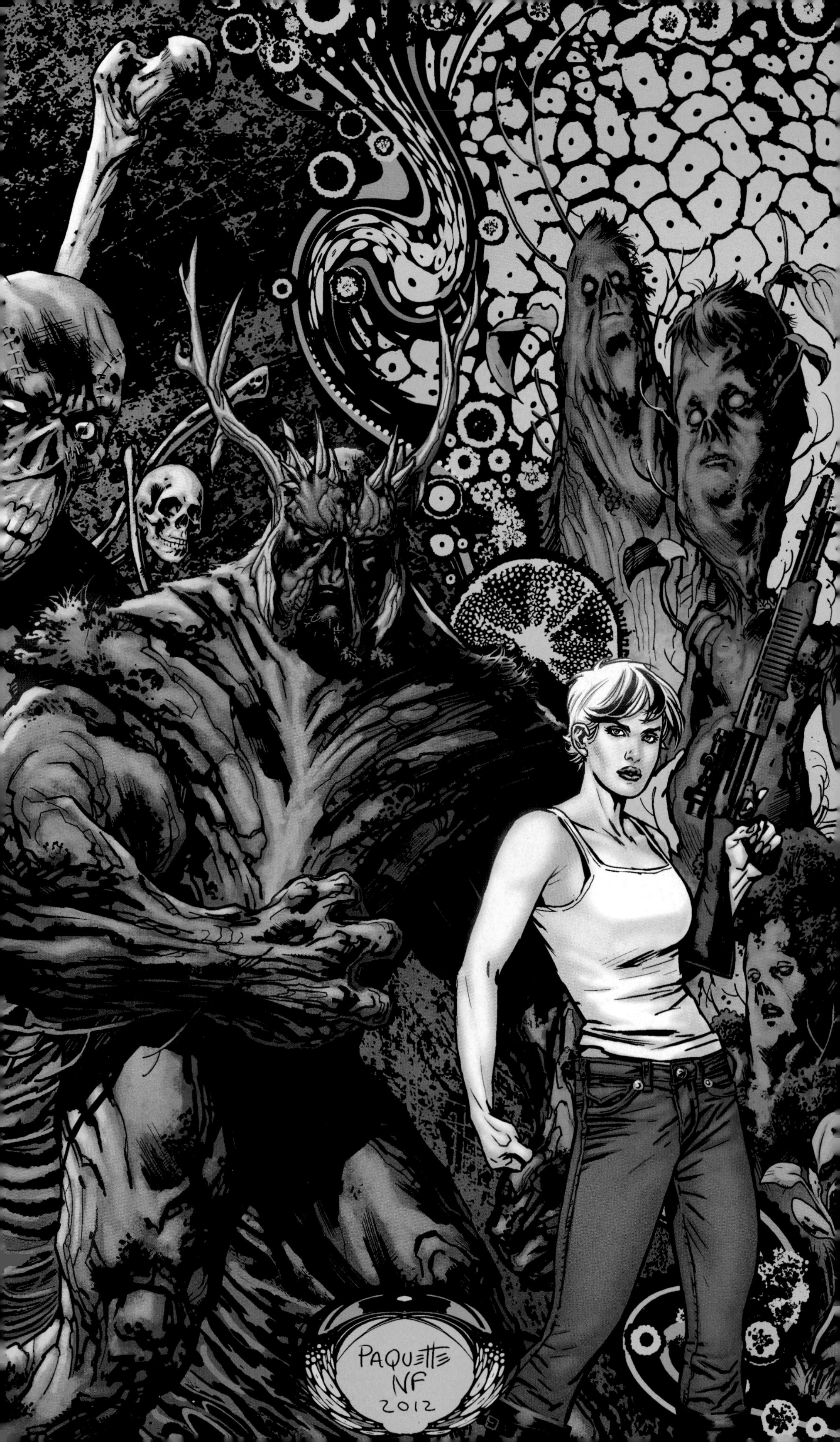
PAQUETTE
NF
2012

SWAMP THING #17 and ANIMAL MAN #17 combined cover by Yanick Paquette, Steve Pugh & Nathan Fairbairn

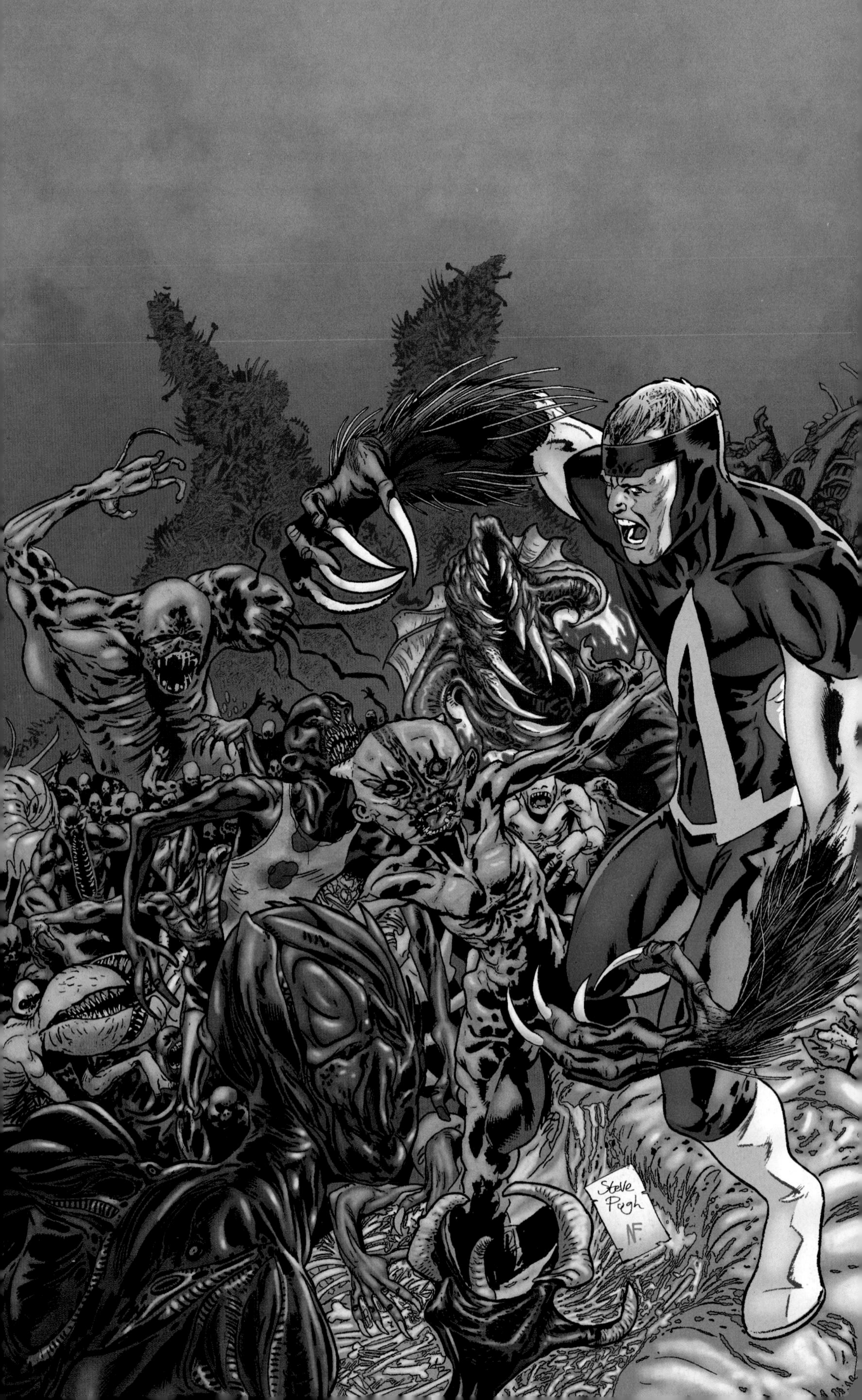
Steve Pugh
NF.

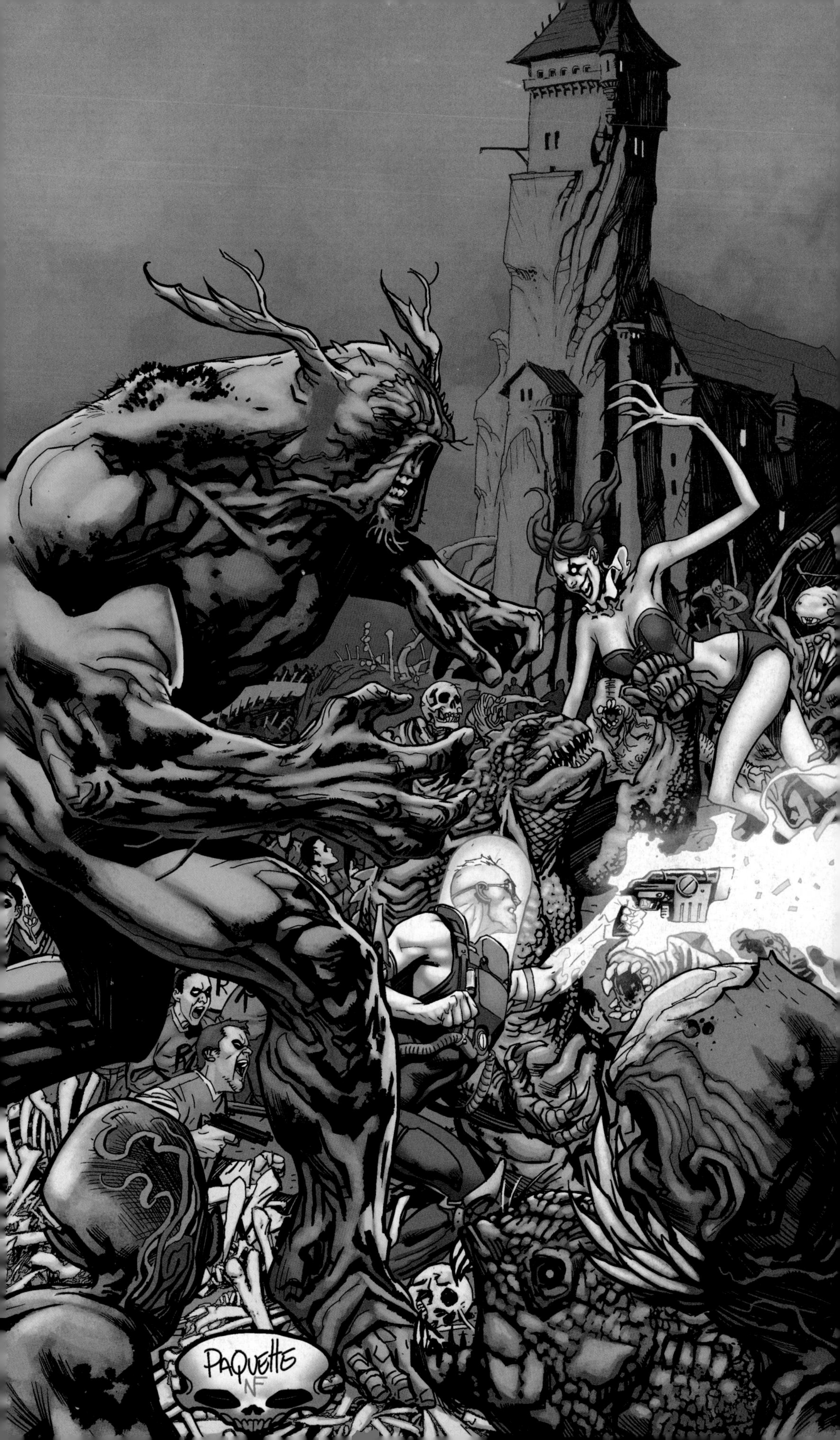
PAQUETTE
NF

SWAMP THING
CHARACTER SKETCHES BY YANICK PAQUETTE

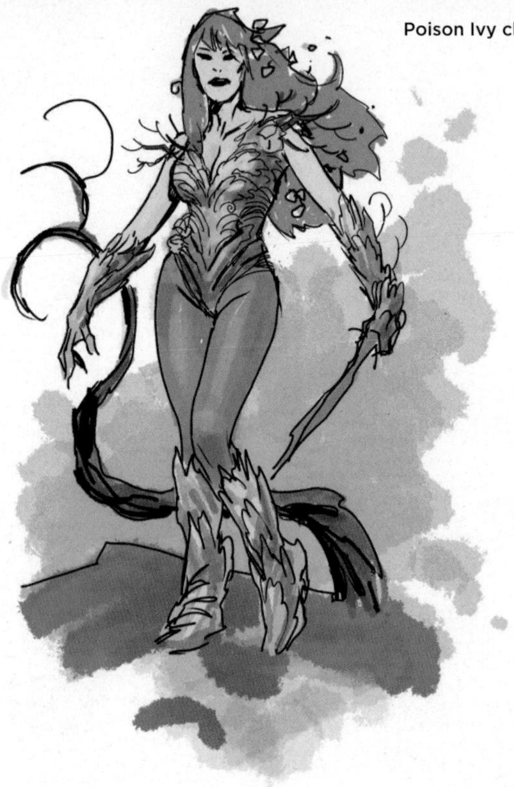

Poison Ivy character design

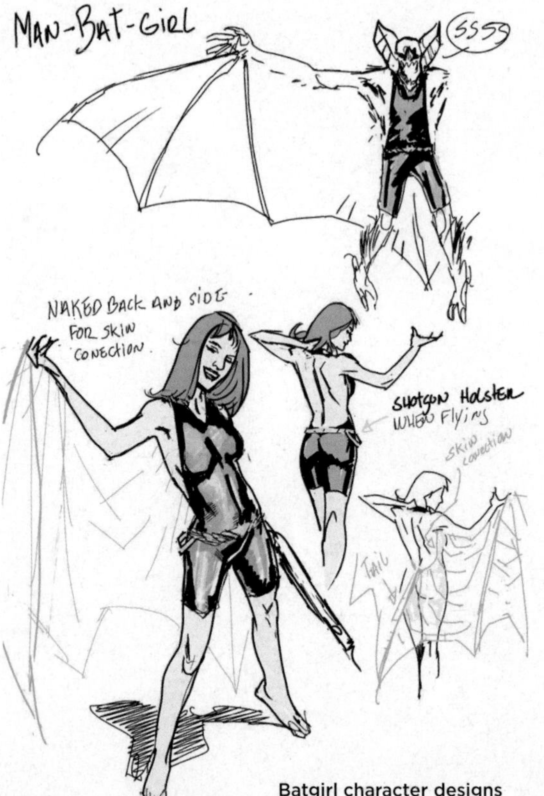
MAN-BAT-GIRL
SSSS
NAKED BACK AND SIDE FOR SKIN CONECTION.
SHOTGUN HOLSTER WHEN FLYING
SKIN CONECTION
TAIL

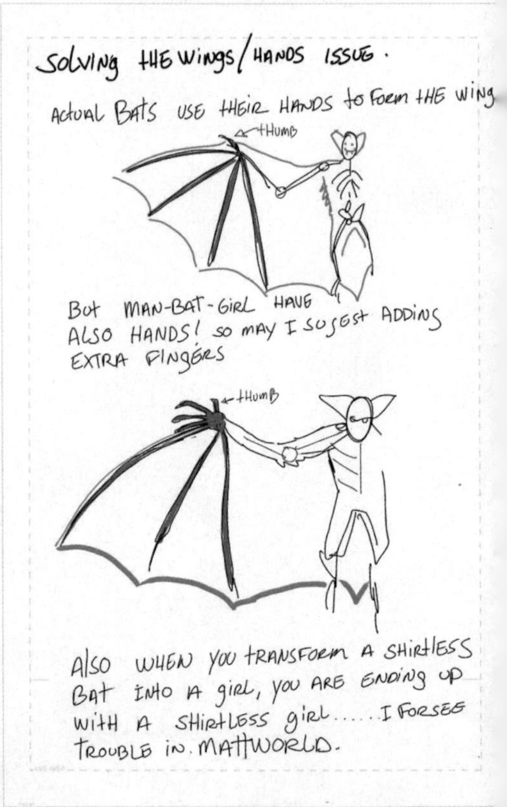
SOLVING THE WINGS/HANDS ISSUE.
ACTUAL BATS USE THEIR HANDS TO FORM THE WING
THUMB
BUT MAN-BAT-GIRL HAVE ALSO HANDS! SO MAY I SUGEST ADDING EXTRA FINGERS
THUMB
ALSO WHEN YOU TRANSFORM A SHIRTLESS BAT INTO A GIRL, YOU ARE ENDING UP WITH A SHIRTLESS GIRL..... I FORSEE TROUBLE IN MATTWORLD.

Batgirl character designs